INTRODUCTION
TO
DATA STRUCTURES
AND
NON-NUMERIC
COMPUTATION

PRENTICE-HALL
SERIES IN AUTOMATIC COMPUTATION

George Forsythe, editor

AHO AND ULLMAN, *Theory of Parsing, Translation, and Compiling, Volume I: Parsing*
ANDREE, *Computer Programming: Techniques, Analysis, and Mathematics*
ANSELONE, *Collectively Compact Operator Approximation Theory and Applications to Integral Equations*
ARBIB, *Theories of Abstract Automata*
BATES AND DOUGLAS, *Programming Language/One*, 2nd ed.
BLUMENTHAL, *Management Information Systems*
BOBROW AND SCHWARTZ, *Computers and the Policy-Making Community*
BOWLES, editor, *Computers in Humanistic Research*
BRENT, *Algorithms for Minimization without Derivatives*
CESCHINO AND KUNTZMAN, *Numerical Solution of Initial Value Problems*
CRESS, et al., *FORTRAN IV with WATFOR and WATFIV*
DANIEL, *The Approximate Minimization of Functionals*
DESMONDE, *A Conversational Graphic Data Processing System*
DESMONDE, *Computers and Their Uses*, 2nd ed.
DESMONDE, *Real-Time Data Processing Systems*
DRUMMOND, *Evaluation and Measurement Techniques for Digital Computer Systems*
EVANS, et al., *Simulation Using Digital Computers*
FIKE, *Computer Evaluation of Mathematical Functions*
FIKE, *PL/1 for Scientific Programmers*
FORSYTHE AND MOLER, *Computer Solution of Linear Algebraic Systems*
GAUTHIER AND PONTO, *Designing Systems Programs*
GEAR, *Numerical Initial Value Problems in Ordinary Differential Equations*
GOLDEN, *FORTRAN IV Programming and Computing*
GOLDEN AND LEICHUS, *IBM/360 Programming and Computing*
GORDON, *System Simulation*
GREENSPAN, *Lectures on the Numerical Solution of Linear, Singular and Nonlinear Differential Equations*
GRUENBERGER, editor, *Computers and Communications*
GRUENBERGER, editor, *Critical Factors in Data Management*
GRUENBERGER, editor, *Expanding Use of Computers in the 70's*
GRUENBERGER, editor, *Fourth Generation Computers*
HARTMANIS AND STEARNS, *Algebraic Structure Theory of Sequential Machines*
HULL, *Introduction to Computing*
JACOBY, et al., *Iterative Methods for Nonlinear Optimization Problems*
JOHNSON, *System Structure in Data, Programs, and Computers*
KANTER, *The Computer and the Executive*
KIVIAT, et al., *The SIMSCRIPT II Programming Language*
LORIN, *Parallelism in Hardware and Software: Real and Apparent Concurrency*
LOUDEN AND LEDIN, *Programming the IBM 1130*, 2nd ed.
MARTIN, *Design of Real-Time Computer Systems*
MARTIN, *Future Developments in Telecommunications*
MARTIN, *Man-Computer Dialogue*

MARTIN, *Programming Real-Time Computing Systems*
MARTIN, *Systems Analysis for Data Transmission*
MARTIN, *Telecommunications and the Computer*
MARTIN, *Teleprocessing Network Organization*
MARTIN AND NORMAN, *The Computerized Society*
MATHISON AND WALKER, *Computers and Telecommunications: Issues in Public Policy*
MCKEEMAN, et al., *A Compiler Generator*
MEYERS, *Time-Sharing Computation in the Social Sciences*
MINSKY, *Computation: Finite and Infinite Machines*
MOORE, *Interval Analysis*
PLANE AND MCMILLAN, *Discrete Optimization: Integer Programming and Network Analysis for Management Decisions*
PRITSKER AND KIVIAT, *Simulation with GASP II: a FORTRAN-Based Simulation Language*
PYLYSHYN, editor, *Perspectives on the Computer Revolution*
RICH, *Internal Sorting Methods Illustrated with PL/1 Programs*
RUSTIN, editor, *Algorithm Specification*
RUSTIN, editor, *Computer Networks*
RUSTIN, editor, *Debugging Techniques in Large Systems*
RUSTIN, editor, *Formal Semantics of Programming Languages*
SACKMAN AND CITRENBAUM, editors, *On-Line Planning: Towards Creative Problem-Solving*
SALTON, editor, *The SMART Retrieval System: Experiments in Automatic Document Processing*
SAMMET, *Programming Languages: History and Fundamentals*
SCHULTZ, *Digital Processing: A System Orientation*
SCHULTZ, *Finite Element Analysis*
SCHWARZ, et al., *Numerical Analysis of Symmetric Matrices*
SHERMAN, *Techniques in Computer Programming*
SIMON AND SIKLOSSY, editors, *Representation and Meaning: Experiments with Information Processing Systems*
SYNDER, *Chebyshev Methods in Numerical Approximation*
STERLING AND POLLACK, *Introduction to Statistical Data Processing*
STOUTMEYER, *PL/1 Programming for Engineering and Science*
STROUD, *Approximate Calculation of Multiple Integrals*
STROUD AND SECREST, *Gaussian Quadrature Formulas*
TAVISS, editor, *The Computer Impact*
TRAUB, *Iterative Methods for the Solution of Polynomial Equations*
UHR, *Pattern Recognition, Learning, and Thought*
VAN TASSEL, *Computer Security Management*
VARGA, *Matrix Iterative Analysis*
VAZSONYI, *Problem Solving by Digital Computers with PL/1 Programming*
WAITE, *Implementing Software for Non-Numeric Application*
WILKINSON, *Rounding Errors in Algebraic Processes*
ZIEGLER, *Time-Sharing Data Processing Systems*

INTRODUCTION TO DATA STRUCTURES AND NON-NUMERIC COMPUTATION

Featuring the WATFOR and WATFIV Compilers

PETER C. BRILLINGER
University of Waterloo
Waterloo, Ontario, Canada

DORON J. COHEN
The Technion
Haifa, Israel

PRENTICE-HALL, INC.
Englewood Cliffs, New Jersey

Library of Congress Cataloging in Publication Data

BRILLINGER, PETER C., 1943–
Introduction to data structures and non-numeric computation.

1. Electronic digital computers—Programming.
2. Electronic data processing. 3. FORTRAN (Computer program language) I. Cohen, Doron J., 1942– joint author. II. Title.
QA76.6.B74 001.6'42 72-5632
ISBN 0-13-479899-6

10 9 8 7 6 5 4

Printed in the United States of America

PRENTICE-HALL INTERNATIONAL, INC., *London*
PRENTICE-HALL OF AUSTRALIA, PTY. LTD., *Sydney*
PRENTICE-HALL OF CANADA, LTD., *Toronto*
PRENTICE-HALL OF INDIA PRIVATE LTD., *New Delhi*
PRENTICE-HALL OF JAPAN, INC., *Tokyo*

To Cathy and Rina

PREFACE

This textbook contains material for an intermediate course on Data Structures and Applications in Computer Science. It assumes a basic knowledge of computer programming, with an emphasis on the FORTRAN language as it is implemented with the WATFOR and WATFIV compilers.

The book provides a comprehensive discussion of data representations and data structures, followed by a detailed study of operations and applications with character strings, linearly linked lists, graphs, and trees. Included is a consideration of algorithms for traversing trees and implementing recursive routines with the use of push-down stacks. This in-depth study of techniques takes the mystery out of list processing by teaching the basic methods usually used by high-level list processing languages. The book concludes with an elementary discussion of programming language translation, covering syntactic analysis, object code generation, and macro processors.

We have addressed this book not only to students at educational institutions but also to industry-oriented programming personnel. Emphasizing techniques and mechanics rather than theory, the book teaches methods and internal representations. Although

FORTRAN was not originally designed for non-numerical programming, many programmers have nonetheless found it a comfortable language for doing so. The book treats this subject in a formal and rigorous manner. To our knowledge, this approach is relatively novel and has not been adopted in previous textbooks.

The FORTRAN language is utilized only as a convenient tool for illustrating the techniques and procedures that are usually implemented in machine language. By using FORTRAN as if it were the actual machine language, the book simplifies the explanation and removes the need for unnecessary details that usually make such techniques difficult to teach or comprehend. The reader, once exposed to the basic concepts and ideas, can proceed to transfer them to other programming languages.

This textbook is the fifth edition of a set of notes originally written by Doron J. Cohen and based on his experience in teaching courses in Non-Numerical Applications in Computer Science at the University of Waterloo during the years 1968 - 1972. During this period, these notes were used at several universities as a sequel to the text FORTRAN IV WITH WATFOR AND WATFIV (written by P. Cress, P. Dirksen, and J.W. Graham, and published by Prentice-Hall).

We are very indebted to Donald F. Weir of the University of Waterloo for his numerous suggestions and invaluable assistance in proof-reading various versions of the manuscript, testing examples on the computer, preparing rough drafts of exercises, and constructing the index. We are also grateful to H. Boom of the University of Alberta for his contributions to the earlier versions of the notes. Finally, we would like to express our sincere thanks to Mrs. Susan Hopkins for her excellent typing of the manuscript.

Peter C. Brillinger

Doron J. Cohen

Waterloo, Ontario, Canada.

CONTENTS

CHAPTER ONE: PRIMITIVE NUMERICAL DATA REPRESENTATION

CHAPTER TWO: LOGICAL OPERATIONS

CHAPTER THREE: CHARACTER STRINGS - REPRESENTATION AND MANIPULATION

CHAPTER FOUR: CHARACTER STRINGS - APPLICATIONS

CHAPTER FIVE: INTRODUCTION TO DATA STRUCTURES

CHAPTER SIX: PROCESSING LINEARLY LINKED LISTS

CHAPTER SEVEN: MULTI-LINKED STRUCTURES

CHAPTER EIGHT: OPERATIONS WITH TREE STRUCTURES

CHAPTER NINE: THE PROGRAM AS AN OBJECT FOR MANIPULATION

APPENDIX A: POSITIONAL NOTATIONS: ARABIC, BINARY, HEXADECIMAL

APPENDIX B: CHARACTER VARIABLES WITH WATFIV

APPENDIX C: SPECTRE MACHINE AND ASSEMBLY LANGUAGE CODING

INDEX

INTRODUCTION TO DATA STRUCTURES AND NON-NUMERIC COMPUTATION

CHAPTER ONE

PRIMITIVE NUMERICAL DATA REPRESENTATION

1.1 COMPUTER MEMORY

How does an electronic digital computer handle and manipulate information? The answer to this basic question is suggested by the nature of all electronic switching devices: a switch is either open or closed; a lightbulb is either on or off; a magnetic material is saturated in either a positive or negative direction. All these are examples of what have come to be known as *TWO-STATE SYSTEMS*. What could be more natural than to denote the states by the two symbols used in the *BINARY* notation, 0 and 1? Since these two symbols form all the elements needed in the binary system of notation, such a system becomes extremely practical for representing numbers by a computer. In fact, the memory unit of a computer is really just a huge collection of bi-stable electronic components, each representative of one binary digit (*BIT*).

A person's initial reaction, perhaps, might be to question the efficiency of using such a notation. Obviously, using 0's and 1's to represent data is not the most efficient method from a pencil-

and-paper point of view. In fact, any number requires more digits to represent it in binary notation than it does in any other system. However, the binary digits are extremely simple. Furthermore, we must admit that efficiency is not always achieved by having more distinct symbols and fewer positions. Otherwise, we would not have adopted the decimal system of notation in preference to other systems having bases larger than ten. At the present time, it is much more economically feasible for a computer to manipulate several two-state devices than to have fewer multi-state devices.

In order to represent information in an organized fashion, we must subdivide the millions of memory bits into smaller groups called *WORDS*. The number of bits comprising one word will vary from one computer to another, depending upon the aims of the manufacturer. Originally, the width of a word depended upon the capacity of the arithmetic unit. Another decision to be made involves the interpretation of the contents of any given word. In the case of numerical data representation, we commonly interpret the bits as representing the coefficients in the polynomial expansion form of a number expressed in binary positional notation. (An expanded description of the binary number system is supplied in Appendix A for interested readers.) However, we can also interpret a string of bits as representing more than just pure numerical data for the machine. Depending upon some arbitrarily chosen code, any combination of bits can represent letters of the alphabet, various symbols, punctuation marks, etc. Instructions to the machine are also coded in abbreviated bit-string form.

1.1.1 IBM S/360 Memory Organization

We often hear that a high-level language such as FORTRAN is machine-independent, implying that programs written in FORTRAN can be processed on any computer for which a FORTRAN compiler exists. Although this would be an ideal situation, in actual fact, there are several variations of FORTRAN. These versions differ slightly, since any specific computer for which a compiler has been created will have its own special features. As a result, programs written in FORTRAN may require modification if they are to yield the same results when processed on different computers. In this chapter, we will be discussing how numerical data may be represented in the memory of any computer. However, since the FORTRAN programs presented throughout this book are written to be processed on an IBM S/360 computer with the WATFIV compiler, we will be concentrating our attention on the particular features of that machine's form of memory representations.

The smallest addressable units in the memory of the S/360 are eight-bit groups called *BYTES*. The size of memory on a specific machine depends on the S/360 model used and on the economic resources of the particular computing installation. Memory sizes vary from many thousand to several million bytes. These bytes are assigned reference numbers called *ADDRESSES*, beginning at zero and increasing in steps of unity. Machine-language instructions obtain access to a particular byte in memory by specifying the address of that byte. Various instructions are designed to operate on adjacent groups of bytes called half-words, full-words and double-words (two bytes, four bytes and eight bytes, respectively). In order to gain access to a particular group of bytes, a machine uses the address of the lowest-numbered byte.

It is a popular misconception that certain computers perform *OCTAL* (i.e., base-8) or *HEXADECIMAL* (i.e., base-16) arithmetic. The S/360, like any other present-day computer, is essentially a binary machine. Octal and hexadecimal notations are merely short and convenient ways of representing large and cumbersome bit-strings. Conversion between binary and octal or hexadecimal notations is extremely easy. (Appendix A presents a detailed discussion of the binary and hexadecimal number systems, their relationship with one another, and conversion algorithms between these notations and decimal notation.)

1.2 FIXED-POINT (INTEGER) REPRESENTATION

A *FIXED-POINT* number is a signed value recorded as a binary integer. It is called fixed-point (equivalent to INTEGER) because of the fixed positioning of the binary point. It is always assumed that the binary point is located at the right end of the bit-string representing the specified number. With such values, the weights (i.e., powers of 2) associated with the various bits are fixed, since the position of the binary point never changes. The rightmost bit-position has a weight of 2^0, the next bit a weight of 2^1, the third bit a weight of 2^2, and so on. For representing positive fixed-point numbers, it is customary practice to use a 0 sign-bit at the left-most end of the string to indicate a positive value. The remaining bit-positions will then designate the magnitude of the number being represented.

Negative fixed-point numbers can be represented in a variety of ways. The most straightforward method is the *SIGNED-MAGNITUDE* scheme used for positive integers, except that the sign-bit 1 is used to indicate a negative value. Using such a scheme, any negative integer would be represented by the same bit-string as its positive counterpart (i.e., absolute value) with the exception of the sign-bit.

A second technique for representing negative integers is *ONE'S COMPLEMENT* notation. In this system, we find the representation of a negative value by inverting each of the bits (i.e., changing all 1's to 0's and vice-versa) in the bit-string representing the absolute value of the negative number.

There is yet a third procedure for representing negative integers, namely *TWO'S COMPLEMENT* notation. For interpreting this notation, we attach a negative weight of -2^{n-1} (assuming a word length of n bits) to the leftmost bit, but leave the weights of the remaining bits unchanged (i.e., 2^{k-1} for the kth bit, where k=1, 2,...,n-1). As a result, fixed-point values with sign-bit 1 are construed as being equal to -2^{n-1} plus the positive integer value represented in positional form by the remaining bits. One way of determining the two's complement representation of a negative fixed-point number involves merely adding unity to the one's complement of the bit-string representing the corresponding positive value.

Figure 1.1 illustrates the use of both one and two's complement notation for representing -26. It assumes that we are using sixteen bits to represent fixed-point values. In such a case, the two's complement form is equivalent to the bit-string yielded by subtracting the number

$$(26)_{10} = (0000000000011010)_2$$

from

$$(2^{16})_{10} = (10000000000000000)_2$$

using ordinary binary subtraction.

There is an alternative algorithm for determining the two's complement form of a negative fixed-point value. We scan the bit-string representing the corresponding positive value from right to left until the first 1-bit is encountered. We leave this 1-bit, together with all the 0-bits to the right of it (if any), unaltered. All the bits to the left of this 1-bit, however, are inverted. This gives us the same representation as the algorithm discussed earlier. As an illustration of the numerical validity of these algorithms, consider the two's complement representation of -26 as indicated in Figure 1.1. The leftmost bit has a weight of $-2^{15} = -32768$, while the remaining fifteen bits represent 32742 in true binary form. It follows that -32768 + 32742 is equal to -26, as we expected.

```
          SIGN
          BIT
           ↓
+26        0  0000000  00011010
Invert:    1  1111111  11100101 (One's complement form)
Add 1:                        1
           ---------------------
-26        1  1111111  11100110 (Two's complement form)
```

Figure 1.1

One and Two's Complement Representation of -26

The advantage of using two's complement notation to represent negative fixed-point values lies in the fact that it reduces the operation of integer subtraction to simple integer addition, as illustrated by Examples (i) through (vi). For the sake of brevity, only eight bit-positions are used, with the leftmost bit corresponding to the sign-bit. All negative values are expressed in two's complement form.

(i)	+57	=	00111001	
	+35	=	00100011	
	+92	=	01011100	
(ii)	+57	=	00111001	Subtracting 35 from 57 is equivalent to adding -35 to 57. Consequently, we add the two integers (one of which is expressed in two's complement form), including the sign-bit, as in ordinary binary addition. We ignore the carry out of the high-order (sign) bit-position.
	-35	=	11011101	
	+22	=	00010110	
(iii)	+35	=	00100011	The sign-bit of the result is 1, thus denoting a negative integer. Consequently, we interpret this notation by using the actual definition of two's complement form [i.e., $(-2^7)_{10} + (1101010)_2 = -128 + 106 = -22$].
	-57	=	11000111	
	-22	=	11101010	
(iv)	-57	=	11000111	Ignore the carry out of the high-order (sign) bit-position.
	-35	=	11011101	
	-92	=	10100100	
(v)	-57	=	11000111	Overflow.
	-92	=	10100100	
	-149	≠	01101011	

(vi) +57 = 00111001 Overflow.

$$\begin{array}{rcl} +57 & = & 00111001 \\ \underline{+92} & = & \underline{01011100} \\ +149 & \neq & 10010101 \end{array}$$

The largest positive integer capable of being stored in eight bit-positions is $2^7-1 = 127_{10}$ (reserving a high-order bit of 0 to indicate a positive value). The smallest integer we can store in eight bits (using two's complement form) is $-2^7 = -128_{10}$. The difference in the magnitudes of the upper and lower bounds is a result of excluding negative zero. In Examples (v) and (vi), the results obtained by regular binary addition (i.e., treating the sign-bit similar to any other bit) are obviously incorrect. This is due to the fact that the actual results lie outside the range of numbers (-128 to +127) which can be accurately represented by eight bit-positions. In such cases of *OVERFLOW*, only the low-order eight bits are left to represent the result. Such truncation would invalidate any subsequent computation involving these values.

1.2.1 S/360 Fixed-Point

In the S/360 memory, fixed-point operands may be recorded in half-word (i.e., sixteen bits) or full-word (i.e., thirty-two bits) lengths. In both cases, the leftmost bit-position represents the sign of the number, following the usual convention of using 0 for positive and 1 for negative values. For positive fixed-point values, the remaining bit-positions (i.e., fifteen for half-words and thirty-one for full-words) indicate the magnitude of the number involved. Two's complement notation is used to represent negative fixed-point values. Figure 1.2 provides several examples of fixed-point numbers as they are represented in a full-word of S/360 memory. The first value is the largest integer that can be represented by thirty-two bits (including a 0 sign-bit), and the last is the smallest integer (expressed in two's complement form).

NUMBER		DECIMAL NOTATION		SIGN BIT	INTEGER
$2^{31}-1$	=	2147483647	=	0	1111111 11111111 11111111 11111111
2^{16}	=	65536	=	0	0000000 00000001 00000000 00000000
2^{1}	=	2	=	0	0000000 00000000 00000000 00000010
2^{0}	=	1	=	0	0000000 00000000 00000000 00000001
0	=	0	=	0	0000000 00000000 00000000 00000000
-2^{0}	=	-1	=	1	1111111 11111111 11111111 11111111
-2^{1}	=	-2	=	1	1111111 11111111 11111111 11111110
-2^{16}	=	-65536	=	1	1111111 11111111 00000000 00000000
$-2^{31}+1$	=	-2147483647	=	1	0000000 00000000 00000000 00000001
-2^{31}	=	-2147483648	=	1	0000000 00000000 00000000 00000000

Figure 1.2

S/360 Fixed-Point Representations

As we can see from Figure 1.2, the storage procedure used for representing integer values in the S/360 memory restricts full-word integer values to the range from -2^{31} to $2^{31}-1$ (i.e., -2147483648 to 2147483647). In the case of half-word integers, the range is -2^{15} to $2^{15}-1$ (i.e., -32768 to 32767), thus allowing a saving in space at the expense of a decrease in magnitude. We might warn the reader that it is the programmer's own responsibility to ensure that results of computations with fixed-point values do not fall outside these ranges, since many compilers give no indication of such occurrences. If, for example, two integers such as 2147483642 and 135 are added, the result cannot be stored in a full-word. The result "overflows" a word (a *FIXED-POINT OVERFLOW* is said to occur). Subsequently, the computer ignores the overflowed part of the result, and proceeds with the least significant part that will fit into a word. This very often leads to unexpected results, as illustrated by Examples (v) and (vi) presented earlier in this section.

1.3 FLOATING-POINT (REAL) REPRESENTATION

In the case of fixed-point notation, the programmer is always fully aware of where the binary point is assumed to be located. The weights associated with the various bits are fixed, since the position of the binary point never changes.

Numbers expressed in this form are easily manipulated for performing arithmetic operations. Unfortunately, however, the range of values which can be represented using this notation is quite limited. On the S/360, for example, we have seen that such numbers can range in magnitude up to slightly more than two billion. However, there are numerous occasions on which we might wish to deal with numbers larger in magnitude than fixed-point notation will permit (assuming, of course, that we are restricted to a reasonable word length). Furthermore, in many situations, it is considerably more convenient to allow the position of the binary point to vary (i.e., float) as the instructions of a program are being executed. With such a scheme, it is necessary to associate with each number some indicator of the appropriate position for the binary point.

The use of *FLOATING-POINT* notation dates back to the Babylonians (eighteenth century B.C.) who developed a sexagesimal (i.e., base-60) floating-point notation with the understanding that the appropriate power of 60 was to be supplied by the context (e.g., 2, 120, 7200, and 1/30 were all written in an identical manner). However, any significant use of floating-point notation was delayed until much later in the seventeenth century when logarithms and the slide rule were invented. Floating-point arithmetic was first incorporated into the design of some of the earliest computers during the 1940's. This availability of built-in floating-point facilities to automatically maintain binary point placement (i.e., scaling) during computation was considered to be a major advance in digital computer design. However, in spite of the fact that the availability of such hardware features considerably simplifies the task of the average programmer, not all computers possess built-in floating-point logic, primarily because of the added complexity in designing the arithmetic unit. Moreover, floating-point operations can be handled by programming alone without any extra hardware. Most large modern computers designed for scientific computation, however, do include built-in facilities for manipulating floating-point values.

The key to floating-point data representation is the separation of the significant digits of a number from the size (scale) of the number. In general, we obtain the base-r floating-point representation of a number N having n digits by expressing N as $f \times r^e$, where e is an integer exponent lying within some specified range, and f is a signed base-r fraction. Normally, we restrict f so that $|f| < 1$, implying that the radix point lies to the left of the positional notation for f. Consequently, the fact that N has n digits indicates that $|r^n f| < r^n$. To illustrate, if we use $r = 10$, we would express -83.2715 as $-.832715 \times 10^2$, and 9999.99 as $.999999 \times 10^4$. When we express N as $f \times r^e$, we refer to f as the *FRACTION* part and to e as the *EXPONENT* part. Some books call these two components the *MANTISSA* and *CHARACTERISTIC* respectively.

A floating-point representation, $f \times r^e$, is said to be *NORMALIZED* when the digit immediately adjacent to the radix point in the representation of f is non-zero (i.e., $1/r \leq |f| < 1$), or when f is zero and e is as small as the specified range will permit. For example, $.321 \times 10^{-3}$ is a normalized form, whereas $.0321 \times 10^{-2}$ is not normalized. It is easy to determine which of two normalized floating-point values is larger in magnitude. We merely compare the exponent parts first, and subsequently we need examine the fraction parts only in the case of equal exponents. Most floating-point routines now available on present-day computers deal almost exclusively with normalized values.

As we have already indicated, numbers expressed in floating-point notation have two parts associated with them, a fraction part for representing the significant digits of the number, and an exponent part to specify the appropriate position of the radix point. Consequently, we must subdivide a word of memory into two parts, allocating one group of bits to represent the fraction and the remaining bits to indicate the exponent. This implies that the computer will represent a floating-point value as a binary fraction multiplied by 2 raised to a binary exponent. The weights (i.e., powers of 2) associated with different bits in the positional representation of the fraction part will be variable (i.e., floating), depending entirely upon the value of the exponent which specifies the proper location of the binary point.

By sacrificing part of the memory word to represent the exponent, we are losing precision, since we will have fewer bits to represent the fraction part. However, we vastly increase the range in magnitude of values which can be handled. For a fixed word length, it is obvious that the range in magnitude involved with such values will vary inversely with the number of significant digits retained.

It appears to be much more advantageous to use signed-magnitude representation for floating-point values than to utilize complement notation. However, there are two signs associated with such a value, one for the fraction part and another for the exponent. One solution would involve designating one of the bits assigned to represent the exponent as a sign-bit. However, a more flexible solution would be to maintain only one sign-bit to be associated with the fraction part. Using such a scheme, we merely add a fixed constant value to our true exponent. For example, if we had two decimal digits available to represent an exponent, we would use excess-50 notation where 50 is added to the true exponent. Consequently, our excess-50 exponent value would be free to range from 00 to 99, thus permitting us to represent true exponents in the range -50 to +49 without requiring a separate sign position. For machine representation, the fixed value to be added to the true binary exponent depends upon the number of bits allocated to represent the exponent part of the floating-point value.

1.3.1 S/360 Floating-Point

For various reasons, the S/360 hardware implementation of floating-point numbers was designed to manipulate bits in groups of four (i.e., half-bytes). Consequently, for representation in the S/360 memory, a floating-point number is expressed as a normalized hexadecimal fraction multiplied by 16 raised to an appropriate power (i.e., $(f)_{16} \times 16^{e}$). For example, $(26.25)_{10} = (1A.4)_{16}$, which is then expressed as $(.1A4)_{16} \times 16^{2}$. Within a specified fraction length, a floating-point arithmetic operation will provide maximum precision if the fraction is normalized. A hexadecimal fraction is normalized when the high-order digit (denoted in computer memory by the first four bit-positions in the bit-string allocated to represent the fraction) is non-zero. During floating-point computation, automatic normalization of intermediate values is provided by built-in machine instructions. Such normalization is accomplished by left-shifting the fraction, four bits per shift, until a non-zero hexadecimal digit occupies the high-order digit position. For each shift of four bits, the hexadecimal exponent part is reduced by unity.

A FORTRAN single-precision floating-point value occupies a full word of memory on the S/360. The fraction part is stored as six hexadecimal digits (i.e., twenty-four bits), $H_1\ H_2\ H_3\ H_4\ H_5\ H_6$, in the three rightmost bytes of the word. The remaining byte (i.e., eight bits) is reserved to represent the exponent and the sign of the fraction.

The fraction's sign is represented by the regular sign-bit of the word, namely the leftmost bit. Following the usual conventions with signed-magnitude notation, a 0 sign-bit indicates a positive fraction, leaving a 1-bit to represent a negative value. The remaining seven rightmost bits of the first byte are allocated to represent the exponent using excess-64 notation. Using this scheme, we merely add $(64)_{10} = (2^6)_{10} = (40)_{16}$ to the true hexadecimal exponent.

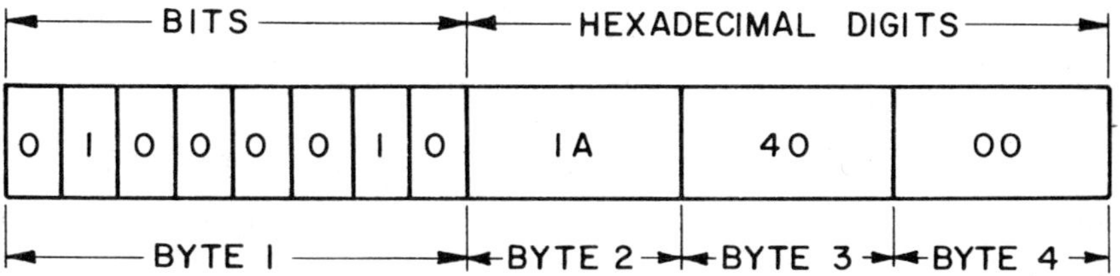

Figure 1.3

S/360 Representation of 26.25

Figure 1.3 portrays the internal memory representation on the S/360 for the floating-point value $(26.25)_{10} = (.1A4)_{16} \times 16^2$. Expressed completely in hexadecimal terms, the bit-string representing 26.25 would be written as $(421A4000)_{16}$. We must realize that the leftmost hexadecimal digit includes the 0 sign-bit. For $(-26.25)_{10}$, the bit-string representation would be identical, except for the sign-bit which would be changed to 1. Expressed in hexadecimal terms, however, we would have $(C21A4000)_{16}$. The hexadecimal digit "C"

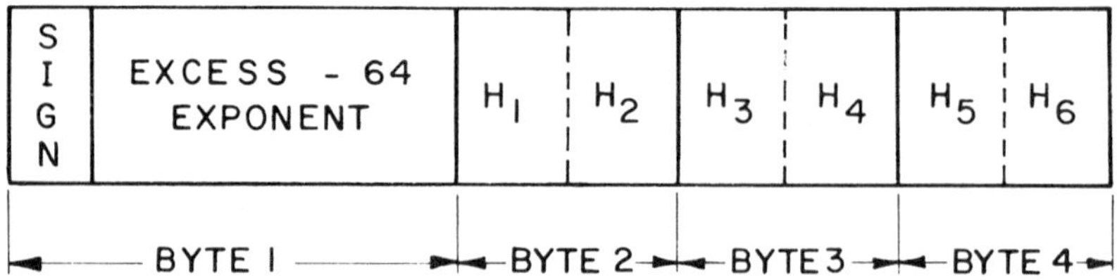

Figure 1.4

General Single-Precision
Floating-Point Format for the S/360

reflects the new sign-bit 1. Figure 1.4 indicates the general internal format for representing single-precision floating-point values on the S/360.

The seven bits available to represent the exponent part of a floating-point number can store any value ranging from 0 to $2^7 - 1 = 127$. By using excess-64 notation, we split this range in half, thus permitting the actual exponent to range from -64 to 63. Consequently, the largest single-precision floating-point number which can be represented on the S/360 is $(.FFFFFF)_{16} \times 16^{63}$ which is approximately 0.7237005×10^{76} using decimal notation. In comparison, the smallest in magnitude (excluding zero which is represented by thirty-two 0-bits) is $(.1)_{16} \times 16^{-64}$, or approximately $0.5397605 \times 10^{-78}$. We might contrast this range in magnitude to that involved with fixed-point representation where values can range in size only as high as $2^{31} - 1 = 2,147,483,647$ (i.e., approximately 2×10^9). This tremendous increase in range achieved by using floating-point notation is gained by sacrificing some precision in the numbers which can be represented (i.e., a drop to seven significant decimal digits from nine or ten). Actually, $(FFFFFF)_{16}$ is equivalent to $2^{24} - 1 = 16,777,215$ in decimal notation. As a result, WATFIV prints out a maximum of seven significant decimal digits for a single-precision floating-point value. Computation with such values, however, carries slightly more accuracy, utilizing the equivalent of about 7.2 decimal digits.

As illustrated in Appendix A, some simple decimal fractions do not have a simple hexadecimal fraction equivalent. In fact, there are numerous simple decimal fractions which cannot be represented exactly by any finite base-16 fraction. Such a phenomenon can cause considerable problems for unsuspecting computer users who write programs involving floating-point arithmetic. Example 1.1 illustrates the type of problems caused by non-exact conversion of decimal data.

```
C EXAMPLE 1.1 - NON-EXACT CONVERSION
C               OF DECIMAL DATA
C
      X = 0.0
    5 PRINT,X
      X = X+0.2
      IF(X.NE.2.0)GO TO 5
      STOP
      END
```

On first examination, it appears that this program will terminate execution after ten loops. However, deeper examination reveals that the program involves an infinite loop. This situation exists because the simple decimal fraction 0.2 cannot be represented exactly by a finite hexadecimal fraction. Actually, $(.2)_{10}$ is equivalent to the infinite hexadecimal fraction $(.333333...)_{16}$. Since WATFIV rounds any single-precision floating-point value to be stored in the S/360 memory at six significant hexadecimal digits, the actual internal memory representation of $(0.2)_{10}$ is equivalent to $(.333333)_{16} \times 16^0$ which is only a truncated approximation to the true value. Consequently, the accumulated error in successive evaluations of the variable X causes the value of X to be slightly less than 2 (after ten increments) rather than exactly equal to 2. In fact, the value of X after ten increments is represented internally as $(.1FFFFF)_{16} \times 16^1$ which is indeed not equal to the internal representation of 2.0, namely $(.200000)_{16} \times 16^1$. As a result, the value of X is never exactly equal to 2.0 from the computer's view-point, thus setting the stage for an infinite loop in the program.

A FORTRAN double-precision value occupies two adjacent words (i.e., eight bytes) of S/360 memory, and is stored using double-precision floating-point notation. This differs from the single-precision form only in that the rightmost four bytes store eight additional hexadecimal digits of precision for the fraction part. The internal storage format of such values is illustrated in Figure 1.5.

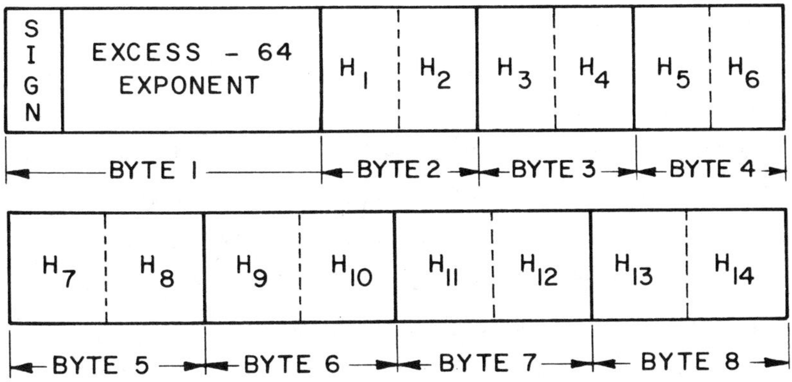

Figure 1.5

S/360 Double-Precision Storage Format

Since the internal representation of the exponent is the same for both double and single-precision floating-point values, the acceptable range of magnitudes for both types of number will be essentially the same. However, there is a considerable gain in the number of significant digits involved with double-precision values. As an illustration, consider the simple decimal constant 2.3. The single-precision representation of 2.3 is equivalent to $(.24CCCD)_{16} \times 16^{1}$ (i.e., rounded to six significant hexadecimal digits). In comparison, the double-precision format for 2.3 is equivalent to $(.24CCCCCCCCCCCC)_{16} \times 16^{1}$ (i.e., WATFIV truncates to fourteen hexadecimal digits). Although neither of these is an exact representation of 2.3, the double-precision form will generate much less of an error in subsequent calculations than its single-precision counterpart.

As we have indicated, the increase in precision is more than double because of the fact that there is no need to use any of the extra four bytes to represent an exponent part. Actually, the value of $(FFFFFFFFFFFFFF)_{16}$ is equivalent to the number $2^{56} - 1 = 72,057,594,037,927,935$ (expressed in decimal notation). Consequently, WATFIV prints out a maximum of sixteen significant decimal digits for a double-precision floating-point value. Computation with such numbers, however, proceeds with the equivalent of approximately 16.7 decimal digits.

1.4 HEXADECIMAL FORMAT - EXAMPLES

Since we use hexadecimal notation as a convenient means of representing bit-strings in the S/360 memory, most FORTRAN compilers (including WATFIV) designed for use with this machine include provision for a special hexadecimal format code. The availability of this Z FORMAT specification allows us to transmit data to and from the computer memory in hexadecimal form. It can be used in conjunction with any variable type, and permits programmers to investigate the actual bit structure used by the computer to represent various values. When using the Z FORMAT code, a programmer must be aware of the number of bytes referenced by the different variable names accompanying the use of such specifications. This special code can be used with READ statements or compile-time initialization statements as a means of constructing specific bit patterns in the computer memory.

```
C EXAMPLE 1.2 - SIMPLE USE OF "Z" FORMAT
C
      I = 29
      A = 29.0
      PRINT 40,I,I,A,A
   40 FORMAT('0',I4,3X,Z8,F5.1,Z10)
      STOP
      END
```

```
b̸b̸29 b̸b̸b̸ 0000001D b̸29.0 b̸b̸421D0000
 I4   3X      Z8      F5.1     Z10
 I            I       A        A
```

(Note: "b̸" will represent a blank space.)

In the output from Example 1.2, the field 0000001D is the hexadecimal representation of the bit-string contained in the full-word of S/360 memory denoted by the INTEGER variable I. Similarly, 421D0000 is the hexadecimal representation of the contents of the word denoted by the REAL variable A. Since a word, or four bytes, is equivalent to eight hexadecimal digits, the rightmost field printed has been filled on the left with two blanks to make up the requested printed field of width ten.

In Example 1.3, the bit structure in the memory word corresponding to both variables X and I (because of the EQUIVALENCE statement) is set to 01111111111111111111111111111111. This bit string, considered as representing an integer, is the S/360 notation for the largest positive integer suitable for memory storage, namely $2^{31} - 1 = 2147483647$.

```
C EXAMPLE 1.3 - SHARING MEMORY STORAGE
C
      EQUIVALENCE (I,X)
      READ 20,I
   20 FORMAT(Z8)
      PRINT 30,I,X
   30 FORMAT('b̸',I12,E15.7)
      STOP
      END
```

```
7FFFFFFF    (data)

b̸b̸2147483647  b̸b̸0.7237005Eb̸76    (output)
 \_________/    \_____________/
     I12             E15.7
      I                X
```

Similarly, the same bit configuration is the floating-point representation of $(.FFFFFF)_{16} \times 16^{63}$ (approximately 0.7237005×10^{76} in decimal form).

```
C EXAMPLE 1.4 - TWO'S COMPLEMENT NOTATION
C
      INTEGER*2 X/-1/
      PRINT 12,X
   12 FORMAT('0',Z6)
      STOP
      END
```

```
b̸b̸FFFF
```

In Example 1.4, the internal bit structure representing $(-1)_{10}$ in a half-word of the S/360 memory is a sequence of sixteen 1-bits corresponding to $(FFFF)_{16}$. The <u>leftmost</u> hexadecimal digit "F" reflects the 1 sign-bit of the two's complement representation.

In Example 1.5, the DATA statement establishes during compilation specific bit patterns in the words symbolically labelled K and J. These bit structures are the internal S/360 memory representations of 2^{16} and -2^{16} respectively.

```
C EXAMPLE 1.5 - CONSTRUCTING BIT PATTERNS
C
      DATA K,J/Z10000,ZFFFF0000/
      PRINT 2,K,K,J,J
    2 FORMAT('0',Z8,I8,Z8,I8)
      STOP
      END
```

```
00010000  b̸b̸b̸65536  FFFF0000  b̸b̸-65536
   Z8        I8         Z8        I8
            2^16                 -2^16
        K                   J
```

In Example 1.6, a floating-point value is read as data and assigned to the single-precision variable X. Prior to being stored in the S/360 memory, such a value must first be converted by the machine into the form $(f)_{16} \times 16^{e}$, where f is a normalized hexadecimal fraction and e is the appropriate exponent expressed in base-10 notation. The printed output from Example 1.6 is the particular value of e associated with the given number X.

```
C EXAMPLE 1.6 - SEPARATION OF AN EXPONENT
C
      EQUIVALENCE (X,IX)
      READ,X
      X = ABS(X)
      IEXP = IX/2**24-64
      PRINT,IEXP
      STOP
      END
```

The EQUIVALENCE statement in Example 1.6 allows us to manipulate the bit-string representing the floating-point value as an ordinary fixed-point representation. In order to obtain the desired value, we must first isolate the seven rightmost bits in the leftmost byte for further manipulation. Provided that the sign-bit is 0, we can accomplish this by dividing the value of IX by 2^{24}. We can ensure that the sign-bit is 0 by replacing X by ABS(X). Such an operation leaves the remaining thirty-one bits unaltered, since floating-point values are recorded using signed-magnitude notation. The quotient of our division by 2^{24} represents the excess-64 exponent involved with the specified value of X. However, since we are seeking the true exponent, we merely subtract 64 to determine the desired value of *e*. As an illustration, if the data value were -0.78125E-02, the printed output would be -1, since $(-0.78125E-02)_{10} = (-.0078125)_{10} = (-.02)_{16} = (-.2)_{16} \times 16^{-1}$.

In the exercises which follow at the end of this chapter, the tables presented in Figures 1.6 and 1.7 should be of considerable assistance.

N	2^N	N	2^N	N	2^N
0	1	11	2048	22	4194304
1	2	12	4096	23	8388608
2	4	13	8192	24	16777216
3	8	14	16384	25	33554432
4	16	15	32768	26	67108864
5	32	16	65536	27	134217728
6	64	17	131072	28	268435456
7	128	18	262144	29	536870912
8	256	19	524288	30	1073741824
9	512	20	1048576	31	2147483648
10	1024	21	2097152	32	4294967296

Figure 1.6

Powers of 2

HEX	BIN	HEX	BIN
0	0000	8	1000
1	0001	9	1001
2	0010	A	1010
3	0011	B	1011
4	0100	C	1100
5	0101	D	1101
6	0110	E	1110
7	0111	F	1111

Figure 1.7

Hexadecimal Digits

1.5 EXERCISES

1. Give the printed output generated by Example 1.7, assuming that columns 1-8 of the four data cards involved contain 00006FAE, 00058132, 00ABCDEF, and B3A89DE7 respectively.

```
C EXAMPLE 1.7 - EXERCISE
C
      DO 2 I=1,4
      READ 1,J
    1 FORMAT(Z8)
      K = -J
    2 PRINT 3,J,K
    3 FORMAT('0',2Z10)
      STOP
      END
```

2. Assuming that the data values involved are -50, 798, -32767 (i.e., $-2^{15} + 1$), -61681, and -2147483647 (i.e., $-2^{31} + 1$) respectively, give the printed output generated by Example 1.8.

```
C EXAMPLE 1.8 - EXERCISE
C
      DO 2 I=1,5
      READ,J
    2 PRINT 3,J,J
    3 FORMAT('0',I15,Z10)
      STOP
      END
```

3. Perform the operation of <u>subtraction</u> on the following pairs of numbers, subtracting the second from the first. <u>Use two's complement</u>

representations to perform this subtraction.
Check your results by converting to decimal and doing base-10 subtraction. All the pairs of numbers given are expressed in base-16. Assume a word length of twenty bits.

(i)		(ii)		(iii)		(iv)		(v)	
	B19C		48AD0		4A5E7		73A		CCCC
	6FF		B3EF		B93C		D50F		4A5E7

4. What is the printed output from Example 1.9? Why do we obtain such an unusual result?

```
C EXAMPLE 1.9 - EXERCISE
C
      I = -2147483648
      J = IABS(I)
      PRINT,I,J
      STOP
      END
```

5. Give the printed output generated by Example 1.10. Explain the reasons for such unusual results.

```
C EXAMPLE 1.10 - EXERCISE
C
      INTEGER*2 I,J
      I = 2**15
      J = 2*I
      PRINT,I,J
      STOP
      END
```

6. Given that columns 1-8 of eight successive data cards contain 41100000, 41200000, 41480000,

C2560000, 437F0000, A4630500, 41833333, and C1833333 respectively, what is the printed output from Example 1.11?

```
C EXAMPLE 1.11 - EXERCISE
C
      DO 2 I=1,8
      READ 1,X
    1 FORMAT(Z8)
    2 PRINT 3,X,X
    3 FORMAT('0',Z10,E18.7)
      STOP
      END
```

7. Suppose we have the following pairs of values punched on five successive data cards:

```
     1.3             1.3
    10.5            10.5
    -1.75           -1.75
     5.11            5.11
   329.354         329.354
```

What would be the printed output from Example 1.12?

```
C EXAMPLE 1.12 - EXERCISE
C
      REAL*4 X
      REAL*8 Y
      DO 1 I=1,5
      READ,X,Y
    1 PRINT 2,X,X,Y
    2 FORMAT('0',E20.7,Z12,Z20)
      STOP
      END
```

8. Give the printed output generated by Example 1.13, assuming a data value -26.25. Explain briefly what the program is designed to do.

```
C EXAMPLE 1.13 - EXERCISE
C
      INTEGER COUNT
      EQUIVALENCE (X,K)
      READ,X
      COUNT = 0
      DO 5 I=1,32
      IF(K.LT.0)COUNT = COUNT+1
    5 K = 2*K
      PRINT,COUNT
      STOP
      END
```

9. Twenty consecutive elements of an INTEGER vector called LOOSE are used to store twenty positive fixed-point constants, each less than 2^8. Write a FORTRAN program which reads twenty such constants into array LOOSE, and then packs them, four per word, into another INTEGER array of five words called PACKED. You can use Z FORMAT for printing the entries of PACKED and LOOSE as a means of testing whether or not your program is correct.

10.(a) Write a FORTRAN program to print in reverse order the string of thirty-two bits which represents the S/360 memory format for a given fixed-point data value (expressed in decimal notation). For example, $(25,829)_{10}$ is represented by the bit-string

00000000000000000110010011100101,

and consequently, the printed output would be

10100111001001100000000000000000.

(b) Instead of merely *printing* the bit-string in reverse order as requested in part (a), change your program to actually create internally in memory a bit-string which is in reverse order to the given data-string. Print out *both* bit-strings, using Z FORMAT, to test whether or not your program is working properly.

CHAPTER TWO
LOGICAL OPERATIONS

2.1 INTRODUCTION

In this chapter, we will be considering data of type *LOGICAL* and the operations which can be performed upon this new data type. A logical quantity is one that can be either "true" or "false". Such quantities may be constant (i.e., always true or always false; e.g., "Five is less than seven." is always true.) or variable (e.g., "I have more than $50 in the bank." may or may not be a true statement.).

Whenever we introduce a new type of data item, our first step should be to define precisely what we mean by constants and variables in this new classification. The two logical constants in FORTRAN are written as .TRUE. and .FALSE.. Logical variables are merely those variables which can be assigned such values, and must be explicitly declared in a type declaration statement such as the following:

```
LOGICAL A,L,X,D(10),B(10,5)
```

The internal memory representation of logical values is completely dependent upon the compiler that is processing the program and the machine for which the compiler was designed. WATFIV, like all the conventional FORTRAN compilers, assigns a full word (i.e., four bytes on the S/360) to each logical variable. It represents the value .TRUE. by eight 1-bits in the leftmost byte, and .FALSE. by eight 0-bits. In both cases, the remaining three bytes are ignored. This is extremely wasteful of memory space, especially if we are dealing with large amounts of logical data. Consequently, WATFIV does allow declarations of the following form:

```
LOGICAL*1 A,L,X,D(10),B(10,5)
```

This saves some memory space, since such variables are now assigned only one byte of memory instead of four. The eight-bit representations of .TRUE. and .FALSE. remain the same, however, even though we really need only one bit (i.e., 1 for .TRUE. and 0 for .FALSE.) to distinguish between the two possible logical values.

Logical constants and variables can be useful in programming to make decisions regarding the proper sequence of instructions to be executed. For example, a fairly common decision we might wish to make involves recognizing the end of a file on a magnetic tape. A logical variable such as ENDFIL could be assigned the value .TRUE. when the last record (i.e., collection of information) has been encountered (i.e., read), and this value could be used to determine the future actions of the program. Such a decision could also be made by testing for a particular value of an arithmetic quantity. For example, we could set EOF = 1 when the last record has been read, and later test variable EOF for the value 1. However, in many cases, the use of logical quantities makes a program more meaningful and easier to understand.

2.2 MANIPULATION OF LOGICAL DATA IN FORTRAN

Once we have defined the constants and variables for a new data type, we can consider the operations which can be performed upon such data items. FORTRAN provides three new operators which can be utilized to combine logical quantities. These operators are defined as follows:

.AND. - The result of X.AND.Y is .TRUE. only if the logical expressions X and Y both have the value .TRUE.. Otherwise, the result is .FALSE..

.OR. - The result of X.OR.Y is .TRUE. if either or both X and Y have the value .TRUE.. If both X and Y are .FALSE., the result is .FALSE..

.NOT. - This unary operator negates the value of a variable. Thus .NOT.X is .TRUE. if X has the value .FALSE., and .FALSE. if X is .TRUE..

These three *LOGICAL OPERATORS* are analogous to the more common multiplication, addition, and unary subtraction operators which are defined for arithmetic data values. They are defined to act upon logical operands rather than numerical ones. Furthermore, they can be combined to produce more complicated expressions. As a result, we must establish a priority rating for these three operators so that there will be no ambiguity as to which operators are applied before others. In the absence of parentheses to indicate otherwise, the logical operators are applied in the following descending order of priority:

(1) .NOT.   (2) .AND.   (3) .OR.

Example (i):

Let X be .TRUE., Y be .FALSE., and Z be .FALSE.. Then X.AND..NOT.Y.OR.Z has the value .TRUE.. Applying .NOT. gives us X.AND..TRUE..OR.Z; then applying .AND. gives us .TRUE..OR.Z which is .TRUE..

Example (ii):

Let X,Y, and Z have the same values as in Example (i). Then consider the following expression:

X.OR..NOT.Z.AND.X.OR..NOT.Y.AND..TRUE.

Here we are faced with two appearances of each of the three operators. To determine which of each pair should be applied first, we adopt the usual FORTRAN convention that operators be applied left-to-right in cases of equal priority. Although parentheses are unnecessary (unless we wish to alter the normal order of operations), we might insert them in this expression to further clarify the order of evaluation. The innermost operators are applied first.

((X.OR.((.NOT.Z).AND.X)).OR.((.NOT.X).AND..TRUE.))

If we apply the operators in the specified order, this expression will have the value .TRUE..

We have considered two examples involving logical-valued expressions which were comprised exclusively of logical operands and logical operators. However, this is not the only type of expression which can have a logical value. For example, consider the expression X.LT.10, where .LT. is a *RELATIONAL OPERATOR* meaning "less than". It is applied to two arithmetic operands to produce a logical result. This expression will have the value .TRUE. if X is indeed less than 10, and the value .FALSE. otherwise. A complete list of the six relational operators available in FORTRAN, together with their meanings and algebraic equivalents, is given in Figure 2.1.

Relational operators in FORTRAN are used exclusively to compare two fixed-point or floating-point operands. They cannot, for instance, be used to compare two complex-valued operands for equality or non-equality, unless we test the two parts of the complex values individually. Furthermore, we cannot use them to test two logical operands for equality or non-equality. We must use the logical operators for this purpose.

RELATIONAL OPERATOR	ALGEBRAIC EQUIVALENT	MEANING
.LT.	$a < b$	less than
.LE.	$a \leq b$	less than or equal to
.EQ.	$a = b$	equal to
.NE.	$a \neq b$	not equal to
.GE.	$a \geq b$	greater than or equal to
.GT.	$a > b$	greater than

Figure 2.1

FORTRAN Relational Operators

We know that relational operators compare the values of two arithmetic operands to produce a logical-valued result. However, in what order do we apply the various operators if one or both of the arithmetic operands involves some computation? To illustrate, consider the following examples:

(i)	A+B.GE.C	$(a+b) \geq c$
(ii)	X.NE.A**2	$x \neq a^2$
(iii)	Y+4.LT.X*Y/Z	$y+4 < xy/z$

In FORTRAN, such expressions are evaluated by applying the arithmetic operators before the relational ones. Consequently, in Examples (i), (ii), and (iii), the arithmetic quantities A+B, A**2, Y+4, and X*Y/Z are computed before their values are compared by the appropriate relational operators. In such cases, of course, the customary priority rules for arithmetic operators are applied.

Not all programming languages, however, follow the same operator priority scheme as adopted in FORTRAN. Some languages, such as APL, follow the convention that each operator is applied as soon as it is encountered in a right-to-left scan of the expression to be evaluated. Furthermore, some languages (e.g., PL/1) include a provision for mixing logical and arithmetic operands in a manner entirely unacceptable in FORTRAN. For example, consider the following assignment statement:

$$y = 0.5 + (x > 7) * 5.6$$

With such languages, the arithmetic operations on mixed operands are defined as if the logical quantities had the numerical values 0 and 1 (corresponding to .FALSE. and .TRUE., respectively). As a result, the value produced by applying the relational operator ">" will be 1 or 0, depending upon the value of the variable x. It follows that variable y will be assigned the value 0.5 if $x \le 7$ and 6.1 otherwise.

A *LOGICAL EXPRESSION* in FORTRAN can be defined as any combination of constants, variables, and operators which produces a logical-valued result when it is evaluated. We have already considered examples of logical expressions involving logical operators (e.g., A.AND.B) and relational operators (e.g., A.LT.B-C). There is nothing to prevent our combining both types of operator to form more complicated expressions. As an illustration, consider:

X.AND..NOT.P.EQ.Q/R*S.OR.L/M.LT.5

We are already aware that arithmetic operators are applied before relational ones. These, in turn, are applied before the logical operators. The arithmetic and logical operators are ranked among themselves with respect to priority of application. The relational operators, however, are applied in order from left to right (i.e., they all share the same priority rating) throughout the expression. The three types of operators are summarized in Figure 2.2.(arranged in descending order of priority).

OPERATOR	OPERANDS	RESULT
Arithmetic	Arithmetic	Arithmetic
Relational	Arithmetic	Logical
Logical	Logical	Logical

Figure 2.2

Summary of FORTRAN Operators

Parentheses can always be inserted to alter the normal priority scheme of the various operations. Once again, although such action is not necessary in this case, we might insert parentheses into our most recent example of a logical expression to further clarify the order of evaluation:

```
((X.AND.(.NOT.(P.EQ.(Q/R*S)))).OR.(L/M.LT.5))
```

The value of such a logical expression can be assigned to a logical variable using a *LOGICAL ASSIGNMENT STATEMENT*. We include some examples of this type of assignment statement.

(i) A = .TRUE.

(ii) B = X.AND..NOT.Y

(iii) KAP = I.LE.J.OR.J.GT.K

(iv) TABLE(1,3) = SIN(X)/(1-SIN(X)**2).GE.0.5

In summary, FORTRAN provides arithmetic operators to manipulate numeric quantities and logical operators to combine logical quantities. Furthermore, it has relational operators to provide conversion from the numeric domain to the logical domain.

Earlier in this chapter we mentioned that logical quantities could be useful to make decisions regarding the flow of execution in a program. Such decisions usually appear in the form of a *LOGICAL IF* statement. This statement has the following general form:

IF (ℓ) S

where "ℓ" is any logical expression, and "S" may be any executable FORTRAN statement except a DO statement or another LOGICAL IF statement. If the value of "ℓ" is .TRUE., then statement "S" is executed. Then, provided control has not been passed to another point in the program, the next instruction executed is the first executable statement following the LOGICAL IF statement. If "ℓ" is .FALSE., however, statement "S" is ignored, and control passes to the first executable statement following the LOGICAL IF. The following examples illustrate some of the possibilities:

```
  (i)  IF(A.GT.B)GO TO 10
 (ii)  IF(ENDFIL)C = C+1
(iii)  IF(X(N)-X(N-1).LT.10.**(-6))RETURN
 (iv)  IF(P.GT.Q**2.OR.BLACK.AND.WHITE)PRINT,X
  (v)  IF(I.EQ.J)CALL SUBR(I)
 (vi)  IF(I.NE.K+5)Y = SIN(X)+Z
(vii)  IF(I**3.LT.1000)READ,J
```

2.3 LOGICAL FUNCTIONS

Now that we have examined the basic concepts involved with logical data, we should be in a position to consider some functions of type logical. Such functions will obviously return to the user a value .TRUE. or .FALSE.. As an illustration, suppose we wanted to know when either X or Y was .TRUE., but not both. The FORTRAN coding for this function, usually referred to as the EXCLUSIVE OR function, is presented in Example 2.1. Function EXOR will return the value .TRUE. if the two logical parameters have different values, and the value .FALSE. otherwise.

```
C EXAMPLE 2.1 - THE "EXCLUSIVE OR" FUNCTION
C               WITH LOGICAL ARGUMENTS
C
      LOGICAL FUNCTION EXOR*1(X,Y)
C
      LOGICAL*1 X,Y
      EXOR = X.AND..NOT.Y.OR.Y.AND..NOT.X
      RETURN
      END
```

If X, Y, and Z all have the value .TRUE., consider the value of the following logical expression:

EXOR(EXOR(X,Y),Z)

EXOR(X,Y) will be .FALSE., and, as a result, the value of this complete expression will be .TRUE.. Consequently, we can conclude that the result of applying function EXOR is .TRUE. whenever it is applied with either one, or three, .TRUE. values.

In general, the EXOR function returns a value .TRUE. if applied to an odd number of .TRUE. values, and .FALSE. if applied to an even number of .TRUE. values. This property can be used in situations where it is necessary to know if we have an odd or even number of bits. Such a situation arises during the transmission of data. For example, a character can be recorded on magnetic tape as nine bits; eight to represent the actual character, plus one extra "check" or "parity" bit which is added to make the total number of 1's either even or odd, depending upon the representation chosen. If there should be an even number of 1's, but the character transmitted has an odd number of 1's, then we know there has been an error in transmission. In a later example, when we simulate binary addition, we will see another use for this counting property of the EXCLUSIVE OR function.

In our earlier discussion of logical declaration statements, we noted that a single bit is sufficient to represent the values .TRUE. (1) and

.FALSE. (0). Following this convention, we can define the logical operators .AND., .OR., and .NOT. by the tables in Figure 2.3. We can also construct such a table for function EXOR (included with Figure 2.3). In this latter case, the result will be 1 whenever either, but not both, of the arguments is 1, and 0 otherwise.

X	Y	.AND.
0	0	0
0	1	0
1	0	0
1	1	1

X	Y	.OR.
0	0	0
0	1	1
1	0	1
1	1	1

X	.NOT.
0	1
1	0

X	Y	EXOR
0	0	0
0	1	1
1	0	1
1	1	0

Figure 2.3

Truth Tables for .AND.,.OR.,.NOT., and EXOR

For two logical (sometimes called Boolean) variables, we have four different combinations of the values 0 and 1. Furthermore, it is clear that we may have two possible results (0 or 1) after performing some operation with each X-Y pair. It follows that there are 2^4, or 16, different possible functions of two logical variables X and Y. Three of these will correspond to the logical operators .AND., .OR., and .NOT., and a fourth will be function EXOR. A complete table of these functions is presented in Figure 2.4. Actually, two of these sixteen functions will be constant values (see columns 0 and 15 in Figure 2.4).

X	Y	0	1	2	3	4	5	6	7	8	9	10	11	12	13	14	15
0	0	0	1	0	1	0	1	0	1	0	1	0	1	0	1	0	1
0	1	0	0	1	1	0	0	1	1	0	0	1	1	0	0	1	1
1	0	0	0	0	0	1	1	1	1	0	0	0	0	1	1	1	1
1	1	0	0	0	0	0	0	0	0	1	1	1	1	1	1	1	1

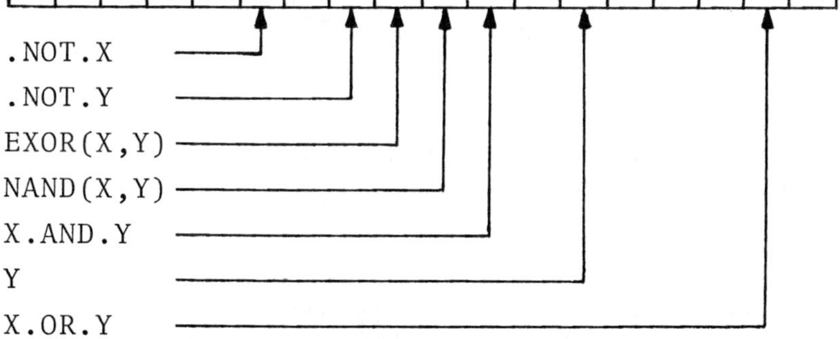

Figure 2.4

Sixteen Logical (Boolean) Functions of Two Variables

It is sometimes desirable in a program to be able to use any one of the sixteen possible functions as defined in Figure 2.4. To this end, we can design a function, BOOL, which accepts as parameters two logical variables, X and Y, and an integer value N (0 to 15), specifying one of the sixteen functions available. Function BOOL returns to the user the logical value obtained from applying function N to variables X and Y. The FORTRAN coding for this function is presented in Example 2.2.

```
C EXAMPLE 2.2 - SIXTEEN LOGICAL (BOOLEAN)
C               FUNCTIONS OF TWO VARIABLES
C
      LOGICAL FUNCTION BOOL*1(X,Y,N)
C
C The table for BOOL is in Figure 2.4.
C
      LOGICAL*1 X,Y,T(4,16)
C
      DATA ((T(I,J),J=1,16),I=1,4)
     2      /F,T,F,T,F,T,F,T,F,T,F,T,F,T,F,T,
     3       F,F,T,T,F,F,T,T,F,F,T,T,F,F,T,T,
     4       F,F,F,F,T,T,T,T,F,F,F,F,T,T,T,T,
     5       F,F,F,F,F,F,F,F,T,T,T,T,T,T,T,T/
C
      J = 1
C
C If X is .TRUE., move to the third row.
C Otherwise, stay in row 1.
C
      IF(X)J = J+2
C
C If Y is .TRUE., move to the second or fourth
C row, depending upon the earlier value of X.
C
      IF(Y)J = J+1
C
C Select the specified function.
C
      BOOL = T(J,N+1)
C
      RETURN
      END
```

Example 2.3 illustrates a possible reference to function BOOL. In this case, the value of variable Z is the result obtained from applying the

NAND (i.e., "NOT AND") function to variables X and Y. For the particular values of these two variables in this example, the result is .TRUE. (i.e., the entry in row 3 and column 8 of matrix T is .TRUE.). We can achieve the same result by using the statement Z=.NOT.(X.AND.Y).

```
C EXAMPLE 2.3 - CALL TO FUNCTION "BOOL"
C
      LOGICAL*1 X,Y,Z,BOOL
      .
      .
      .
      X = .TRUE.
      Y = .FALSE.
      Z = BOOL(X,Y,7)
```

2.4 BIT-STRING OPERATIONS

We have already indicated how logical operators can be applied to logical operands with values .TRUE. or .FALSE.. Furthermore, we have considered some examples (Figure 2.4) of various logical functions which can act upon pairs of logical values. However, the basic unit which we usually wish to manipulate in a program is a word which, for the S/360, is comprised of thirty-two bits. Since each bit can be either 0 or 1, we can consider a word as representing thirty-two logical (Boolean) quantities. It follows that we will want to have functions which perform various operations upon these bits.

Most FORTRAN compilers for the S/360 (including WATFIV) provide four built-in <u>functions</u> which operate on bit-strings of length 32. These functions operate on given bit-strings to produce a new bit-string. The actual variable names associated with these bit-strings may be of any type for which a full-word of memory is assigned (i.e., fixed-point, floating-point, logical). The four built-in functions and their descriptions are listed below:

(i) AND - This function accepts as parameters two bit-strings of length 32, and produces as its value a third bit-string. Each bit in the resulting string is obtained by performing an .AND. operation on all pairs of corresponding bits in the given strings. This function should not be confused with the logical operator .AND. which operates on two <u>logical</u> operands.

<u>Examples</u>:

```
....1001    ....1111
....1100    ....0101
....1000    ....0101
```

<u>Note</u>: In these examples, all bit-strings are assumed to be of length 32. However, for convenience, only a few bits are actually shown. Furthermore, the last line represents the resulting bit-string produced by the function.

(ii) OR - This function operates on two bit-strings simultaneously to produce a third bit-string whose individual bits are obtained by performing an .OR. operation on all pairs of corresponding bits in the given strings. Once again, this function should not be confused with the logical operator .OR. which operates on two <u>logical</u> operands.

<u>Examples</u>:

```
....0011     ....101111
....1001     ....000100
....1011     ....101111
```

(iii) EOR - This EXCLUSIVE OR function operates on two bit-strings to produce a third one. However, in this case, the bits in this new string are obtained by performing an EXCLUSIVE OR operation on all pairs of corresponding bits in the given strings. We must be careful not to confuse this new function with our logical-valued function, EXOR, which <u>we wrote</u> to operate on <u>logical</u> parameters.

<u>Examples</u>:

```
....001111     ....000011
....011010     ....100101
....010101     ....100110
```

(iv) COMPL - This "complement" function operates on <u>one</u> bit-string to produce another. The bits in this new string are obtained by negating the bits in the original string (i.e., performing a .NOT. operation on each of the original bits).

<u>Examples</u>: 00001111 0101011
....11110000 1010100

Each of the built-in functions AND, OR, EOR, and COMPL produces a new bit-string as its value. The type of the result in each case is <u>REAL</u>, since all variable names beginning with the letters A, O, E, and C are considered by FORTRAN compilers to be <u>REAL</u>. This is unfortunate, since we often wish to use the resulting string as an integer quantity in an assignment statement or for a comparison. We can overcome this obstacle, however, by using an EQUIVALENCE statement as illustrated in Example 2.4.

```
C EXAMPLE 2.4 - FUNCTION "AND" OPERATING
C               ON BIT-STRINGS
C
      EQUIVALENCE (A,IA)
      .
      .
      .
      A = AND(J,K)
      B = IA.NE.0
```

In Example 2.4, the variables A and IA are just two names for the same bit-string. When we refer to this string by the name A, the computer regards this string as representing a REAL value. Conversely, when we use the name IA, this same string of bits is considered to represent an INTEGER quantity. When we produce this bit-string using the AND function, we assign it to the variable A (to prevent any tampering with the string corresponding to a REAL-to-INTEGER mixed-mode conversion). However, for comparing this string of bits to zero, we use the name IA. To illustrate, suppose the bit-string produced by the AND function contains a single 1-bit somewhere in the seven rightmost bit-positions in the leftmost byte (i.e., the part representing the exponent of a floating-point value) and 0's elsewhere. Then the expression A.NE.0.0 would be .FALSE., since the twenty-four bits representing the fractional part of A would indeed be zero. However, using IA.NE.0 will indicate to us that the bit-string is not all 0's, since the value of this expression will be .TRUE..

We have seen that functions AND, OR, EOR, and COMPL can be used to form new bit-strings by acting upon other bit-strings. We can also make use of these functions to determine or change the value of a particular bit in a string without altering the other bits. For example, suppose we want to set the Jth bit (J = 1,2,...,32) of a string represented by variable I to have the value 1, without disturbing any of the remaining bits. This can be achieved by using the following coding:

```
EQUIVALENCE (I,X)
X = OR(I,2**(J-1))
```

Once again, we are using an EQUIVALENCE statement to avoid the problem of a mixed-mode conversion of the bit-string produced by the OR function. However, this is not the main issue. We have to consider the reason for using the OR function with the string represented by I and the string representing 2**(J-1). Whenever we apply the .OR. operation to two bits, one of which is 1, the result will always be 1. Similarly, applying this operator to two bits, one of which is 0, will always produce a result which is identical to the other bit. Consequently, the presence of a 1 in position J and 0's elsewhere in the string representing 2**(J-1) will ensure that the string produced by function OR will have a 1 in position J and that the remaining thirty-one bits will be the same as the corresponding bits in string I.

As a second illustration, suppose we want to set the Jth bit in a string represented by variable I to have the value 0, without disturbing the other bits. The following coding will achieve this for us:

```
EQUIVALENCE (I,X)
X = AND(I,COMPL(2**(J-1)))
```

Whenever we apply an .AND. operation to two bits, one of which is 0, the result will always be 0. Similarly, applying this operator to two bits, one of which is 1, will always produce a result which is identical to the other bit. Consequently, if we can apply the AND function to string I and a second string which has a 0 in bit-position J and a 1 in each of the remaining thirty-one positions, we can ensure that the resulting bit-string will have a 0 in position J and that the remaining bits will be the same as the corresponding bits in string I. The string produced by COMPL(2**(J-1)) satisfies the necessary properties of this second string, since it is the complement of a string having a 1 in position J and 0's elsewhere.

Now that we have examined methods by which we can set a particular bit to 0 or 1 without altering the rest of the string, we might consider how to complement the Jth bit of a string without changing the rest of the bits. To see how this can be accomplished, consider the following segment of coding:

```
EQUIVALENCE (I,X)
X = EOR(2**(J-1),I)
```

Whenever we perform an EXCLUSIVE OR operation on two bits, one of which is 1, the result will be exactly the opposite of the other bit. Conversely, applying this operation to two bits, one of which is 0, will always produce a result which is identical to the other bit. We know that the string representing 2**(J-1) has a 1 in position J and 0's elsewhere. Consequently, by using 2**(J-1) with string I as arguments for function EOR, we ensure that the Jth bit in the resulting string will be the complement of its counterpart in string I and that the remaining bits will be unchanged from those in string I.

Finally, suppose we want to write an integer-valued function to count the number of 1-bits in the string represented by a parameter K. In order to determine such a count, we must examine each bit individually to see whether or not it is a 1. We make such a decision by using the AND function with our given bit-string and a special string called MASK as parameters. This special string will have a 1 in the bit-position which we want to examine in string K, and 0's in the remaining thirty-one positions. For example, if we are checking for a 1 in bit-position three of string K, then MASK would be 0.....0100. In general, if we are examining the Jth bit-position of string K, then the bit-string MASK represents the integer 2^{J-1}. By using MASK and K as parameters for the AND function, we are ensuring that the resulting bit-string will have 0's in all bit-positions other than position J. Furthermore, we are guaranteeing that the Jth bit in the resulting string will be identical to its counterpart in string K. Prior to examining each new bit-position in string K, we generate a new value for MASK by multiplying the previous value by 2. This shifts the single 1-bit in MASK one position to the left, as desired. By generating thirty-two successive values of MASK (i.e., $2^0, 2^1, 2^2, \ldots$), we can examine each of the bits in string K on an individual basis. For each application of the AND function with parameters K and MASK, if the resulting string is not all 0's, we know that we have encountered an additional 1-bit in string K, with the result that we increment our counter, COUNT. The FORTRAN coding for this function is given in Example 2.5.

```
C EXAMPLE 2.5 - COUNTING 1-BITS IN
C               A BINARY STRING
C
      INTEGER FUNCTION COUNT(K)
C
      EQUIVALENCE (A,IA)
C
      COUNT = 0
      IF(K.EQ.0)RETURN
C
C Initialize MASK to 2**0.
C
      MASK = 1
C
C Examine the 32 bits of K individually.
C
      DO 1 J=1,32
C
C Compare K with proper value of MASK.
C
      A = AND(MASK,K)
C
C If there is a 1 in bit-position J of K,
C increment the counter.
C
      IF(IA.NE.0)COUNT = COUNT+1
C
C Now move the 1 in MASK to the next
C higher bit-position.
C
    1 MASK = MASK*2
C
      RETURN
      END
```

2.5 SIMULATION OF BINARY ADDITION

In this section, we develop a FORTRAN program which uses logical functions to simulate binary addition as it is performed by the circuitry in a digital computer. In order to add two binary numbers, we have to add pairs of corresponding bits, beginning at the right end of the bit-strings. For each pair of bits, we must also include in the addition a "carry" bit from the addition of the preceding pair of bits. For the first pair of bits, the carry-bit is obviously considered to be 0. Figure 2.5 defines the addition of two bits, A and B, together with a previous carry-bit, to produce an appropriate sum-bit and a new carry.

A	B	OLD CARRY	NEW CARRY	SUM
0	0	0	0	0
0	0	1	0	1
0	1	0	0	1
0	1	1	1	0
1	0	0	0	1
1	0	1	1	0
1	1	0	1	0
1	1	1	1	1

Figure 2.5

Summary of Binary Addition

Notice that the sum-bit is always a 1 whenever there is an odd number of 1's on the left side of the table in Figure 2.5. This means that the sum-bit will be 1 whenever only one of the three bits is 1, as well as whenever all three bits are 1. Otherwise, the sum-bit will be 0. Furthermore, we can discover a similar pattern with the carry-bit. If at least two of the three bits being added are 1's, then the carry-bit is 1. Otherwise, it is 0. We will design our program to recognize these conditions so that it can determine the sum and carry-bits.

Logical function ADDER (Example 2.6) simulates the addition of two bits, A and B, together with a CARRY bit. Actually, the variables ADDER, A, B, and CARRY are all logical variables. They assume the value .TRUE. or .FALSE., corresponding to the value 1 or 0, respectively, of the bits they represent. The function returns, via its name, a logical value corresponding to the sum-bit produced by adding the bits represented by A, B, and CARRY. Furthermore, it returns an additional value to the user via its parameter list. The value of CARRY is updated inside the function to reflect the new carry-bit produced by the addition operation. We use logical function EXOR to ascertain whether there is an odd number of bits to be added. This will determine the value of ADDER. In order to decide the new value of CARRY, we use the logical operators .OR. and .AND. to determine whether at least two of the bits to be added are 1's.

```
C EXAMPLE 2.6 - SIMULATING THE ADDITION OF
C               TWO BITS WITH A CARRY-BIT
C
      LOGICAL FUNCTION ADDER*1(A,B,CARRY)
C
C This function adds two bits, A and B, and
C a CARRY to produce the sum in ADDER
C and a new CARRY.
C
      LOGICAL*1 A,B,CARRY,EXOR
C
C Find the sum of A, B, and the old CARRY.
C
      ADDER = EXOR(EXOR(A,B),CARRY)
C
C Now compute the new CARRY.
C
      CARRY = A.AND.B.OR.A.AND.CARRY.OR.B.AND.CARRY
C
      RETURN
      END
```

Now that we have a logical function to simulate the addition of two bits and a carry-bit, we can proceed to consider a program which simulates the addition of two binary numbers, each containing thirty-two bits. Figure 2.6 presents a basic diagram of a binary adder. The bits of the two numbers being added, J and K, are labelled (from right to left) $J_0, J_1, J_2, \ldots, J_{31}$ and $K_0, K_1, K_2, \ldots, K_{31}$ respectively. For the addition of bits J_i and K_i, the resulting sum and carry-bits are denoted by S_i and C_i respectively. For each of the thirty-two pairs of bits to be added, our simulator program will invoke function ADDER to supply the proper sum and carry-bits. The coding for this program is given in Example 2.7.

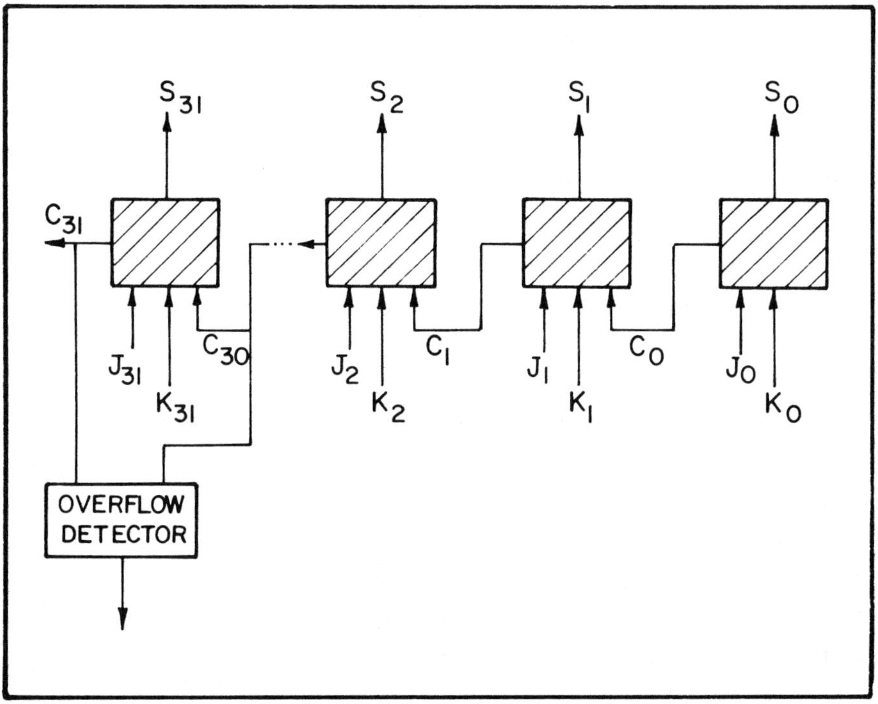

Figure 2.6

<u>A Binary Adder</u>

Once again, the variables ADDER, A, B, and CARRY in Example 2.7 are logical variables, each assuming a value .TRUE. or .FALSE., depending upon the value of the bit it is representing. They are used to simulate the addition of two numbers, J and K, with the sum being assigned to variable I. The initial carry-bit is 0 (i.e., CARRY = .FALSE.). Then we must proceed through the thirty-two pairs of bits in strings J and K, considering one pair at a time. In order to assign appropriate values to variables A and B which will be used to represent

```
C EXAMPLE 2.7 - SIMULATING BINARY ADDITION
C               OF TWO NUMBERS (I = J+K)
C
      EQUIVALENCE (X,JX),(Y,KY),(ZI,I)
      LOGICAL*1 A,B,CARRY,LCARRY,ADDER,EXOR
C
C Initialize the carry-bit to zero.
C
      CARRY = .FALSE.
C
      READ,J,K
      I = 0
C
C MASK will take the values 1,2,4,8,16,...,2**31
C in the following loop.  We look for 1's in the
C successive positions of J and K.
C
      MASK = 1
C
      DO 10 L=1,32
C
C JX will have a 1 in position L
C if J has a 1 in position L.
C
      X = AND(MASK,J)
C
C KY will have a 1 in position L
C if K has a 1 in position L.
C
      Y = AND(MASK,K)
C
C A and B will be the bits we wish to add together.
C
      A = JX.NE.0
      B = KY.NE.0
C
C If the sum-bit is 1, add MASK to I.
C
      IF(ADDER(A,B,CARRY))ZI = OR(I,MASK)
C
C Save the second-to-last carry (LCARRY).
C
      IF(L.EQ.31)LCARRY = CARRY
C
      MASK = MASK*2
   10 CONTINUE
C
      PRINT,J,K,I
```

```
C
C Test for overflow.
C
      IF(EXOR(CARRY,LCARRY))PRINT 20
C
   20 FORMAT('0','OVERFLOW HAS OCCURRED')
C
      STOP
      END
```

each pair of bits, we must first determine the actual values (i.e., 0 or 1) of the two bits. To ascertain the values of these bits, we use a special bit-string, MASK. This string plays the same role here as it did in Example 2.5, when we were trying to count the number of 1-bits in a string. If we are adding the Nth pair of bits in J and K, then MASK has the value 2^{N-1}. By using MASK and J as parameters for function AND, we can determine the state of the appropriate bit in string J, and consequently assign the proper value to variable A. We perform a similar operation with MASK and K to ascertain the value of variable B. Once we have determined the values of the bits to be added, we call function ADDER to give us the sum-bit and a new carry. If the sum-bit is 1 (i.e., ADDER returns a .TRUE. value), we insert a 1 in the appropriate position of string I by using the OR function with arguments MASK and the preceeding value of I. I is initialized, of course, to zero, at the beginning of the program.

We have also included in Example 2.7 a provision for determining when an "overflow" has occurred. This situation will arise whenever the result of adding the two numbers, J and K, lies outside the acceptable range for fixed-point values (i.e., -2^{31} to $2^{31} - 1$ for the S/360). In Section 1.2, we considered six examples of binary addition (using an eight-bit word). Careful examination of these examples will reveal the conditions under which an overflow will occur. In essence, the presence or absence of an overflow condition will depend entirely on the two carry-bits generated by the additions of the leftmost two pairs of bits in strings J and K. If these two carry-bits are both 0's or both 1's, there will be no overflow (see Examples (i) to (iv) in Section 1.2). On the other hand, if only one of these two carry-bits is 1, then an overflow situation will arise. It does not matter which of the two carry-bits is 1 (see Examples (v) and (vi) in Section 1.2). In Example 2.7, we save the second-to-last carry (LCARRY) for comparison with the last carry (i.e., the value of CARRY upon exit from the DO loop). Then we use function EXOR, with LCARRY and CARRY as operands, to determine whether they have different values. If they do, then an overflow condition exists, and we print an appropriate message.

2.6 EXERCISES

1. Given X = .TRUE., Y = .FALSE., and Z = .TRUE., evaluate the following logical expressions:

   (a) X.OR..NOT.Z
   (b) Y.AND.X.OR..NOT.(X.OR.Z)
   (c) Z.AND.X.AND.Y.OR..NOT.X.OR..NOT.Y.AND..NOT.Z
   (d) .TRUE..OR..NOT.(X.AND.Y.OR.Z).AND..FALSE.

2. If P = 1.0, Q = 2.0, R = 3.0, S = 1.5, and T = 2.0, evaluate the following logical expressions:

   (a) P+3.0.GE.Q**2
   (b) R*S.NE.T*2*R
   (c) P/T*R.LT..5.OR..TRUE.
   (d) Q*P*R.EQ.(Q+T)*S.AND.S.GE.0.5
   (e) (P-Q)*S.EQ.T/P.AND..TRUE..OR.Q.LE.S**2

3. The logical function IMP (number 11 in Figure 2.4) is defined as follows:

   IMP(X,Y) = .NOT.X.OR.Y

   Using the values of X, Y, and Z from Exercise 1, evaluate the following logical expressions:

   (a) IMP(Y,X).OR.IMP(X,Z)
   (b) IMP(.NOT.X.AND.Y,X)
   (c) IMP(X,.NOT.Z).AND.IMP(X,.NOT.X)
   (d) EXOR(IMP(EXOR(X,Y),Z),.TRUE..OR.X.AND..NOT.Z)

4. Assuming a string length of five bits, perform the following bit-string operations with X = 10111 and Y = 00101:

   (a) AND(X,Y)
   (b) COMPL(Y)
   (c) NOR(X,Y) - The corresponding logical function (number 1 in Figure 2.4) is defined as .NOT.(X.OR.Y)
   (d) NAND(X,Y)- The corresponding logical function (number 7 in Figure 2.4) is defined as .NOT.(X.AND.Y)
   (e) OR(X,Y)
   (f) EOR(X,Y)
   (g) IMP(X,Y) - See Exercise 3 for the corresponding logical function.

5. Punch a card deck for the simulated binary addition program, and test it with the following data values:

   (a) J = 5 K = 6
   (b) J = 3 K = -10
   (c) J = -15 K = -10
   (d) J = -75 K = -2147483600
   (e) J = 648 K = 2147483000
   (f) J = 2**31 K = -2**31

   Use assignment statements rather than data cards for (f).

   Note: Insert a PRINT statement after IF(CARRY...)... to check the sum-bit at each bit-position.

6. Given an eight-bit string in the rightmost byte of a word, write a logical function to determine if that group of eight bits contains an odd number of 1-bits. Do not use function COUNT (Example 2.5).

7. Given a bit-string of length 32, write a FORTRAN program which uses at least one of the four built-in functions, AND, OR, EOR, and COMPL, to produce in memory the reverse bit-string.

Example: 0....0110010011100101 (data)
         1010011100100110....0 (output)

8. Write a logical function to simulate subtraction of two binary numbers.

9. What is the output from Example 2.8? What is this program actually doing?

```
C EXAMPLE 2.8 - EXERCISE
C
      A = 0.375621E+17
      B = 0.936264E-19
      PRINT,A,B,
      A = EOR(A,B)
      B = EOR(A,B)
      A = EOR(A,B)
      PRINT,A,B
      STOP
      END
```

CHAPTER THREE
CHARACTER STRINGS
REPRESENTATION AND MANIPULATION

3.1 CHARACTER STRINGS

In this chapter, we will be considering the representation and manipulation of yet another data type - the *CHARACTER STRING*. Such data consists of ordered sets of alphanumeric characters, with the basic unit of data being a single character. A character can be any one of the twenty-six letters of the alphabet (lower or upper case), a digit (0 - 9), or any one of several special characters (+, -, $, #, *, etc.). The set of all possible characters available under a particular computer system (or subsystem) is called a *CHARACTER SET*. The size of these character sets varies considerably from one system to another. For example, common keypunches do not provide lower case letters, with the result that their character set is smaller than the one available on some line printers.

Throughout this book we will be designating character string constants by enclosing the set of characters within a pair of single quotation marks. The reason for this convention will become obvious later in this chapter. For example, the character string containing the characters A, B, and C (in that order) will be written as 'ABC'. Similarly, 'X=A+2' is a character string composed of the characters X, =, A, +, and 2. We associate with each string an integer value specifying the length of that string (i.e., the number of characters in it). The previous two examples have lengths 3 and 5 respectively, while the string, 'I DO', is of length 4, including the special character blank ' '. This character will be designated by 'b̸' for future examples in cases of possible ambiguity.

Usages and applications of character string data are very widespread. It is quite obvious that, when programs are designed to aid in editing of text or automatic control of type-setting machines, the data is naturally represented by character strings. Furthermore, the input data to translators (assemblers, compilers, or interpreters) is always in the form of character strings representing the source language to be translated. Moreover, if we take a close look at most input/output devices currently used for transmission of information between users and the computer, we will find that all of these devices provide the computer with character strings as input, and they expect the output from the computer to be in character string form. It is the responsibility of the I/O routines to convert these strings into their internal representation upon input, and to convert the data from its internal representation into character strings for output. Images of cards punched by users are transmitted to the computer in the form of character strings containing eighty characters. Data to be printed on a line printer is first converted into character strings of lengths compatible with the width of the paper currently mounted on the line printer. Communication between key-board terminals (teletypes and the like) and the computer (both input and output) is achieved via character strings transmitted back and forth through the telephone line. (In reality, only one character at a time is transmitted. It is the responsibility of the communication control unit to assemble the characters received from the terminals into character strings, and to decompose the strings produced by the computer into individual characters for transmission.)

In summary, the character string is the only data type which is directly comprehensible to the human user. All other data types have to be converted into character strings before they can be delivered to the output media. Similarly, all information generated by the user is in character string form, and it has to be converted into its internal machine representation before it can be manipulated by the computer. This generalization, of course, does not apply to those programs which are specifically designed to manipulate character strings as actual character strings, ignoring any numeric information possibly contained in them.

At this point, we might consider some examples of programs in which we will be mainly concerned with the manipulation of character strings. First, suppose a data card contains an arithmetic assignment statement in which the expression on the right-hand side contains a number of left and right parentheses. We might be asked to determine whether or not the parentheses are properly matched. The solution to this problem involves a relatively simple algorithm. After initializing a counter (N) to 0, examine the characters punched on the card, one at a time, scanning from left to right. Every time a left (i.e., opening) parenthesis is encountered, increase the counter by unity. Conversely, for each right parenthesis found in the expression, the counter should be similarly decreased. If, at the end of the scan, N has the value 0, we can conclude that the parentheses are properly matched, provided, of course, that N has remained non-negative all through the scanning procedure.

Example:

```
X = A * ( B + C / ( (D - E) / (D - F) ) )
N = 0   1         2 3       2   3     2 1 0
```

Whenever a compiler encounters a source card like the one presented in our example, it must perform numerous other operations on the character string in addition to checking whether the parentheses are properly matched. For example, it must isolate all the variable names contained in the expression (A, B, C, etc.), as well as identify the various operators (+, -, /). Furthermore, if the expression contains constant numeric values, they will have to be converted into their appropriate representations according to the relevant type (INTEGER, REAL, etc.).

In this context, we should make a distinction between character strings that can be converted into numerical values and others that cannot. The first type would be called *NUMERICAL CHARACTER STRINGS*. Examples of such strings are:

```
'2'
'-32.5'
'0.13245E-07'
'14789A8F'
'1.0974224567821D+23'
```

Each of these strings has an equivalent numeric value that can be represented inside the machine's memory by some other data type (as discussed in Chapter One). In general, we can say that strings containing only digit characters ('0', '1', ..., '9') are definitely numeric strings. Extension of this definition to include the special characters '.', '+', and '-', or the characters 'E' and 'D', has to be restricted, to preclude strings like '0.2+5-5' or 'E05.6.7'. Any attempt to convert regular strings into numeric values (i.e., through FORMAT statements in FORTRAN) will result in a "conversion" error which will usually terminate execution of the program.

Another area in which we might consider a problem involving character strings is text editing. Suppose we wish to write a program to aid us in the preparation of technical letters or any other printed material. Given character strings which represent the sentences of the text, we would like our program to provide us with the facilities to correct typing or spelling mistakes. Once again, we will have to develop techniques to operate on character strings so that we can identify and isolate the parts of the sentences to be corrected and actually perform the desired corrections. All these operations will be required in addition to the usual I/O operations requiring character string handling. When we use high-level languages like FORTRAN, such I/O operations are implied by the FORMAT statements and performed automatically by the run-time routines provided by the compiler.

Before we can begin to study the various operations on character strings, we have to be aware of how such data is represented in the machine. Like all other data types, characters are represented in the memory of the computer by some combination of bits; and strings of characters are stored in groups of consecutive memory locations. In Section 3.2, we examine in detail the actual internal representation of characters, with emphasis on the technique used in the IBM S/360.

3.2 CHARACTER REPRESENTATION

As we have already indicated, the individual characters in a character string are each represented inside the memory of the computer by a particular code. There is a specific combination of bits to represent each of the characters in the character set. Since these bit patterns have (almost) no numerical meaning, we can assign code values to characters in a manner that will help us to simplify the processing of character data. In order to determine the number of bits that will be needed for the representation of each character, we have to know the required range for our codes. In essence, we have to decide how many different characters we want to be able to represent. Including upper and lower case letters, digits, and the more common special symbols, we find that we need about sixty-four different code values for representing a character set. This can be done by using six bits to represent each character (since $2^6 = 64$). Actually, many computer systems and devices use a six-bit code for the representation of characters. The S/360, however, being a byte-addressable machine, allocates a single byte for the representation of each character. Figure 3.1 contains the complete set of character codes used with the S/360. It is worthwhile noticing that only 89 of the 256 (i.e., 2^8) possible code values are used for the representation of these characters. The rest are considered invalid characters for the usual character set but can be used whenever a larger character set (i.e., more special symbols) is needed. Some of these unused codes are employed as control characters in communicating with I/O devices (carriage-return, back-space, etc.).

SPECIAL SYMBOLS			LOWER CASE			UPPER CASE			DIGITS		
CHAR.	HEX. code	DEC. value	CHAR.	HEX. code	DEC. value	CHAR.	HEX. code	DEC. value	CHAR.	HEX. code	DEC. value
b̸	40	064									
¢	4A	074	a	81	129	A	C1	193	0	F0	240
.	4B	075	b	82	130	B	C2	194	1	F1	241
<	4C	076	c	83	131	C	C3	195	2	F2	242
(	4D	077	d	84	132	D	C4	196	3	F3	243
+	4E	078	e	85	133	E	C5	197	4	F4	244
|	4F	079	f	86	134	F	C6	198	5	F5	245
&	50	080	g	87	135	G	C7	199	6	F6	246
!	5A	090	h	88	136	H	C8	200	7	F7	247
$	5B	091	i	89	137	I	C9	201	8	F8	248
*	5C	092	j	91	145	J	D1	209	9	F9	249
)	5D	093	k	92	146	K	D2	210			
;	5E	094	l	93	147	L	D3	211			
¬	5F	095	m	94	148	M	D4	212			
-	60	096	n	95	149	N	D5	213			
/	61	097	o	96	150	O	D6	214			
,	6B	107	p	97	151	P	D7	215			
%	6C	108	q	98	152	Q	D8	216			
_	6D	109	r	99	153	R	D9	217			
>	6E	110	s	A2	162	S	E2	226			
?	6F	111	t	A3	163	T	E3	227			
:	7A	122	u	A4	164	U	E4	228			
#	7B	123	v	A5	165	V	E5	229			
@	7C	124	w	A6	166	W	E6	230			
'	7D	125	x	A7	167	X	E7	231			
=	7E	126	y	A8	168	Y	E8	232			
"	7F	127	z	A9	169	Z	E9	233			

Figure 3.1

S/360 Character Codes (EBCDIC)

Regardless of whether characters are represented by six, seven, or eight bits, each character will always utilize only a small portion of the computer's full word. (Exceptions, of course, are mini-computers with small machine words and some decimal computers designed to process only one digit at a time.) Consequently, when we are considering manipulation of character strings with word-addressable machines, we have to pack several characters into every machine word in order to economize on storage usage. For example, assuming that six bits are used to represent each character, we can pack six characters into a single word of size thirty-six bits. Character strings will occupy several consecutive words, with the last word only partially filled if the number of characters in the string is not evenly divisible by six. Packing and unpacking character strings is the responsibility of the programmer, a fact which makes processing of character strings in word-addressable machines quite cumbersome.

Character handling is much simpler for the S/360, where the basic memory unit is the byte. Characters can be addressed either as single characters, or collectively as strings having up to 256 characters. (The length of the string to be processed is defined by a field in the machine language instruction.) For example, the character string, '2+2 is FOUR', will be represented (in hexadecimal notation) in the machine as a sequence of eleven bytes as follows:

```
F2 4E F2 40 89 A2 40 C6 D6 E4 D9
```

We can gain access to any character in this string by merely adding its index (indicating its sequential position) in the string to the address of the string. This address is actually the address of the first byte in the string (i.e., the one containing the first '2'). For example, if we wish to replace the '+' by a '-', we need merely insert the code "60" in the byte whose address is offset by unity from the beginning of the string.

To summarize what we have learned about the internal representation of information in the S/360 memory, suppose we have selected at random a group of four bytes (aligned on word boundaries) from an S/360 memory unit. We might be interested in knowing what information is contained in these four bytes. After careful consideration, we come to the obvious conclusion that, without further information, there is nothing we can say about the contents of these bytes. It is essential that we know the interpretation that the programmer has associated with them. For example, suppose the contents of the four bytes (expressed in hexadecimal and binary notation) is as follows:

```
  D    4      C    1      E    3      C    8
 11010100    11000001    11100011    11001000
```

If we are told that this string of bits represents an INTEGER number, then we can interpret it as being a 32-bit binary number expressed in two's complement form. Evaluating it as such, noticing that the sign-bit is 1, we obtain the negative number -725490744 (expressed in decimal notation).

If we know, however, that these four bytes represent the value of a REAL variable, we have to interpret the contents as being a floating-point number. Since the sign-bit is 1, we know that the number is negative. Furthermore, the exponent part is 1010100, which denotes an exponent value of 20 (expressed as 84 in excess-64 notation). Finally, we are aware that the remaining twenty-four bits, 110000011110001111001000, represent the fractional part of the number, assuming that the binary point is located at the immediate left of the string. After evaluating this binary string to obtain 12706760, we divide by 2^{24} to arrive at 0.7573819. Consequently, the value of the floating-point number is 0.7573819×16^{20}, or equivalently 0.9156186E+24.

If we consider these same four bytes as representing a character string, then the interpretation of the contents does not involve any calculations. By examining the four bytes individually, and looking up the corresponding character codes in Figure 3.1, we obtain the string 'MATH'.

Before we go on to investigate character manipulation in FORTRAN, let us discuss a simple algorithm for evaluating the equivalent decimal value of a given character string. As we will see later, in standard FORTRAN we usually store character strings as INTEGER type variables. It is quite possible that, for some manipulations, we will have to know the equivalent integer value of a specific character string. Furthermore, when writing FORTRAN statements to manipulate characters, we might have to calculate manually the equivalent integer value of a full-word containing a string of characters.

A simple method for performing this type of conversion would be to consider the characters as digits of a number represented in base-256 notation and use the equivalent decimal values given in Figure 3.1. One difficulty for which we must be prepared will arise in cases where the leftmost character has a bit-string representation in which the leftmost bit is 1. (Most of the characters in Figure 3.1 belong to this category.) When we are considering the equivalent numerical value of the character string, this particular bit is interpreted as the sign-bit. In such cases, we will have to evaluate the two's complement value. Consequently, we begin by initializing our sum value to 0 or -256, depending upon whether the sign-bit is "off" (0) or "on" (1) respectively. In other words, we begin with 0 if the decimal value of the first character is less than 128, or with -256 if the decimal value of the first character is greater than or equal to 128. (You should be able to see why this is correct.) Subsequently, we implement the number conversion by the usual iterative method (discussed in Section A.6) of multiplying by the base (256 in our case) and adding the value of the next digit (i.e., character). We now examine the step-by-step application of this procedure to the character string 'MATH':

	−256	('M'=$D4_{16}=212_{10}>128$)
Add first digit:	+212	
	−44	
Multiply by base:	×256	
	−11264	
Add second digit:	+193	('A' = 193_{10})
	−11071	
Multiply by base:	×256	
	−2834176	
Add third digit:	+227	('T' = 227_{10})
	−2833949	
Multiply by base:	×256	
	−725490944	
Add last digit:	+200	('H' = 200_{10})
	−725490744	

i.e., $(\text{'MATH'})_{10}$

$$= -256^4 + 212\times256^3 + 193\times256^2 + 227\times256 + 200$$

$$= -256 + 212\rceil 256 + 193\rceil 256 + 227\rceil 256 + 200$$

$$= -725490744_{10}$$

Actually, the conversion routines in FORTRAN which are part of the I/O run-time routines can do the above conversion for us. The FORTRAN coding which reads as data a character string of length four and prints its equivalent integer value expressed in decimal notation is very simple:

```
   READ(5,99)K
99 FORMAT(A4)
   WRITE(6,86)K
86 FORMAT(I12)
```

It is important to realize, however, that such conversion can be done only with input/output operations which have the conversion routines implied by the FORMAT statements. In the previous sequence of FORTRAN statements, the FORMAT code, A4, instructs the READ routines to move the first four characters from the input card to the memory location indicated by the symbolic name K <u>without</u> conversion. The A FORMAT code is the only one that specifies no conversion. In the following output statement, however, we find an I FORMAT code which directs the output routines to perform the following steps:

(i) Consider the memory location indicated by the symbolic name K, and interpret those four bytes as representing a fixed-point binary number.

(ii) First, convert this number to its decimal equivalent form. Then convert the decimal number to a character string whose characters are the digits of the decimal representation with a possible minus sign in front. Insert as many blanks on the left as are necessary to fill the field to its requested twelve positions.

(iii) Finally, move this character string into the first twelve positions of the print buffer. Then issue a command to transfer the data in the buffer to the printer. (Before requesting that the contents of the buffer be written, WATFIV checks whether the first character is a valid carriage control character. If not, it inserts a blank in its place. The I/O routines of other FORTRAN compilers may or may not do this.)

We are aware that the I/O procedures of FORTRAN have a set of conversion routines built into them that can transform information from its external representation (which is always in character string form) into its internal representation according to the FORMAT specified (or implied). Another set of I/O routines will perform the conversion of information from its internal representation into character string form for output. When we are dealing with character strings, it is often desirable to perform such conversion operations on character strings held in memory. Since the coding of such routines might be very cumbersome, we would like to use the conversion routines imbedded in the I/O processors of FORTRAN. Standard FORTRAN does not allow us to make use of these routines. WATFIV, however, provides an extension to the I/O operations called *CORE-TO-CORE I/O*. This extension allows us to perform the conversion to and from character strings by moving the strings into and out of memory as character string variables. We illustrate this new type of data conversion and transmission in Section 3.3.3. Further information about this feature is also available in Appendix B.

3.3 CHARACTER MANIPULATION

When the FORTRAN language was originally conceived, most of the computers available were word-addressable machines whose word length was the width of the channel connecting the arithmetic unit to the memory. All operations performed by the arithmetic unit were on data of fixed length (i.e., one machine word). We have already noticed that character string data is different from the other data types discussed in Chapters One and Two, in light of the fact that character string data can assume different lengths. As a result, each operation on character string data might well involve different amounts of memory storage. Since it is difficult to implement character string data on word machines, and, since FORTRAN is primarily a numerical scientific programming language, the proper definition of FORTRAN did not provide facilities for the representation or manipulation of character strings. When using standard FORTRAN, the user is forced to employ unconventional methods in order that he may be able to manipulate character data.

The byte addressability of the S/360 simplifies considerably the manipulation of character strings. Furthermore, the hardware is equipped with machine instructions for handling strings of bytes of variable lengths (up to 256). Consequently, it is a straightforward addition to the FORTRAN language to include a new data type (i.e., character strings) and some basic operations for the manipulation of such data. Such an extension to FORTRAN is available with WATFIV. (We discuss this feature in more detail later in this section. Additional information is also supplied in Appendix B.) It should be emphasized, however, that character handling facilities have been added to FORTRAN as an "after-thought", and that the features supported by WATFIV are very basic and elementary. Other languages (e.g., SNOBOL) have been designed to handle character strings as their principal data type, while still others (e.g., PL/1, APL) have character handling facilities in the original definition of the language, thus providing a much wider scope of operation.

Whenever we discuss a new data type, there are three main issues that we have to consider:

(i) The internal representation of the data.
(ii) The form of data constants.
(iii) Operations to be performed on the specified data type.

For example, when we considered INTEGER data, we covered these three areas by specifying that such data is represented in two's complement fixed-point binary form; that constants are the integer numbers 0, 1, 2, ... in the range -2^{31} to $2^{31} - 1$; and finally, that the operations which we want to perform on integers are addition, subtraction, multiplication, etc.. Since we have already explained in Section 3.2 how character string data is stored in memory, we are left to consider how we designate character string constants and assign them to variables. The definition of some basic operations on character strings analogous to the arithmetic operations on integers will be discussed in Section 3.4.

It is a convention with S/360 to designate character string constants by enclosing the characters comprising the string inside a pair of single quotation marks. This convention is carried into the FORTRAN language by those compilers which allow for character string constants. Conventional FORTRAN, however, requires that character string specification be done only in the form of an H FORMAT code. For example, the character string, 'STRING', would be designated by 6HSTRING. WATFIV allows both methods of specification in an attempt to be compatible with standard FORTRAN.

3.3.1 Character Data In Standard FORTRAN

At this point, it would be well worthwhile to review how we store and reference character data in standard S/360 FORTRAN without taking advantage of the extensions provided by the WATFIV compiler. These ideas can be summarized as follows:

1. Character data may be stored using any of the four types of variables: REAL, INTEGER, LOGICAL, COMPLEX. The length specification of the type (i.e., the number of bytes associated with it) indicates the maximum number of characters that

can be represented using that particular variable type.

2. Character data can be assigned at compile time using DATA statements, or at execution time by the READ statement with an A FORMAT code.

3. Character strings are stored in memory locations beginning at the leftmost byte. If the string is longer than the length specification of the variable to which the string is assigned, it is truncated. Conversely, if the string is shorter than the associated length specification, it is padded on the right with blanks.

Example (i):

```
DATA I/2H23/,J/'ABCDEF'/
```

The four bytes referenced by variable I represent the string '23bb', whereas the four bytes designated by J represent 'ABCD'.

Example (ii):

```
  DOUBLE PRECISION X
  READ 2,X
2 FORMAT(A10)
  PRINT 3,X
3 FORMAT('0',A8)

  ABCDE.+FGH   (data)

  CDE.+FGH     (output)
```

Since X is a double-precision variable, the character string contained in columns 1-10 of the data card is truncated to eight characters before it is stored in the eight bytes referenced by variable X.

4. Careful examination of the character codes in Figure 3.1 reveals that they have been chosen in such a manner that they reflect alphabetical ordering. If we let I_A, I_B, I_C, ... denote the integer values representing the characters A, B, C, ..., then we can see that

$$I_{\not{b}} < I_A < I_B < I_C < \ldots < I_Z < I_0 < I_1 < I_2 < \ldots < I_9.$$

5. As a general rule, INTEGER variables are used to represent character data whenever these variables are to be used in comparisons of character strings.

We are now in a position to consider more carefully a FORTRAN program that solves the problem of determining whether parentheses are properly matched within a given arithmetic expression. The coding for such a program is given in Example 3.1. As the data card is read, each character (i.e., column) is stored in a separate component of the vector CARD. Each character is stored in the <u>leftmost byte</u> of the memory word to which it is assigned. Then, by comparing them with the character strings defined in the elements LEFT and RIGHT, the entries of CARD are searched, one at a

```
C EXAMPLE 3.1 - TEST FOR PROPERLY
C               MATCHED PARENTHESES
C
      INTEGER CARD(80),COUNT,LEFT,RIGHT
      DATA LEFT/'('/,RIGHT/1H)/
C
      READ 1,CARD
    1 FORMAT(80A1)
      PRINT 7,CARD
    7 FORMAT(1X,80A1)
C
      COUNT = 0
C
C Examine the input characters one at a time.
C
      DO 2 J=1,80
C
C Search for left or right parentheses.
C
      IF(CARD(J).EQ.LEFT)COUNT = COUNT+1
      IF(CARD(J).EQ.RIGHT)COUNT = COUNT-1
C
C An extra right parenthesis makes COUNT negative.
C
      IF(COUNT.LT.0)GO TO 4
C
    2 CONTINUE
C
      IF(COUNT.NE.0)PRINT 3
    3 FORMAT('0','EXTRA LEFT PARENTHESES')
C
      IF(COUNT.EQ.0)PRINT 8
    8 FORMAT('0','PARENTHESES ARE MATCHED')
C
      STOP
C
C J indicates location of the extra right parenthesis.
C
    4 PRINT 6,J
    6 FORMAT('0',I2,'TH COLUMN CAUSED ERROR')
C
      STOP
      END
```

time, for a left or a right parenthesis. The value of COUNT is increased and decreased according to the algorithm discussed in Section 3.1.

Example 3.1 illustrates some of the inefficiencies involved with processing character data in standard FORTRAN. We read the input card in the form of eighty single characters, and store them, one character per element, in an INTEGER vector with eighty components. In other words, we are using 320 bytes of storage where eighty would suffice. This consideration might become very important as the size and number of character strings processed becomes larger. The technique usually used to overcome this obstacle is packing. However, this makes the processing very slow and cumbersome. As an illustration, we could change the coding in Example 3.1 so that we use an INTEGER vector having only twenty components to store the input characters (four characters per element). In our subsequent scan of the string, however, we would have to calculate the location in memory of each character that we wish to examine. In addition to determining the word in which the character is stored, we would also need to ascertain its byte position inside that word. The FORTRAN coding to process our character string in this packed form is presented in Example 3.2.

In Example 3.2, we know that the characters in the input string are stored in groups of four per word. Consequently, in order to consider one particular character, we have to isolate that character by itself in a separate word of memory.

```
C EXAMPLE 3.2 - PARENTHESES CHECK BY PACKING THE
C                INPUT CHARACTERS 4 TO A WORD
C
      INTEGER CARD(20),COUNT,LEFT,RIGHT
      EQUIVALENCE (AN,N)
C
C Initialize variables LEFT and RIGHT for future
C comparisons with the various input characters.
C The rightmost 3 bytes in each case are set to
C zero.
C
      LEFT = 77*(256**3)
      RIGHT = 93*(256**3)
C
      READ 10,CARD
   10 FORMAT(20A4)
      PRINT 9,CARD
    9 FORMAT(1Hb,20A4)
C
      COUNT = 0
C
      DO 2 J=1,80
C
C Determine which component (K) of vector CARD
C contains the Jth character.
C
      K = 1+(J-1)/4
C
C L indicates the byte position in CARD(K) of the
C Jth character (L = 3, 2, 1, or 0).  To isolate
C the Jth character, we use function AND with
C CARD(K) and MASK (comprised of one byte of 1's
C and three bytes of 0's).
C
      L = 4*K-J
      MASK = 255*2**(8*L)
      AN = AND(MASK,CARD(K))
C
C The isolated character in N is now
C shifted to the leftmost byte of N.
C
      N = N*2**(8*(3-L))
C
C N now contains the Jth character aligned in its
C leftmost byte with the remaining 3 bytes being
C filled with zeros.  We can now compare the Jth
C character with variables LEFT and RIGHT as was
C done in Example 3.1.
```

```
      IF(N.EQ.LEFT)COUNT = COUNT+1
      IF(N.EQ.RIGHT)COUNT = COUNT+1
      .
      .
      .
      END
```

The first five statements inside the range of the DO loop in Example 3.2 accomplish this isolation for us. The particular character of interest is isolated in the leftmost byte referenced by the INTEGER variable N, with the remaining three bytes containing all zeros. However, in order to determine whether this character is a left or right parenthesis, we have to compare the character string represented by variable N with two character strings (represented by variables LEFT and RIGHT) whose leftmost bytes represent a left and right parenthesis respectively. Furthermore, since the rightmost three bytes of variable N contain all zeros, we must arrange for the corresponding three bytes of variables LEFT and RIGHT to be filled with zeros as well. We cannot accomplish this initialization by using a DATA statement such as the one employed in Example 3.1, since such a statement would fill the rightmost three bytes of LEFT and RIGHT with blanks instead of zeros. Instead, we can obtain the character codes for a left and right parenthesis (77 and 93 respectively) from Figure 3.1. Then we can make the proper initialization by using the method discussed in Section 3.2, where we evaluate the equivalent integer value of a specified character string.

It is obvious that this method of packing and unpacking the characters is not a convenient solution either. Ideally, we would like to be able to define a vector having eighty character strings as its components, each string being one character (i.e., byte) in length, and to have the facilities to compare the individual characters with other single-byte data items. We now examine how the WATFIV extension to FORTRAN provides the facilities to support such operations.

3.3.2 Character Data With WATFIV

WATFIV recognizes character data as a legitimate data form which can be manipulated to a limited extent. The remainder of this section illustrates some of the rules and ideas relating to the use of CHARACTER variables. Appendix B contains a more formal description of this material for further reference.

As with any new data type, we should first consider the proper form of constants and how such values can be assigned to variables. To illustrate, consider the following examples of valid CHARACTER constants:

(i)	'AB'	(iv)	'THE NAME IS'
(ii)	'12345678'	(v)	'X'
(iii)	'A-B+C*D'	(vi)	'IT''S'

These examples clearly illustrate the reason for our convention adopted earlier in this chapter of designating character strings by enclosing the set of characters comprising the string within a pair of single quotation marks. Example (vi) indicates that, if a quote mark is required as one of the characters in the character string, it must be duplicated (i.e., the characters in the string are IT'S) to distinguish it from the two quote marks which define the string.

Variables capable of being assigned CHARACTER constants are called CHARACTER variables. Such variables can be any valid FORTRAN symbolic names which are declared in a CHARACTER type-declaration statement. For example, the statement

```
CHARACTER A*4,B*6,C*30(40)
```

declares A and B to be CHARACTER variables of length 4 and 6 characters (i.e., bytes) respectively. Furthermore, C is declared to be a one-dimensional array having forty components, each of length 30 characters.

WATFIV allows the combining of compile-time initialization with type-declaration statements as an extension to standard FORTRAN. This extension applies to all type-declarations (including CHARACTER), as illustrated in Examples (i) to (iv) below. Notice that, if no length is specified in a CHARACTER declaration statement, the length is assumed to be one character.

```
  (i) REAL I/5.3/,J/6.8/
 (ii) INTEGER X(10)/10*0/,Y,Z/'JUMP'/
(iii) CHARACTER A,B*8/'WELLbNOW'/
 (iv) CHARACTER ARRAY*5(2)/'HELLO','THERE'/
```

In Example (i), I and J are declared to be single-precision floating-point variables whose values are initialized to be 5.3 and 6.8 respectively at compile time. In Example (ii), variables X, Y, and Z are all designated as type INTEGER. Furthermore, X is declared to be a vector having ten components, all initialized to zero, and Z is initialized to represent the character string 'JUMP'. In Example (iii), A and B are specified as CHARACTER variables of length 1 and 8 respectively. In addition, B is initialized to represent the character string 'WELLƀNOW'. Finally, in Example (iv), ARRAY is defined to be a CHARACTER vector having two components (of length 5 characters) which are initialized as 'HELLO' and 'THERE' respectively.

The CHARACTER assignment statement is very straightforward. However, given the statement, A = B, where A and B are CHARACTER variables of length m and n respectively, something should be said about the case when $m \neq n$. If $m < n$, only the leftmost m characters of B are stored in A. If $m > n$, A is padded on the right with blanks.

Example:

If m = 3, n = 2, and B = 'XY',

then the assignment statement A = B causes 'XYƀ' to be stored in A. Similarly, if n = 3, m = 2, and B = 'XYZ', then the assignment statement A = B causes 'XY' to be stored in A.

Whenever a CHARACTER variable appears in the list of a format-free PRINT statement, the associated character string is printed. Most printers, however, do not have the feature that allows them to print all 89 standard characters in the character set. As a result, they can only print a subset of these characters, and any non-printable characters in the string will be printed as blanks. Character strings may also appear as elements in a PRINT list as illustrated by the following statement:

```
PRINT,'I=',I,'X=',X
```

The READ statement may be used to assign character strings to CHARACTER variables. In this case, the CHARACTER constants are punched on data cards, separated by a comma or at least one blank column. (Recall that a CHARACTER constant is a string of characters <u>enclosed in quotes</u>.) Of course, character strings can also be read or printed using the A FORMAT code.

<u>Example (i)</u>:

```
CHARACTER A*6,B*4
READ,A,B
PRINT,A,B

'XYZ12'   'BILLS'   (data)

XYZ12b̸    BILL      (output)
```

Example (ii):

```
      CHARACTER A*6,B*4
      READ 1,A,B
    1 FORMAT(A5,A5)
      PRINT 2,A,B
    2 FORMAT('b̸',A6,2X,A4)

      XYZ12BILLS       (data)

      XYZ12b̸b̸b̸ILLS     (output)
        A6   2X A4
```

Notice that the character string 'BILLS' is truncated differently using A FORMAT than is done with format-free input. Furthermore, no surrounding quote marks are used to define the character strings on the data card if A FORMAT is used.

3.3.3 Core-to-Core Input/Output

As we mentioned at the end of Section 3.2, one of the features that has been introduced with CHARACTER variables is core-to-core input/output. We know that the usual I/O routines of FORTRAN have built-in conversion procedures for transforming information from character string form into its internal representation, and vice versa, according to some implied or special FORMAT. With the extension of core-to-core I/O, however, we can now perform such conversions on information held in memory. In essence, we are now able to transmit data from one location in core to another location in core (where it is stored in a converted form from its original form) under the control of a FORMAT statement. The two diagrams in Figure 3.2 compare the information flow under normal I/O with that under core-to-core I/O.

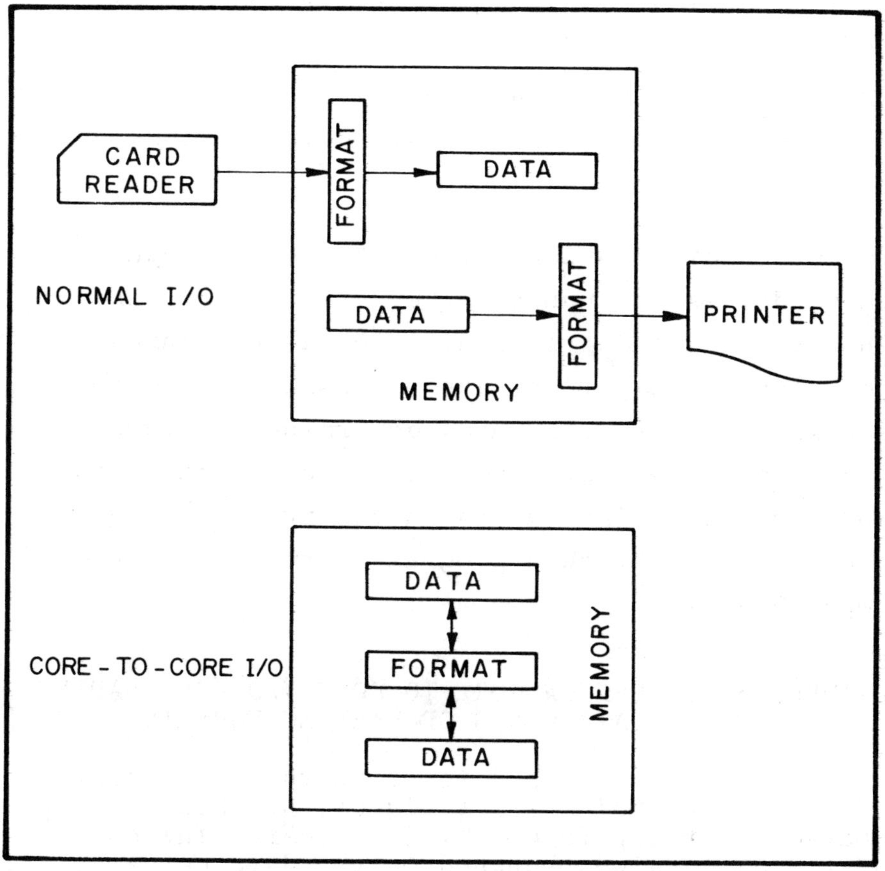

Figure 3.2

Information Flow for Normal and Core-to-Core I/O

To demonstrate one simple use of core-to-core I/O, suppose we consider a set of data cards, each of which falls into one of three different categories:

1. Four integer values punches using I4 FORMAT.
2. Four floating-point values punched using F9.2 FORMAT.
3. Four integer values and four floating-point numbers punched alternatively using I4 and F9.2 FORMAT.

In order to distinguish between the three types of data cards, we can punch either a 1, 2, or 3 in column 80 of each data card to denote the three types respectively. We have to design a program which will read a data card, determine its type, and subsequently store integer values in the array N and floating-point values in the array A. The FORTRAN coding for this program is presented in Example 3.3.

```
C EXAMPLE 3.3.- USE OF CORE-TO-CORE I/O FOR READING
C               DATA CARDS OF VARYING FORMATS
C
C Arrays N and A are used to store the actual data.
C BUFF contains columns 1 to 79 of the data card in
C character string form.  TYPE indicates the mode
C of the data values punched on the data card.
C
      INTEGER N(4),TYPE
      REAL A(4)
      CHARACTER*79 BUFF
C
   10 READ 30,BUFF,TYPE
   30 FORMAT(A79,I1)
C
      GO TO (1,2,3),TYPE
C
```

```
C Read back from the data card image in INTEGER mode.
C
    1 READ(BUFF,31)N
   31 FORMAT(4I4)
      GO TO 100
C
C Read back from the data card image in REAL mode.
C
    2 READ(BUFF,32)A
   32 FORMAT(4F9.2)
      GO TO 100
C
C Read back from the data card image in alternating
C INTEGER and REAL modes.
C
    3 READ(BUFF,33)(N(I),A(I),I=1,4)
   33 FORMAT(4(I4,F9.2))
C
C Statement 100 initiates the processing of the data
C values after they have been read.
C
  100 .
      .
      .
      .
      END
```

In Example 3.3, the first 79 columns of each data card are assigned as a single character string to the CHARACTER variable BUFF. Column 80, the type indicator, is assigned to the INTEGER variable TYPE which is used as an index to transfer to the appropriate core-to-core READ statement. Each of these READ statements takes the data values from BUFF (which is merely a character string image of the data card) and stores them in the desired array(s). Notice that the core-to-core READ statements are similar to the generalized READ statement, except that the CHARACTER variable name BUFF is used instead of a unit number. For example, the statement

```
READ(BUFF,31)N
```

causes the data, in character form, to be transmitted to the array N (in internal fixed-point form) using FORMAT statement 31.

A second use for core-to-core I/O, namely generating FORMAT statements at execution time, can be illustrated by considering a program (Example 3.4) which generates and prints several rows of Pascal's triangle in triangular format. The calculation of the actual values in the triangle involves relatively simple programming. We can use a vector to represent the successive rows of the triangle, one row at a time. This vector has all its entries initialized to 1 at the beginning of the program. It follows that the first two rows of the triangle require no computation. However, from the third row onwards, each element of the triangle is equal to the sum of the two elements immediately above it (see Figure 3.3). This calculation of the elements in each new row is accomplished in Example 3.4 by repeated execution of the statement

```
C(J) = C(J)+C(J-1)
```

for decreasing values of J. (Notice that we proceed backwards in the vector to calculate new entries. Why can we not proceed in a forward direction?)

The main obstacle, however, is to print the values in a triangular format. This means that we have to use a different FORMAT specification for each row that we have to print. In Example 3.4, the CHARACTER variable FMT is used to store the suitable FORMAT which has to be modified for each row.

```
C EXAMPLE 3.4 - PROGRAM TO GENERATE AND PRINT
C               SEVERAL ROWS OF PASCAL'S TRIANGLE
C               IN TRIANGULAR FORMAT (USING CORE-
C               TO-CORE I/O TO CONSTRUCT AN
C               EXECUTION-TIME FORMAT)
C
C Vector C is used to store the successive rows of
C the triangle.  All its entries are initialized to
C be 1.  FMT is a CHARACTER variable used to store
C the FORMAT specifications constructed during
C execution.
C
      INTEGER C(20)/20*1/
      CHARACTER FMT*20(1)
C
C N represents the space count preceding the first
C entry printed in each new row.  N = 50 for the
C first row.
C
      N = 50
C
C Generate and print 11 rows of the triangle.
C
      DO 10 I=1,11
C
C Calculate the entries of the new row by proceeding
C backwards through vector C.
C
      J = I
    3 J = J-1
      IF(J.LT.2)GO TO 6
      C(J) = C(J)+C(J-1)
      GO TO 3
C
C Construct the FORMAT statement for row I using
C core-to-core I/O.
C
    6 WRITE(FMT,9)N
    9 FORMAT('(1H0,',I3,'X,20I4)')
C
C Print row I and reduce the space
C count for the next row.
C
      WRITE(6,FMT)(C(L),L=1,I)
   10 N = N-2
C
      STOP
      END
```

```
                    1
                  1   1
                1   2   1
              1   3   3   1
            1   4   6   4   1
          1   5  10  10   5   1
        1   6  15  20  15   6   1
      1   7  21  35  35  21   7   1
    1   8  28  56  70  56  28   8   1
  1   9  36  84 126 126  84  36   9   1
1  10  45 120 210 252 210 120  45  10   1
```

Figure 3.3

Pascal's Triangle (Output from Example 3.4)

In Example 3.4, it is necessary to declare FMT a vector in accordance with the language specifications which decree that an array must be used to store a variable (execution-time) FORMAT. The character string assigned to FMT will include all the characters which normally comprise a FORMAT statement (including the exterior parentheses but excluding the actual word "FORMAT"). Suppose we decide that the initial entry in each new row is to be printed two spaces to the left of the first entry in the preceding row. Then, assuming that the entries in the various rows are uniformly spaced, the only change to the FORMAT statement for each new row will be the space count preceding the first entry to be printed (i.e., 50X, 48X, 46X, 44X, etc., for successive rows). This varying space count is represented by N in Example 3.4.

3.4 BASIC OPERATIONS ON CHARACTER STRINGS

In earlier sections of this chapter, we have discussed the internal representation of character data and the form of this new data type as it is implemented with WATFIV. We are now in a position to consider some basic operations on character strings analogous to the arithmetic operations on numerical data. It is obvious that the standard arithmetic operations (+,-,*,/) have no real significance when we are dealing with character strings. However, there are certain specialized operations on character strings which will prove very useful to us. Unlike some languages (e.g., SNOBOL, APL, PL/1), WATFIV does not include these operations as part of the language. Consequently, we have to discuss such operations in terms of subprograms.

For our purposes, we will introduce three basic operations which involve manipulation of one or more character strings. Other character string operations can be created by combining these three basic operations in various ways.

Extraction of a Substring From a Given String

In this operation, a specified portion of an already existing character string is extracted, thus creating a new character string. Such an operation requires that we specify the length of the substring and the position of its first character in the original character string. Later in this section, we shall consider a subroutine, SUBSTG, which implements this extraction operation in FORTRAN.

As an illustration, consider the character string 'AB+C1'. For notational convenience, we can let (m,n) represent a substring of length n characters beginning at position m in the original string. Some sample substrings are indicated in Examples (i) to (iv):

(i) The (3,2) substring is '+C'.

(ii) The (1,3) substring is 'AB+'.

(iii) The (4,6) substring is 'C1bbbb'. This substring, beginning at position 4 of the original string, is specified to be 6 characters in length. However, the original string contains fewer than 9 characters, with the result that the substring is padded on the right end by blanks (similar to a CHARACTER assignment statement).

(iv) The (6,6) substring is the empty string. However, since we cannot implement this concept in WATFIV, we have to use 'bbbbbb'.

Position of a Substring Within a String

It is often useful to be able to determine the (starting) position of a specified substring inside a second character string. Such knowledge could be used, for example, to modify certain portions of a given character string, by replacing all appearances of a particular character (or group of characters) with some other character(s). Later in this section, we shall consider a function subprogram, INDEX, which performs this look-up operation.

To illustrate, consider the following character string:

'ABC=56.E-01E'

(i) '=' is in the 4th position.

(ii) 'C=5' begins in the 3rd position.

(iii) 'E' appears in the 8th position. Although 'E' occurs twice in the original string, we shall restrict ourselves to indicating only the first appearance of the specified substring.

(iv) 'ABD' is considered to begin at position zero, since it does not appear anywhere in the original string.

Concatenation of Strings

The operation of *CONCATENATION* involves forming one longer character string from two shorter strings. The second of the two shorter strings is added to the right end of the first string. For example, the concatenation of 'XYZ' and '12345' is the character string 'XYZ12345'. Similarly, the concatenation of 'CXDE' and 'ƀƀ2ƀ3' is 'CXDEƀƀ2ƀ3'. We will be discussing this operation further in Section 3.5 when we consider a subroutine, CONCAT, which implements this procedure in FORTRAN.

Subroutine SUBSTG

One possible FORTRAN implementation of the substring extraction operation is presented in Example 3.5. Subroutine SUBSTG requires six parameters which are summarized below:

TO: The name of the new character string (in CHARACTER vector form) to be created.

LTO: The total length of the new string as declared in the mainline program.

FROM: The name of the original character string from which the substring is to be extracted.

LFROM: The total length of the original string as declared in the mainline program.

START: The starting position from which extraction begins.

N: The desired number of characters to be extracted.

```
C EXAMPLE 3.5 - SUBSTRING EXTRACTION OPERATION
C
      SUBROUTINE SUBSTG(TO,LTO,FROM,LFROM,START,N)
C
      INTEGER START
      CHARACTER*1 TO(LTO),FROM(LFROM)
C
C N represents the desired number of characters
C to be extracted.  However, the maximum number of
C characters that can be extracted from string FROM
C is LFROM-START+1.  Furthermore, string TO can
C accommodate only LTO characters.  Consequently,
C the actual number of characters to be extracted
C is the minimum of these 3 values, or zero if this
C minimum is negative (START>LFROM).
C
      N = MAX0(0,MIN0(LTO,N,LFROM-START+1))
C
C If we cannot extract any characters from FROM,
C then we fill TO exclusively with blanks.
C
      IF(N.EQ.0)GO TO 15
C
C Extract the appropriate characters.
C
      DO 10 I=1,N
   10 TO(I) = FROM(START+I-1)
C
C If LTO and N are now the same, there will
C be no padded blanks at the end of TO.
C
      IF(N.EQ.LTO)RETURN
C
C K represents the number of padded blanks
C needed to fill out string TO.
C
   15 K = LTO-N
C
C Pad with blanks if the actual number of
C characters extracted is less than LTO.
C
      DO 20 I=1,K
   20 TO(N+I) = 'b̸'
C
      RETURN
      END
```

In Example 3.5, the two character strings are stored, one character per element, in two CHARACTER vectors. Such isolation of the characters in separate vector components permits us easy access to the characters on an individual basis. However, this approach tends to oversimplify the problem. Ideally, the user should be free to pass each character string to the subroutine as a complete entity (i.e., a variable of type CHARACTER**n*) rather than being forced to store it as a series of individual characters representing the elements of a CHARACTER*1 vector.

In Example 3.5, the first step is to determine the actual number of characters which can be extracted from FROM. This will depend on the values of LTO and N, as well as the value of START relative to that of LFROM. We can invoke the library functions MAX0 and MIN0 to assist us in making this decision. Once we have extracted the characters from string FROM, we can insert the appropriate number of blanks to fill out string TO. It is worthwhile noticing that the original value of N (as passed to the subroutine by the user) represents the number of characters which the user wishes to extract from string FROM. However, in various situations (e.g., N is larger than LFROM-START+1), it may not be possible to extract that many characters. Upon exit from the subroutine, the value of N is the number of characters which have actually been extracted.

As an illustration of the use of subroutine SUBSTG, consider the string A = 'ABCFGH', and suppose that we wish to extract the string B = 'BCF' from the longer string. (i.e., Starting from the second character in string A, we want to extract three consecutive characters to form string B.) Our mainline program would need to include the following invocation of the subroutine:

```
CALL SUBSTG(B,3,A,6,2,3)
```

Function INDEX

One version of a FORTRAN function subprogram to determine the location of a specified substring inside another character string is presented in Example 3.6. This coding for function INDEX assumes that the length of the substring to be located is only one character. The first parameter required by INDEX is a CHARACTER vector (STRING) containing the character string (one character per component) which is to be searched for the presence of a particular character, namely the third parameter (LOCATE). The second parameter (N) specifies the number of characters in the overall string. The function returns as its value the position of the first appearance of substring LOCATE in STRING.

To illustrate the use of function INDEX, suppose we wanted to determine the position of the substring '-' inside the string A = '72-34A'. We could invoke the function from a mainline program as follows:

```
INDEX(A,6,'-')
```

If the specified substring does not appear anywhere in the overall character string, we would like function INDEX to so indicate by returning some arbitrary value. This would be the case, for example, if we were to ask the function to locate the character '$' in the string '2345CDE'. In PL/1, the value returned in such instances is zero. By comparison, the APL implementation returns the value N+1 (where N is the length of the overall string). Our simplified version of function INDEX has followed the PL/1 convention of returning a zero value.

```
C EXAMPLE 3.6 - INDEXING OPERATION
C
      INTEGER FUNCTION INDEX(STRING,N,LOCATE)
C
      CHARACTER*1 LOCATE,STRING(N)
C
      DO 1 INDEX=1,N
    1 IF(LOCATE.EQ.STRING(INDEX))RETURN
C
C Normal exit from the above DO loop indicates
C that LOCATE does not appear anywhere in STRING.
C
      INDEX = 0
C
      RETURN
      END
```

At this stage, we are not including sample FORTRAN coding to implement the concatenation operation on character strings, since we will be considering a more general approach in Section 3.5. Furthermore, after reading the next section, the reader should be in a position to attempt more generalized versions of subprograms SUBSTG and INDEX (see Exercises 19, 20 and 21).

3.5 VARIABLE LENGTH CHARACTER STRINGS

We have already seen that character string data items are different from all the other data types we have considered in that character strings can assume different lengths. Furthermore, we have indicated that each character string has a length attribute associated with it. The WATFIV compiler allows us to declare character data to be of length *n*, where *n* is an integer constant defined at compile time. During execution of a program, the lengths of the character string data items can not be altered. For many applications, however, it is desirable to be able to manipulate the length of a character string as well as its content. For other applications, memory storage can be better utilized if character string data is permitted to occupy only the necessary number of bytes containing relevant information.

As an illustration, suppose that we wish to concatenate two character strings, A and B, and store the result in string C. The length of string C should become the sum of the lengths of A and B. However, if we program such a procedure in a language that does not support dynamic manipulation of string length, we might obtain undesirable results. For example, consider the following coding:

```
CHARACTER A*5,B*4,C*10
A = 'ABC'
B = '12345'
.
:   (coding to concatenate A and B into C)
.
```

The actual character string values assumed by A and B after execution of these two assignment statements might not reflect the true intentions of the programmer. Since all CHARACTER variables have fixed lengths, truncation or padding of blanks occurs as the consequence of a string assignment involving incompatible lengths. The actual values of A and B are 'ABCbb' and '1234' respectively. Furthermore, because the concatenation subprogram has no information regarding the actual lengths of the data items in character strings A and B, the resulting character string after assignment to C would be 'ABCbb1234b', whereas the desired result would be 'ABC12345'. This difficulty could be overcome if we were to maintain the length of each character string variable as an integer variable, and update it whenever a new value is assigned to the associated character string variable.

As a further illustration, modern programming languages do not restrict the length of the identifiers used by the programmer to a small number of characters like six as imposed in FORTRAN. The theoretical definition of ALGOL, for example, does not place any restriction on identifier length, while S/360 implementations of ALGOL and PL/1 restrict them to a maximum of 256 characters. At this point, we might examine the implications that the removal of identifier length restrictions has on the design of a compiler. The compiler program maintains a list of all identifiers used in the subject program, along with information regarding the type and addresses of the variables or functions designated by the identifiers. This list is called a *SYMBOL TABLE*. The restriction of six characters in FORTRAN identifiers stems from the fact that 36-bit machines could conveniently pack six characters into one machine word. Each entry in the symbol table has to contain the identifier name, and when we allow for arbitrarily long identifiers, we cannot assign a single word for each one. However, when identifiers can have from one to 256 characters, it would be very inefficient to reserve the maximum 256 bytes for each entry. Once again, the solution involves implementation of variable length character strings. Within this context, each entry in the table contains an integer indicating the length of the identifier, and then that number of bytes is used to store the identifier itself.

In summary, we have indicated that it is often desirable to have data items of type *VARIABLE LENGTH CHARACTER STRING* whereby we can manipulate the length of the strings during execution time. Such data types are supported by several general-purpose programming languages (e.g., PL/1, APL), and they constitute the major data type in special-purpose string manipulation languages (e.g., SNOBOL).

What are the difficulties involved in the implementation of variable length character strings? First, we cannot predict at compile time the storage requirements of such variables. Second, whenever we perform an operation on this type of variable, the program must have information about its <u>current</u>

length, and when a new value is assigned to it, its length has to be updated to reflect the change. We can simplify the problem of storage management by requiring the programmer to declare the maximum length of each one of his character strings so that we can reserve that much storage space for it. This is, of course, defeating the goal of efficient storage utilization, but it simplifies the program and saves on its running time (another case of time versus storage trade-off). This method was adopted by PL/1, thus allowing the programmer the option of declaring a character string to be of variable length, but forcing him to specify its maximum length. With each of these variables, the compiler associates a descriptor (invisible to the user) in which it records the current and maximum lengths of the string. The current length is modified when a new value is assigned to the string variable, and the maximum length is used for checking against possible string-overflow.

Other languages (e.g., APL), which have more flexible run-time facilities for allocation and liberation of storage, allocate a new storage area to a character string whenever its value is changed. A small part of the storage area contains the current length of the string, so that, when reference is made to that string, the program can determine its length.

At this stage, we might consider how we could implement (i.e., simulate) the two approaches to variable length character strings in WATFIV. The first approach is quite simple and can be implemented by associating an integer variable with each fixed-length WATFIV string. We will be discussing this approach in more detail in the remainder of this section. The second approach, illustrated in Section 8.5, is somewhat more complicated, since it requires the use of storage management routines for better use of memory. These routines employ list processing techniques which we will study and illustrate in later chapters.

What steps are involved in the simulation of the fixed maximum length approach to the implementation of variable length character strings in WATFIV? First, we have to decide the maximum length of each string, and we might choose 132, since that is the line size of our printer. Second, we have to specify the maximum number of variable length strings that our program will have to handle (e.g., 100). Then we can use the following declarations:

```
CHARACTER*132 STRING(100)
INTEGER*2     LENGTH(100)
```

At any given stage, the variable LENGTH(I) represents the current length of STRING(I), where $0 \leq LENGTH(I) \leq 132$. Furthermore, all the characters in STRING(I) between the $(LENGTH(I)+1)^{st}$ and the 132nd positions are ignored. In our program, we reference a particular character string by means of its index in the array STRING. Figure 3.4 contains a typical example in tabular form.

STRING NUMBER	STRING	LENGTH
1	YOU'VE HEARD ABOUT THE WILD	27
2	CHRISTMAS PARTY IN A	20
3	COMPLETELY AUTOMATED COMPANY -	30
4	THE COMPUTER GOT DRUNK AND	26
5	TRIED TO UNDO THE	17
6	ELECTRIC TYPEWRITER'S RIBBON.	29
.	.	.
.	.	.
.	.	.
.	.	.

Figure 3.4

Sample Variable Length Character Strings

We are now in a position to study how we can implement the basic operations on character strings using our method of representing variable length strings. Example 3.7 illustrates the concatenation operation. The other two operations, INDEX and SUBSTG, are left as exercises (see Exercises 20 and 21).

In Example 3.7, subroutine CONCAT requires three parameters which designate the two strings to be concatenated and the resulting string respectively. Two other parameters, STRING and LENGTH, are passed to the subroutine using COMMON storage. An EQUIVALENCE statement is used so that the program can gain access to each of the strings involved, either as a complete unit or on a character-by-character basis, depending upon the action to be performed.

```
C EXAMPLE 3.7 - CONCATENATION OPERATION WITH
C               VARIABLE LENGTH CHARACTER STRINGS
C
      SUBROUTINE CONCAT(IT,BY,INTO)
C
C IT, BY, and INTO are INTEGER values.  The relevant
C part of STRING(IT) is concatenated with the
C relevant part of STRING(BY), and the result is
C stored in STRING(INTO).  LENGTH(INTO) is set
C accordingly, after checking for overflow and
C truncating the result if necessary.
C
      CHARACTER*132 STRING(100),BYS,INTOS
      INTEGER*2 LENGTH(100),IT,BY,INTO
C
      COMMON STRING,LENGTH
C
C Align storage so that we can access each string
C as a complete unit or character-by-character.
C
      CHARACTER*1 BYC(132),INTOC(132)
      EQUIVALENCE (BYS,BYC),(INTOS,INTOC)
C
      INTOS = STRING(IT)
      LIT = LENGTH(IT)
      LENGTH(INTO) = MIN0(132,LIT+LENGTH(BY))
C
C If LENGTH(IT) is 132, there is no actual
C concatenation to perform.
C
      IF(LIT.EQ.132)GO TO 20
C
      BYS = STRING(BY)
      LBY = LENGTH(INTO)-LIT
C
C LBY now contains the number of characters in
C STRING(BY) which have to be moved to the
C concatenated string.
C
      DO 10 I=1,LBY
   10 INTOC(LIT+I) = BYC(I)
C
C Put the concatenated string into its proper place.
C
   20 STRING(INTO) = INTOS
C
      RETURN
      END
```

Example 3.7 has illustrated how we can manipulate our representation of variable length character strings. Each string data item consists of two FORTRAN items, namely the actual character string and its length. We associate them as being one item by the fact that they have the same index in the arrays STRING and LENGTH. Although this technique does allow us to perform the length manipulation we are seeking, we do, however, lose the ability to reference string variables by separate symbolic names. We have to refer to each string by its number (i.e., its index) in the arrays. Further examples of this technique will be presented in Chapter Four when we discuss text editing programs.

3.6 EXERCISES

1. Ignoring possible alignment problems, how many bytes are required in the S/360 implementation of WATFIV to represent the following variables?

```
INTEGER INT,INTA(20)
REAL X,Y(32)
CHARACTER A,B,C*8,D*4(8,4)
CHARACTER*8 E(10),F(2,4)
EQUIVALENCE (INTA,E),(Y,D)
COMMON X,INT,F
```

2. What will be the output from Example 3.8? (Notice that the overflow occurring in statement 10 does not cause execution to terminate, nor does it invalidate any of the results.)

```
C EXAMPLE 3.8 - EXERCISE
C
      INTEGER K,N
      CHARACTER*4 CHAR
      EQUIVALENCE (N,CHAR)
      CHAR = 'M240B'
      K = 0
      DO 10 I=1,32
      IF(N.LT.0)K = K+1
   10 N = N+N
      PRINT,K
      STOP
      END
```

3. What will be the output from Example 3.9?

```
C EXAMPLE 3.9 - EXERCISE
C
      CHARACTER*8 C
      INTEGER*2 N(4)
      REAL R(2)
      EQUIVALENCE (C,N,R)
      C = 'ȻPEA'
      N(3) = N(3)-31867
      N(4) = N(4)-16448
      PRINT 99,N,R(2)
   99 FORMAT('Ȼ',3A2,I8,F8.0)
      STOP
      END
```

4. What will be the output from Example 3.10?

```
C EXAMPLE 3.10 - EXERCISE
C
      CHARACTER*8 C,D
      INTEGER N(2)
      REAL R(2)
      EQUIVALENCE (C,N,R)
      C = 'OVERCOME'
      R(1) = EOR(R(1),R(2))
      R(2) = EOR(R(1),R(2))
      R(1) = EOR(R(1),R(2))
      D = C
      N(1) = N(1)+2087283726
      N(2) = N(2)-153
      PRINT 9,D,N
    9 FORMAT('Ȼ',A8,2A4)
      STOP
      END
```

5.(a) Write a logical-valued FORTRAN function subprogram called TEST which accepts a single input parameter, CHAR. CHAR is a CHARACTER*1 variable representing one alphanumeric character. TEST should return the value

.TRUE. if CHAR is a vowel and .FALSE. otherwise. Use a compile-time initialization statement to create the vowels (in a vector) for the comparisons.

5.(b) Write a mainline program which reads a series of data cards, each containing eighty alphanumeric characters (some of which may be blanks). The program should determine the number of times that two consecutive vowels appear for <u>each</u> card.

<u>Note</u>: Three consecutive vowels count as two appearances of two consecutive vowels; four consecutive vowels count as three occurrences; etc..

Use function TEST from part (a) to determine whether a character is a vowel. For each data card, the output should be the contents of the data card and the number of appearances of two consecutive vowels on that card. Your program should terminate execution upon encountering a data card with eighty blank columns.

<u>Example</u>:

HELLO THERE	0
SHIELD	1
BEAUTIFUL	2
AQUEOUS	3

6. (a) Write a program to read a data card containing a sequence of arithmetic operator symbols (i.e., +, -, *, and /). This program should print the number of occurrences of each character.

(b) Alter your program for part (a) to include the following provision: If two asterisks (*) appear adjacently, they should be counted as only one character.

7. The characters listed in Figure 3.1 are listed in four categories: special symbols, lower case alphabet, upper case alphabet, and digits. Write a program to read a data card containing eighty characters selected randomly from Figure 3.1. This program should determine how many of these eighty characters belong to each of the four categories [i.e., how many are special symbols, how many are lower case alphabet (assuming such characters were available on the keypunch), etc.].

8. Write a FORTRAN program that accepts as input two integers, I and J, and then prints a rectangle of width I and length J, using the asterisk as the character to outline the rectangle. Thus, if I = 10 and J = 4, your

program should print out a rectangle which has ten asterisks across the page and four down the page.

```
**********
*        *
*        *
**********
```

9. Write a set of WATFIV subprograms to carry out conversions between any two of the following number representations:

   DEC - Optionally signed string of (up to nine) decimal characters (0 - 9).

   BIN - A string of thirty-two binary characters (0 or 1) representing the two's complement binary representation of the number.

   HEX - A string of eight hexadecimal characters (0 - F) representing the number in two's complement form.

   Your main routine should read numbers in any one of these representations from data cards, one number per card, and print out their values in all three representations. To identify the type of the number being read, you should punch 'DEC', 'BIN', or 'HEX' in the first three columns of each card, followed by the number itself in any format you find convenient. Do not use Z FORMAT.

Example: DEC -32 (data)

```
DEC = -32   (output)
BIN = 11111111111111111111111111100000
HEX = FFFFFFE0
```

Test your program on the following data:

```
DEC  -72
HEX  ABCDEF78
BIN  10001000100111100101001100111001
DEC  1731940
HEX  AAAAAAAA
```

In this chapter, we have discussed the fact that the I/O procedures of FORTRAN have a set of conversion routines built into them that transform information from its external representation (i.e., character strings) into its internal form, and vice versa, according to a specified or implied FORMAT. Furthermore, we have shown how the core-to-core I/O feature of WATFIV allows us to make similar conversions on data held in memory. Exercises 10-17 illustrate various forms of data conversion without using core-to-core I/O.

10. Write the coding for the following WATFIV subroutine:

```
SUBROUTINE CHRHEX(CHAR,LC,HEX,LH)
CHARACTER*1 CHAR(LC),HEX(LH)
```

The input parameters to this subroutine are CHAR, LC, and LH. CHAR is a CHARACTER*1 vector containing a sequence of LC characters. The output parameter is HEX, a CHARACTER*1 vector having LH components. Subroutine CHRHEX assigns characters, each of which is either a digit (0-9) or one of the upper case letters A-F, to vector HEX on the following basis:

The two characters representing the hexadecimal code in Figure 3.1 for CHAR(I) are assigned to HEX(2*I) and HEX(2*I-1), where I=1,2,...,LC.

<u>Example</u>: CHAR: 'AB2$'

HEX: 'C1C2F25B'

CHARACTER	CODE
A	C1
B	C2
2	F2
$	5B

If LH<2*LC, an appropriate error message should be printed. Do <u>not</u> use core-to-core I/O in this subroutine.

11. Write the coding for the following WATFIV subroutine:

```
SUBROUTINE HEXCHR(CHAR,LC,HEX,LH)
CHARACTER*1 CHAR(LC),HEX(LH)
```

This subroutine performs the reverse operation to that of subroutine CHRHEX. In this case, the input parameters are HEX, LH, and LC. HEX is a CHARACTER*1 vector containing a sequence of LH characters, each of which is either a digit (0-9) or one of the upper case letters A-F. The output parameter is CHAR, a CHARACTER*1 vector having LC components. Subroutine HEXCHR assigns characters to vector CHAR on the following basis:

The characters in vector HEX are interpreted as being hexadecimal digits. The character in Figure 3.1 represented by the character code specified in HEX(2*I-1) and HEX(2*I) collectively is assigned to CHAR(I), where I=1,2,...,LC.

Appropriate error messages should be included to indicate if LH is odd (Why?), LH<2*LC, or if any pair of successive characters in vector HEX represents an invalid character code (e.g., DO). Do <u>not</u> use core-to-core I/O in this subroutine.

12. Write the coding for the following WATFIV function:

```
INTEGER FUNCTION CHRINT(CHAR)
CHARACTER*10 CHAR
```

CHAR is a string of ten characters, each of which should be one of the digits 0-9, a blank, or one of the two special characters '+' and '-'. CHAR represents, in character string form, a FORTRAN INTEGER constant expressed in decimal notation. Function CHRINT, ignoring any blanks trailing the rightmost digit character in CHAR, returns, in numerical form, this INTEGER value.

If any of the characters in CHAR are invalid, or if the value represented by CHAR is outside the range -2^{31} to $2^{31} - 1$, an error message should be printed. Do not use core-to-core I/O in this function.

```
C EXAMPLE 3.11 - SAMPLE MAINLINE ROUTINE
C                FOR FUNCTION CHRINT
C
      CHARACTER*10 CHAR/'ƀƀƀ-235'/
      INTEGER CHRINT
      I = CHRINT(CHAR)
      PRINT 1,CHAR,I
    1 FORMAT('0',A10,I10)
      STOP
      END

      ƀƀƀ-235ƀƀƀƀƀƀƀ-235  (output)
```

13. Write the coding for the following WATFIV subroutine:

```
SUBROUTINE INTCHR(INT,STRING)
CHARACTER*10 STRING
INTEGER INT
```

INT represents a valid FORTRAN INTEGER constant. This subroutine produces a character string, STRING, whose characters, right-justified, are the digits of the decimal representation of INT, possibly including a minus sign immediately preceding the leftmost digit. Do not use core-to-core I/O in this subroutine.

```
C EXAMPLE 3.12 - SAMPLE MAINLINE ROUTINE
C                FOR SUBROUTINE INTCHR
C
      INTEGER INT/-10987/
      CHARACTER*10 STRING
      CALL INTCHR(INT,STRING)
      PRINT 1,INT,STRING
    1 FORMAT('b̸',I10,A10)
      STOP
      END

      b̸b̸b̸b̸-10987b̸b̸b̸b̸-10987    (output)
```

14. Write the coding for the following WATFIV function:

```
REAL FUNCTION HEXFLT(HEX)
CHARACTER*8 HEX
```

HEX is a string of eight characters, each of which should be either a digit or one of the upper case letters A-F. These eight characters can be interpreted as being the hexadecimal representation of the contents of a specified group of four bytes in the S/360 memory. Furthermore, we can consider these four bytes as representing a floating-point value. Function HEXFLT returns, in numerical form, this floating-point value. If any of the characters in HEX cannot be interpreted as a hexadecimal digit (i.e., 0-9,A-F), an error message should be printed. Do <u>not</u> use core-to-core I/O in this function.

```
C EXAMPLE 3.13 - SAMPLE MAINLINE ROUTINE
C                FOR FUNCTION HEXFLT
C
      CHARACTER*8 HEX/'421A4000'/
      X = HEXFLT(HEX)
      PRINT,HEX,X
      STOP
      END

      421A4000    0.2625000E 02  (output)
```

15. Write the coding for the following WATFIV function:

```
REAL FUNCTION CHRFLT(CHAR)
CHARACTER*14 CHAR
```

CHAR is a string of fourteen characters, each of which should be a digit or one of the characters 'b̸', '.', '+', '-', and 'E'. CHAR represents, in character string form, a FORTRAN REAL (single-precision) constant. This constant may be expressed in any format which is acceptable under FORTRAN specifications. Function CHRFLT, ignoring any blanks trailing the rightmost non-blank character in CHAR, returns, in numerical form, this constant value. If CHAR contains any invalid characters, or if the constant represented is not REAL, an error message should be printed. Do not use core-to-core I/O in this function.

```
C EXAMPLE 3.14 - SAMPLE MAINLINE ROUTINE
C                FOR FUNCTION CHRFLT
C
      CHARACTER*14 C1/'b̸b̸b̸24.6'/,C2/'-4.2Eb̸3'/
      X = CHRFLT(C1)
      Y = CHRFLT(C2)
      PRINT,X,Y
      STOP
      END

      0.2460000E 02   -0.4200000E 04  (output)
```

16. Write the coding for the following WATFIV subroutine:

```
SUBROUTINE FLTCHR(FLT,STRING)
CHARACTER*14 STRING
REAL FLT
```

The input parameter to FLTCHR is a floating-point value FLT. The subroutine produces a character string, STRING, whose characters, right-justified, represent the normalized form of the decimal representation of FLT, possibly including a minus sign immediately preceding the leftmost digit. Do not use core-to-core I/O in this subroutine.

```
C EXAMPLE 3.15 - SAMPLE MAINLINE ROUTINE
C                FOR SUBROUTINE FLTCHR
C
      CHARACTER*14 STR1,STR2
      REAL FLT1/-236.78/,FLT2/0.005/
      CALL FLTCHR(FLT1,STR1)
      CALL FLTCHR(FLT2,STR2)
      PRINT,STR1,STR2
      STOP
      END
      -0.2367800E 03  b̸0.5000000E-02   (output)
```

17. Write the coding for the following WATFIV subroutine:

```
SUBROUTINE FFMT(FLT,CHAR,W,P)
INTEGER W,P
CHARACTER*1 CHAR(W)
REAL FLT
```

This subroutine simulates F FORMAT. The three input parameters are FLT, W, and P. FLT represents a floating-point value specified by the user. The subroutine converts FLT into a character string having W characters. These characters represent the value of FLT, expressed in F FORMAT, with P digits to the right of the decimal point. You should incorporate a check to insure that $0 \le P < W-1$. Furthermore, the values of W and P may cause loss of significance, as indicated by the following examples:

(i)	W = 3	P = 1	FLT = 16.5	1 [6.5]
(ii)	W = 5	P = 3	FLT = -2.	- [2.000]

(FLT = +2. would not result in a loss of significance here.)

Your program should provide error diagnostics in such cases. Do <u>not</u> use core-to-core I/O in this subroutine.

18. Write a WATFIV subroutine, CONCAT, to concatenate two character strings, A and B, and form a new string C. The subroutine has arguments as shown:

```
SUBROUTINE CONCAT(A,LA,B,LB,C,LC)
CHARACTER*1 A(LA),B(LB),C(LC)
```

If LC>LA+LB, pad the right end of C with blanks. If LC<LA+LB, truncate the rightmost portion of the concatenated string, and print a message:

```
'STRING TOO LONG - TRUNCATED'
```

19. Write the coding for the following WATFIV function:

```
INTEGER FUNCTION INDEX(STRING,LS,THING,LT)
CHARACTER*1 STRING(LS),THING(LT)
```

Function INDEX returns the numerical position of the first complete occurrence of THING in STRING. If LT>LS, or THING is not found in STRING, the function returns a zero value to the calling program.

20. Write a WATFIV function subprogram to implement the INDEX operation on variable length character strings:

```
INTEGER FUNCTION INDEX(IN,IT)
CHARACTER*132 STRING(100)
INTEGER*2 LENGTH(100)
COMMON LENGTH,STRING
:
:
```

This function should find the position index of the variable length character string referenced by IT in the string referenced by IN. If LENGTH(IT)>LENGTH(IN), or STRING(IT) does not appear anywhere in STRING(IN), the function returns a zero value.

21. Implement the SUBSTG operation on variable length character strings:

```
SUBROUTINE SUBSTG(IT,START,N,INTO)
CHARACTER*132 STRING(100)
INTEGER*2 LENGTH(100)
COMMON LENGTH,STRING
.
.
.
```

Beginning at position START, this subroutine extracts from STRING(IT) a substring having N characters for storage in STRING(INTO). LENGTH(INTO) is modified to represent the number of relevant characters in STRING(INTO) after the assignment has been completed.

22. Pairs of words with a letter in common can be written as in a crossword puzzle. In the following example, 'S' is the letter in common:

```
    T
    E
E A S Y
    T
```

We can refer to 'EASY' as the "horizontal" word and to 'TEST' as the "vertical" word. We can extend this idea to three dimensions by introducing a "normal" word (e.g., 'CASE'). Since 'S' is the letter in common, the letters 'C' and 'A' would appear above the plane of this paper and the letter 'E' below this plane.

Write a FORTRAN program to do the following:

(i) Read three 9-character words into variables HOR, VERT, and NOR, each of which is declared CHARACTER*9. Each character is either a letter of the alphabet or a blank.

(ii) Terminate execution upon encountering a trio of words which contains at least one completely blank word.

(iii) Determine and print all non-blank intersections of the three data words. The form of the output should conform to that illustrated below.

(iv) Return to step (i) upon completion of step (iii).

Example 1:

HORIZONTAL	VERTICAL	NORMAL
1 2 3 4 5 6 7 8 9	1 2 3 4 5 6 7 8 9	1 2 3 4 5 6 7 8 9
b̸ b̸ E A S Y b̸ b̸ b̸	T E S T b̸ b̸ b̸ b̸ b̸	b̸ b̸ b̸ b̸ C A S E b̸

INTERSECTION NUMBERS

HORIZONTAL	VERTICAL	NORMAL
3	2	8
5	3	7

Example 2:

HORIZONTAL	VERTICAL	NORMAL
1 2 3 4 5 6 7 8 9	1 2 3 4 5 6 7 8 9	1 2 3 4 5 6 7 8 9
A R T S b̸ b̸ b̸ b̸ b̸	b̸ b̸ b̸ b̸ M A T H S	b̸ H I S T O R Y b̸

INTERSECTION NUMBERS

HORIZONTAL	VERTICAL	NORMAL
3	7	5
4	9	4

23. Write a FORTRAN program to read thirty 5-letter words from data cards and store them in an array [CHARACTER*5 WORD(30)]. Then the program should create and print all possible 5×5 crossword puzzles which use ten words (i.e., five vertically and five horizontally) chosen from the given thirty words. (See the example displayed on the following page.)

    Note: Can you solve this problem without using any other arrays than WORD?

Example:

MARSH
ENROL
MINER
RELAX
LEVER
OUTDO
YANKS
APPLE
TRAIL
MILKY
ALTAR
PLANE
KNEAD
STEAK
TROLL
AROMA
EXERT
SMOTE
HERDS
SMART
PERIL
ALERT
IRATE
MOURN
LATER
ORATE
MOLAR
RADIO
ARENA
RAVEN

M A R S H
I R A T E
L E V E R
K N E A D
Y A N K S

M I L K Y
A R E N A
R A V E N
S T E A K
H E R D S

(The above two puzzles are transposes. There are at least two other puzzles and their transposes for this example.)

CHAPTER FOUR
CHARACTER STRINGS APPLICATIONS

4.1 CHARACTER SORTING

In this section, we will concentrate on one example of character manipulation - the sorting of character strings. We will demonstrate how a sorting algorithm can be implemented to order a list of fixed-length character strings with both standard FORTRAN and WATFIV. Throughout the rest of this book, we will be using only the CHARACTER facilities of WATFIV, trusting that the examples given in this chapter will assist those who do not have access to a WATFIV compiler to code the exercises in standard FORTRAN.

Before we can proceed to discuss sorting of character strings, we should briefly consider the general problem of sorting. Sorting of data according to the values of a certain item (sometimes called the *KEY*) is a very common operation throughout the computer applications field. In most instances, the data is organized in records, each record being a collection of several data items. The problem is to place the records in order according to the key item in the records. If a sort in ascending order is required, the result of the sorting operation should place record *i* before record *j* if the key in record *i* is smaller than the key in record *j*, where *i* and *j* represent all possible pairs of records in our data.

The classical example where sorting is required is that of personnel records, where each record contains information about an employee, including his name, I.D. number, type of job, or salary. In many instances, we would like to sort such data according to the alphabetical order of the employee names or according to their I.D. numbers. When sorting according to a numeric key, the definition of "greater than" or "smaller than" is obvious. When sorting a series of character strings, however, a clearer definition of the relationship has to be made. We have a conventional way of ordering character strings alphabetically, grading the 'b̸' as the smallest character, followed by the letters 'A' to 'Z' in that order. The appropriate place in this ordering for the digits and the special characters will vary according to the specific application. Furthermore, for sorting purposes, character strings are considered as if they were sequences of digits, with the leftmost character considered the most significant one. When character strings of different lengths are compared, the shorter string is padded on the right with blanks to make it equal in length with the other one.

We are all aware that comparison of character strings plays an important role in sorting. For such purposes, we have to test the relationship between two character strings (e.g., .GT., .LT., .EQ., etc.) as we do for numeric variables. We have already seen that the internal representation chosen for characters maintains the kind of ordering we want when considering the individual equivalent integer values of the various characters. Generally, we are able to compare character strings by comparing the integer values of the machine words in which they are stored. This is usually done in standard FORTRAN, where character string operations are not available. WATFIV, however, allows comparison of actual character strings, thus eliminating some problems that might arise as a result of comparing the equivalent integer values of the character strings.

To illustrate the kind of problems that might be encountered in standard FORTRAN, suppose we consider the character strings, 'JOHN' and 'DAVE', to see how their equivalent integer values compare. If we use two INTEGER variables to store these two character strings, we will actually be comparing their equivalent integer values which are -744453035 and -993925691 respectively. Since the sign-bit is 1 (for all strings beginning with a character other than a special character or a blank), both numbers are interpreted as negative values. However, the comparison still produces the results which we desire, since the second number is more negative than the first, with the result that the second will be found to be less than the first one. This ordering preserves the alphabetic sequence which we are seeking.

If we compare the two strings, 'DANȸ' and 'ȸDAN', however, we do not get the desired results produced by the previous pair of character strings, since the new respective integer values are -993929920 and 1086636501. By comparing such values, the second string will be considered larger than the first, because the representation of the 'ȸ' as the first character makes the corresponding integer value positive, thus yielding an undesirable result. We should emphasize that a 'ȸ' at any position other than the leftmost byte in a word will yield a correct comparison, since it will not affect the sign-bit. Representing character strings by REAL or COMPLEX variables in standard FORTRAN does not solve the problem. Consequently, when comparing character strings in standard FORTRAN, a programmer has to include special coding to handle situations like the one just considered, if the conventional ordering of character strings is to be maintained.

For our discussion of sorting algorithms, we are making some simplifying assumptions. First, we assume that the record to be sorted contains only a single item which is a character string (e.g., a list of names to be sorted). In addition, we assume that the character strings are sorted in an array so that the ordering is to be done with respect to the subscripts by which individual entries are identified within the array. In later chapters, we will adopt the sorting algorithms discussed here to accommodate different relationships between the sorted records.

4.1.1 A Primitive Sort

The most straightforward way to go about sorting a list into ascending numerical order (actually, alphabetical in our case) is to search the list for its smallest member, which is subsequently exchanged with the first entry in the list. Then, beginning with the second entry in the list, the rest of the list is examined to find the smallest number. This entry is then exchanged with the element currently in the second position of the list. This searching process is repeated a total of N-1 times for a list having N entries, each time beginning with the entry immediately following the position where the previous pass was initiated. For each pass, the smallest entry found is exchanged with the entry at which the pass began. Upon completion of the last pass, all the entries in the list will be properly sorted.

The first pass in this sorting algorithm is performed over the entire list, with the result that it requires N-1 comparisons. The second pass, however, covers only the last N-1 entries in the list, and consequently it requires only N-2 comparisons. Each successive pass, since it is performed on one less entry, requires one less comparison than the preceding pass. The last pass, of course, involves only the last two entries in the list and requires a single comparison. As a result, this type of sorting algorithm requires a total of

$$(N-1)+(N-2)+....+1 = \frac{N(N-1)}{2}$$

comparisons. In most cases, this might be too time-consuming a process, especially when N is very large. Furthermore, this algorithm makes no provision for cases where the list might already be partially ordered. At any given step in this sorting process the list might have reached its final sorted state, and thus require no further modification. This algorithm, however, does not include any provision for checking the state of the list at the end of each pass, and consequently, it continues to complete N-1 passes.

4.1.2 Bubble Sort

We will now describe in detail one of the adaptive sorting algorithms which take advantage of partially sorted data. This algorithm is sometimes called a *BUBBLE SORT*, since the smaller key values tend to "bubble" to the top locations in the array at the same time as the larger values are shifted towards the bottom. During each pass, consecutive entries are compared, and, if they are out of order, interchanged. The list is scanned at most N-1 times, with each pass progressing from the top of the list down towards the bottom. The first pass, since it considers all the entries in the list, involves N-1 comparisons. One certain result of the first pass, however, is the relocation of the largest entry in the last position of the list.

For example, if the largest member is initially in the ith position of the list, it is compared with the $(i+1)^{st}$ entry. Then, since these two elements are out of order (i.e., the first is larger than the second), an interchange is performed, with the result that the largest entry is now located in the $(i+1)^{st}$ position. The next comparison is performed with the $(i+1)^{st}$ and $(i+2)^{nd}$ entries, once again causing an interchange which moves the largest entry one position further down the list (i.e., into position $i+2$). Finally, after the first pass has been completed, the largest entry is relocated in the Nth position of the array.

Since we know that the largest entry is in its proper position at the end of the first pass, the second pass need be performed only upon the first N-1 entries of the list (involving N-2 comparisons). This pass insures that the second largest entry in the list is relocated in the $(N-1)^{st}$ position. Similarly, the third largest entry is relocated in the $(N-2)^{nd}$ position. This process is repeated a maximum of N-1 times, each pass involving one less element than the previous one. The $(N-1)^{st}$ pass, of course, compares only the first two elements in the list. We have already mentioned, however, that it is quite possible for the list to have reached its final sorted form at some intermediate stage in the algorithm. This condition will be reflected by the fact that a pass has been completed without any interchanges having been made. Since the list, in such cases, is already in the proper order, no further passes are necessary.

The advantage of this method of sorting over the previous one is obvious. If we are lucky enough to be considering a list which is already in order, a single pass will be sufficient, since no interchanges will be performed. Furthermore, only in some cases, where the list is completely out of order, will the maximum N-1 passes be required. Depending upon the extent to which the list is already pre-sorted, the potential difference in efficiency becomes considerably greater with larger lists.

Nevertheless, the average number of comparisons performed with the bubble sort on random data is still proportional to N^2, and increases significantly with N. There are other sorting algorithms for which the average number of comparisons involved is proportional to $N\log_2 N$. However, it is more difficult with these algorithms to take advantage of partially sorted lists. We shall be implicitly using a tree sort with logarithmic properties in our discussion of bitree symbol tables in Section 7.5.

Now that we have discussed the operation of the bubble sort, let us consider how to implement this algorithm in standard FORTRAN. The coding for such a program is presented in Example 4.1. We assume that the names are 16 characters long and that there are no more than 100 names in the list. Since we need four INTEGER variables to represent 16 characters, we store the names, one per row, in an INTEGER array, WORD, of size 100 by 4. In order to make the program complete, as well as to illustrate character I/O in standard FORTRAN, we have included the necessary statements to read the names and print them, both before and after the sorting process. The variable, FLAG, is used to indicate whether an interchange has occurred during the most recent pass. Consequently, if the value of FLAG is .TRUE. at the end of a particular pass, and providing the pass just completed is not the (N-1)st, the scanning procedure is repeated. The next pass, however, covers one less element (N = N-1).

```
C EXAMPLE 4.1 - BUBBLE SORT IMPLEMENTED
C               IN STANDARD FORTRAN
C
      INTEGER WORD(100,4),TEMP
      LOGICAL FLAG
C
C Read the data and save the value of N
C for later output.  The value of N is
C modified several times in the program.
C
      READ,N
      NN = N
C
      READ 9,((WORD(I,J),J=1,4),I=1,N)
    9 FORMAT(4A4)
C
      PRINT 8,((WORD(I,J),J=1,4),I=1,N)
    8 FORMAT(1H0,12HINITIAL DATA(/1Hb̸,4A4))
C
C Prepare the values of N and FLAG for the
C next pass.  FLAG is used to indicate whether
C any interchanges occur during each pass.
C Its value is set to .FALSE. at the beginning
C of each new pass.  Each new pass covers one
C less element than the previous one.
C
    2 N = N-1
      FLAG = .FALSE.
C
C Compare each pair of names, 4 characters at a time.
```

```
      DO 4 J=1,N
      DO 5 K=1,4
C
      IF(WORD(J,K)-WORD(J+1,K))4,5,3
C
    5 CONTINUE
C
C Natural exit from inner DO loop above indicates
C that the two names being compared are identical.
C
      GO TO 4
C
C Perform an interchange with the two names, and
C reset the value of variable FLAG.
C
    3 FLAG = .TRUE.
C
      DO 6 L=1,4
      TEMP = WORD(J,L)
      WORD(J,L) = WORD(J+1,L)
    6 WORD(J+1,L) = TEMP
C
C Control passes to statement 4 when it is time
C to compare the next pair of names.
C
    4 CONTINUE
C
C Determine whether any further passes are necessary.
C
      IF(FLAG.AND.N.GT.1)GO TO 2
C
      PRINT 11,((WORD(I,J),J=1,4),I=1,NN)
   11 FORMAT(1H0,11HSORTED DATA(/1Hb,4A4))
C
      STOP
      END
```

In Example 4.1, all operations on the character strings are performed upon the INTEGER variables used to represent them. As a result, all I/O operations, interchanges, and comparisons of the strings require DO loops to iterate through the four components of matrix WORD in which each name is stored. Each comparison is made, four characters at a time, by examining the equivalent integer values of the substrings. As we discussed earlier, such comparisons might yield undesirable results (e.g., 'JOHNSTON' will be listed after 'JOHNSTONE').

Example 4.2 illustrates how the same program can be written with WATFIV. We use a character string vector, WORD, to represent the names, with the result that each comparison is performed using complete strings (rather than examining individual substrings), thus contributing to the efficiency of the program and eliminating undesirable sorting results. Our algorithm for the bubble sort is modified slightly to improve the speed of the sorting process. This modification is based on the premise that it is often possible to shorten the length of each successive pass by more than just one entry. Actually, we know that the bottom part of the list, from the point of the last interchange down, must already be in the proper order. (If it were not, an interchange would have been performed.) Consequently, we record the position of the last interchange during the pass just completed, and we use this value to indicate the last entry to be compared in the next pass. In Example 4.2, we use two INTEGER variables, LAST and LATEST, the former to indicate the position of the last entry to be covered in the current pass, and the latter to store the position of the most recent interchange performed. If, at the end of a particular pass, the value of LATEST is not smaller than that of LAST, we know that no interchange has taken place during the pass just completed, and the sorting

```
C EXAMPLE 4.2 - IMPROVED BUBBLE SORT IMPLEMENTED
C               WITH WATFIV'S CHARACTER VARIABLES
C
      CHARACTER*16 WORD(100),TEMP
C
      READ,N
      READ,(WORD(I),I=1,N)
C
C The data cards require a pair of single quote
C marks surrounding each name unless we use a
C format for input.
C
      PRINT,'INITIAL DATA'
      DO 10 I=1,N
   10 PRINT,WORD(I)
C
C Initialize the values of LAST and LATEST.  LAST
C indicates the final entry to be considered in
C the forthcoming pass.  LATEST indicates the
C position of the most recent interchange performed.
C
      LATEST = N
    2 LAST = LATEST
C
C Begin the next pass through the list of names.
C
      DO 4 J=2,LAST
C
      IF(WORD(J-1).LE.WORD(J))GO TO 4
C
C Perform the interchange when necessary.
C
      LATEST = J-1
      TEMP = WORD(J-1)
      WORD(J-1) = WORD(J)
      WORD(J) = TEMP
C
    4 CONTINUE
C
C Determine whether any further passes are necessary.
C
      IF(LATEST.LT.LAST.AND.LATEST.GT.1)GO TO 2
C
      PRINT 11,(WORD(I),I=1,N)
   11 FORMAT('0','SORTED DATA'(/'b̸',A16))
C
      STOP
      END
```

process is terminated. Alternatively, if LATEST has the value 1, we know that the last interchange involved the first two entries in the list, and again we can terminate the sorting procedure. This modification makes a significant improvement in the performance of the sorting algorithm.

However, we can make a still further improvement in the performance of our sorting routine. For example, for those cases in which the smallest entry is initially located in the last position of the list, we still have to perform the maximum N-1 passes, even if the rest of the list is in perfect order. By reversing the direction of the subsequent scan at the end of each pass (i.e., the first pass progresses from the top of the list down, whereas the second moves from the bottom upwards, etc.), we can eliminate this unfortunate possibility. To do this, we keep two indicators, FIRST and LAST, to mark the position of the last interchanges made during the passes up and down the list respectively. This modification requires a significant addition to the program, quite possibly involving a different set of coding for the passes proceeding in opposite directions. We leave the detailed programming of this improved algorithm as an exercise (see Exercise 2).

4.2 SOURCE SCANNING

Computer programs that accept text of one language as input, and produce its translation in another language as output, are called *TRANSLATORS*. A compiler, for example, is just one special type of translator. Its input consists of statements in a high-level programming language, and its output is the equivalent machine language code. The input to a translator is called the *SOURCE*, and it is usually in character string form.

One of the first tasks of a translator is to read the source and break it down into its components, sometimes called *SYNTACTIC UNITS*. For a programming language, these syntactic units are the symbolic names of variables, subroutines and functions, key words (e.g., INTEGER, DO, RETURN), and numeric or character string constants. The syntactic units in the source are separated by delimiters. These may consist of a sequence of blanks, or be any one of the special characters recognized as operators in the translated language (+, -, (, *, etc.). The process by which the translator locates the delimiters in the source and isolates the syntactic units is called *SOURCE SCANNING*.

The source is transmitted to the translator in units, usually cards containing 80 characters each. These are not necessarily the same as the logical units of the translated language (i.e., sentences in natural languages or statements in programming languages). Modern programming languages allow several statements to be punched on a single card or one statement to overflow onto several cards. Consequently, source scanners usually consider the source as one long character string containing all the statements of the subject program, with a special delimiter (e.g., semi-colon in ALGOL and PL/1) separating the statements. Most translators perform the translation one statement at a time, leaving the responsibility to signal "end of statement" with the source scanner routine.

The output from the text scanner might be in the form of a table containing the syntactic units in order of their appearance in the source statement, together with their associated delimiters. In such cases, the table created for a particular statement is processed immediately by the translator. Subsequently, this table is erased, and a new table is created for the next statement. Other translators might process one syntactic unit at a time, thus eliminating the need for such tables. A table of syntactic units and their delimiters is sometimes called an *OPERATOR-OPERAND TABLE*.

As an illustration, suppose we consider the following FORTRAN source statement:

```
ALPHA = SIN(X**2/(2.0*PI))+0.345E-5
```

The resulting operator-operand table produced by the scanner for this statement is presented in Figure 4.1.

Delimiter	Length	Unit
#	5	ALPHA
=	3	SIN
(	1	X
**	1	2
/	0	
(	1	2
.	1	0
*	2	PI
)	0	
)	0	
+	1	0
.	4	345E
-	1	5
$	0	

Figure 4.1

Simplified Operator-Operand Table

Each row of Figure 4.1 contains three entries: a syntactic unit, the length of that unit, and the delimiter that precedes that unit in the source. The '#' and '$' are two special delimiters which indicate the beginning and end of the statement respectively.

Actually, the operator-operand table will probably contain more information than is shown in Figure 4.1. For example, along with each entry, we would like to have some indication of the type of the syntactic unit, distinguishing mainly between character and numeric units. Another task, usually performed by the scanner, is the conversion of the different numeric constants from their external character string form into their equivalent numeric representation. If these additional steps are performed on the example illustrated by Figure 4.1, the output from the scanner might be as presented in Figure 4.2.

Delimiter	Type	Length	Unit
#	1	5	ALPHA
=	1	3	SIN
(	1	1	X
**	3	4	00000002_{16}
/	0	0	
(	4	4	41200000_{16}
*	1	2	PI
)	0	0	
)	0	0	
+	4	4	$3C39E1A3_{16}$
$	0		

Figure 4.2

Detailed Operator-Operand Table

In Figure 4.2, the entries from the first table which comprised a single numeric value are combined to form a single entry in the new table. The result of the conversion from character string to numeric is also stored in the revised version. Furthermore, an additional column is used to indicate the type of the operand. In Figure 4.2, we have chosen 0 to indicate that no operand is present, 1 to indicate a symbolic operand, 3 for an integer constant, and 4 for a floating-point number. It should also be noted that the length field in the new table indicates the number of bytes occupied by the corresponding syntactic unit.

With our previous example, we have illustrated scanner operations similar to those performed by the scanner routines of the WATFOR and WATFIV compilers. This is by no means, however, the only way by which source scanning can be performed, nor is it the best method. The amount and type of processing performed by the scanning routine depends on many factors, such as the type of language translated, or the type of compiler (in-core, batch, incremental, etc.). Nevertheless, the common operation performed by all scanners is that of examining the source, character by character, and breaking it into its separate syntactic units. Since a character-by-character scan is an expensive process, we want to make sure that it is performed only once, and consequently, we design the scanner to produce an output that does not have to be re-scanned.

4.2.1 Scanning For Symbolic Names

At this stage in our discussion, we can illustrate source scanning operations by implementing a simplified version of this process in FORTRAN. We will be isolating symbolic names from the source deck and storing them in a table. Tables of this type, which contain symbolic names accompanied by their associated attributes, are called *SYMBOL TABLES*. These tables comprise the mechanism by which compilers can record the different names generated by the programmer and locate the variables associated with them. We will be discussing the implementation and application of symbol tables in further detail in Chapter Eight.

Usually, the creation of a symbol table is performed after the scanning process has been completed so that the symbolic names can be obtained from the operator-operand table. In our present example, however, we will by-pass the intermediate step of generating an operator-operand table and enter syntactic names directly into the symbol table. Furthermore, we will simplify the problem by assuming that we have only one possible delimiter, namely a blank or a sequence of blanks. For the actual scanning process, we will introduce a function called NECAR (i.e., NExt ChARacter) that will be invoked once per input character for the purpose of determining whether it is a delimiter.

The version of function NECAR presented in Example 4.3 maintains a storage area for one card at a time, IN(72), assuming that each card contains 72 source characters. In addition, the function maintains a pointer, IP, pointing at the character currently being scanned. When it is invoked, the function will increment the pointer and examine the next source character. NECAR returns a 0 value if the character being considered is a blank, and the value 1 otherwise. Whenever a card has been

```
C EXAMPLE 4.3 - SOURCE SCANNING ROUTINE
C
      INTEGER FUNCTION NECAR(CC)
C
C IN contains the 72 source characters on the
C card.  CC represents the specific character
C being scanned.  CARNO contains the 8
C characters in columns 73-80 of the card.
C
      CHARACTER*1 IN(72),CC,CARNO*8
      INTEGER IP/72/
C
C Assume the next character to be scanned is
C not a blank until proven otherwise.
C
      NECAR = 1
C
C Increment IP to point at the next character to
C be scanned.  IP has been initialized to 72 so
C that the first source card will be read when
C the function is invoked for the first time.
C
      IP = IP+1
      IF(IP.LE.72)GO TO 20
C
C After completing the scan of one source card,
C read the next card.  Make a listing of the source.
C
   10 READ 13,IN,CARNO
   13 FORMAT(72A1,A8)
C
      PRINT 16,IN,CARNO
   16 FORMAT('b̸',72A1,A8)
C
C Ignore comment cards with '*' in column 1.
C
      IF(IN(1).EQ.'*')GO TO 10
C
      IP = 1
C
   20 CC = IN(IP)
C
C Return a zero function value if CC is a blank.
C
      IF(CC.EQ.'b̸')NECAR = 0
C
      RETURN
      END
```

completely scanned (i.e., IP>72), a new source card will be read and the pointer reset to 1.

We have included another feature with function NECAR to permit the insertion of "comment cards" in the source deck. We assume that all source cards with the character '*' in column 1 are comment cards, and consequently, they should be ignored. The single parameter of the NECAR function, CC, is a character string of length 1, and it is used to return the source character just scanned to the calling program.

```
C EXAMPLE 4.4 - SCANNING A SOURCE DECK TO
C               CONSTRUCT A SYMBOL TABLE
C
      CHARACTER*6 TABLE(100)/100*'b̸'/,SYM
      CHARACTER*1 CC,S(6)
C
C TP indicates the last entry used in table.
C
      INTEGER TP/0/
C
C SYM and S are used to obtain the syntactic
C units.  S permits us access to each character
C individually, while SYM gives us access to
C the complete symbolic name after it has
C been selected from the source.
C
      EQUIVALENCE (SYM,S)
C
C Function NECAR is invoked repeatedly until a
C non-blank character is encountered.
C
   10 IF(NECAR(CC).EQ.0)GO TO 10†
C
C Initialize SYM to be all blanks.
C
      SYM = 'b̸'
C
C Create the next symbolic name in SYM, one
C character at a time, until a blank is found,
```

```
C or until 6 consecutive non-blank characters
C have been encountered.
C
      DO 20 I=1,6
      S(I) = CC
      IF(NECAR(CC).EQ.0)GO TO 30
   20 CONTINUE
C
C Truncate symbolic names which exceed 6 characters.
C
      PRINT,' SYMBOL TOO LONG - TRUNCATED ',SYM
C
C Invoke NECAR repeatedly as long as non-blanks
C are encountered (i.e., discard excessive characters
C at the right end of an overly long symbolic name).
C
   25 IF(NECAR(CC).NE.0)GO TO 25†
C
C Test for the 'END' card to terminate the process.
C
   30 IF(SYM.EQ.'END')GO TO 50
C
C Store the new symbolic name in TABLE.  Then resume
C the scanning procedure to find a new unit.
C
      TP = TP+1
      TABLE(TP) = SYM
      GO TO 10
C
C Print the entries in the symbol table.
C
   50 DO 55 I=1,TP
   55 PRINT,I,TABLE(I)
C
      STOP
      END
```

† Because of a "bug" in the current version of the WATFIV compiler, this statement should be replaced by:

```
xx CONTINUE
   IF(NECAR(CC)....)GO TO xx
```

Example 4.4 presents a sample main program illustrating the use of function NECAR for isolating symbolic names within a source deck and storing them in a symbol table. A source card containing an 'END' is used to terminate the process. The program includes a provision for recognizing symbolic names which are longer than six characters, with the result that only the first six characters of the name are stored in the symbol table. A sample output listing from the program is provided in Figure 4.3.

```
*    THIS IS AN EXAMPLE OF A LIST OF SYMBOLS.
LOADER       LOOP   SCAN       FAUST    FETCH STORE
COURSE MATH23    WILL HAVE     A       MIDTERM
    SYMBOL TOO LONG - TRUNCATED  MIDTER
EXAMINATION
    SYMBOL TOO LONG - TRUNCATED  EXAMIN
OPEN         BOOK              END

1      LOADER
2      LOOP
3      SCAN
4      FAUST
5      FETCH
6      STORE
7      COURSE
8      MATH23
9      WILL
10     HAVE
11     A
12     MIDTER
13     EXAMIN
14     OPEN
15     BOOK
```

Figure 4.3

Sample Output Listing From Example 4.4

We could generalize the scanning routine NECAR to recognize other delimiters in addition to blanks (e.g., (,), +, =, -, etc.). In these cases, function NECAR would be designed to return a separate numeric code to identify each delimiter. A list of possible choices is provided in Figure 4.4. We employ such an extended NECAR function in later chapters when we discuss compilation techniques.

Code	Character
-2	a digit
-1	a letter
0	b̸
1	+
2	-
3	*
4	/
5	=
6	.
7	(
8	)
9	,
10	'

Figure 4.4

Delimiter Codes For Function NECAR

4.3 TABLE SEARCHING

We have illustrated how a compiler can collect the symbolic names from a source program and store them in a table. However, whenever we entered a new symbolic name into the table, we did not check to see whether an entry with the same name already existed in the table. Furthermore, a compiler adds and extracts information to and from the symbol table as it proceeds and has to locate table entries associated with symbolic names. In order to carry out these actions, a *SEARCHING* operation has to be performed. We can define the general searching operation as follows: given a data item (e.g., a character string) and a table (e.g., symbol table), determine whether an entry with the same data item exists in the table, and, if it does, find its location (i.e., index) in the table.

Searching operations have a wide scope of applications in addition to symbol table lookups. Moreover, there are numerous searching techniques which can be used. However, in this section, as a further illustration of character string operations, we shall confine ourselves to discussing a basic searching method as it is applied to symbol tables.

4.3.1 Linear Search

The most straightforward technique for searching is the *LINEAR SEARCH*. In essence, we iterate through successive entries of the table, comparing each entry with the symbol we are seeking, until we either find a match or the table is exhausted. However, this is obviously an inefficient technique for searching. If we assume that each symbol in the table has the same chance of being sought as any other, the average number of comparisons involved with a linear search is (N+1)/2, where N represents the number of entries in the table. This number becomes inhibitively large for large values of N.

4.3.2 Binary Search

In trying to arrive at a better searching technique, we might first observe how human beings perform a search through a dictionary. Knowing that the entries in the dictionary are sorted alphabetically, we open the book (somewhat at random) and compare the first entry encountered with the term we are seeking. If that particular entry comes after our term in alphabetical sequence, we turn some pages to the left (assuming an English dictionary). By comparison, if that entry precedes our term in alphabetical sequence, we turn to the right in the dictionary. This procedure is performed repeatedly until the desired entry is located.

We can easily write a program to simulate this type of searching process. However, a necessary condition to make such a searching algorithm feasible is the pre-sorting of the entries in the table. If we can afford to maintain the table in alphabetical order at all times, we are in a good position to employ this efficient searching technique. Furthermore, in our computerized algorithm, we can eliminate the random element inherent in the human dictionary-searching method by systematically "opening the dictionary" in the middle. In other words, we always bisect the range over which our search is to be performed. Beginning with a range that covers the entire table, we compare the symbol to be located with the entry in the middle of our range. If the symbol we are seeking precedes in alphabetical sequence (i.e., is numerically less than) the entry with which it is being compared, we re-define the search range to cover the lower half of the old range. However, if the opposite is true (i.e., the middle entry precedes in sequence the symbol we are seeking), we use the upper half of the old range as our new searching domain. This searching process is terminated whenever an exact match is encountered, or when the search range is reduced to zero entries, in which case the search fails (i.e., the symbol we are seeking is not in the table). This method, known as the *BINARY SEARCH* technique, is used for a large variety of other applications as well.

The binary search procedure is much more efficient than the linear search. In fact, for some applications, this has been found to be the most efficient method of searching. It is worthwhile noticing that, for the <u>worst</u> possible case (i.e., either a match is found only on the last comparison or no match is encountered at all), the number of comparisons performed in this type of search is

$$1+\mathrm{CEIL}(\mathrm{LOG}_2 N) ,$$

where CEIL(X) represents the smallest integer equal to or larger than X. This value is much smaller than the number of comparisons involved with a linear search, especially for large values of N. This advantage is further emphasized when we remember that (N+1)/2 is the <u>average</u> number of comparisons required with a linear search, whereas $1+\mathrm{CEIL}(\mathrm{LOG}_2 N)$ is the <u>maximum</u> number of comparisons involved with a binary search. Figure 4.5 illustrates the relative efficiencies of the two searching algorithms by comparing values of (N+1)/2 and $\mathrm{LOG}_2 N$ for various values of N.

N	(N+1)/2	$\mathrm{LOG}_2 N$
4	2	2
8	4	3
16	8	4
32	16	5
⋮	⋮	⋮
1024	512	10
4096	2048	12

Figure 4.5

<u>Comparison of Linear and Binary Searches</u>

The superiority of the binary search technique over the linear search is obvious. However, the price we pay for the ability to use this method is the cost of sorting, and this price usually becomes too high to justify the use of the binary search technique. This is especially true for those applications in which the contents of the table change frequently (e.g., a compiler symbol table), since a new sort is required after every new entry has been added to the table. In Chapter Seven, we will propose a method whereby we can eliminate this expensive sorting process without surrendering the advantages of a binary-like search.

In Example 4.5, we present a FORTRAN program that can be used to perform a binary search on the table created in Example 4.4. We assume that the table has been sorted prior to invoking our search routine, perhaps by using one of the methods discussed in Section 4.1. Function BISRCH returns as its value the location (i.e., subscript) of the entry in TABLE where the symbolic name SYM is found. In the event SYM does not yet appear in TABLE, BISRCH returns a zero value as a signal to the calling program. Variables UB and LB represent the external upper and lower bounds respectively of the search range. If there is at least one entry in the search range (i.e., UB-LB≥2), I is set to point at the middle of that range, so that TABLE(I) is compared with SYM. The search range is subsequently redefined, if necessary, according to the results of the comparison.

```
C EXAMPLE 4.5 - BINARY SEARCH
C
      INTEGER FUNCTION BISRCH(SYM)
C
      CHARACTER*6 TABLE(100),SYM
      INTEGER TP,UB,LB
      COMMON TABLE,TP
C
C We are seeking to locate SYM in TABLE (having
C TP entries).  UB and LB represent the upper
C and lower bounds respectively of the search range.
C
      LB = 0
      UB = TP+1
C
C Assume SYM is not present in TABLE until
C proven otherwise.
C
      BISRCH = 0
C
C Return control to the calling program if there
C are no entries left in the search range.
C
   10 IF(UB-LB.LT.2)RETURN
C
C Find the mid-point of the new search range.
C
      I = (UB+LB)/2
C
C Determine how SYM compares with TABLE(I).
C
      IF(SYM.LT.TABLE(I))GO TO 20
      IF(SYM.GT.TABLE(I))GO TO 30
C
C If control reaches the next statement, a match
C has been found between SYM and TABLE(I).
C
      BISRCH = I
      RETURN
C
C Redefine the new search range.
C
   20 UB = I
      GO TO 10
   30 LB = I
      GO TO 10
C
      END
```

4.4 TEXT EDITING

Another common application for character data is *TEXT EDITING*. For this purpose, we maintain in storage, in the form of character strings, the text of various reports, business letters, source programs, etc. What would be the typical operations for this particular application? First, we would like to have the facilities to modify specific portions of the data selected on the basis of their contents. When correcting a misspelled word, for example, we would like to indicate which word is to be corrected and how (i.e., what the misspelled word should be replaced with). We do not want to reference the portion of the data to be processed by using its integer location (i.e., index) in the character string, since it may well be very inconvenient for us to determine its exact position. Instead, we would like merely to specify a character string which is a substring of our data, and designate a replacement for it. This replacement could be performed for all occurrences of the subject string, or just for one of its appearances, usually the first.

The text is usually stored in units [e.g., lines to be printed, sentences, or statements (in the case of programming languages)]. In general, it is advantageous to store the units in the form of variable length character strings, especially when specifying portions of existing strings to be processed. Moreover, when the sizes of the units are not fixed, variable length strings are essential for efficient storage utilization.

In order to gain some understanding of the type of operation employed in text editing, suppose we examine a FORTRAN implementation of the replacement operation, assuming that the text is stored in (fixed maximum-length) variable length character string form as introduced in Section 3.5. Assuming that the text to be processed is comprised of source statements for a FORTRAN compiler, and that each statement is contained on a single card, we can safely define the maximum length of our character strings to be 80 characters.

The detailed coding for our replacement function (REPL) is presented in Example 4.6. Function REPL has three variable length character string parameters. (Actually, the parameters are integer values (indices) designating the positions of three variable length character strings in the vector CARD.) The first parameter (IN) indicates the string to be modified, while the second parameter (IT) designates the substring whose occurrences in the first string should each be replaced by the third parameter string (BY). The function, after replacing <u>all</u> appearances of IT in IN by BY, returns as its value a count of the number of times a replacement has been performed. If IT does not appear anywhere in IN, a zero value is returned to the calling program.

```
C EXAMPLE 4.6 - TEXT EDITING REPLACEMENT OPERATION
C
      INTEGER FUNCTION REPL(IN,IT,BY)
C
C CARD is a vector containing the source statements,
C one statement per component.  Variables ITS, BYS,
C INS, and RES will permit us access to the 3 input
C strings and the revised version of CARD(IN) as
C complete entities.  Vectors ITC, BYC, INC, and
C REC will permit us access to these 4 strings on
C a character-by-character basis.
C
      CHARACTER*80 CARD(500),ITS,BYS,INS,RES
      CHARACTER*1 ITC(80),BYC(80),INC(80),REC(80)
      EQUIVALENCE (ITS,ITC),(BYS,BYC),(INS,INC)
      EQUIVALENCE (RES,REC)
C
      INTEGER*2 LENGTH(500),IT,BY,IN,LIT,LBY,LIN
C
      COMMON CARD,LENGTH
C
C This function replaces all occurrences of CARD(IT)
C in CARD(IN) by CARD(BY).  REPL counts the number
C of such replacements.
C
      ITS = CARD(IT)
      BYS = CARD(BY)
      INS = CARD(IN)
C
      LIT = LENGTH(IT)
      LBY = LENGTH(BY)
      LIN = LENGTH(IN)
C
C LIMIT indicates the latest position in CARD(IN)
C that CARD(IT) can possibly appear.  M represents
C the difference in size between CARD(IT) and CARD(BY).
C
      LIMIT = LIN-LIT+1
      M = LBY-LIT
C
C Check the validity of LIMIT and LIT.
C
      REPL = 0
      IF(LIMIT.LT.1.OR.LIT.LT.1)RETURN
C
C IP is a pointer scanning along the characters in
C CARD(IN).  IR is a similar pointer for RES.
C
```

```
      IP = 1
      IR = 1
C
C Test for an appearance of CARD(IT).
C
   10 DO 20 J=1,LIT
      IF(ITC(J).NE.INC(IP+J-1))GO TO 50
   20 CONTINUE
C
C An occurrence of CARD(IT) has been located
C if control arrives at the next statement.
C
      REPL = REPL+1
C
C Determine if making an actual replacement
C will create an overflow condition.
C
      IF(LENGTH(IN)+M.LE.80)GO TO 30
C
C Indicate the overflow situation.
C
      REPL = -REPL
      GO TO 60
C
C Readjust LENGTH(IN) to reflect the
C replacement which is forthcoming.
C
   30 LENGTH(IN) = LENGTH(IN)+M
C
C Perform the actual replacement operation.
C (It is possible that LBY is zero.)
C
      J = 1
   40 IF(J.GT.LBY)GO TO 45
      REC(IR+J-1) = BYC(J)
      J = J+1
      GO TO 40
C
C Readjust the pointers for CARD(IN) and RES.
C
   45 IR = IR+LBY
      IP = IP+LIT
      GO TO 55
C
C Insert another character from CARD(IN) into RES.
C Then adjust the appropriate counters.
C
```

```
   50 REC(IR) = INC(IP)
      IR = IR+1
      IP = IP+1
C
C Test whether there is any need to look further
C for more appearances of CARD(IT).
C
   55 IF(IP.LE.LIMIT)GO TO 10
C
C Move any remaining characters in CARD(IN) to
C the right end of RES.
C
   60 REC(IR) = INC(IP)
      IR = IR+1
      IP = IP+1
      IF(IP.LE.LIN)GO TO 60
C
C Place the revised version of CARD(IN) back
C where it belongs.
C
      CARD(IN) = RES
C
      RETURN
      END
```

Because of the maximum length restriction imposed on our character strings, a replacement operation might fail in situations where it could cause an overflow. (This can occur only in cases where LENGTH(BY)>LENGTH(IT).) In such cases, function REPL terminates the replacement process, and notifies the main program of this condition by returning a negative function value. In order that the overflow be avoided and LENGTH(IN) remain valid, this check for possible overflow is performed before the actual replacement operation is executed.

Now that we have examined in detail the replacement operation, suppose we consider some other operations which we might expect a text editing system to perform.

INPUT: There are two distinct types of input to a text editing system: data and commands. The data is the text proper, whereas the commands are editing or I/O instructions. One of these instructions is the "replace" command which results in the activation of a function similar to REPL which prints error messages in case of an overflow.

ERASE: This command is used to erase one or more units of text. It should be applied only to complete units, since erasure of individual portions of strings can be achieved by employing a replacement command with the null string (LENGTH(BY)=0) as the replacement string.

COPY: This command can be used to create a duplicate of any part of the text.

MOVE: This command changes the order of the units in the text.

OUTPUT: Once again, we have two types of output. The first type is the printing of the text or portions of it, while the second is the saving of the complete text on some sort of secondary storage device, usually disk. This second form of output comprises an important part in any text editing system, since there is very little sense in editing text if it can not be saved and reused at a later date.

Text editors sometimes provide additional string operations to the ones we have just described, one of which is *PATTERN MATCHING*. A simplified version of the operation is introduced as an exercise in Section 4.5 (see Exercise 9).

All the actions which we have considered in this section involve various operations on units of text. We have avoided thus far any discussion concerning the problem of how several units can be associated together to form a single text piece. The methods used for this purpose involve list processing, a topic which we study in subsequent chapters.

4.5 EXERCISES

1. Rewrite Example 4.1 to yield a correct sort (i.e., 'JOHNSTON' before 'JOHNSTONE') without using the character manipulation facilities of WATFIV.

2. Rewrite the bubble sort routine of Example 4.2 to perform the odd sorting passes top-down and the even passes bottom-up. Assess the relative efficiency of this method as compared to the top-down-only method originally described in Example 4.2.

3. Determine the full character set available on the printer at your installation by writing a FORTRAN program to generate and print the table entries of Figure 3.1. Each line of output should be of the form:

   ddd hh c

   where 'ddd' and 'hh' are the equivalent decimal and hexadecimal representations of the character 'c'. Do <u>not</u> use CHARACTER variables, compile-time assignment statements, or input data cards.

4. Write a program that will accept as input a variable number of FORTRAN assignment statements,

one per card (use the 'END=' parameter in a READ statement to halt execution of your program), and produce a delimiter-operand table (as described in Section 4.2) for each assignment statement. Declare the table entries as follows:

```
CHARACTER DEL*1(100),OPER*10(100)
INTEGER TYPE(100),LEN(100)
```

DEL contains the delimiters.

TYPE contains the operand codes.

LEN contains the operand lengths.

OPER contains the operands.

Assume that the constants are only of the following types:

INTEGER
REAL
CHARACTER*n (n < 10).

Your program should also detect the following error conditions:

(i) The occurrence of an invalid delimiter pair (e.g., *+ or */, etc.) as disallowed by WATFIV (You should print an error message and continue processing.). Specify those you consider invalid in your documentation, and try to check for every possible error (e.g., ***).

(ii) The occurrence of a variable name having more than 6 characters. Truncate it to the 6 left-most characters, and print an error message.

(iii) Unmatched parentheses and unmatched quotes.

Your program should use a revised version of function NECAR as discussed in Section 4.2.1. This version should return a numeric code identifying the delimiter according to the table in Figure 4.4.

Example: For the assignment statement

A1 = BETA+(0.14925E+03*XYZ)/298

the table entries would be as follows:

DEL	TYPE	LEN	OPER
#	1	2	A1
=	1	4	BETA
+	0	0	
(	2	1	0
.	2	6	14925E
+	2	2	03
*	1	3	XYZ
)	0	0	
/	2	3	298
$	0	0	

Note: Use # and $ as beginning and end-of-statement marks respectively.

For the present time, the TYPE column will contain only the following information:

0 if no operand is present
1 if the first character of the operand is alphabetic
2 if the first character of the operand is a digit.

5. In Exercise 4, we have simulated the analysis which is usually performed during the so-called first pass through the source data. Now write a program to perform a second pass through the table of delimiter-operand pairs produced in Exercise 4, converting all decimal constants to their internal hexadecimal representation, and produce a new table. Consequently, decimal constants will be represented as a character string of eight hexadecimal digits (i.e., characters 0-9,A-F). INTEGER constants will, of course, be expressed in two's complement form. REAL constants may be converted to their internal excess-64 hexadecimal form using core-to-core I/O and Z FORMAT; though as an added challenge, you might try to devise your own algorithm for the conversion.

   Using these conversions, your program should produce a revised operator-operand table, deleting extraneous entries. Do not create a new table. Instead, delete entries from the old table, and then shift all succeeding entries up one position. You should also revise the operand codes to:

   0 if no operand is present
   1 if the operand is a symbolic name
   3 if the operand is an INTEGER number
   4 if the operand is a REAL number
   5 if the operand is a CHARACTER constant.

During the second pass, your program should also detect invalid numeric constants, print an appropriate error message, and then continue processing.

Example: For the sample table given in Exercise 4, the output from the second pass should be as follows:

DEL	CODE	LEN	OPER
#	1	2	A1
=	1	4	BETA
+	0	0	
(	4	4	42954000
*	1	3	XYZ
)	0	0	
/	3	4	0000012A
$	0	0	

Notice that column LEN now represents the number of bytes needed for the operand.

6. Before a FORTRAN program can be executed, it must first be translated into machine language. Part of this translation process involves determining the type of FORTRAN statement to be translated. Write a program to read a data deck of FORTRAN source statements, one at a time. For each statement, devise an algorithm to determine the statement type. You may wish to use a bracket count routine similar to the one

presented in Example 3.1. The output should include the source statement, followed by one of the following messages:

```
SPECIFICATION STATEMENT
ARITHMETIC ASSIGNMENT STATEMENT
IF STATEMENT
CONTROL STATEMENT
I/O STATEMENT.
```

Test your program on Example 4.7.

```
C EXAMPLE 4.7 - SAMPLE SOURCE STATEMENTS
C               AS DATA FOR EXERCISE 6
C
      REAL X,READ
      DIMENSION X(10),READ(10)
      INTEGER A(10)/10*0/,IF(10,5),PRINT
      READ,READ,X
      PRINT = 1
   10 IF(1,(PRINT+1)/2) = A(PRINT)
      IF(X(PRINT).EQ.READ(PRINT))STOP
      PRINT = PRINT+1
      IF(PRINT.LE.10)GO TO 10
      PRINT,X,(IF(1,I),I=1,5)
      STOP
      END
```

Note: Follow the FORTRAN convention of ignoring all blanks.

7. Write the coding for the following function:

INTEGER FUNCTION SCAN(OPRD,LENG,TYPE)

This function should use the extended version of the NECAR function to isolate complete syntactic units. The value returned by the function is a numerical code identifying the operator <u>following</u> the syntactic unit being scanned. The codes to be used are presented in Figure 4.6.

<u>CODE</u>	<u>OPERATOR</u>	
0	$ (end of statement)	
1	+	
2	-	
3	*	
4	/	
5	=	
7	(	
8	)	
9	,	
11	**	
12	.NE.	
13	.EQ.	
14	IF	only if first in the statement and <u>not</u> followed by an '='.
15	DO	

Figure 4.6

<u>Delimiter Codes For Function NECAR</u>

OPRD is a character string containing the syntactic unit. LENG is the number of bytes needed to store the syntactic unit. TYPE is the operand code as specified in Exercise 5.

<u>Example</u>: Consider the following statement:

```
IF(UU.EQ.'N+T')ALPHA = X(I,J+5)*BB-0.341
```

Function SCAN will be invoked twelve times, returning to the calling program the values listed in Figure 4.7.

SCAN	OPRD	LENG	TYPE
14		0	0
7		0	0
13	UU	2	1
8	N+T	3	5
5	ALPHA	5	1
7	X	1	1
9	I	1	1
1	J	1	1
8	5	4	3
3		0	0
2	BB	2	1
0	0.341	4	4

Figure 4.7

Output From Example In Exercise 7

8. Using either the SCAN function (from Exercise 7) or an operator-operand table, write a program to read source cards and store the symbolic names in a symbol table. Before entering a new symbolic name into the table, check to determine that an entry with the identical symbol does not already exist in the table. Use each of the following search techniques:

   (a) Linear Search.

(b) Binary Search - In this case, if the search fails, save the location of the last comparison. Then rearrange the table so that the new entry is inserted immediately before, or after, the location of the last comparison, depending upon the result of that comparison. This would ensure that the table is always maintained in the proper order.

9. Write a program to determine whether a sentence (represented in variable length character string form) corresponds to a particular pattern. For example, consider the following:

THE _____ BELONGS TO THE ___.

Sentences which would match this pattern are:

THE HORSE BELONGS TO THE MAN.
THE CAT BELONGS TO THE OLD LADY., etc.

We can define a variable length character string to represent a pattern by using a specified symbol (e.g., '$') to identify the blank parts (i.e., variants) of the pattern. For example, the pattern described above can be represented as follows:

THE $ BELONGS TO THE $.

Assuming that a pattern can have only two blank variants, write the coding for the following FORTRAN function:

LOGICAL FUNCTION MATCH(SENT,PATR,VAR1,VAR2)

The four parameters identify four variable length character strings. The first, SENT, is the sentence which is being considered to determine whether it matches the specified pattern, PATR. In the event a match is found, the two variants are stored in the two strings, VAR1 and VAR2. Function MATCH returns a .TRUE. value if a match is found, and .FALSE. otherwise.

<u>Example</u>:

```
PATR = 'IF($.EQ.$)GO TO 10'
SENT = 'IF(UU-75.EQ.X**2)GO TO 10'
```

The value returned by function MATCH would be .TRUE., since a match would be found. Furthermore, VAR1 would be set to 'UU-75' and VAR2 to 'X**2'.

CHAPTER FIVE
INTRODUCTION TO DATA STRUCTURES

5.1 INTRODUCTION

A *DATA STRUCTURE* is a means of representing information in a computer. The simplest data types already encountered are the representations of fixed-point values, floating-point numbers, logical values, and characters, all represented as sequences of bits. We may consider these elementary data types to be *PRIMITIVE* data structures. The computer is usually equipped with machine instructions to manipulate such primitive data items. However, to provide for processing of more complex information, we must construct more complicated data structures to serve as the internal representation of the information. Data structures are merely aggregates of primitive data types combined to create new data items.

We are designing data structures to meet two basic requirements:

(i) To represent the external information in a unique and unambiguous fashion.

(ii) To facilitate efficient manipulation of the data by the computer.

In order to satisfy the first requirement, we must program conversion routines to transform the given information from its external form into an appropriate data structure. In essence, we are merely transforming the information from a form readily comprehended by humans into a form which is more suitable for processing by a computer. The second requirement implies that the design of a data structure is highly dependent upon both the type of processing required and the particular processing facilities provided by the computer.

In Chapters Six through Eight, we discuss various techniques used for creating complicated data structures from primitive data types. Furthermore, we will examine the underlying considerations involved during the design of such data structures.

In order to fully utilize the advantages of a complicated data structure built from primitive ones, we must pay particular attention to two basic mechanisms. Initially, we require a technique for creating the entire structure from a collection of independent component parts. Subsequently, we need a procedure for discriminating between the various parts which comprise the total structure so that we can gain access to any particular component. As a result, we must design two basic types of functions: *CONSTRUCTORS* to actually create the complete data structure, and *SELECTORS* to provide a method of referencing the individual components within the total structure. We usually refer to the individual components of a data structure as its *FIELDS*.

Before discussing any examples of complicated data structures, we should consider two simple illustrations of elementary data structures with which we are already familiar, namely arrays and complex numbers. These simple data structures are supported by all modern FORTRAN compilers.

5.2 ARRAYS

The fields of an array are its individual elements. By using a DIMENSION or type-declaration statement in FORTRAN, we can associate a collection of primitive variables of identical type as members of a larger block to be identified using a single variable name. In response to such instructions, the compiler will allocate a contiguous group of memory words for the entire array. By recording its dimensions along with the name of the array, the compiler can remember that the programmer considers this group of primitive variables as a single entity. The individual components of the array are associated with one another through the fact that they occupy consecutive locations in the memory of the computer. This method of association provides a very simple mechanism for referencing individual components in the array. As we will observe later in this chapter, however, such an arrangement might impose some restrictions on the efficiency with which these data structures can be utilized.

FORTRAN does not provide execution-time constructors for arrays. Instead, the program begins execution with several pre-defined arrays already in existence. Since the nature of these arrays is specified at compile time, it is impossible to construct new arrays or modify the dimensions of existing arrays during execution of the program. We should be aware that some programming languages (e.g., PL/1, ALGOL) do provide execution-time constructors for arrays by making declaration statements executable. Such statements are supported by having execution-time routines for the allocation and liberation of memory locations occupied by arrays.

FORTRAN does, however, provide selectors for arrays by allowing the programmer to use a subscript with the array name. The value used as a subscript designates an individual element within the vector. By remembering the initial memory location of the block allocated to the vector and the size of the individual components within the array, the FORTRAN compiler provides a mechanism for calculating the location in memory of the particular element specified by the subscript. A similar mechanism is invoked to select a particular component from a multi-dimensional array when a group of integer subscripts is supplied by the programmer. For every array used in a program, the compiler gathers information regarding its dimensions and the size of its individual elements. This information must be available during execution time to determine the appropriate memory location specified by a particular set of subscripts. For example, if we had INTEGER A(10,15), then A(I,J) would reference the $[(J-1)10+I]^{th}$ memory location in the block allocated to array A.

A particular field selected through the subscripting mechanism can appear on either side of the assignment operator in FORTRAN. This implies that it can be used either as a destination, in which case its value is changed, or as a source from which a value is obtained. This dual flexibility is one of the most important characteristics of true selectors.

5.3 COMPLEX NUMBERS

FORTRAN provides both a constructor and selectors for complex numbers. The constructor is the built-in function CMPLX. It accepts two floating-point values as arguments, and produces as its value a single complex number which has two fields, namely a real part (i.e., the first argument) and an imaginary part (i.e., the second argument). CMPLX, however, is not as powerful as we might wish, since it provides only a complex constant, and not a new complex variable. In essence, the CMPLX function can only combine two floating-point values and store them as the fields of an already existing complex number. To select a single field from a specified complex number or variable, FORTRAN supplies the two built-in pseudo-functions REAL and AIMAG. However, these functions can only be used on the right side of assignment operators to indicate a source of information. They cannot appear on the left side of such operators to specify a destination for some numerical value. Consequently, they are not true selectors.

For every variable declared of type COMPLEX, the compiler allocates two consecutive full-words of memory (four words for double-precision complex variables), one for each of the two floating-point values which comprise a complex number. Furthermore, the compiler recognizes such variables whenever they are encountered in the computation, and invokes the appropriate processing routines. In Example 5.1, the two assignment statements look very similar. However, we know that the object code generated for each would be completely different from the other. The first would translate into a short sequence of machine-language instructions, since integers are primitive data items, and the computer is equipped with machine instructions to manipulate them. Complex numbers are not primitive data structures, however, and the compiler would have to generate a calling sequence to invoke a built-in routine to perform the complex multiplication. Alternatively, some compilers might choose to insert the multiplication routine as in-line code. If, in the future, computers are built with hardware capabilities to handle complex numbers, we will then consider them as primitive data types.

```
C EXAMPLE 5.1 - INTEGER VS. COMPLEX PROCESSING
C
      COMPLEX A,B,C
      .
      .
      .
      K = I*J
      C = A*B
      .
      .
      .
      END
```

In many programming languages, such as FORTRAN, PL/1, and ALGOL60, selectors are either hidden within other language features, or they are called pseudo-variables. Unfortunately, FORTRAN does not permit the definition of new selectors. PL/1, however, has a better (but still not complete) facility, with its based structures and pointer variables. ALGOL68 seems to have extended the concept nearly as far as it seems likely to go.

5.4 INADEQUACIES OF ARRAYS

In earlier sections of this chapter, we have seen that a FORTRAN compiler will permit us to create some simple data structures subject to two major constraints:

(i) All the fields must be of the same type.

(ii) The number of fields and their locations in memory are pre-defined during the compilation phase.

There are several common applications for which these simple data structures are inadequate. Since they result in ineffective processing, we would like to develop more complex data structures which will facilitate more efficient processing.

Suppose we are asked to computerize the operation of a rent-a-car company. In particular, we are required to maintain an up-to-date record of the status of each of its cars. We must be aware at all times of whether each car is in storage awaiting rental, in the service department being repaired, or else out on rental to a customer. To maintain an accurate record of the necessary information, we should have at least three lists:

(i) A list of cars in storage awaiting rental, sorted in ascending order of mileage so that the cars with the lowest mileage can be rented first.

(ii) A list of cars in the service department, sorted according to the expected completion date of the necessary repairs.

(iii) A list of cars currently rented, sorted by expected return date so that we know when they will be available for further rental or possible repair.

It will be our task to develop methods of representing such lists so that the necessary information can be processed in the most efficient manner.

The most straightforward method available to us involves having one single-dimension array to represent each of our three lists. To handle the extreme cases, we have to ensure that each of these three arrays is large enough to contain all the cars owned by the company. At any given time, we must also be aware of how many cars belong in each list so that we know to what extent the various arrays are filled. Consider, for a moment, what steps we must take whenever one of the rented cars is returned:

(i) Locate that particular car on the rented list.

(ii) Remove that car from the rented list.

(iii) Shift all the cars previously following that car on the rented list forward one position in the array to fill the space left vacant by the removal of the car being returned.

(iv) By noting the mileage when the car is returned, locate the position in the list of cars available for rental into which the newly available car should be inserted.

(v) Create a space on the rental list for the recently returned car by shifting the appropriate cars down one position in the list. We are assuming here, of course, that the car being returned does not need any repairs before being rented again. Otherwise, this car has to be inserted on the servicing list according to the amount of time required to repair it.

(vi) Insert the new arrival into the proper position in the new list as indicated in Step (v). We cannot simply insert the car being returned at the end of the new list, since each of the three lists is always sorted in a particular order.

Such manipulation of cars in the various lists can involve considerable time and effort. Furthermore, we must be prepared to deal with a possible decision by the company to buy several new cars or else sell some of their existing cars. Standard arrays in FORTRAN are not well-suited to such manipulation. Since consecutive elements of an array occupy successive memory locations, any removal or deletion of a single entry in a sorted array necessitates shifting large sections (perhaps all) of the remainder of the array to accommodate such changes. The data structures which we develop to maintain our various car lists should be designed to minimize the amount of shifting within lists, since the status of most of the cars will be constantly changing from one day to the next.

Suppose we examine another problem which does not lend itself well to the use of standard arrays in FORTRAN, namely calculations with polynomials. We might wish to write programs for manipulating polynomials in two variables. For example, we might want a program to add two polynomials, say $x^2+2xy+5y^2$ and $x^2-2xy+y$, to produce the answer $2x^2+5y^2+y$. Equally likely, we might also want to design programs to subtract, multiply, divide, differentiate, and integrate polynomials.

How can we represent polynomials internally in the computer memory so that they can be processed more efficiently? The answer to this basic question is the key to solving our problem. In order to manipulate polynomials efficiently, we must be able to isolate individual terms, variables, coefficients, exponents, etc.. The data structures which we use to represent polynomials must be compatible with such demands.

One of the first representations which may be suggested is character strings. Using this type of structure, a polynomial such as x^2-2xy would be represented as 'X**2-2*X*Y'. At first glance, such a scheme might appear to be a simple solution to our dilemma. However, the extraction of variables, coefficients, exponents, etc. from a lengthy character string involves considerable difficulty.

Using another approach, we might construct a matrix of coefficients to represent the polynomial. In such a matrix, the entry in row i+1, column j+1, is the coefficient of the term involving $x^i y^j$. As an illustration, if we assume that the exponents for x and y are restricted to a maximum of 9, then the 10×10 matrix of coefficients representing the polynomial $4x^2+2x^3-7xy+y^9$ is presented in Figure 5.1.

Such a storage structure makes it extremely easy to isolate coefficients. However, there will usually be a large number of zeros in the matrix.

0	0	0	0	0	0	0	0	0	1
0	-7	0	0	0	0	0	0	0	0
4	0	0	0	0	0	0	0	0	0
2	0	0	0	0	0	0	0	0	0
0	0	0	0	0	0	0	0	0	0
0	0	0	0	0	0	0	0	0	0
0	0	0	0	0	0	0	0	0	0
0	0	0	0	0	0	0	0	0	0
0	0	0	0	0	0	0	0	0	0
0	0	0	0	0	0	0	0	0	0

Figure 5.1

Matrix of Polynomial Coefficients

For example, Figure 5.1 contains only four non-zero entries out of the 100 elements in the matrix. In addition to representing an enormous waste of memory space, these extra zeros also waste a considerable amount of computer time, since all the entries in the matrix must be processed whenever the polynomial is involved with any computation. Furthermore, we do not want to be forced to place arbitrary restrictions on the number of terms and the size of the exponents for x and y permitted with any of our polynomials. Such limitations would be annoying, especially when we remember that computation with polynomials can often involve results of unpredictable complexity. For example, if we divide x^8-1 by x+1, the quotient polynomial obtained from this division of two simple binomials involves eight terms.

5.5 LINKED LISTS

We would like to develop an improved procedure for handling situations such as those described in Section 5.4. In our first example of a rent-a-car company, we had data whose organization changed rapidly (i.e., every time a car was rented, returned by a customer, or else released from the service department), each time causing extensive manipulation of various lists. In our second example of polynomial manipulation, we had a small amount of data, but no method of packing it into a small amount of memory space. Furthermore, when a new polynomial was generated as the result of computation with other polynomials, we had to provide storage for it. As we indicated in Section 5.4, these types of problems are not easily handled when we attempt to use standard arrays in FORTRAN.

These, and similar problems, can be solved using *LINKED LIST STRUCTURES*. With this type of data structure, related data items need not be stored in consecutive memory locations, but can be spread all over memory. In essence, a linked list structure is composed of numerous items called *NODES*, each containing several *FIELDS*. A field can contain a primitive data item, such as a character string, a fixed-point value, or a floating-point value, or else it can contain a *POINTER* to another node. A pointer is merely a means of identifying and manipulating a particular node. Consequently, for our purposes, we can consider a pointer to be a new type of primitive data item. A node is usually represented as a single block of storage in which its fields are stored side by side. The machine address of this block of storage is then utilized as a pointer.

Figure 5.2 illustrates a sketch of a linked list structure. In such a diagram, nodes are drawn as boxes, and the individual fields within each node are merely subdivisions of that box. If a field contains a data item, that information is merely inserted in the appropriate part of the box. As a pointer, we use a dot with an arrow leading from it. Each arrow will lead to the node indicated by the pointer value in the node from which the arrow originates.

As indicated in Figure 5.2, the various nodes in a linked list structure need not all be the same size. In fact, the nodes may even contain different types of fields. However, it is considerably more difficult to handle lists having a varying node structure (see Section 8.5). Storage allocation and processing are much easier for a linked list if all its nodes are the same size and contain the same types of fields. For this reason, we shall concentrate most of our attention on linked lists which have a uniform node structure.

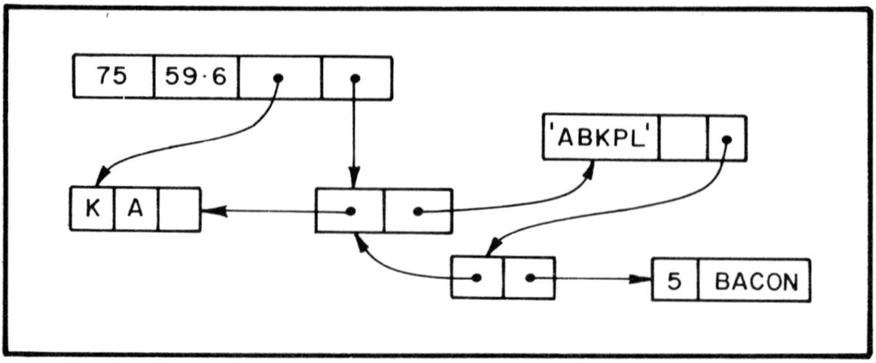

Figure 5.2

Sample Linked List Structure

Now that we are no longer forced to use contiguous storage locations for successive items in a list structure, we should be able to alleviate the various difficulties we encountered with our earlier examples of a rent-a-car company and polynomial manipulation. In the rent-a-car example, we can set up one node for each car which will contain the significant parameter values for that particular car. In addition to having separate fields for the mileage, license number, and date of expected return from rental or the service department, we should include an extra field for a pointer which will serve to link the nodes together. Figure 5.3 presents an example of a linked list structure containing four nodes (i.e., cars). In this particular example, the first car in the list has license number U63.592; the second car has license number U29.112; the third U29.663; and the fourth U59.611. In the pointer field of the last car, however, we have inserted the word "null". Such an action indicates that this field should contain a special entry that cannot be confused with any valid pointer value. This special pointer value cannot be interpreted as pointing to another node, and consequently, we can employ such a device to identify the last node in the list. This type of linked list structure, where each node contains one pointer to indicate the next node in the list, is called a *LINEARLY LINKED LIST*.

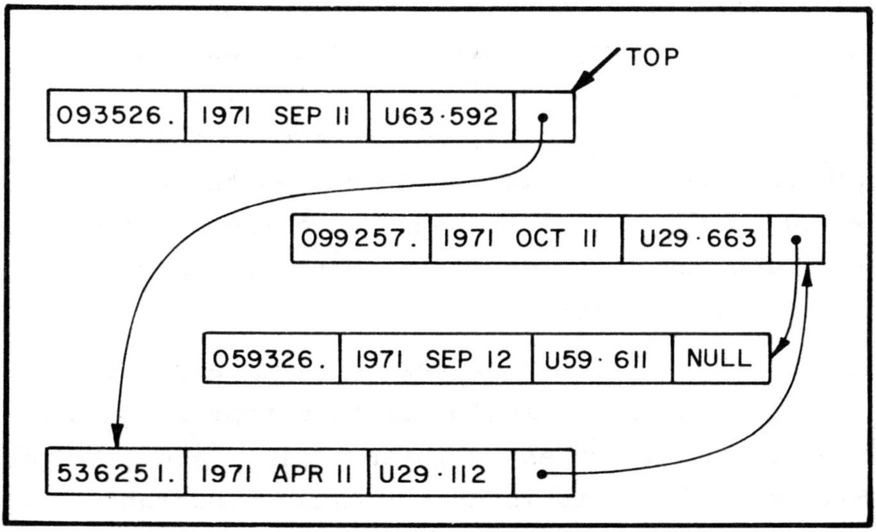

Figure 5.3

Linearly Linked List of Four Cars

Since we can now use a pointer with each node to identify the next node in the list, we are no longer forced to keep the various nodes physically in core storage in precisely the same order as that in which they are processed. As a result, whenever it is necessary to insert a new node or remove a current node within a specified list, we are not required to shift the entire list (or even a large part of it) after the action has been completed. For example, to insert a new node, we merely allocate part of the available storage to represent that node. Then we must alter the pointer in the node which will immediately precede the newly inserted node in the list, so that it will subsequently point to the new member. The only adjustment remaining for us to make involves setting the pointer in the newly inserted node so that it will point to the node succeeding it in the list (i.e., the node previously identified by the pointer in the node which now precedes the newly inserted one). Such a sequence of actions does not necessitate any major movement of the various data items in the list structure.

Furthermore, we can now identify any particular list by using a single variable representing a pointer to the first entry in that list (e.g., TOP in Figure 5.3). This is an extremely important simplification, since we can now essentially treat some variables not as if they were fixed-point, floating-point, or character type, but as if they were "car-list" variables. Variables of this type would be very useful in any program dealing with lists of cars.

In our polynomial manipulation example, we can again overcome our various difficulties by using list processing techniques. In this case, however, the main advantage to us is not the ease of rapid rearrangement of data. Instead, we gain compactness of representation and a certain freedom from arbitrary restrictions on the complexity of the polynomials involved in the computation. We have indicated that the complexity of the results obtained from a long sequence of additions, multiplications, integrations, etc., is not easily predictable when we are working with polynomials. If we use standard arrays in FORTRAN, we are required to estimate detailed core storage requirements for every intermediate and final result at the time we are writing the program. However, the dynamic nature of linked list structures frees us from having to make such estimates in advance.

By assigning one node to represent each term, we can use a linked list to represent an entire polynomial. This implies that each node will contain a pointer (to link the terms together), a coefficient (i.e., a floating-point number), and one exponent (i.e., a fixed-point value) for each variable. We can easily increase the number of variables associated with our polynomials by simply inserting additional fields in each node for the extra exponents. Figure 5.4 illustrates a linearly linked list representation of a polynomial in three variables. (Consider, for a moment, what adjustments we would have to make in order to represent a polynomial of three variables using an extension of our earlier matrix representation.)

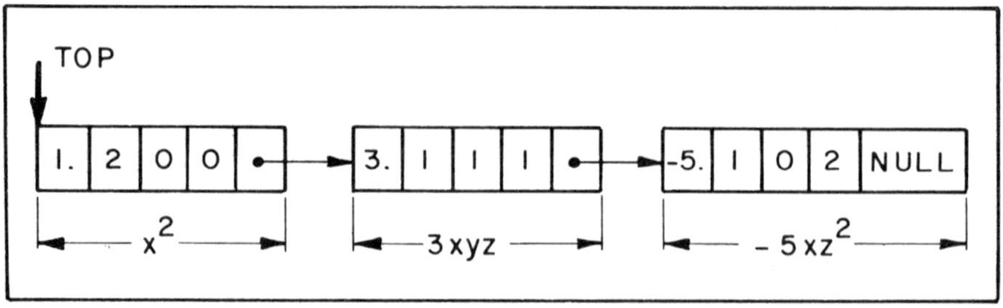

Figure 5.4

Linked List Representation of $x^2+3xyz-5xz^2$

As was the case with our rent-a-car example, we can now identify a particular polynomial by a single variable, namely a pointer to its first term (e.g., TOP in Figure 5.4). Actually, it is possible to extend a programming language so that it has variables whose values are, essentially, polynomials in three variables. In fact, ALGOL68 permits such extensions very easily, and FORMULA ALGOL already has these extensions incorporated into the language.

Efficient utilization of memory space is one of the more significant advantages of linked lists. Whenever a list structure is used, we maintain a special list of unused nodes called the *AVAILABILITY LIST*. By removing nodes from this list and linking them as required, we can construct new lists or add new nodes to existing lists. On the other hand, when we no longer need a particular list, or some part of that list, we can return the nodes which are no longer needed to the availability list. Subsequently, we can reuse the same nodes for the construction of new lists. If we maintain close control over the utilization of nodes, by returning nodes to the availability list as soon as they are no longer needed, we can realize a significant saving in the amount of storage used.

It is precisely this feature that makes linearly linked lists a more suitable representation for polynomials. The amount of storage used to represent various polynomials is highly dependent on the type of operations involved. Consequently, we would like to minimize the number of nodes actually used at any step of the calculation. Consider, for example, the evaluation of a polynomial expression such as P = R+Q*P-S, where P, Q, R and S are polynomials. To perform such a computation, we will generate several intermediate temporary polynomials, namely the product of polynomials Q and P, the sum of that product and the polynomial R, and finally the difference of that sum and the polynomial S. As soon as the new polynomial expression has been assigned to P, there will be several surplus lists representing the temporary polynomials and the previous polynomial expression for P. The nodes in these redundant lists can be returned to the availability list for possible use at some later time. (Actually, it is possible to evaluate any polynomial of any complexity by using only two temporary polynomials.)

We have examined two situations where list processing techniques can be applied to best advantage. However, there are numerous other areas where linked list structures are particularly useful. For example, list processing techniques are employed by operating systems to control storage utilization in multiprogramming environments. When several programs or users compete for the usage of memory, the operating system maintains a record of storage allocation by creating separate lists of used and unused memory. These lists have nodes of different sizes according to the various blocks of memory required by the users. When a request for memory arrives from a user, the system scans the list of free storage in an attempt to satisfy the request. Similarly, when execution of a particular program is terminated, the system shifts the block of storage used by that program to the list of available memory.

We should mention that storage management in a list processing environment becomes considerably more complicated when *NON-LINEAR* lists are used. In the examples of linearly linked lists which we have discussed, each node is linked to one, and only one, node. Consequently, it is easy to determine when a particular node can be released to the availability list. In non-linear lists, however, each node contains more than one pointer, so that the various nodes are linked in several different ways (i.e., each node is a member of several independent lists). As a result, in order to determine which nodes can be released to the availability list, we must institute some additional actions. Such a cleanup operation could become very involved, since we might have to scan through all existing lists in order to collect the nodes that can be deleted. Such an operation is often called *GARBAGE COLLECTION*.

We should emphasize, however, that list processing techniques do not always represent the best solution for all data processing situations. Although such techniques often provide numerous advantages, they do involve extra costs. Every data item has extra information (i.e., one or more pointers) associated with it that takes up extra space. Generally, for any specific situation, list processing techniques are justified only if one or both of the following conditions is satisfied:

(i) A significant decrease in running time, storage consumption, or program complexity is achieved by the use of pointers.

(ii) In an extreme case, the problem is just too complex for any other way of handling it to be practical.

Recall our rent-a-car example again. If cars are not renting well on a short-term basis, the company may well decide to convert its operations to become a long-term lease-a-car company. Since transactions will now become much less frequent, the extra trouble of maintaining links is no longer justified. Changes to the various lists will now occur only rarely, with the result that we can easily afford the cost of shifting the necessary entries.

5.6 OPERATIONS WITH LINKED LISTS

Before discussing the programming techniques involved with the utilization of linked lists, we should examine the various construction, selection, and manipulation operations we might wish to perform with such lists. In Chapter Six, we will develop several examples illustrating how we can implement these operations using a FORTRAN representation of linked lists.

In general, we can distinguish three major categories of operations on linked list data structures:

1. Utilities: These are the data-independent operations, such as storage management (i.e., construction and deletion of nodes), or selector mechanisms which allow us to select a particular node from a given linked list. Programming languages that support list processing usually provide all of these operations, either in the form of built-in functions or in-line compiler-generated code.

2. Input/Output: These operations represent the interface between the processing operations and the user. Input operations convert the data from a format comprehensible to the user into the internal representation of the data for machine manipulation. Conversely, output operations make a similar transformation of the data in the reverse direction. These

routines are data dependent, in the sense that they must take into account the interpretation that we attach to the data structures. List processing languages usually support only some basic general-purpose operations of this type. The user is left with the task of designing any additional I/O routines he may require.

3. Processing Operations: These operations represent the ultimate purpose of our programs. Since we write these routines to manipulate the data expressed in its internal structural form, the design of these operations depends entirely upon our interpretation of the data structures. The user is always required to write the subprograms to implement the processing of his data.

To be more specific, suppose we examine our earlier polynomial manipulation example. Under each of the three categories just described, we define the various operations which we will apply to this particular situation. In Chapter Six, we will present detailed FORTRAN subroutines which implement these operations.

Utilities for Polynomials

CNS: This routine constructs a new node. Given the values to be inserted into the fields of the node, it acquires the necessary free storage from the availability list and creates a new node.

DLT: This routine deletes a specified node from a particular list. It returns the deleted node to the availability list so that the storage may be used again later.

LAST: This routine returns a pointer identifying the last node in a specified list.

NTH: This routine is a generalization of LAST. It returns a pointer to the Nth node of a given list (provided the list has at least N nodes).

We should emphasize that, conceptually, all of these routines are data independent. For any given type of list structure, say linearly linked lists, we can use them without being aware of what interpretation is associated with the nodes in the list. It is immaterial whether a specific node represents one term in a polynomial or a car belonging to some rent-a-car company. Such interpretations will have no effect on the design of these routines.

Input/Output of Polynomials

READ: This routine reads the coefficients and exponents of the terms in the polynomial from data cards. Then, through successive invocations of the CNS routine, it creates a new internal representation of the given polynomial in the form of a linked list.

PRINT: This routine simply scans through a linked list and prints its terms on the line printer in an appropriate format.

Processing Routines for Polynomials

We can easily visualize a large collection of processing operations for lists which represent polynomials. Such operations include addition, subtraction, multiplication, and division of two polynomials, and possibly differentiation or integration of a single polynomial.

ADD: This routine creates a new linked list to represent the sum polynomial obtained by adding two polynomials already represented by two existing lists. We could design similar routines (i.e., SUB, MULT, DIV) for subtraction, multiplication, and division of two existing polynomials.

DERV: This routine creates a new linked list to represent the derivative of a given polynomial with respect to any one of its variables. A similar routine could be designed for integration of a specified polynomial.

We should now be in a position to understand the motivation behind the development of general-purpose list processing languages. These languages take a flexible and commonly used list structure and provide the utilities, in the form of standard compiler facilities, for managing that type of structure. Consequently, the user must adopt this structure for the representation of his data, and subsequently develop the desired processing routines for it. However, since the compiler provides all the standard storage management and selection routines, his task is considerably easier.

In addition to the general-purpose list processing languages, there exist special-purpose languages that concentrate on the processing of a specific type of data. As a result, these languages also provide all the relevant processing routines, leaving to the user the simple task of invoking these routines according to his own individual needs. In Chapter Six, we will develop two specialized languages dedicated to the processing of data representing polynomials and graphic structures. To illustrate some of the programming techniques used to manipulate linked lists, we use FORTRAN as the lower-level language in which we implement all the operations we need.

CHAPTER SIX
PROCESSING LINEARLY LINKED LISTS

6.1 FORTRAN REPRESENTATION OF LISTS

In this chapter, we will be considering how to implement in FORTRAN the various list processing techniques which make use of the concepts of nodes and pointers. As we have indicated before, a node is merely a group of data items, some of which are pointers linking the node into particular list structures. The items in a node are usually of different types. FORTRAN, however, does not provide us with any mechanism to associate primitive data items that are not of the same type. Pointers represent another feature not directly supported by FORTRAN. Pointers are understood to be addresses, and consequently, we say that a pointer P is pointing at node N if, and only if, its value represents, in some way, the location of the node N. When we are writing programs in assembly language or using languages that provide pointers, we can obtain the memory address of one of the items in a node, and subsequently use that address as a pointer to that particular node. With FORTRAN, however, we will use the subscripting mechanism to provide us with necessary addresses. Once we have developed techniques for representing nodes and pointers in FORTRAN, we will have to decide how to use these techniques in the selection and construction operations. With these selector and constructor mechanisms, we can manipulate various lists according to the data they represent.

We will use a set of FORTRAN vectors to represent the various fields comprising the nodes in a linked list structure. A single node will be represented as a cross-section of these vectors across the same subscript, and this common subscript will serve as a pointer to that node. Consequently, the vector names will serve as the field selectors, while the pointers will be used as subscripts for the various vectors.

In order to be more specific, suppose we re-examine our car rental problem introduced in Chapter Five. We want four fields in each node:

MILAGE: A floating-point number representing the mileage figure on the car represented by the node.

DATE: A fixed-point value representing the expected return date of that car, either from rental or the servicing department.

LICENS: A character string (of length 8) representing the license number of the car.

LINK: A fixed-point value representing a pointer to the next car in the appropriate list.

After estimating the largest number of nodes we shall ever need (e.g., 200), we can write the declarations describing the representation of our nodes as indicated in Example 6.1. As an illustration of a pointer implemented by subscripts, if P has the value 5, we say that it is pointing to a node composed of MILAGE(5), DATE(5), LICENS(5), and LINK(5). Similarly, if we wish to link this node to another node identified by a pointer Q, we merely set LINK(P) = Q.

```
C EXAMPLE 6.1 - LIST STRUCTURE DECLARATIONS
C
      REAL MILAGE(200)
      INTEGER DATE(200),LINK(200)
      CHARACTER*8 LICENS(200)
```

In Figure 5.3, we presented a sketch of a typical linked list structure representing four cars. Figure 6.1 contains a representation for this list. The integer value 3 would serve as a pointer to identify this list (since it points to the top node in the list). We can gain access to the list, whenever we wish to do so, by merely using this pointer. The last node in the list, as identified by the pointer value 68, has a value 0 in its link field, thus indicating the end of the list. We have chosen 0 to represent the null pointer, since 0 is a guaranteed illegal subscript, and consequently, it cannot possibly be interpreted as a valid pointer value.

This method of denoting nodes will provide us with the necessary mechanism to create and

```
MILAGE( 3) =   093526.          DATE( 3) = 710911
LICENS( 3) = 'U63.592'          LINK( 3) =     99

MILAGE(19) =   099257.          DATE(19) = 711011
LICENS(19) = 'U29.663'          LINK(19) =     68

MILAGE(68) =   059326.          DATE(68) = 710912
LICENS(68) = 'U59.611'          LINK(68) =      0

MILAGE(99) =   536251.          DATE(99) = 710411
LICENS(99) = 'U29.112'          LINK(99) =     19
```

Figure 6.1

Nodes of Car List in Figure 5.3

manipulate linked lists. However, we should note that this method deviates from the original idea of nodes. In Chapter Five, we implied that all the items associated with a single node are stored in consecutive memory locations. Based on this assumption, a pointer to a node is simply the address of the first memory location occupied by the fields of that node. This is the natural implementation of the concepts of nodes and pointers, and it should be used whenever pointers and such storage structures are available. Our FORTRAN implementation, however, does not locate the fields of a node in consecutive memory cells. In fact, the items comprising a node are scattered in memory among the various vectors used to represent the fields. Although this internal representation of nodes is not the natural one, it will not have any effect on the techniques that we use to process our lists. Actually, the subscripting mechanism calculates the address for each selection operation that is performed. With the conventional representation of a node, where the fields are stored consecutively, selecting a particular field requires the addition of a certain displacement factor (which is a function of the selected field) to the original pointer value indicating the first item of the node. By comparison, in the FORTRAN implementation, the selection of a field requires the addition of a certain displacement factor (now a function of the node we choose) to the address of the vector representing that particular field.

The actual numerical values of the subscripts used as FORTRAN pointers are not really significant within the context of list processing. In Figure 6.1, we chose to illustrate the idea of subscripts-as-pointers by explicitly showing the actual subscript values. However, in the following sections, we will deliberately avoid any reference to the subscript values. We will simply indicate that a pointer P is pointing at a certain node. However, we will not be able to derive any significance from the actual integer value of P. For example, although DO loops represent the natural mechanism for processing standard FORTRAN arrays, we will not be able to use them to process our vectors representing nodes. The reason for this statement should be obvious, especially if we remember that the paramount concept of linked lists is the association of data items through pointers rather than by computation of their relative addresses. The expression P+1, where P is a pointer, is completely meaningless, since the node identified by P+1 bears no relation whatsoever to the node indicated by P.

Indeed, for all we know, such a node may not even exist in the list containing node P.

6.2 SELECTORS AND CONSTRUCTORS FOR LINEARLY LINKED LISTS

Using the FORTRAN implementation of linked lists described in Section 6.1, the selector mechanism is a very straightforward operation. To select a particular field in a specified node, we merely use the pointer to that node as a subscript for the vector corresponding to the desired field. For example, if P is a pointer, then MILAGE(P) selects the mileage field in the node designated by P. These selectors can be used on either side of an assignment operator in a FORTRAN statement. Furthermore, they can be nested to any level we wish. For example, MILAGE(LINK(P)) selects the mileage field of the node directly linked to the node P (i.e., the node succeeding node P in the list). To illustrate, suppose P = 3 within the context of the list portrayed in Figure 6.1. MILAGE(LINK(P)) will yield the value 536251 (i.e., the mileage figure in node 99) if it is employed on the right side of an assignment operator. By using this term on the left-hand side of an assignment operator, we can insert a new value into the mileage field of node 99.

The construction mechanism for our FORTRAN implementation of linked lists is not as straightforward as that used for selectors. A constructor routine has to accept as arguments a number of values to be inserted into the fields of the new node. Prior to inserting these arguments, it must first find storage for the new node. Once the routine has obtained an unused node from the availability list, however, it is a simple matter to fill in the necessary fields.

As we indicated in Chapter Five, we maintain control over storage utilization by keeping all the unused nodes chained together into a single list, namely the availability list. When we need additional storage, we remove the first node from this list. Furthermore, when we are finished with a particular node, we return it to the availability list. General mechanisms exist for reclaiming storage for the availability list (e.g., the garbage collector in LISP), but they are rather clumsy to use unless they are actually built into the programming language. In this chapter, since we are only dealing with linear lists, we can adopt a simplified approach toward the reutilization of nodes. We will provide a subroutine called DLT to return nodes to the availability list. It will be the programmer's own responsibility to invoke this routine whenever a node is no longer needed.

As part of the initialization procedure, we must create the availability list. At this point, since none of the nodes are being used, we can simply chain together all the nodes by using a simple loop which scans through the declared nodes and sets the pointers accordingly. An appropriate set of FORTRAN coding is given in Example 6.2. This initialization is the only exception for which we can use a DO loop to iterate through the nodes of a list. Actually, we are free to perform the initial chaining of the availability list in any order we desire. Sequential linkage just happens to be the most convenient way of creating the list. Furthermore, we set the pointer field of the last node to the null value (0) to indicate the end of the list. We also initialize the AVAIL pointer (1) so that it points to the topmost node in the availability list. The value of this pointer will be updated every time we remove nodes from, or return nodes to, the availability list.

```
C EXAMPLE 6.2 - INITIALIZING THE
C               AVAILABILITY LIST
C
      DO 10 I=1,199
   10 LINK(I) = I+1
      LINK(200) = 0
      AVAIL = 1
```

Now we can examine in detail how a new node can be obtained from the availability list. The appropriate FORTRAN coding is given in Example 6.3. Initially, we check to see whether there are any nodes left in the availability list. If we find a node, we remove it by making the pointer NEW point to that node, and subsequently updating the AVAIL pointer to indicate the next node on the list. The constructor routine will take the node NEW, insert the data into its fields, and then link it into the appropriate list structure by modifying LINK(NEW) as required.

```
C EXAMPLE 6.3 - OBTAINING A NEW NODE FROM
C               THE AVAILABILITY LIST
C
      IF(AVAIL.EQ.0)GO TO ... (no available nodes)
    1 NEW = AVAIL
    2 AVAIL = LINK(AVAIL)
```

Example 6.4 provides the necessary FORTRAN coding to return a node to the availability list. The node to be returned to the list is identified by the pointer OLD. We set its link to point to the current topmost node in the availability list, as indicated by the pointer AVAIL. Then we update AVAIL so that it will point to the newly returned node, since this node (i.e., node OLD) has now become the new topmost node in the availability list. The node previously at the top of the list has now become the second node in the list.

```
C EXAMPLE 6.4 - RETURNING A NODE TO
C               THE AVAILABILITY LIST
C
    1 LINK(OLD) = AVAIL
    2 AVAIL = OLD
```

Figure 6.2 illustrates the availability list before and after the two operations described in Examples 6.3 and 6.4. Note the conventions used in this diagram. We will follow them throughout the remaining chapters in this book. A node is shown as a rectangular box divided into sections according to the fields of the node. We will always include one "legend" node to identify the various fields in a typical node. Pointers are shown as arrows, each originating from the proper field of a node and pointing towards another node.

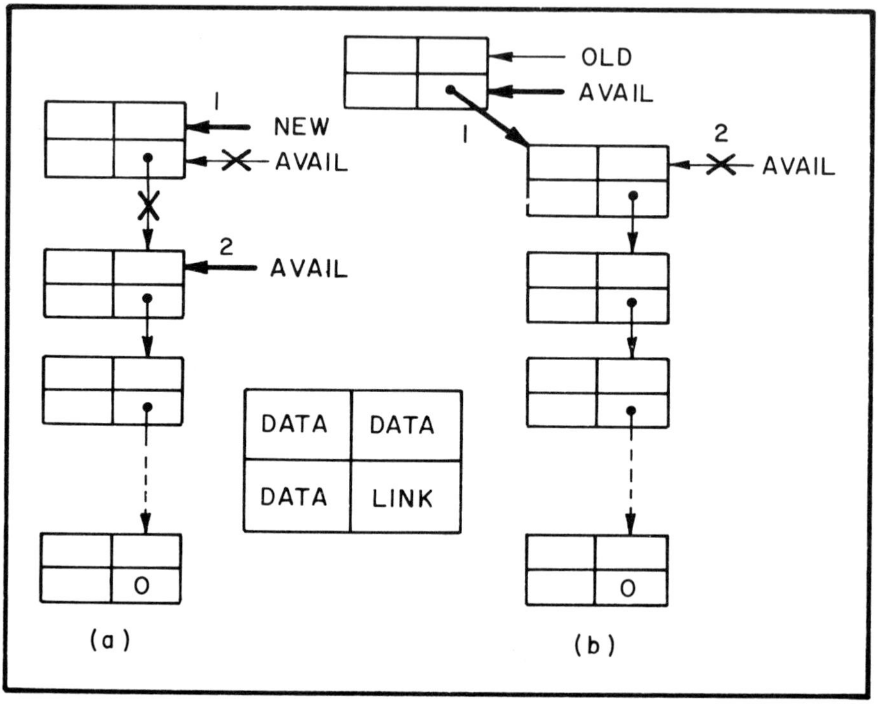

Figure 6.2

<u>Availability List Before and After Obtaining a NEW Node (a) and Returning an OLD Node (b).</u>

6.2.1 Node Construction Routine

We are now in a position to write the FORTRAN coding for a constructor routine for the creation of nodes in our list structures. As an illustration, we will demonstrate the constructor used for nodes in the polynomial problem introduced in Chapter Five. Recall that a typical node will represent one term in the polynomial. Each node will contain five fields, assuming that our polynomials contain three variables. Three of these fields will contain integer values, A, B, and C, representing the exponents of variables x, y, and z, respectively. The fourth field will contain a floating-point value, CF, to represent the coefficient of that term, while the fifth field will contain an integer pointer, LINK.

To construct a new node for us, we need an INTEGER function called CNS which will accept as arguments the five values to be assigned to the fields of the new node. The value returned by function CNS will represent a pointer to the newly created node. In the FORTRAN coding of this function (i.e., Example 6.5), the vectors CF, A, B, C, and LINK (comprising the fields of the nodes) are placed in COMMON storage so that we can write several subroutines to operate on these vectors without having to pass them every time as arguments.

We now have the basic machinery required to manipulate the list structures that represent polynomials. Furthermore, we should note that it is possible to have several different polynomials in

```
C EXAMPLE 6.5 - CONSTRUCTOR ROUTINE FOR NODES
C
      INTEGER FUNCTION CNS(CFN,NA,NB,NC,NLINK)
C
C The list structure declarations.
C
      REAL CF(200)
      INTEGER A(200),B(200),C(200),LINK(200),AVAIL
      COMMON CF,A,B,C,LINK,AVAIL
C
C Check whether AVAIL is empty.
C
      IF(AVAIL.GT.0)GO TO 10
      PRINT,'INSUFFICIENT STORAGE'
      STOP
C
C Pick off a node to be used.
C
   10 CNS = AVAIL
C
C Take the node off the list of available storage.
C
      AVAIL = LINK(AVAIL)
C
C Fill in the fields for the new node.
C
      A(CNS) = NA
      B(CNS) = NB
      C(CNS) = NC
      CF(CNS) = CFN
      LINK(CNS) = NLINK
C
      RETURN
      END
```

storage simultaneously, spread over the same storage areas CF, A, B, C, and LINK, distinguished only because each is identified by a different pointer. These pointers, in fact, can be considered to represent the polynomials. As a result, we can create an extension to the FORTRAN language, by developing a collection of subroutines, which will enable us to perform calculations with polynomials.

By using function CNS, we can construct a complete list structure to represent a polynomial. For example, a linked list to represent the polynomial "$6x^2+2yz-x$" can be created by using the coding given in Example 6.6.

```
C EXAMPLE 6.6 - POLYNOMIAL CONSTRUCTION
C
    1 POLY = CNS(-1.,1,0,0,0)
    2 POLY = CNS(+2.,0,1,1,POLY)
    3 POLY = CNS(+6.,2,0,0,POLY)
```

In Example 6.6, variable POLY represents a pointer to the resulting polynomial. The value of POLY is updated as a result of each call to function CNS after it is used as the link value of the new node. The step-by-step construction of the complete polynomial is illustrated in Figure 6.3.

Before we continue, we should agree on a convention that the polynomial with no terms be considered as the "zero polynomial". This fits in with our decision to suppress any terms in a polynomial that have zero coefficients. As a result, the polynomial with no terms will be represented by an empty list (i.e., the null pointer). It is quite conceivable that such a zero polynomial could arise, for example, as a special case when we subtract two polynomials (i.e., subtraction of a polynomial from itself). Using our FORTRAN implementation of linked lists, the zero polynomial will be identified by the null pointer 0.

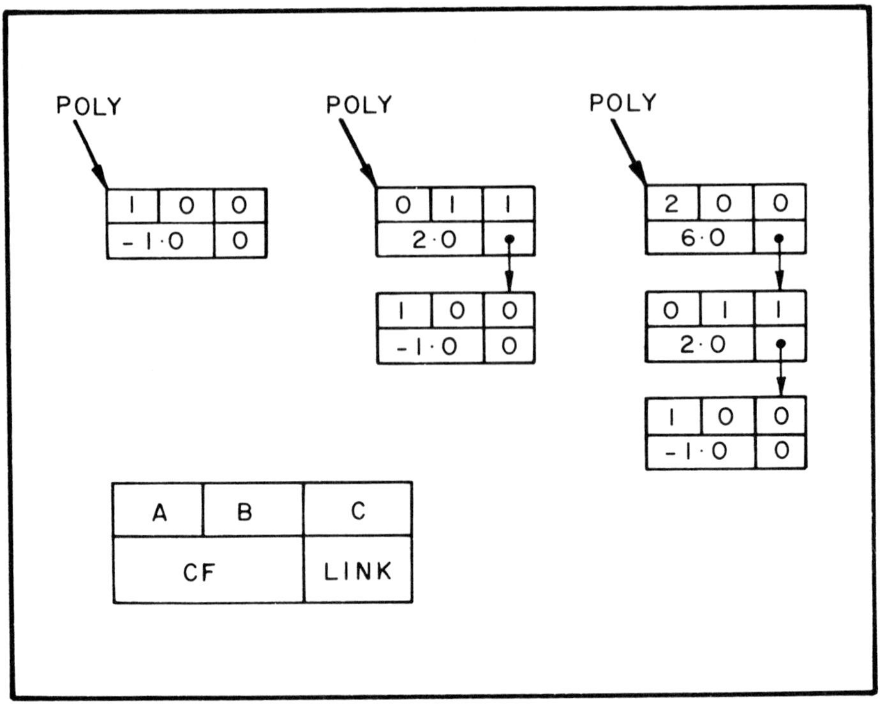

Figure 6.3

Polynomial Construction Using Function CNS

6.3 OTHER DATA-INDEPENDENT OPERATIONS ON LINEARLY LINKED LISTS

Now that we have defined our FORTRAN representation of linked lists and developed selectors and constructors for them, we can proceed to become more familiar with list processing operations. In this section, we will discuss some data-independent operations. These operations can be applied to any type of linearly linked list, since the fields mainly involved in these operations are those containing the pointers.

6.3.1 Sequencing Through Linked Lists

We identify a particular list by a pointer designating the topmost node of that list. Such pointers are integers which we can pass as parameters to the FORTRAN subroutine performing the operations. For our purposes, we shall refer to these pointers as *TOP POINTERS*. A top pointer represents the only access we have to a list. With linearly linked lists, all operations must begin with the top node, and, by following the links, proceed down the list. This is one of the major deficiencies of linearly linked lists. (In Chapter Seven, we will see what adjustments we can make to cope with this problem.) If we wish to operate on the nodes near the end of a long list, we will be spending a significant amount of time searching sequentially for these nodes. Unlike arrays, where a component can be directly accessed by calculating its address, with linearly linked lists we are forced to perform a search every time we look for a particular node. Every such search must begin from the top of the list. This is part of the price we pay for the conveniences provided by linked lists.

To demonstrate the mechanism by which we "iterate" through the nodes of a linked list, we should consider an example. If we wish to operate on the first node in a list, we can simply use the top pointer for gaining access to it. However, it is sometimes necessary to operate on the last node in a list. As a result, we need a function that accepts a top pointer as a parameter, and returns as its value a pointer to the last node in the list identified by that top pointer. The FORTRAN coding for this function is given in Example 6.7.

```
C EXAMPLE 6.7 - LOCATING THE LAST NODE IN A LIST
C
      INTEGER FUNCTION LAST(TOP)
      .
      : (declaration of data fields)
      INTEGER....LINK(200),...
      COMMON....LINK,...
C
      INTEGER TOP,P
C
      P = LAST = TOP
   10 IF(P.EQ.0)RETURN
      LAST = P
      P = LINK(P)
      GO TO 10
C
      END
```

When we write the coding for function LAST, we once again place the vectors representing the various fields of the nodes in COMMON storage. This will be standard practice for us with all our subprograms which operate on any of these vectors. Such action will make it unnecessary to pass these vectors as arguments every time we reference any of our subroutines. The first step in the LAST routine involves initializing the pointer P so that it will point to the top node in the list specified by TOP. Then we perform a complete search until we encounter the last node in the list. We proceed from one node to the next by simply writing P = LINK(P). As we encounter each new node, we test for the null pointer (0) which will identify the end of the list.

6.3.2 Concatenation of Lists

Now that we have function LAST available to us, we can proceed to use it as part of other utility operations. For example, it is sometimes desirable to concatenate two lists into one. Such an action will involve chaining the two lists together so that the last node of the first list points to the first node of the second list. Function CHAIN, as coded in Example 6.8, performs this concatenation for us. It accepts two top pointers, TOP1 and TOP2, as parameters, and returns as its value a pointer to the topmost node in the chained list. Provided that TOP1 is not equal to zero, the value returned is that of TOP1, since the top node in the first list is now considered to be the topmost node in the chained list. Otherwise, the value returned by CHAIN is that of TOP2.

The FORTRAN coding for function CHAIN provides an excellent example of nested selectors. By using LAST(TOP1), we are employing function LAST to select the last node from the first list. This pointer value is then used to select the LINK field of that node so that its value can be updated (it was 0 to indicate the end of the first list) to point to the top node in the second list (i.e., TOP2). This action will connect the last node in the first list to the top node in the second list, thus forming one concatenated list.

```
C EXAMPLE 6.8 - CHAINING TWO LINEARLY LINKED LISTS
C
      INTEGER FUNCTION CHAIN(TOP1,TOP2)
      :  (other declarations)
      INTEGER....LINK(200),...
      COMMON....LINK,...
C
      INTEGER TOP1,TOP2
C
      IF(TOP1.NE.0)GO TO 5
      CHAIN = TOP2
      RETURN
C
    5 LINK(LAST(TOP1)) = TOP2
      CHAIN = TOP1
      RETURN
C
      END
```

We could include another safety measure in the coding for function CHAIN to avoid chaining one list to itself, thus creating a circular list. A test for TOP1.EQ.TOP2 could be inserted to produce an appropriate error message if the two top pointers designate the same list. Any reader who needs further convincing that such a chained list would produce disturbing results should consider the following example of an infinite loop:

```
      TOP = CHAIN(TOP1,TOP1)
        P = LAST(TOP)
```

6.3.3 Deletion of Nodes

We can now consider writing a second storage management routine to complement the action of function CNS. This subroutine, called DLT, will remove a designated node from a specified list and return its storage to the availability list. In order to ensure the continuity of the list after the removal of the specified node, we should design our routine to link the preceding node to the succeeding node. Subroutine DLT accepts two parameters, a pointer (P) identifying the node to be deleted and a top pointer (TOP) designating the list from which the particular node should be removed. The coding for this routine is presented in Example 6.9. Figure 6.4 contains a diagram illustrating the pointer adjustments involved with subroutine DLT.

Subroutine DLT illustrates two inefficiencies inherent in our current implementation of linked lists. First, we have to include a special segment of code to accommodate the special case where we wish to delete the top node from the list. In Section 6.5, we will introduce a technique to eliminate the need for having this extra code. Second, searching for the predecessor of node P involves a loop which might well be very time consuming, especially if the node we are deleting is located near the end of a long list. We will suggest a possible solution to this problem in Chapter Seven.

```
C EXAMPLE 6.9 - DELETION OF A NODE FROM A
C               LINEARLY LINKED LIST
C
      SUBROUTINE DLT(P,TOP)
      .
      : (other declarations)
      .
      INTEGER....LINK(200),AVAIL
      COMMON....LINK,AVAIL
C
      INTEGER TOP,P,Q,R
C
C Consider special case of deleting node TOP.
C
      IF(P.NE.TOP)GO TO 10
C
C Modify TOP pointer to point
C at the next node down.
C
      TOP = LINK(TOP)
      GO TO 20
C
C At 10 we are searching for the predecessor of P.
C
   10 Q = TOP
   11 R = Q
      Q = LINK(Q)
      IF(Q.EQ.0)GO TO 30
      IF(Q.NE.P)GO TO 11
C
C We have found the predecessor (R);
C so link it around P.
C
      LINK(R) = LINK(P)
C
C Return node P to the availability list.
C
   20 LINK(P) = AVAIL
      AVAIL = P
      RETURN
C
C Error condition; P not found in TOP.
C
   30 PRINT 99,P,TOP
   99 FORMAT(' DLT ERROR-NODE',I4,'NOT IN LIST',I4)
C
      RETURN
      END
```

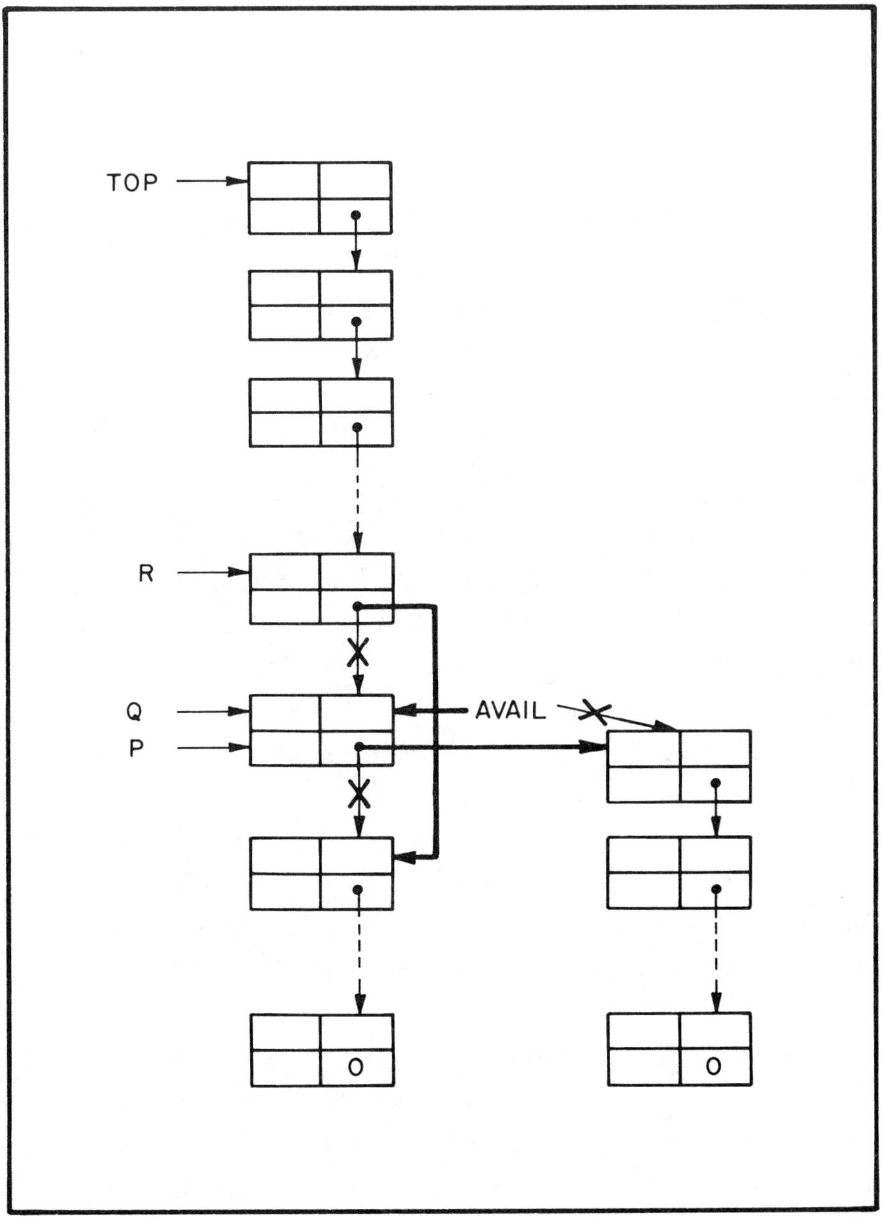

Figure 6.4

<u>Deletion Operation On Linearly Linked Lists</u>

In situations where we wish to delete an entire list, rather than just a single node, we need not invoke subroutine DLT. By using

AVAIL = CHAIN(AVAIL,TOP)

we can return the complete list identified by TOP to the availability list. We should exercise considerable caution at this point, however, since we might still have some other pointers pointing at list TOP or some of its nodes. Subsequent use of these nodes after the deletion operation might yield some very unpleasant results.

With our FORTRAN implementation of linearly linked lists, we have already indicated that it is the programmer's own responsibility to return nodes to the availability list as soon as they are no longer needed. However, it should be noted that the garbage collection technique used by actual list processing languages utilizes a complementary approach. Only when the construction function finds the availability list empty is the garbage collection routine invoked. It scans through all the lists and returns to the availability list those nodes which are not pointed at by any pointer in the program. Consequently, the user is freed from the burden of having to liberate unused nodes. It would be very impractical, however, to implement a garbage collection scheme within the framework of our linearly linked lists. To begin with, the garbage collection procedure is a very time-consuming one, even if it is employed only when there are no nodes remaining in the availability list. Secondly, we use regular FORTRAN integers as pointers, with the result that there is no way of determining which nodes are not pointed at by pointers external to the linked lists. *EXTERNAL POINTERS* are those pointers which are not fields of a node. Included in this category are all top pointers, as well as pointers to individual nodes within a list (e.g., P, Q, and R in Example 6.9). By comparison, we will refer to those pointers which are actually fields of a node (i.e., the entries of vector LINK) as *INTERNAL POINTERS*. Implementation of a garbage collection scheme would involve incorporating some method of distinguishing between regular fixed-point variables and external pointers.

6.3.4 Reproduction of Lists

Finally, we can consider another utility function, DUP, which we will use for duplicating lists. Despite the fact that it does reference particular data fields, we can still consider this routine to be (conceptually) data independent. This function is useful when we wish to modify the contents of a particular list (TOP) without actually destroying the original list. In such cases, we can use DUP to duplicate the appropriate list, and subsequently be free to operate on the new copy of the list. The coding for function DUP is presented in Example 6.10. The value returned by this function is a pointer to the duplicated list.

```
C EXAMPLE 6.10 - DUPLICATING A LINEARLY LINKED LIST
C
      INTEGER FUNCTION DUP(TOP)
      .
      :  (other declarations)
      .
      INTEGER....LINK(200),...
      COMMON....LINK,...
C
      INTEGER CNS,P,TOP
C
      DUP = 0
      P = TOP
   10 IF(P.LT.1)RETURN
C
      DUP = CNS(....data values of node P....,DUP)
      P = LINK(P)
      GO TO 10
C
      END
```

Using function DUP as coded in Example 6.10, we produce a duplicated list whose nodes are in the reverse order to those of the original list (i.e., the top node of the original list becomes the last node in the duplicated list, etc.). For many operations, we are not really concerned with the order of the nodes in the list. However, for those cases where we are concerned, we can modify the coding for DUP so that it maintains the order of the nodes in the duplicated list. This will require the use of an additional pointer to the end of the duplicated list so that we can attach the new nodes to it (see Exercise 12 in Section 6.6).

Function DUP can now be used within other function calls. For example, if we wish to create a new list (TOP) to be the concatenation of two other lists (TOP1,TOP2) without actually linking the original lists, we can use the following coding:

```
TOP = CHAIN(DUP(TOP1),DUP(TOP2))
```

Another data-independent routine which we mentioned in Chapter Five is a function called NTH. This function returns as its value a pointer to the Nth node in the list specified as a parameter to the routine. If, by any chance, there are fewer than N nodes in the designated list, the routine should return the null pointer. The FORTRAN coding for this function is left as an exercise for interested readers (see Exercise 13 in Section 6.6).

In Section 6.4, we will be discussing additional operations with linked lists representing polynomials. These operations will be data dependent in the sense that their design will depend upon the interpretation we assign to the data structures. Following this discussion, Section 6.5 introduces another common application of linked lists, namely computer graphics. In our examination of this topic, we will be considering the design of the various routines we need to process such data items.

6.4 FORMAL MANIPULATION OF POLYNOMIALS

In this section, we will develop several data-manipulation operations for a programming language which processes polynomials as regular data types. For example, in FORTRAN, we can use the following coding to read and manipulate complex values:

```
COMPLEX A,B,C
READ,A,B,C
C = A+B*C
.
.
.
```

Ideally, we would like to be able to operate on polynomials in a similar manner. To do so, we should be able to write, in our hypothetical language, statements such as the following:

```
polynomial p,q,r
read,p,q,r
r = p+q*r
.
.
.
```

We know that the FORTRAN compiler invokes special complex arithmetic routines to operate on data of type COMPLEX, represented in memory by pairs of full (or double) words. In the same way, we want the compiler for our hypothetical language to invoke data-manipulation routines specifically designed to operate on data of type POLYNOMIAL, represented internally in the form of linearly linked lists. Complex numbers are referenced by using the address of the first word of the pair of memory words. Analogously, a polynomial can be referenced by using a pointer to the topmost node in the linked list representing it.

In our FORTRAN representation of linked lists, we use fixed-point values to represent our pointers. It follows that we use INTEGER variables to serve as pointers to the tops of the various linked lists. Since we are not yet in a position to modify the FORTRAN compiler to accept new types of data declarations (i.e., POLYNOMIAL), we will have to declare our polynomials as type INTEGER. We are faced with a similar obstacle with our operations on polynomials. Since the compiler will not understand that our integer pointers represent polynomials, we must invoke the various operations by using subroutine and function calls. For example, the FORTRAN coding to implement the operations discussed earlier in this section with polynomials p, q, and r, is given in Example 6.11.

In Example 6.11, we have declared variables P, Q, and R as type INTEGER, even though, in reality, we mean to declare them as type POLYNOMIAL. The same is true with functions ADD and MULT. Each of these functions operates on linked lists representing polynomials, and returns as its value a new polynomial (i.e., a pointer) which is the result of the operation (i.e., addition or multiplication) with the two polynomials supplied as parameters to the function. Following these initial declarations, we insert additional declaration statements for the various fields of the nodes in our linked lists. The subroutine READ then takes (from data cards) the coefficients and exponents

```
C EXAMPLE 6.11 - POLYNOMIAL MANIPULATION
C                IN FORTRAN
C
      REAL CF(200)
      INTEGER A(200),B(200),C(200),LINK(200),AVAIL
      COMMON CF,A,B,C,LINK,AVAIL
C
      INTEGER P,Q,R,ADD,MULT
C
      CALL READ(P)
      CALL READ(Q)
      CALL READ(R)
      R = ADD(P,MULT(Q,R))
      :
```

of certain polynomials, and subsequently constructs for us linked lists as the internal representations of those polynomials. As an argument for each call to subroutine READ, we supply a top pointer to identify the list constructed for the appropriate polynomial. This will permit us to reference this list later within the context of our computations.

6.4.1 Input/Output Routines

As a first step, we might write the actual coding for the I/O operations. Whenever we are developing a large system of programs, it is always advisable to write these routines first. This will make any subsequent debugging an easier task for us. The FORTRAN coding for our output routine is given in Example 6.12. Subroutine PRINT accepts as a parameter a top pointer for a linked list, and prints the nodes of that list on the line printer, one node per line. The program consists of a single loop to scan through the nodes of the list, printing the various fields of each node as it is encountered. Actually, whenever we are debugging a program, it might be helpful to print the LINK along with each node, and possibly even the number of each node.

```
C EXAMPLE 6.12 - PRINT ROUTINE FOR POLYNOMIALS
C
      SUBROUTINE PRINT(POLY)
C
C Declaration of the nodes.
C
      REAL CF(200)
      INTEGER A(200),B(200),C(200),LINK(200),AVAIL
      COMMON CF,A,B,C,LINK,AVAIL
C
      INTEGER POLY,P
C
C First check whether the polynomial has any terms.
C
      IF(POLY.GT.0)GO TO 10
      PRINT,'0'
      RETURN
C
C Initialize the loop pointer P and begin printing.
C
   10 P = POLY
   20 PRINT 99,CF(P),A(P),B(P),C(P)
   99 FORMAT(' ',F11.4,'*X**',I5,'*Y**',I5,
     1'*Z**',I5)
C
C Proceed to the next node.
C
      P = LINK(P)
C
C Test for end of list; if not, loop back.
C
      IF(P.GT.0)GO TO 20
      RETURN
C
      END
```

The READ routine (Example 6.13) is equally simple. Once we have decided on the input format, we have to define some criterion to indicate the end of the list. Since polynomials can have an arbitrary number of terms, we might use a dummy data card with a coefficient 0.0 to signal the end of the input for a particular polynomial.

```
C EXAMPLE 6.13 - READ ROUTINE FOR POLYNOMIALS
C
      SUBROUTINE READ(POLY)
C
      REAL CF(200)
      INTEGER A(200),B(200),C(200),LINK(200),AVAIL
      COMMON CF,A,B,C,LINK,AVAIL
C
      INTEGER POLY,CNS
C
      POLY = 0
C
   10 READ(5,99,END=20)CFI,IA,IB,IC
   99 FORMAT(F12.4,3I6)
      IF(CFI.EQ.0)RETURN
C
C Construct a new node and
C return to read the next card.
C
      POLY = CNS(CFI,IA,IB,IC,POLY)
      GO TO 10
C
   20 RETURN
      END
```

Notice that the list created by READ to represent the polynomial will have its nodes arranged in the reverse order to that of the terms on the data cards. It is clear that the first data card contains the values that will be found in the fields of the last node in the list. Conversely, the data values to be used as the fields of the top node are obtained from the last data card preceding the dummy one (which contains a zero for the coefficient).

6.4.2 Reduction to Canonical Form

Now that we have written our I/O routines, we can concentrate our attention on a most important polynomial manipulation routine, the simplification function. This routine will be used by almost all other polynomial manipulation functions. It will sort the linked list to put the polynomial in a *CANONICAL* form. This implies that the terms in the polynomial will be arranged in descending order, according to the exponents, A, B, and C, respectively. Furthermore, function SIMP will detect and merge pairs of terms with identical exponents. Upon completion of the sorting procedure, it will also delete from the list all terms with zero coefficients. The FORTRAN coding for function SIMP is given in Example 6.14.

```
C EXAMPLE 6.14 - SIMPLIFICATION OF POLYNOMIALS
C
      INTEGER FUNCTION SIMP(POLY)
C
      REAL CF(200)
      INTEGER A(200),B(200),C(200),LINK(200),AVAIL
      COMMON CF,A,B,C,LINK,AVAIL
C
      INTEGER POLY,CNS,P,Q,R
C
C Check for a zero polynomial.
C
      IF(POLY.LT.1)RETURN
C
C First, we create an extra node at the start.
C This makes it possible to look at 3 nodes at
C a time, work on the second two, and not
C lose our place.  It will be deleted later.
C
      POLY = CNS(0.,0,0,0,POLY)
C
```

```
C LATEST will indicate the position in the list
C where the most recent interchange of nodes
C has occurred.  LAST will indicate the position
C where the final exchange of nodes occurred
C during the previous pass.  We need go no further
C than this point during the next pass.
C
      LATEST = 0
   10 LAST = LATEST
C
C P points to the first of the three
C nodes we are examining.
C
      P = POLY
C
C At the beginning of each sorting pass, we
C initialize the 3 pointers to the top 3 nodes in
C the list.  We check each time to see whether the
C end pointer has reached the top.
C
      Q = LINK(P)
      IF(Q.EQ.LAST)GO TO 90
   25 R = LINK(Q)
      IF(R.EQ.LAST)GO TO 90
C
C Next we compare the two nodes, Q and R.
C If the exponents of R are greater than those
C of Q, we have to perform an interchange (70).
C If they are equal, we merge the nodes Q and R
C into Q, and then delete R.
C
   30 IF(A(R)-A(Q))80,40,70
   40 IF(B(R)-B(Q))80,50,70
   50 IF(C(R)-C(Q))80,60,70
C
C The next statements are executed only
C if all exponents are equal.
C
   60 CF(Q) = CF(Q)+CF(R)
      CALL DLT(R,POLY)
C
C Go to statement 25 to compare the newly merged
C node with the one now following it to
C preserve sorting order.
C
      GO TO 25
C
```

```
C The next statements perform the interchange.  We
C only modify the links to reflect the change.
C There is no data movement. (See Figure 6.5.)
C The value of LATEST is also reset.
C
   70 LATEST = Q
      LINK(P) = R
      LINK(Q) = LINK(R)
      LINK(R) = Q
C
C Advance the pointers along the links of the list.
C
   80 P = LINK(P)
      Q = LINK(P)
      R = LINK(Q)
C
C If the last pointer R has not yet reached the end
C pointer, loop back to continue the sorting pass.
C
      IF(R.NE.LAST)GO TO 30
C
C Check to see if another pass is necessary.
C If unordered nodes have been found,
C go back to perform another pass.
C
   90 IF(LAST.NE.LATEST)GO TO 10
C
C Here we scan the list for the terms with
C zero coefficients and delete them.
C
      Q = POLY
    3 P = Q
    4 Q = LINK(P)
      IF(Q.EQ.0)GO TO 5
      IF(CF(Q).NE.0)GO TO 3
      CALL DLT(Q,POLY)
      GO TO 4
C
C Set the value of pointer SIMP.
C
    5 SIMP = LINK(POLY)
C
C Delete the dummy node we added at the beginning.
C
      CALL DLT(POLY,POLY)
      RETURN
C
      END
```

The sorting algorithm employed for function SIMP is a version of the well-known bubble sort, very similar in principle to that used for sorting character strings in Chapter Four. To simplify the coding, we create a dummy header node at the top of the list. Prior to returning control to the user, our routine deletes this extra node. With the aid of three pointers, P, Q, and R, which point to three consecutive nodes in the list, we scan through the list several times. We examine nodes in pairs (i.e., first and second, second and third, etc.), each time comparing the related exponents. For each pair of nodes (i.e., Q and R), we first compare the exponents of variable x (i.e., the values of A). If the exponents of x are the same, we compare the exponents of variable y. If both pairs of exponents are the same, we consider the exponents of variable z. In cases where all three exponents are the same, we combine the two terms into one. This merging of terms is achieved by the addition of the coefficient in the second node (i.e., CF(R)) to the coefficient in the first node (i.e., CF(Q)), and the subsequent deletion of the second node (i.e., node R) from the list. Then we proceed to compare the exponents of the newly merged node (i.e., node Q) with those of the node now succeeding it in the list. If, however, we encounter two consecutive nodes which are out of order, relative to one another, we interchange them. (A typical exchange of nodes, using the pointers from Example 6.14, is shown in Figure 6.5.) Otherwise, we leave them alone, and proceed to examine the next pair of nodes.

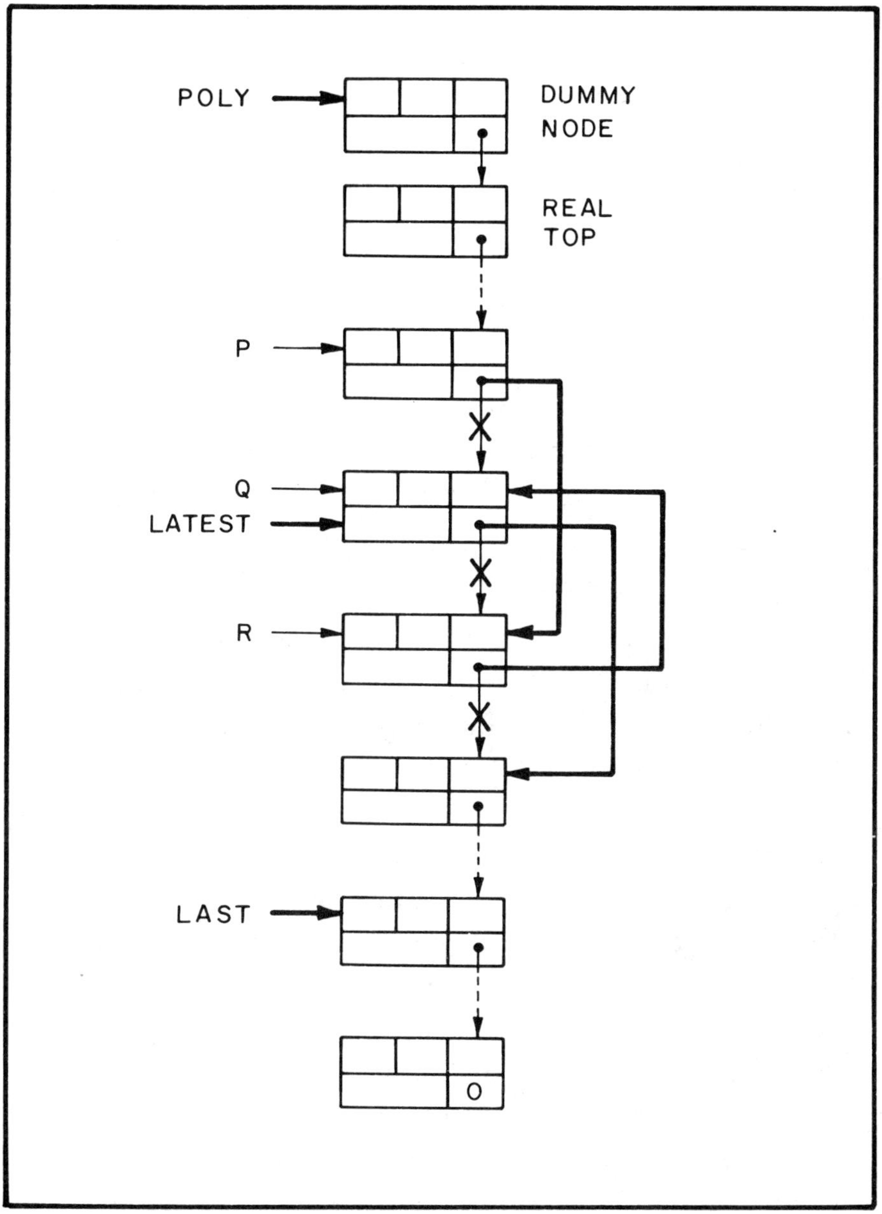

Figure 6.5

Interchange Of Nodes In Function SIMP

It is important to realize that changing the relative position of two consecutive nodes in the list does not involve any actual data movement. To make such an exchange, we merely alter the appropriate pointers (i.e., links) to reflect the change in order. This was not the case in Chapter Four when we used a similar sorting algorithm to sort character strings. In that instance, there was an actual shifting in memory of the two character strings to be interchanged. However, with linked lists, we know that consecutive elements in a list need not be stored in contiguous memory locations.

Each time that we scan through the list in this manner, making node interchanges whenever necessary, we ensure that at least one (and perhaps more) of the nodes is located in its proper position in the ordered list. In essence, as we make repeated iterations through the list, we are sorting the nodes into proper order, beginning at the end of the list and working backwards. Consequently, it is not necessary for us to continue to the end of the list each time when comparing coefficients of consecutive nodes. During each pass through the list, we need go no further than the point of the last interchange made during the previous pass (as indicated by LAST in Example 6.14). We know that the nodes following that point are already in their proper positions in the list. In order to determine when we can terminate our sorting procedure, we maintain a pointer, LATEST, to the position in the list where we made our most recent exchange. As soon as we manage to complete a pass through the nodes without performing a single interchange (i.e., when LAST is equal to LATEST at the end of the pass), we can stop making any further comparisons, since all the nodes are now properly sorted within the list.

6.4.3 Addition Routine

Now that function SIMP is available to us, we can use it as part of other polynomial processing operations. As an illustration, consider the addition operation performed by function ADD in Example 6.15. This routine accepts as parameters two top pointers identifying the polynomials to be added, and returns as its value a pointer to the list representing the sum polynomial.

```
C EXAMPLE 6.15 - ADDITION OF POLYNOMIALS
C                 (THE ARGUMENTS ARE DESTROYED)
C
      INTEGER FUNCTION ADD(POLY1,POLY2)
C
      REAL CF(200)
      INTEGER A(200),B(200),C(200),LINK(200),AVAIL
      COMMON CF,A,B,C,LINK,AVAIL
C
      INTEGER POLY1,POLY2,SIMP
C
C If POLY1 is zero, return POLY2.
C
      ADD = POLY2
      IF(POLY1.EQ.0)RETURN
C
C If POLY2 is zero, return POLY1.
C
      ADD = POLY1
      IF(POLY2.EQ.0)RETURN
C
```

```
C If neither of the polynomials is zero, concatenate
C them.  The simplified version of the concatenation
C is the sum.
C
      LINK(LAST(POLY1)) = POLY2
      ADD = SIMP(POLY1)
C
      RETURN
      END
```

Although the coding for function ADD is very straightforward, it does not take into account the fact that POLY1 and POLY2 were probably in canonical form before we performed the addition. If we assume this condition, we can program the addition more efficiently by using a merge sort on the two lists. Function MERGAD (Example 6.16) performs the addition using this method. Notice that the sum polynomial is in reversed canonical form.

It is important that we notice, however, that the two lists representing the original polynomials have been destroyed by both the ADD and MERGAD routines. This might not be acceptable if we want to include the ADD function in the polynomial processing language which we discussed at the beginning of this section. To avoid this obstacle, we can use the DUP function introduced in Section 6.3. As a result, whenever we want to perform an addition of two polynomials without losing the lists representing these polynomials, we can use the following invocation to function ADD:

```
R = ADD(DUP(P),DUP(Q))
```

```
C EXAMPLE 6.16 - ADDITION OF POLYNOMIALS BY MERGING
C                (THE ARGUMENTS ARE DESTROYED)
C
      INTEGER FUNCTION MERGAD(POLY1,POLY2)
C
      REAL CF(200)
      INTEGER A(200),B(200),C(200),LINK(200),AVAIL
      COMMON CF,A,B,C,LINK,AVAIL
C
      INTEGER POLY1,POLY2,PTR1,LINK1,PTR2,LINK2
C
      MERGAD = 0
C
C Check that POLY1 and POLY2 are non-zero.
C
   10 IF(POLY1.GT.0.AND.POLY2.GT.0)GO TO 40
C
C If POLY2 is zero, check POLY1.
C
      IF(POLY2.LE.0)GO TO 30
C
C If POLY2 is non-zero at this point, then POLY1
C must be zero.  Set POLY1 equal to POLY2.
C
      POLY1 = POLY2
C
C Concatenate the top node of POLY1 to the top node
C of the sum polynomial MERGAD.
C
   20 PTR1 = LINK(POLY1)
      LINK(POLY1) = MERGAD
      MERGAD = POLY1
      POLY1 = PTR1
C
C If POLY1 is zero, return to the calling program.
C
   30 IF(POLY1.GT.0)GO TO 20
      RETURN
C
C Compare the exponents of the top nodes
C of POLY1 and POLY2.
C
   40 IF(A(POLY1)-A(POLY2))80,50,90
   50 IF(B(POLY1)-B(POLY2))80,60,90
   60 IF(C(POLY1)-C(POLY2))80,70,90
C
```

```
C If the exponents are identical, add the
C coefficients and move the resulting node to the
C top of MERGAD.  Then delete the obsolete node(s).
C
   70 CF(POLY1) = CF(POLY1)+CF(POLY2)
      CALL DLT(POLY2,POLY2)
      IF(CF(POLY1).NE.0.)GO TO 90
      CALL DLT(POLY1,POLY1)
      GO TO 10
C
C If the exponents of the top node of POLY1 are
C less than those of the top node of POLY2, move
C the top node of POLY2 to MERGAD.
C
   80 PTR2 = LINK(POLY2)
      LINK(POLY2) = MERGAD
      MERGAD = POLY2
      POLY2 = PTR2
      GO TO 10
C
C If the exponents of the top node of POLY1 are
C greater than those of the top node of POLY2,
C move the top node of POLY1 to MERGAD.
C
   90 PTR1 = LINK(POLY1)
      LINK(POLY1) = MERGAD
      MERGAD = POLY1
      POLY1 = PTR1
      GO TO 10
C
      END
```

With this adjustment, the original lists representing polynomials P and Q will not be destroyed. However, what about the previous value of R? If R was a pointer to another list, we would like to return the nodes of this list to the availability list before calling upon the ADD routine to update the value of R. This can be achieved quite easily by using a scratch routine (discussed in Section 6.3) to return the old nodes of list R (if there were any) to the availability list. Alternatively, we could devise a special-purpose routine, ASSIGN, that will check initially whether any nodes are pointed at by an external pointer (R in this case) before assigning a new list to it. The old nodes are returned to the availability list for further use. We could invoke such a routine to handle our problem as follows:

```
CALL ASSIGN(R,ADD(DUP(P),DUP(Q)))
```

All our storage management routines should be activated by the compiler of our polynomial manipulation language. In addition to the deletion of unused lists, we are also faced with a problem of having storage occupied by temporary lists. For example, in processing the expression R = P+Q*R, we generate a temporary polynomial for the product of Q and R. Consequently, in order to use the facilities provided to us by FORTRAN, we will have to use a slightly more complicated code to process this expression:

```
R = ADD(DUP(P),MULT(DUP(Q),R))
```

Function MULT produces the product polynomial from a copy of Q and the old value of R. As a result, we need not worry about returning the old nodes of R to the availability list. Similarly, function ADD forms the sum polynomial from a duplicate of P and the nodes of the temporary product of Q and R. This implies that we do not have to return the nodes in the temporary list to the availability list either.

In summary, we should now be able to code in FORTRAN all the necessary operations with polynomials. Besides having addition (ADD) and multiplication (MULT) routines, our polynomial manipulation language would include routines for dividing two polynomials, evaluating polynomials for specific values of the variables, differentiating a polynomial with respect to one of its variables, integrating a polynomial, etc.. We leave the detailed coding of such operations (as well as the coding for function MULT) as exercises for interested readers. (See Section 6.6.)

6.5 COMPUTER GRAPHICS

- EXAMPLE OF LINEARLY LINKED LISTS

One of the more exciting applications of list processing is the field of *COMPUTER GRAPHICS*, an area where we would like to create, manipulate, and output (i.e., draw) data structures representing graphic data. The graphic entity can be anything which usually requires a pencil and a sheet of paper to be drawn: curves of mathematical functions, technical drawings of machine parts, or even funny cartoons, to mention only a few. From a computer point of view, the common aspect of different graphic structures is the fact that they can all be represented as a collection of points on the two-dimensional plane X-Y. We would like to devise a simple data structure that will provide for easy manipulation of graphic data. The kind of manipulation desired on graphic data can always be reduced to the basic operations of adding points to, and deleting points from, the description of the graphic structure.

6.5.1 Representation of Graphic Entities

For our purposes, a graphic entity will be represented as a linked list of nodes, each representing a single point on the X-Y plane. Consequently, each node contains two data items, the X and Y coordinates of the point it represents. Modifications can be easily performed by adding or deleting nodes (i.e., points) within the linked list. The advantage of using linked list structures lies in the efficient way in which they yield to additions and deletions. This is demonstrated in the discussion which follows.

For representing a line connecting the two points, (0.0,0.0) and (4.0,3.0), it would be ideal if we could create a list containing representations of <u>all</u> the points along the line, one node for each point. This is clearly impractical, however, since theoretically there is an infinite number of points along any line. As a result, we have to define the smallest unit of distance which we can handle, and then spread the points along the line, one unit of distance apart. For simplicity, we choose 1.0 as our unit of distance. We should notice, at this stage, that the distance between the two points is then exactly five units. As a result, we create a linked list having six nodes (since we must include both end points) to represent the line, as demonstrated in Figure 6.6. A pointer, LINE1, indicates the topmost node in the list representing our straight line. We use a dummy node as the first node of our list to simplify the coding of the subroutines which we will write to manipulate these lists (this will be demonstrated later). Following the header node, we have six nodes containing the appropriate X and Y coordinates of the six points along the line.

Figure 6.6 also illustrates a second line drawn from (0.0,3.0) to (4.0,0.0). The list representing this line is indicated by a pointer, LINE2. Following our usual convention, we will identify lists by the names of their top pointers. We now have two lists, LINE1 and LINE2, each representing one line. By calling a print routine, we can have these lists printed for us, one at a time.

However, instead of having the two lines drawn for us separately, we might use the two lists as primitives for the creation of more elaborate graphic structures. For example, suppose we wish to draw a cross, in the shape of an X, centered at the point (10.0,10.0). We can construct a list to represent such a structure in two steps. First, we should chain the two lists representing the individual lines into one list. This new list is the representation of a cross (as the intersection of the two lines) centered at the point (2.0,1.5).

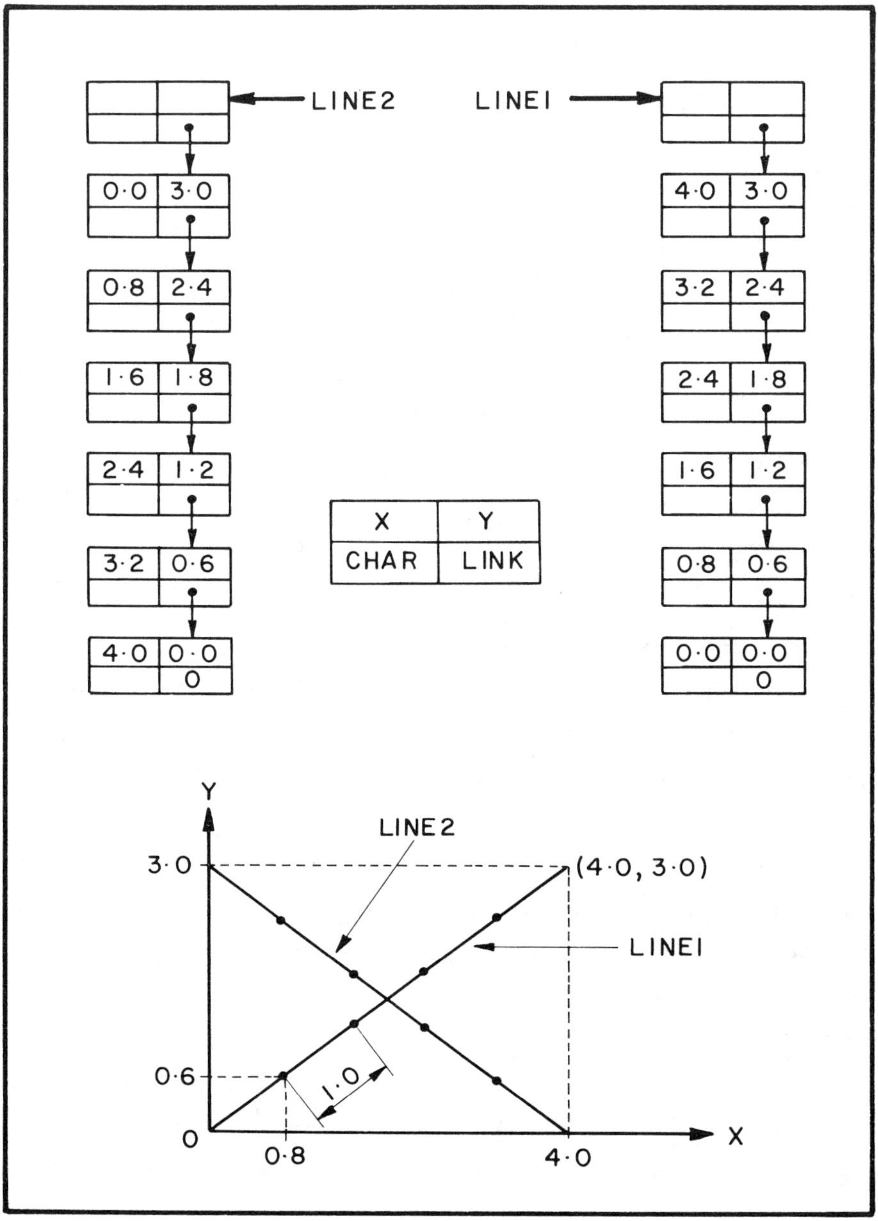

Figure 6.6

Representation Of Two Straight Lines

The second step involves moving the cross so that its center will lie at the point (10.0,10.0). This shift is achieved by adding 8.0 to all the X coordinates and 8.5 to all the Y coordinates of the new list.

Figure 6.7 shows the resulting list structure before and after the shifting operation. The chain operation which we need here will be slightly different from the one we discussed in Section 6.3. The new version of the CHAIN routine must remove the dummy header node before concatenating the two lists. Later in this section, we will examine how this removal can be accomplished in an efficient manner.

As indicated in the previous paragraph, it is a relatively straightforward procedure to superimpose two graphic data items. If, for any reason, we need the representation of the original lines for further use, we can create duplicates of these lists, and concatenate the copies to form the cross. Furthermore, shifting a graphic entity on the X-Y plane is performed by simply looping through the nodes of the corresponding list, following the links, and adding the proper constants to all the coordinates. Once again, if two versions are required (i.e., one shifted and the other unshifted), a duplicate can be made before the shifting operation. In such cases, if we wish to print the two crosses as parts of a single total structure, we have to perform another concatenation of the lists representing the two crosses.

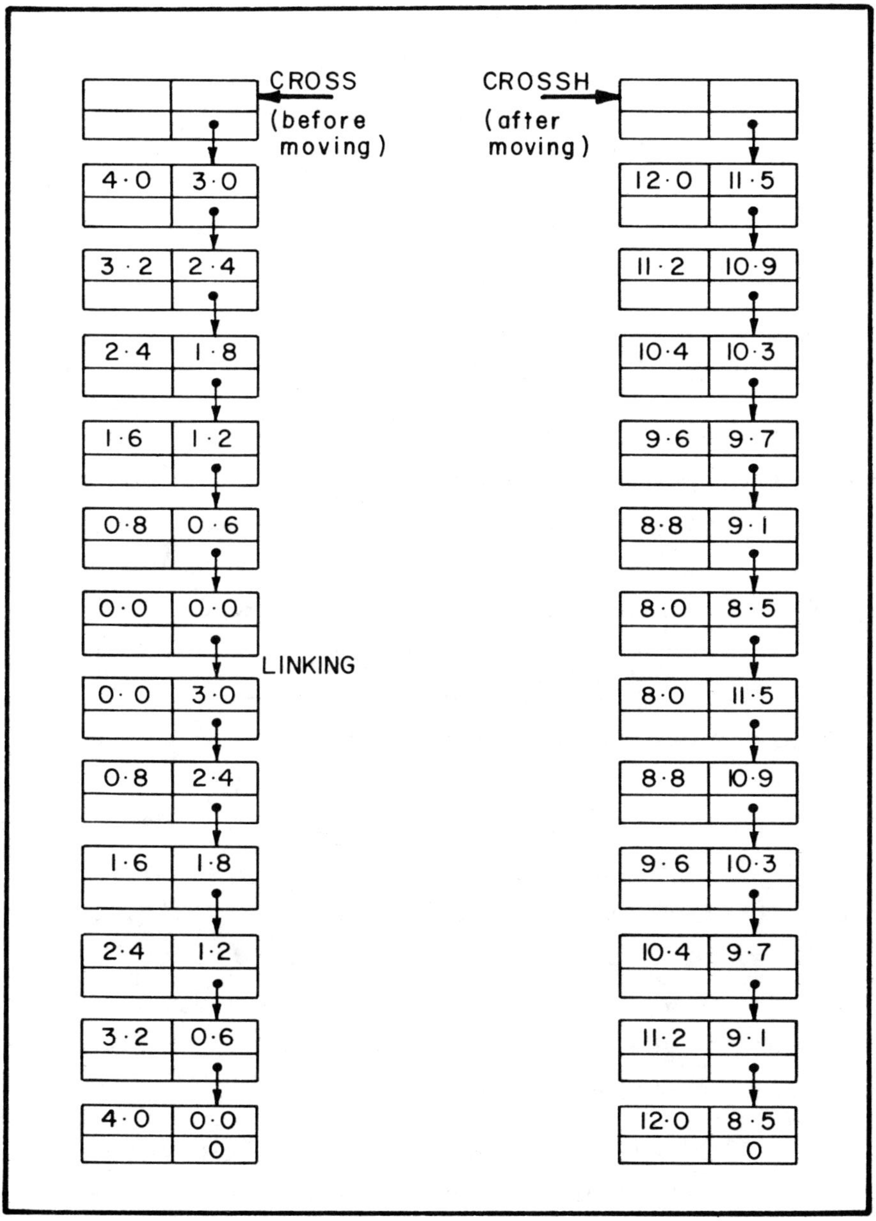

Figure 6.7

Creating A Cross From Two Lines And Moving It

With our example involving lines and crosses, we have attempted to demonstrate some of the justification for employing linked lists for the representation of graphic data. The additional memory space invested in the links is well worthwhile, since it simplifies to a considerable extent the kind of operations required for graphic data.

6.5.2 Graphics Processing System

Once again, as we did in Section 6.4, we can visualize a special-purpose programming language which includes provision for processing a new type of data. In this instance, we want to develop a language to manipulate data of type GRAPHIC. The internal representation of this data is again in the form of linearly linked lists. Whenever we discuss data types, we always commence by defining variables and constants. For example, in FORTRAN, I, J, and K are INTEGER variables, and the numbers 1, 2, 3, ... are INTEGER constants. A variable can assume a value which is one of these constants. Similarly, in the case of our special language to process graphic data, we will have variables of type GRAPHIC. Furthermore, constants will be primitive graphic items like lines and circles.

In the same way that we define arithmetic operations with integers, we should define various operations with graphic data. For example, we can define addition of two graphic items as the merging operation. To illustrate, consider our earlier example of two lines merged into a cross. We could indicate that we want this operation performed by using the following line of coding in our new language:

cross = line1 + line2

As a further example, consider the shifting operation which we have already introduced. This operation involves data of two different types, graphic (i.e., the structure to be shifted) and arithmetic (i.e., the vertical and horizontal distances through which the graphic structure is to be shifted). Consequently, we can consider the shift operation to be a "mixed-mode" operation. We can define such operations so that they are interpreted according to our wishes. In a manner similar to the way in which we mix logical and arithmetic operations in FORTRAN, we might define a shift operator (.*s*.) for moving graphic entities. We could then utilize this operator to create CROSSH from Figure 6.7 by using the following coding in our new language:

crossh = (line1 + line2) .s. (8.0,8.5)

To summarize, in order to implement a special-purpose language for processing graphic data, we will have to write, in addition to all the utility routines we have studied in Section 6.3, two types of data-manipulation routines. Initially, we will need routines to create the constants of our language, namely the primitive graphic items. Once we have written these basic routines, we have to develop several processing operations, similar to those introduced with the polynomial example, to operate on existing variables and to create new graphic variables from them.

6.5.3 FORTRAN Implementation

At this stage, we are in a position to consider how a graphic processing system can be implemented in FORTRAN. For our implementation, we will use the line-printer as the drawing medium. This necessitates imposing the following conditions on our graphic representations:

(i) We define the X-axis to be the horizontal axis (i.e., across the width of the output page) and the Y-axis to be the vertical axis (i.e., up and down the length of the output page).

(ii) We assume that a single line on the printer consists of 120 characters, with the result that the X coordinates of the points in our graphic structure must all lie within the range $1 \le X \le 120$.

(iii) Using the printer, we can specify the character to be printed at any particular point. As a result, we add a third data field to the nodes representing the points which comprise our structure. This new field will contain the single character which is to be printed at the point specified by the X and Y coordinates contained in the other two data fields of the node.

(iv) Since our Y-axis runs vertically along the length of our output page(s), each printed line corresponds to a specific coordinate (y) along this axis. As we proceed down the output page(s), each new print line is associated with a smaller Y coordinate than that of the previous line. Prior to printing line y, we must collect all the points in the list whose Y coordinate is y, so that they can all be printed before we continue to the next print line. Furthermore, if $y_1 > y_2$, then all the points with coordinate y_1 must be printed before those points with coordinate y_2. Consequently, in order to simplify the design of our print routine, we will sort the nodes of a list in descending order, according to their Y coordinates, prior to printing the graphic structure represented by the list. The print routine will scan down the list, collecting all points with the same Y coordinate (such values will be adjacent to one another after the sorting procedure) into a single 120-character buffer. As soon as a node with a different Y coordinate is encountered, the entire buffer is printed. Subsequently, if the new Y coordinate is more than one unit smaller than the previous one encountered, the appropriate number of blank lines will be printed to precede the line containing points with the new Y coordinate.

Now that we have established the ground rules for our graphic representations, we can consider the declarations of our list structures to be included in all of our graphic manipulation routines. These declarations are listed in Example 6.17. We allocate 1000 nodes, assuming this is enough to accommodate all the graphic structures we would like to create during a single run. Each node is comprised of four fields, represented by the vectors CHAR, X, Y, and LINK. The entries of vector CHAR will indicate the characters that we wish to print at the various points represented by nodes in the list. The coordinates of these points will be represented by vectors X and Y. The entries of LINK will serve as pointers to connect consecutive nodes in various lists. Finally, the special pointer AVAIL, as before, will always point at the topmost node in the availability list containing unused nodes.

```
C EXAMPLE 6.17 - DECLARATIONS OF LIST STRUCTURES
C                FOR GRAPHIC DATA
C
      CHARACTER CHAR(1000)
      REAL X(1000),Y(1000)
      INTEGER LINK(1000),AVAIL
      COMMON CHAR,X,Y,LINK,AVAIL
```

At the beginning of each job, we have to initialize the fields of the nodes in the list structure. After we have inserted some initial values in the data fields of the nodes, we link all the allocated nodes together into the availability list. The FORTRAN coding performing this initialization is given in Example 6.18.

```
C EXAMPLE 6.18 - INITIALIZING LISTS
C                FOR GRAPHIC DATA
C
      DO 10 I=1,1000
      CHAR(I) = 'b̸'
      X(I) = 0.
      Y(I) = 0.
   10 LINK(I) = I+1
C
C After linking all the nodes we place the
C terminal zero in the link of the last
C node and point AVAIL to the first node.
C
      LINK(1000) = 0
      AVAIL = 1
```

6.5.4 Creation of Primitive Graphic Items

Once again, we will need a CNS routine to construct new nodes for us. This function should accept as parameters the four items to be inserted in the new node, and return as its value a pointer to the newly created node. The FORTRAN coding for this function will be very similar to that used in Example 6.5, with appropriate changes in the parameter names to reflect the new interpretation associated with the nodes.

Function CNS can be used in several ways, to create new graphic items, or to add new points to existing structures. For example, suppose we wish to create a list of four points with coordinates (X1,Y1), (X2,Y2), (X3,Y3), and (X4,Y4) respectively. At each point, we want to print an asterisk (*). We can create a linked list to represent this structure, identified by pointer HEAD, by making five calls to function CNS (i.e., once for each of the four points plus once for the dummy header node).

The actual FORTRAN coding to create this list is given in Example 6.19.

```
C EXAMPLE 6.19 - CREATING A LIST TO
C                REPRESENT 4 POINTS
C
C Create the first node indicated by pointer
C HEAD.  Zero is copied into the link of this
C new node.  On return from the function,
C HEAD is updated to point at the new node.
C
      HEAD = CNS('*',X1,Y1,0)
C
C Create the second node whose link points at
C the first node.  Then HEAD is updated to
C point at the second node.
C
      HEAD = CNS('*',X2,Y2,HEAD)
C
C Similarly, create the other two nodes and
C link them to the first two.  HEAD points
C at the new node each time.
C
      HEAD = CNS('*',X3,Y3,HEAD)
      HEAD = CNS('*',X4,Y4,HEAD)
C
C Create a dummy node with a blank character.
C HEAD points to the header and we are done.
C
      HEAD = CNS('b̸',1.,1.,HEAD)
```

By utilizing the fact that CNS returns as its value a pointer to the newly created node, we can create the same list of four points with only a single statement:

```
 HEAD = CNS('b̸',1.,1.,CNS('*',X4,Y4,CNS('*',X3,Y3,
1  CNS('*',X2,Y2,CNS('*',X1,Y1,0)))))
```

This one statement, containing five nested calls to function CNS, is equivalent to the five statements in Example 6.19. The innermost reference to function CNS [i.e., the one for (X1,Y1)] is evaluated first, resulting in the creation of the first node which will eventually be at the end of the list. The pointer returned from this first call is then utilized in the second call as the link parameter for the second node. This process is repeated for each successive call, until the header node is created with a link to the rest of the nodes. Such a practice certainly leads to shorter programs. However, in general, we do not recommend it, since it makes the coding extremely unreadable and difficult to debug.

We have already considered the usage of function CNS to create new graphic structures. Suppose, however, that we wish only to insert a new point into the list between two already existing points. For example, the new point to be inserted might have coordinates (7.7,9.0), and we might wish to print the character 'Z' at this point. Furthermore, the node representing this new point is to be inserted into the list following node P. We can accomplish this insertion with the following single line of coding:

```
LINK(P) = CNS('Z',7.7,9.0,LINK(P))
```

This call to function CNS will result in the creation of a new node containing the specified data items and a pointer value, LINK(P). As a result, the new node will point to the node previously succeeding node P in the list, assuming, of course, that node P was not the last node in the list. If P was the last node, however, LINK(P) would have the value zero, thus identifying the recently created node as the new last node in the list. In any case, when control is returned from function CNS, the value of LINK(P) will be modified so that node P will subsequently point to the newly inserted member of the list.

Now that we have examined the procedure for creating new points within the framework of our graphic structures, we should consider a routine for removing nodes from a particular list and returning them to the availability list. We will use a modified version of subroutine DLT (introduced in Section 6.3) to erase points from our graphic data items. The coding for this new version of DLT will be slightly simpler than that presented earlier in Example 6.9, since we are now including a dummy header node at the top of each list. This eliminates the need for DLT to include separate coding to handle the special case where the node to be deleted is the top node. Otherwise, the two versions of subroutine DLT should be identical, except for minor changes in the declarations of the appropriate vectors.

We mentioned earlier that the constants of our graphic processing language would be primitive graphic items such as lines and circles. At this stage in the development of the various routines which will comprise such a language, we can consider the functions which will create for us these primitive data items. For example, function LINE

```
C EXAMPLE 6.20 - CREATING A LIST TO REPRESENT A LINE
C
      INTEGER FUNCTION LINE(CHARL,X1,Y1,X2,Y2)
C
C CHARL is the character to be placed in all the
C points of the line.  X1,Y1 and X2,Y2 are the
C coordinates of the two end points of the
C line to be created.
C
      CHARACTER CHAR(1000)
      REAL X(1000),Y(1000)
      INTEGER LINK(1000),AVAIL
      COMMON CHAR,X,Y,LINK,AVAIL
C
      CHARACTER CHARL
      INTEGER CNS
C
      LINE = 0
      XD = X2-X1
      YD = Y2-Y1
C
C Calculate the distance between the two end points.
C
      DS = 1./SQRT(XD**2+YD**2)
C
C Now we must create 1/DS nodes in the list line.
C The index SI will start at 0 and will be
C incremented by DS until it reaches 1.0.
C
      SI = 0
C
C Create a node for the list.  The X and Y
C coordinates are calculated as a function
C of SI using the linear properties of the line.
C
   10 LINE = CNS(CHARL,X1+SI*XD,Y1+SI*YD,LINE)
C
C Increment SI and loop back if SI.LE.1.
C
      SI = SI+DS
      IF(SI.LE.1.)GO TO 10
C
C Add the header and return.
C
      LINE = CNS(' ',1.,1.,LINE)
      RETURN
C
      END
```

will be used to create a linked list representing a straight line. The parameters passed to this routine specify the coordinates of the two points between which the line is to be drawn, as well as the character to be utilized for printing the line. Function LINE, as coded in Example 6.20, returns as its value a pointer to the header node of the list representing the line in question. Interested readers might consider ways in which function LINE could be written in a more efficient manner.

As an illustration of how we might use function LINE, consider the following line of code:

```
TOP = LINE('X',0.,0.,4.0,3.0)
```

This invocation of the LINE routine will result in the creation of a linked list to represent a straight line between the points (0.0,0.0) and (4.0,3.0). This list will be identified by the pointer TOP which will indicate the header node in the list. Furthermore, when it is printed, the line will consist of 'X' characters. In a similar manner, we can design other routines to generate graphic constants for us (e.g., circles). We leave the actual coding for such routines as exercises for interested readers. (See Section 6.6.)

6.5.5 Manipulation of Graphic Structures

Before concentrating our attention on how we might construct more complicated graphic entities, suppose we consider some of the "mixed-mode" operations through which we can modify existing graphic items by using some specified arithmetic values. Three such operations are listed below:

SHIFT: This routine creates a shifted version of a graphic structure.

ROTATE: This function rotates a graphic entity around a particular point through a specified angle.

SCALE: This routine creates a magnified (or contracted) version of a graph.

It should be well worthwhile for us to describe in detail one of these operations, namely the SHIFT operation. The remaining two routines can be left as exercises. Function SHIFT, accepting as a parameter a pointer to the header node of an existing list, creates a new version of the graphic structure shifted along the X and Y-axes by amounts specified as two additional parameters to the function. This routine returns as its value a pointer to the header node of the new shifted version. In our version of SHIFT, presented in Example 6.21, the original list remains unaltered.

Even though we are leaving the actual FORTRAN coding of function ROTATE to the reader, we will be making use of this routine in a later example. Consequently, we should formalize the description of this operation:

```
INTEGER FUNCTION ROTATE(TOP,CHARR,ALPHA,XC,YC)
```

```
C EXAMPLE 6.21 - SHIFT OPERATION
C
      INTEGER FUNCTION SHIFT(TOP,CHARS,SX,SY)
C
C TOP is the pointer to the header of the original
C list.  CHARS is the character to be used for
C the shifted version.  SX and SY are the quantities
C by which the graph is to be shifted.
C
      CHARACTER CHAR(1000)
      REAL X(1000),Y(1000)
      INTEGER LINK(1000),AVAIL
      COMMON CHAR,X,Y,LINK,AVAIL
C
      CHARACTER CHARS
      INTEGER TOP,P,CNS
C
C P is the wandering pointer which will scan
C down the list.  It is initialized to the
C first node following the header.
C
      P = LINK(TOP)
      SHIFT = 0
C
C Create a node of the new list.  The new
C coordinates are calculated by adding the
C shift values to the coordinates in
C the original list.
C
   10 SHIFT = CNS(CHARS,X(P)+SX,Y(P)+SY,SHIFT)
C
C Advance the pointer P along the links of the list.
C
      P = LINK(P)
C
C If the last node has not been reached, loop back.
C
      IF(P.GT.0)GO TO 10
C
C Create the header for the new list and return.
C
      SHIFT = CNS(' ',1.,1.,SHIFT)
      RETURN
C
      END
```

This routine creates a new linked list to represent a rotated version of the graph identified by pointer TOP. CHARR indicates the character to be printed at every point in the newly created structure. The new graph is merely an image of the old one, rotated about point (XC,YC) through an angle of ALPHA degrees. The function returns as its value a pointer to the header node of the newly created list.

```
C EXAMPLE 6.22 - MERGING TWO GRAPHIC STRUCTURES
C
      INTEGER FUNCTION MERGE(TOP1,TOP2)
C
C TOP1 and TOP2 are pointers to the headers of
C the two lists which we wish to concatenate.
C The function returns as its value a pointer
C to the header of the concatenated list.
C
      CHARACTER CHAR(1000)
      REAL X(1000),Y(1000)
      INTEGER LINK(1000),AVAIL
      COMMON CHAR,X,Y,LINK,AVAIL
C
      INTEGER TOP1,TOP2
C
C We alter the link of the last node of TOP1 to
C point to the first node of TOP2 following the
C header node.
C
      LINK(LAST(TOP1)) = LINK(TOP2)
C
C Return the header of TOP2 to available storage.
C
      LINK(TOP2) = AVAIL
      AVAIL = TOP2
C
C Return a pointer to the header of TOP1.  This
C has now become the header of the merged list.
C
      MERGE = TOP1
      RETURN
C
      END
```

Up to this point in our discussion of computer graphics, we have learned how to create and manipulate lists representing simple graphic items. Now we want to construct more involved graphs by merging several of the basic structures that we have already created. The actual merging operation (i.e., graphic addition) is a very straightforward one. This routine will concatenate for us two lists into one. In fact, it is no different from the utility function CHAIN, introduced in Example 6.8, except for the removal of the dummy header node in the second list and its subsequent return to the availability list. The FORTRAN coding for function MERGE is presented in Example 6.22.

Recall the example illustrated in Figure 6.7. We had two straight lines, one extending from (0.0,0.0) to (4.0,3.0), and the other running from (0.0,3.0) to (4.0,0.0). These two lines intersected at point (2.0,1.5). We wanted to print these two lines, in the form of a cross, centered at point (10.0,10.0). The FORTRAN coding to create a list representing this shifted cross, using functions LINE, MERGE and SHIFT, is presented in Example 6.23.

As a further illustration of constructing a more complicated graphic entity, suppose we want to draw a 3×3 square board for a tic-tac-toe game, with corners at the points (0.0,0.0), (0.0,24.0), (24.0,24.0), and (24.0,0.0) respectively. There are several approaches through which we could attack this problem. The most straightforward approach (although not the most sophisticated one)

```
C EXAMPLE 6.23 - CODING FOR STRUCTURE IN FIGURE 6.7
C                (CREATING A CROSS AND SHIFTING IT)
C
C Create the two lines.
C
      LINE1 = LINE('A',0.,0.,4.,3.)
      LINE2 = LINE('B',0.,3.,4.,0.)
C
C Join the two lines into a cross.
C LINE1 and LINE2 are lost.
C
      CROSS = MERGE(LINE1,LINE2)
C
C CROSSH will point at a new version of CROSS
C shifted to be centered at point (10.,10.).
C
      CROSSH = SHIFT(CROSS,'X',8.,8.5)
```

would involve invoking the LINE function eight times, once for each of the eight lines comprising the table. Then we would call upon the MERGE routine to chain the various lists together into one list. However, this would necessitate seven calls to function MERGE (why?).

```
C EXAMPLE 6.24 - CREATION OF A LIST TO
C                REPRESENT VERTICAL LINES
C                IN A TIC-TAC-TOE BOARD
C
      VLINE = LINE('*',0.,0.,0.,24.)
      VLINE = MERGE(VLINE,SHIFT(VLINE,'*',8.,0.))
C
C At this point VLINE contains two parallel
C vertical lines 8.0 units apart.  We will
C create two more vertical lines by another
C shift and merge
C
      VLINE = MERGE(VLINE,SHIFT(VLINE,'*',16.,0.))
```

As a second alternative, we might create one vertical line from (0.0,0.0) to (0.0,24.0), and then merge it with a shifted copy of itself which runs from (8.0,0.0) to (8.0,24.0). We can create a shifted copy of these two parallel lines by moving them sixteen units to the right. Then we merge these two pairs of parallel lines into one list. The FORTRAN coding for creating these four vertical lines is presented in Example 6.24. Upon completion of this merging operation, we can create a list to represent the four horizontal lines in an analogous manner. Then we can merge these two lists, each representing a set of four parallel lines, to create a list to represent the entire board.

Instead of using similar coding to that of Example 6.24 to create the four horizontal lines, we might generate a copy of the four vertical lines rotated through an angle of 90 degrees around the center of the table [i.e., point (12.0,12.0)]. Then we can merge these two lists (i.e., one for the horizontal and one for the vertical lines) into one long list. These latter two steps can be accomplished with the following single line of code:

```
TABLE = MERGE(VLINE,ROTATE(VLINE,'*',90,12.0,12.0))
```

Figure 6.8 illustrates the table created by any of these three approaches. As well, Exercise 19 at the end of this chapter discusses yet another approach for solving problems such as this one.

Figure 6.8

Tic-Tac-Toe Board

6.5.6 Graphics Output Routine

In any situation where we are dealing with graphic data, we will want to print out (i.e., draw) our graphic structure as soon as we have completed the creation of the necessary linked list(s) to represent it. Towards this end, we should develop two routines, one for sorting the nodes in the list according to their Y coordinates in preparation for printing, and the other to actually print the graphic entity represented by that list.

The sorting routine developed here is almost identical to that used for function SIMP in Example 6.14. The FORTRAN coding to implement this new version (SORT) is presented in Example 6.25. Both of these sorting routines employ the same version of a bubble sort. In fact, both programs utilize the same pointers, P, Q, R, LATEST, and LAST. However, subroutine SORT compares only the

Y coordinates of successive nodes to determine whether they should be interchanged in the list. To ensure proper printing of our graphic structure, the nodes of the list are sorted into descending (actually non-increasing) order, according to their Y coordinates. Our printout routine will take advantage of this ordering within the list to ensure that points with larger Y coordinates will be printed before those with smaller ones.

```
C EXAMPLE 6.25 - SORT ROUTINE (TO BE USED AS
C                PART OF A PRINT ROUTINE)
C
      SUBROUTINE SORT(TOP)
C
      CHARACTER CHAR(1000)
      REAL X(1000),Y(1000)
      INTEGER LINK(1000),AVAIL
      COMMON CHAR,X,Y,LINK,AVAIL
C
C TOP is a pointer to the header of the list
C to be sorted.  P, Q, and R are the 3
C pointers moving along the list.
C
      INTEGER TOP,P,Q,R
C
C Check for empty list.
C
      IF(TOP.LT.1)RETURN
C
C See function SIMP (Example 6.14) for the
C roles of LAST and LATEST.
C
      LATEST = 0
   10 LAST = LATEST
C
C P points to the first of 3 nodes under examination.
C
      P = TOP
C
C At the start of each sorting pass, initialize the
C 3 pointers to the top three nodes.  Check each time
C whether the end pointer has reached the top.
```

```
      Q = LINK(P)
      IF(Q.EQ.LAST)GO TO 90
      R = LINK(Q)
      IF(R.EQ.LAST)GO TO 90
C
C If the nodes Q and R are in order, proceed
C to compare the next nodes.
C
   20 IF(Y(Q).GE.Y(R))GO TO 30
C
C The following statements perform the interchange.
C We only modify the links to reflect the change.
C There is no data movement.  (See Figure 6.5.)
C Also reset the value of LATEST here.
C
      LATEST = Q
      LINK(P) = R
      LINK(Q) = LINK(R)
      LINK(R) = Q
C
C Advance the pointers along the links of the list.
C
   30 P = LINK(P)
      Q = LINK(P)
      R = LINK(Q)
C
C If the last pointer R has not yet reached the end
C pointer, loop back to resume the sorting pass.
C
      IF(R.NE.LAST)GO TO 20
C
C Check to see if another pass is necessary.
C Return to perform another pass if unordered
C nodes have been found.
C
   90 IF(LATEST.NE.LAST)GO TO 10
      RETURN
C
      END
```

Note: How does the inclusion of a dummy header node simplify the design of subroutine SORT?

Subroutine PRINT is the last routine we have to discuss in our collection of graphic processing operations. As indicated in Example 6.26, this routine does not assume that the given list has been sorted, and, as a result, calls upon subroutine SORT to prepare the list for printout. It accepts five parameters, the last four of which are luxury features and not essential to the operation of the actual printing function. The first parameter is a pointer (TOP) to the header node of the list representing the graphic structure to be drawn. The other four parameters are scale and displacement factors which affect the size and positioning of the graph on the output page. Through the use of these values, we can scale our standard unit of distance (either to magnify or shrink it), or shift a graph to a new position, just for one printing without actually altering the list representing that structure.

To illustrate the use of the scale and displacement factors, suppose we have evaluated a function for a series of X values spaced at intervals of 0.1. If we do not magnify the scale for our graph of these function values, every ten points will be printed along a single vertical line, since the smallest unit of distance distinguished by the printer is 1.0. (Subroutine PRINT rounds all coordinates to an integer value prior to printing.) Specifying SCAX = 10.0 as a parameter to the PRINT routine will have the effect of scaling each printer unit as 0.1. Furthermore, it is quite possible that one or more of the (scaled) X values will lie beyond the interval 1≤X≤120, in which case the corresponding function values (represented by points) will not be printed. However, by specifying an appropriate value for DISPX, we should be able to move the entire graph into the range of the printed page.

```
C EXAMPLE 6.26 - PRINT ROUTINE FOR DRAWING
C                GRAPHIC STRUCTURES
C
      SUBROUTINE PRINT(TOP,SCAX,DISPX,SCAY,DISPY)
C
C A subroutine to print out a set of points
C as a picture on the printer:  TOP points to
C the list of points;  SCAX and SCAY are scale
C factors;  DISPX and DISPY are constant
C displacements along the X and Y-axes.
C
      CHARACTER CHAR(1000)
      REAL X(1000),Y(1000)
      INTEGER LINK(1000),AVAIL
      COMMON CHAR,X,Y,LINK,AVAIL
C
C BUF is a vector of single characters used to
C store a single line before it is printed.
C BUFFER is a character string of length 120
C overlayed on BUF so that we can handle the
C buffer as a single character string as well
C as handle the individual characters in it.
C
      CHARACTER BUF(120),BUFFER*120
      EQUIVALENCE (BUF,BUFFER)
      INTEGER P,XC,YC,NYC,TOP
C
C Sort the points into proper order.
C
      CALL SORT(TOP)
C
C Initialize P to the node following the header.
C
      P = LINK(TOP)
C
C YC is the row number (Y coordinate) currently
C being printed.  We modify the Y found in the
```

```
C first node by the scale and displacement to
C derive the first row number to be printed.
C
C Since the modified value of Y is rounded to
C an integer by assigning it to the integer
C variable YC, several different Y's can result
C in the same YC.
C
      YC = Y(P)*SCAY+DISPY+0.5
C
C NYC will contain the row number of the next
C row to be printed.  We initialize it to the
C value of the first YC.
C
      NYC = YC
C
C Clear the buffer to contain 120 blanks.
C
   10 BUFFER = 'b̸'
C
C If we find that the next line to be printed
C is different from the current line, we
C transfer to 30 where we print the blank line.
C
      IF(YC.NE.NYC)GO TO 30
C
C XC is the coordinate of X in the buffer
C and is calculated like YC.
C
   12 XC = X(P)*SCAX+DISPX+0.5
C
C Only if the calculated X coordinate is
C within the range of our line buffer do we copy
C the character into its place in the buffer.
C
      IF(XC.GT.0.AND.XC.LE.120)BUF(XC) = CHAR(P)
C
C Advance the pointer.
C
   15 P = LINK(P)
C
C If there are no more nodes in the list, go to 30
C to print the last line and terminate the
C subroutine call.
C
      IF(P.LT.1)GO TO 30
C
C Determine the next Y coordinate to be printed.
```

```
      NYC = Y(P)*SCAY+DISPY+0.5
C
C Compare the old Y coordinate with the new
C one and take action accordingly.
C If they are equal, we continue to insert
C characters into the buffer as we still wish
C to print on the same line (12).  If the old
C is less than the new one, a sorting error
C has occurred (20).  If the old Y is greater than
C the new Y, we know that there is nothing to add
C to the current line.  Go to 30 to print it out.
C
      IF(YC-NYC)20,12,30
C
C Print the message.  Then go to 15 to
C proceed with the next node.
C
   20 PRINT 98,P,Y(P),NYC,'-',YC
   98 FORMAT(' SEQUENCE ERROR',I6,F8.3,I6,A1,I6)
      GO TO 15
C
C Print the buffer here.
C
   30 PRINT 99,BUFFER
   99 FORMAT(' ',A120)
C
C Decrement the current Y coordinate.  If the
C last node has not been reached yet, we will
C continue (10) to clear the buffer.  We
C will print blank lines until YC becomes
C equal to NYC.
C
      YC = YC-1
C
C Halt when the last node is reached.
C
      IF(P.GT.0)GO TO 10
      RETURN
C
      END
```

6.6 EXERCISES

Write the FORTRAN routines described in the following exercises.

1. REAL FUNCTION EVAL(POLY,X,Y,Z)

   The first parameter to this routine is a pointer identifying a particular polynomial in three variables. The remaining three parameters are all floating-point values for which the polynomial is to be evaluated. The numerical result of this evaluation is to be returned as the value of the function.

2. INTEGER FUNCTION ADD(POLY1,POLY2)

   This function returns as its value a pointer to a newly created list which represents, in canonical form, the sum polynomial obtained by adding the two polynomials, POLY1 and POLY2, using a merge sort. This version of ADD does <u>not</u> destroy the lists representing POLY1 and POLY2.

3. INTEGER FUNCTION MULT(POLY1,POLY2)

   This routine is similar to function ADD, except that the polynomial generated is the <u>product</u> of POLY1 and POLY2.

4. INTEGER FUNCTION SCALE(POLY,D)

This routine generates a new polynomial which is equal to the polynomial POLY multiplied by the floating-point constant D. The function returns as its value a pointer to the newly created list representing this polynomial.

5. INTEGER FUNCTION SUB(POLY1,POLY2)

This routine generates the difference polynomial obtained by subtracting POLY2 from POLY1. The function returns as its value a pointer to the list representing this newly created polynomial. Write two versions of this routine:

(a) using routines SCALE and ADD.

(b) using only function SIMP (i.e., multiplying all coefficients in POLY2 by -1 inside routine SUB without using function SCALE).

6. INTEGER FUNCTION DERV(POLY,WHICH)

The first parameter to this routine is a polynomial (POLY) in three variables, say X, Y, and Z. The second parameter, WHICH, is an integer whose value is assumed to lie between 1 and 3 inclusive. This routine creates a new list to represent the derivative polynomial of POLY with respect to one of X, Y, or Z, depending upon whether WHICH has the value 1, 2, or 3 respectively. The function returns as its value a pointer to this new polynomial.

7. Use function DERV from Exercise 6 and some sample polynomials to illustrate the validity of the relationship

$$\frac{\partial(P \cdot Q)}{\partial x} = P \cdot \frac{\partial Q}{\partial x} + Q \cdot \frac{\partial P}{\partial x}$$

8. INTEGER FUNCTION INT(POLY,WHICH)

This routine creates a new list to represent the polynomial obtained from evaluating the integral

$$\int_0^u (\text{POLY})\,\partial u$$

where POLY is a polynomial in three variables, X, Y, and Z, and "u" represents <u>one</u> of X, Y, or Z, depending upon whether the value of the INTEGER parameter WHICH is 1, 2, or 3 respectively. The function returns as its value a pointer to this newly created polynomial.

9. INTEGER FUNCTION DIV(POLY1,POLY2,REM)

This routine divides the polynomial POLY1 by the polynomial POLY2. The quotient polynomial generated by this division is to be identified by the pointer DIV. Similarly, the remainder polynomial should be identified by the pointer REM. Restrict your solution to polynomials of a single variable.

10. Rewrite the various utility routines, as well as routines READ, PRINT, MULT, and SIMP, to manipulate polynomials in two variables instead of three. Then write the following function:

```
INTEGER FUNCTION SUBS(POLY,POLYX,POLYY)
```

The parameters POLY, POLYX, and POLYY represent three separate polynomials. This function returns as its value a pointer to a newly created polynomial generated by this routine. This new polynomial is obtained by formally substituting the polynomial POLYX for the X variable in POLY and POLYY for the Y variable in POLY.

e.g., $POLY(X,Y) = 3X^2+7Y^2$

$POLYX(A,B) = A+B$

$POLYY(A,B) = A-B$

$$\therefore POLY(A,B) = 3(A+B)^2+7(A-B)^2$$
$$= 3(A^2+2AB+B^2)+7(A^2-2AB+B^2)$$
$$= 10A^2-8AB+10B^2$$

Function SUBS will perform this substitution, and return as its value a pointer to a newly created list representing the polynomial $10A^2-8AB+10B^2$.

Note: You *may* wish to write the following function for use with routine SUBS.

INTEGER FUNCTION PWR(P,K)

This routine returns as its value a pointer to a polynomial formed by raising polynomial P to the (integral) power K. If you do decide to code this function, minimize the utilization of nodes by deleting unused lists as soon as they are no longer needed in the subsequent computation.

11. Find directly the power series for SIN and COS by integrating their differential equations

$$\frac{d \sin x}{dx} = \cos x, \quad \frac{d \cos x}{dx} = - \sin x \; .$$

First, we integrate to get

$$\sin x = \int_0^x \cos x \, dx$$

$$\cos x = 1 - \int_0^x \sin x \, dx.$$

The initial conditions are $\sin 0 = 0$
$\cos 0 = 1.$

Start with the first (very inaccurate) approximation

$$\sin x \approx 0.$$

Integrate:

$$\cos x \approx 1 - \int_0^x \sin x \, dx \approx 1 - 0 = 1.$$

Integrate:

$$\sin x \approx \int_0^x \cos x \, dx \approx \int_0^x 1 \, dx = x$$

$$\cos x = 1 - \int_0^x \sin x \, dx \approx 1 - \int_0^x x \, dx = 1 - \frac{x^2}{2}$$

$$\sin x = \int_0^x \cos x \, dx \approx \int_0^x \left(1 - \frac{x^2}{2}\right) dx = x - \frac{x^3}{6}$$

etc.

Write a FORTRAN program that will fill the power series for sine and cosine in this way.

Do the same to find a power series solution to some other differential equation.

12. INTEGER FUNCTION DUP(TOP)

In Example 6.10, we provided coding to produce a duplicate copy of the linked list identified by TOP. However, the nodes in this duplicated list were in reverse order compared to those in the original list. Write a new version of this function to preserve the original order of the nodes in the duplicated list.

13. INTEGER FUNCTION NTH(TOP,N)

This function returns as its value a pointer to the Nth node in the list TOP. If there are fewer than N nodes in the specified list, the value returned to the user is the null pointer.

14. INTEGER FUNCTION CHANGE(TOP)

This routine accepts as a parameter a linked list, TOP, and reverses the order of the nodes in this list (i.e., it reverses the links without forming a new list). The function returns as its value a pointer to the new top-most node in the revised version of the list (i.e., the node previously at the end of the list).

15. INTEGER FUNCTION ROTATE(TOP,CHARR,ALPHA,XC,YC)

This graphic processing routine creates a new linked list to represent a rotated version of the graph identified by TOP. CHARR indicates the character to be printed at each point in the newly created structure. The new graph is merely an image of the old one, rotated about the point (XC,YC) through an angle of ALPHA degrees. The function returns as its value a pointer to the newly created list.

16. INTEGER FUNCTION CIRCLE(CHARC,XC,YC,R)

This routine creates a list representing a circle with radius R and centre (XC,YC). The character CHARC will be used to draw the circle. The function returns as its value a pointer to the header node of the newly created list.

Hint: The following relationships can be used to find the coordinates of a point (X,Y) on a circle:

X = XC + R*COS(A)

Y = YC + R*SIN(A).

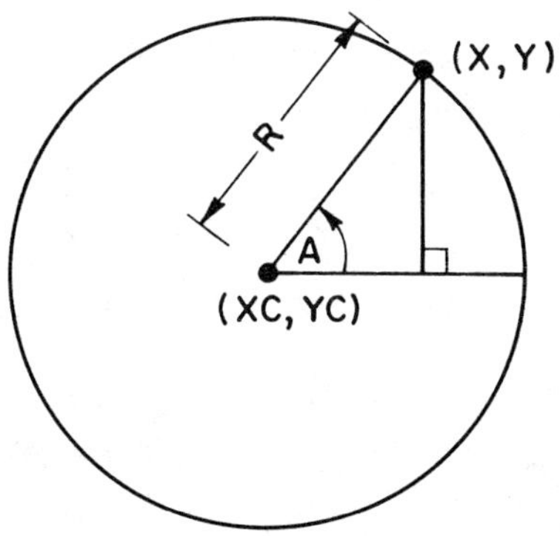

17. INTEGER FUNCTION SCALE(TOP,CHARS,XC,YC,XS,YS)

This routine creates a magnified or contracted version of a graph (TOP) relative to the fixed point (XC,YC). For each point, (X,Y), on the original graph, the corresponding point on the new graph is determined by scaling the horizontal and vertical distances of the point (X,Y) from the point (XC,YC) by factors of XS and YS respectively. Notice that XS and YS need not be equal. Such will be the case if you wish to distort the shape of the graph. The character CHARS is to be printed at each point on the new graph. The value returned to the user by this function is a pointer to the newly created graph. The list representing the original graph remains unaltered.

18. Using only one call to function CIRCLE of Exercise 16, write a program which calls upon function SCALE of Exercise 17 to draw a series of four concentric circles. These circles should have radii 5, 15, 25, and 35 units respectively, all centered at point (10,10).

19. INTEGER FUNCTION DRAW(TOP)

    TOP is a pointer to a list of points, $P_1, P_2, P_3, \ldots, P_n$. DRAW will point to a newly created list which connects these n points in a continuous zigzag line. The line consists of the individual segments P_1P_2, $P_2P_3, \ldots,$ $P_{n-1}P_n$ respectively. To actually draw the line segment P_iP_{i+1}, this routine uses the character to be printed at point P_i.

Thus, if TOP represents

```
P1*          =P3



      (P2
```

then the list created by function DRAW will represent

```
         =
*       (
 *     (
  *   (
   * (
    (
```

20. Use some or all of our graphic processing functions to draw your initials. DRAW should prove to be especially useful

    <u>Thought</u>: How could function DRAW be used to draw disconnected figures using only <u>one</u> call to this routine?

21. Draw a significant figure wit h the graphics routines we have developed up to this point. Some suggestions are listed below, although you should feel free to select any drawing that interests you.

    a pentagram
    the Olympic symbol
    a bicycle
    a cartoon figure

22. What major or minor changes could be made in the entire set of graphics routines to increase efficiency? What are the bottlenecks in the system which consume so much time, and how can they be eliminated?

23. Experiment with computer-generated art. What can be done if a picture is generated partly by careful design and partly by random factors? Try a random number generator to provide random arguments for circle-drawing routines, etc.. You might write routines that draw various objects and use them in the picture. What can you accomplish? No restrictions!

CHAPTER SEVEN
MULTI-LINKED STRUCTURES

7.1 MULTI-LINKED LISTS

Up to this point in our discussion of linked lists, we have used list structures in which only one field in each node was a pointer. However, our original definition of a list structure in terms of nodes and fields in no way imposes such a restriction. In fact, for certain operations, there are definite advantages to be gained by using more than one pointer in a node. For example, whenever we use only a single link, the nodes fall into a natural one-after-the-other order, thus confining us to processing our linked lists only in a sequential fashion. In such a structure, each node has a unique successor which is designated by its pointer value. In those instances where this is an undesirable restriction, we can employ more than one link in each node.

Furthermore, there are numerous applications in which we are mainly interested in the *STRUCTURAL INFORMATION* imbedded in the data structures rather than in the values stored in them. The amount of structural information that can be represented by singly linked nodes is very limited. However, before we discuss such applications further, we should investigate various methods by which the processing of linear lists can be improved through the utilization of multiple links.

7.1.1 Back-Linked Lists

The first modification considered is the inclusion of a second link in each node to point at its predecessor. The first link is retained to point at the successor of the node. Such a list is illustrated in Figure 7.1. The addition of this second pointer enables us to process the list in two directions, progressing through the nodes in either a forward or a backward sequence. The list remains a linear list, and it does not represent any more structural information than its equivalent single-linked list. However, several operations can be performed much more efficiently through the use of the additional back link. More specifically, all those operations in which we need to know the predecessor of a certain node benefit from the retention of this extra link. If we use only a single link, the identification of the predecessor of a particular node requires a linear search, beginning at the top node and progressing down through the list until a node is encountered whose link points at the designated node. If the list is a long one, this can be a very time-consuming operation. The inclusion of a back link eliminates this linear search, in exchange for the price of additional storage in each node for the second link.

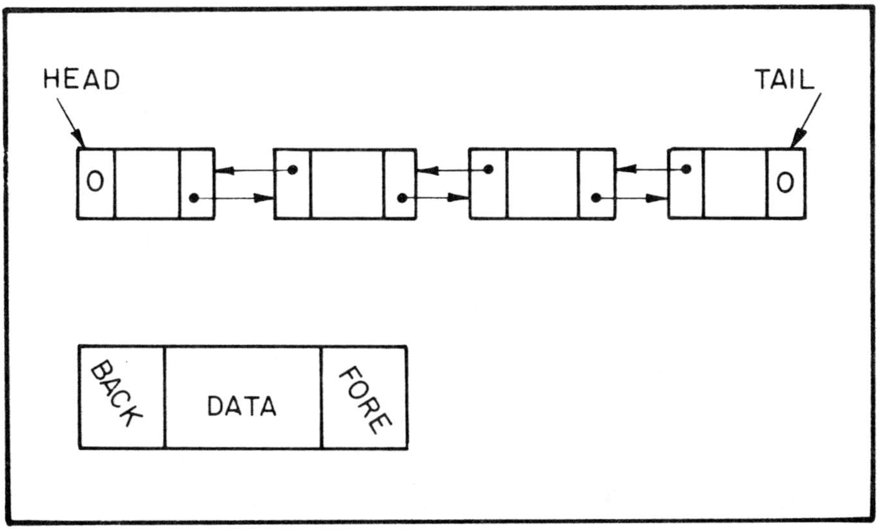

Figure 7.1

Back-Linked List

The deletion operation, for example, as performed by the DLT function on single-linked linear lists (Example 6.9), spends most of its time searching for the predecessor of the node to be deleted. The deletion operation with back-linked lists is much more efficient, since such a search is no longer necessary. Furthermore, the routine does not require a pointer to the top node of the list from which the node is to be deleted. If the two pointer fields in the back-linked list are designated FORE and BACK respectively, and we want to delete node P, the linkage around node P can be quite simply achieved by using the following coding:

```
FORE(BACK(P)) = FORE(P)
BACK(FORE(P)) = BACK(P)
```

This is another case of storage-versus-time trade-off. Before deciding to utilize a back-linked list structure to represent the data, one has to justify the use of the additional storage for the back links. In general, we suggest that back-linked lists should not be used for the representation of linearly linked lists under any of the following conditions:

(i) Storage is at a premium compared to machine time.

(ii) The lists are expected to be relatively short, thus allowing a fast search for predecessors.

(iii) Operations that require references to predecessors of nodes are very infrequent. For example, suppose we have maintained a personnel file in the form of a linearly linked list, and that the only operation which benefits from quick access to predecessors is the delete operation. Furthermore, we know that the company for which we have designed the file dismisses very few employees each year. In such a situation, there would be no justification for the use of back-linked lists.

Finally, we should note that there is an additional cost involved in retaining back links. Whenever we add a node to a list, we have to initialize its own BACK and FORE links, as well as the FORE link of its predecessor and the BACK link of its successor. This amounts to two additional operations when compared to single-linked lists.

However, the cost of such operations can be considered negligible relative to the cost of the additional storage.

7.1.2 Multiple Linear Lists With The Same Set of Nodes

If we have a set of nodes which have to be processed in several different orders, we would like to be able to maintain these nodes as elements in various distinct linearly linked lists. By having more than one pointer available, we can evidently link the nodes into several lists, with each link in a node connecting it to its successor in a different list.

As an illustration, suppose we consider a class of students for which we would like to have three different lists, one classified according to student surnames sorted in alphabetical order, a second arranged in descending order according to final marks, and a third listing the students in ascending order of age. Each student in the class can be represented by a single node which contains six fields, one for each of his name, final mark, and age, and three pointers, each serving as a link for a different order. We maintain three top pointers; one to the node representing the student whose name appears first in the alphabet, H1; a second to the node representing the student with the highest mark, H2; and a third identifying the node associated with the youngest student, H3. To proceed through the list in alphabetical sequence, we begin with the node designated by H1, and follow the pointers in LINK1 until we eventually reach the node containing the name which appears last in the alphabet (i.e., the node in which LINK1 has the null value). Similarly, for traversing the list in descending order of marks or ascending order of age, we begin with node H2 or H3, and follow LINK2 or LINK3 respectively.

Figure 7.2 illustrates a class list of seven students. Despite its complicated appearance, this structure is simply a composite of three linearly linked lists, each of which can be manipulated almost independently. Only when an addition or a deletion of a node is performed do we have to consider all three links and their values in order to maintain the proper sequences within the three different lists. Deletion of a node, for example, would require three searches for three different predecessors so that we could "heal" the wounds inflicted upon the lists by the deletion.

In our example of a class list, all of the nodes were entries in all three lists. However, this example illustrates just one of many ways in which several linearly linked lists can be constructed from the same set of nodes. Another application for additional links might involve subdividing one list into several sublists. Our rent-a-car example of Section 6.1 could be cited as an application of such lists. In that example, we had three lists: rented cars, available cars, and cars being serviced, all using the same link (since a

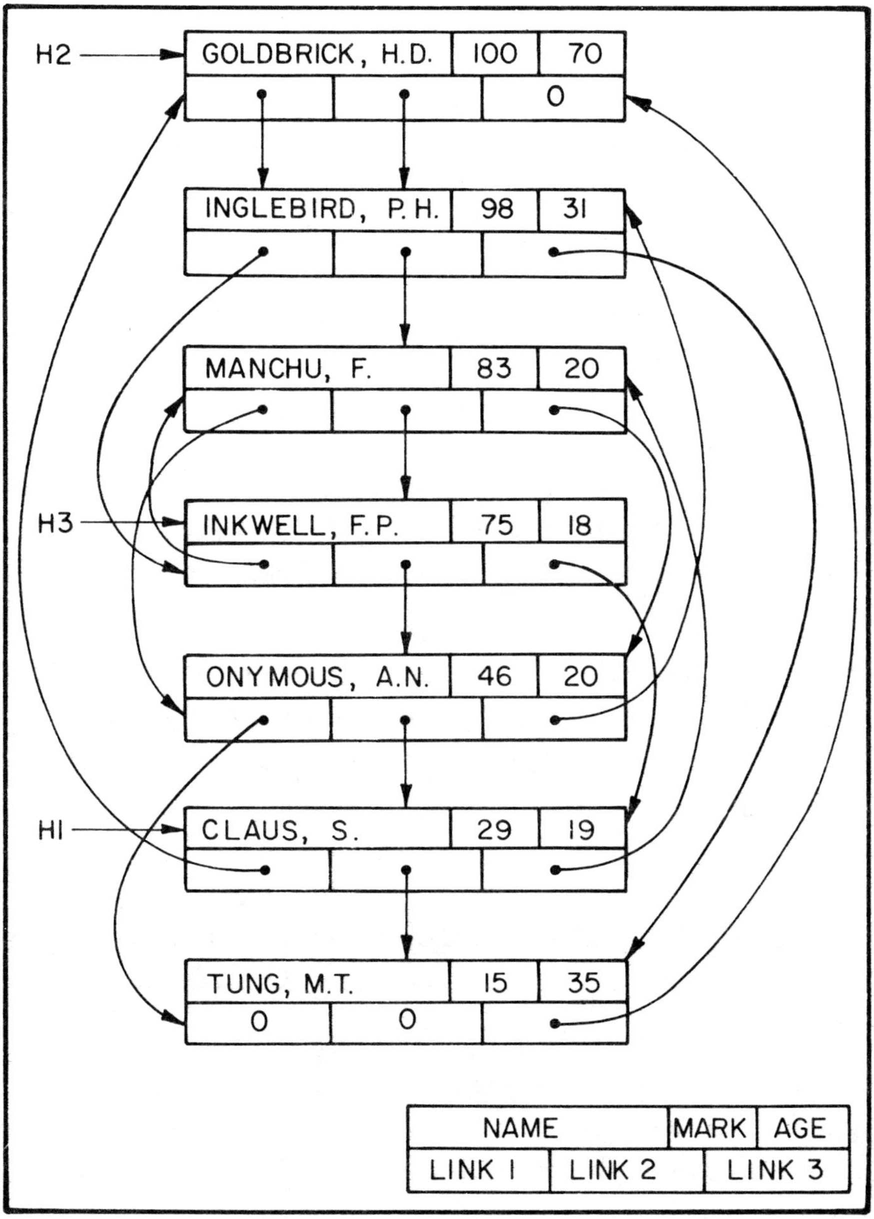

Figure 7.2

Class Sublists

car could be in only one of those lists at any given time). However, if the company were to grow and acquire many rental outlets, we might be required to know such information as the number of cars scheduled to be returned to a particular parking lot on a specified day. Consequently, we would like to subdivide the list of cars currently rented into various sublists according to the station to which they are expected to be returned. As illustrated in Figure 7.3, this can be achieved by including an additional link in each node, LINK2, and retaining a set of top pointers, one for each station. The other link continues to serve its original purpose of connecting the nodes in the rented list.

In a similar manner, we could use the same additional link to subdivide the list of available cars according to the parking lot in which they are located, and the list of cars being serviced according to the service station repairing them. Once again, the investment in an additional set of links is justified only if operations requiring this additional information are frequent and cannot tolerate the time delay involved in linear searches.

Sublists do not have to consist exclusively of nodes from one specific list. For example, suppose our rent-a-car company has several branches, each owning its own cars. The manager of each branch will want to be able to determine the status and location of his cars at any given time. This problem can be overcome by retaining a third set of

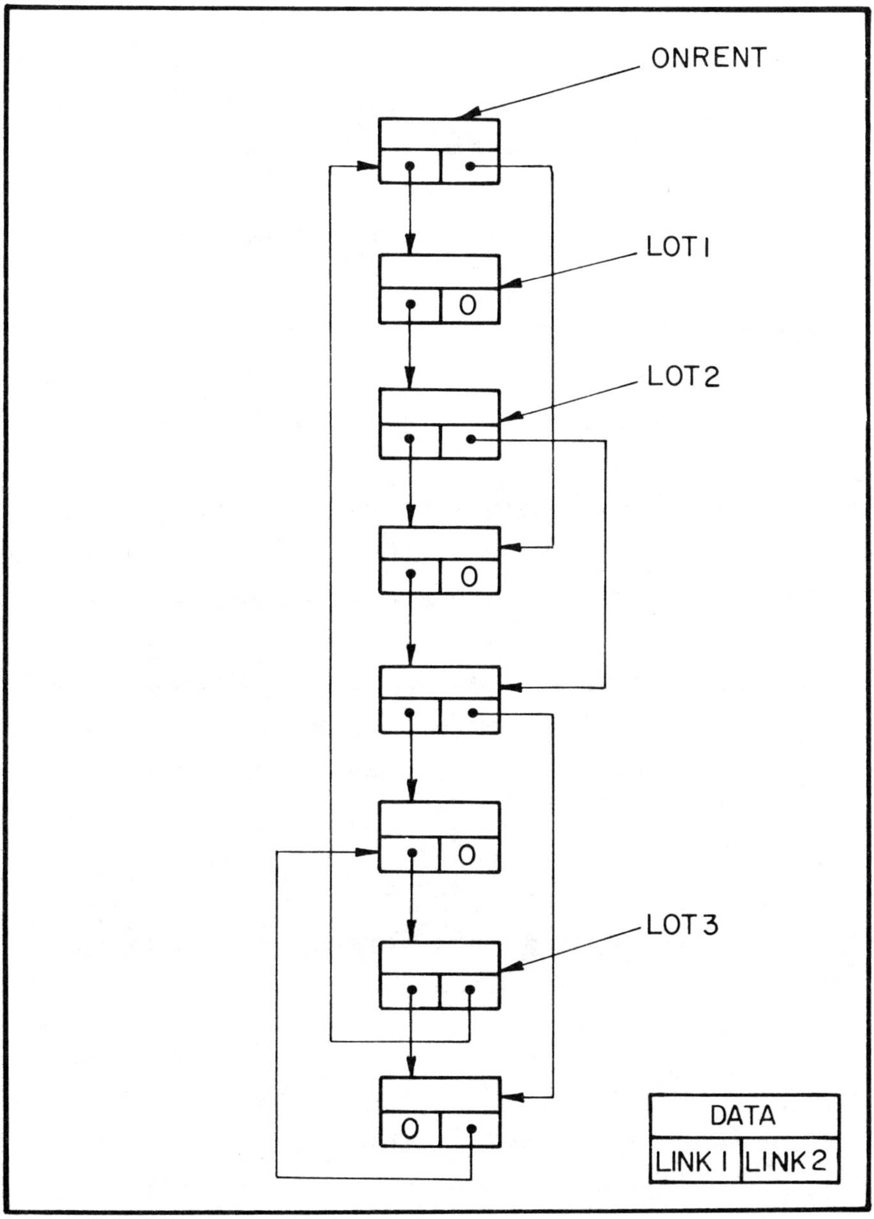

Figure 7.3

Rent-a-Car Sublists

pointers to link the cars belonging to a specific branch as another distinct linked list. In the sample structure presented in Figure 7.4, BRANCH1, BRANCH2, and BRANCH3 are the top pointers for these new lists. (To avoid unnecessary complexity, we have omitted LINK2 in the diagram, since we are primarily concerned at this point with the sublists linked by LINK3.)

Although multi-linked lists like the ones we have described can be very useful, we must avoid the temptation to use so many links that the resulting structures become too cumbersome to maintain. Extra links can cost more storage and time than they save. For example, suppose that our rent-a-car company changes its mode of operation so that, instead of renting cars on a short-term basis, it leases cars for extended periods of time, say at least a year. Transactions now become much less frequent, with the result that the extra trouble and cost of maintaining links are no longer justified. The cost of moving and reordering the lists can now be easily afforded, since the necessity for such actions occurs so rarely.

7.1.3 Circular Lists

A further improvement in linearly linked lists can be achieved by "closing" them in ring-like structures. This is accomplished by replacing the null pointer in the last node of a list with a pointer to the topmost node of that list. In its simplest form, a circular list does not need any additional links. Figure 7.5 illustrates single-

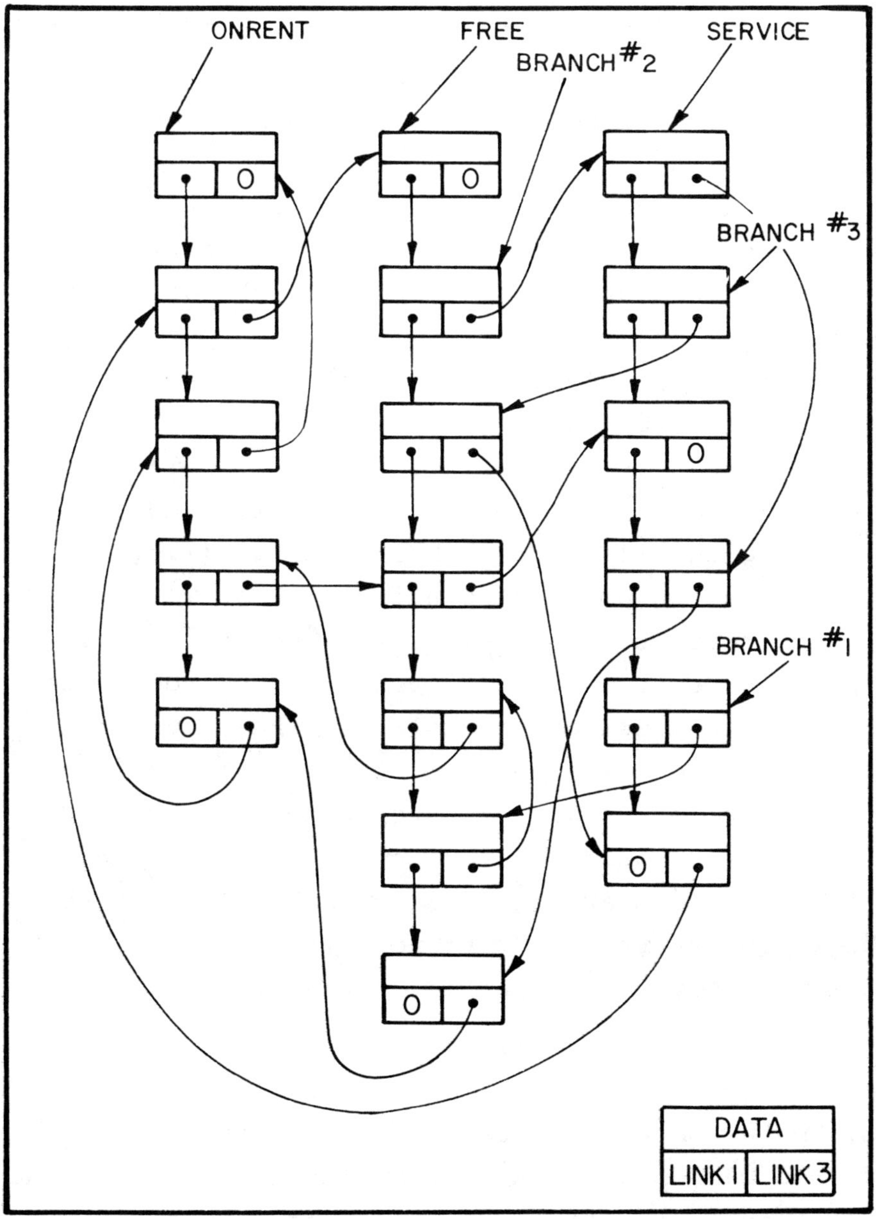

Figure 7.4

Rent-a-Car Sublists

linked and back-linked lists in circular form.

The advantages of a circular list stem from the fact that each node is accessible from any other node in the list. This is definitely not the case with our standard linearly linked lists. With the latter type of list, we can arrive at a particular node only by beginning our search from the topmost node in the list, thus making it necessary to provide a top pointer to all procedures which are expected to operate on arbitrary nodes in the list. The deletion operation on a single-linked circular list, for example, can be performed on any given node without knowing the list to which it belongs (i.e., without having a top pointer identifying the list from which the node is to be deleted). The search for its predecessor can be initiated from the node itself. However, such a search will always take longer than one originating with the topmost node. The average search which begins with the top node will be over (N+1)/2 nodes, where N is the number of nodes in the list. By comparison, in a circular list where we begin the search from the node itself, the search will always cover all N nodes of the list.

For back-linked lists, the circular structure offers a fast way of finding the last node in the list. As a comparison, recall the linear search performed by function LAST (Example 6.7) to determine the last node of a single-linked list. In a circular list, the back link of the top node points directly at the last node. This makes chaining operations much more efficient.

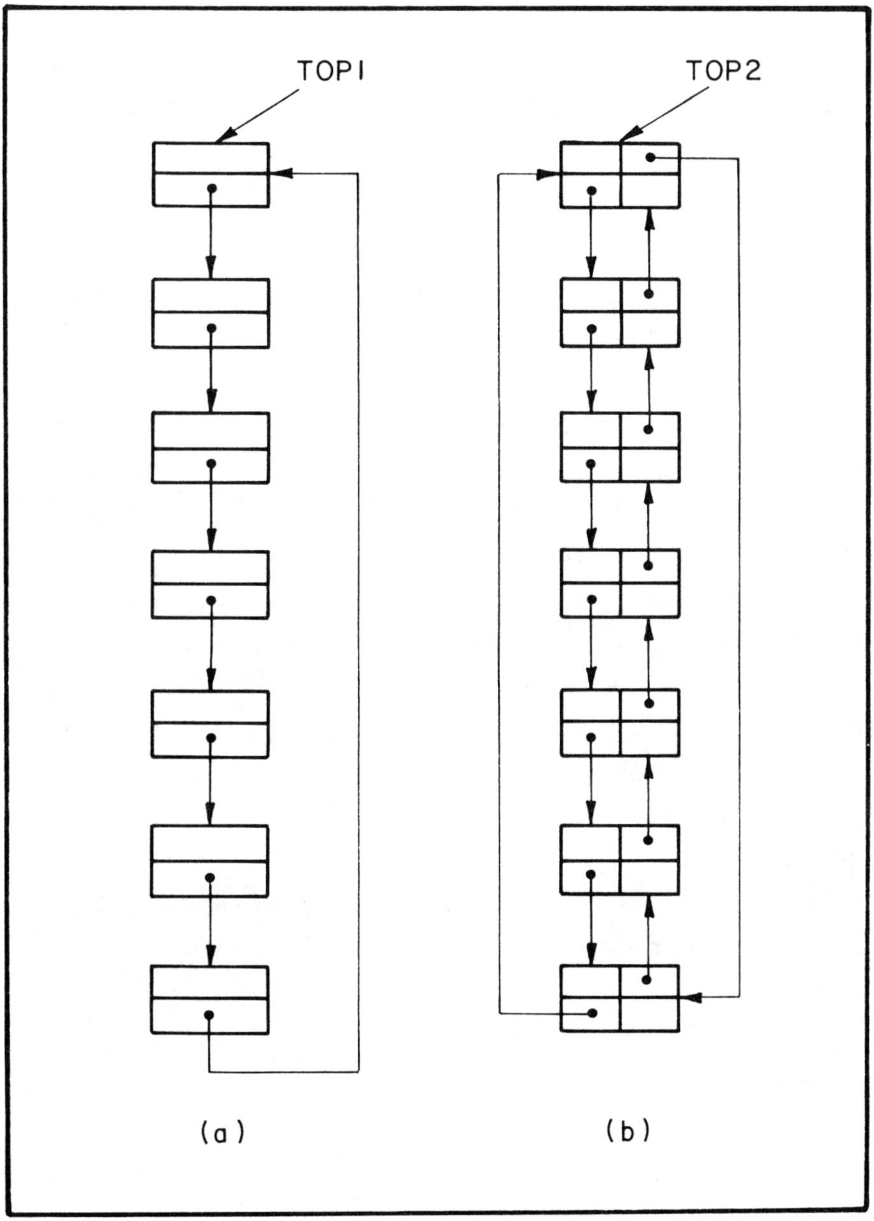

Figure 7.5

<u>Circular Lists</u>

The only disadvantage of circular lists lies in the slight complication that they impose on the coding of their operations. It is very easy to have a small inaccuracy in the coding which will result in a disastrous indefinite looping through a circular list.

One example of a circular multi-linked structure is the representation of sparse matrices (i.e., large matrices having only a few non-zero components). For matrices of this type, it is advantageous to employ linked list techniques in order to conserve storage. As an illustration, if we had a 100×100 matrix in which only 200 components were non-zero, it would be most unwise, and most of the time impossible, to dedicate 10,000 words for its representation. However, we would have to record information about the row and column positions, as well as the values, of all the non-zero components. Figure 7.6 illustrates a possible representation of sparse matrices using a two-way composite of circular lists. The particular matrix represented by this structure is as follows:

0	13	0	27	0	0
0	0	0	0	8	31
0	0	0	2	0	0
0	0	0	0	0	0
15	73	0	0	0	0
0	0	0	0	32	0
0	14	0	0	0	0
0	0	0	0	47	0

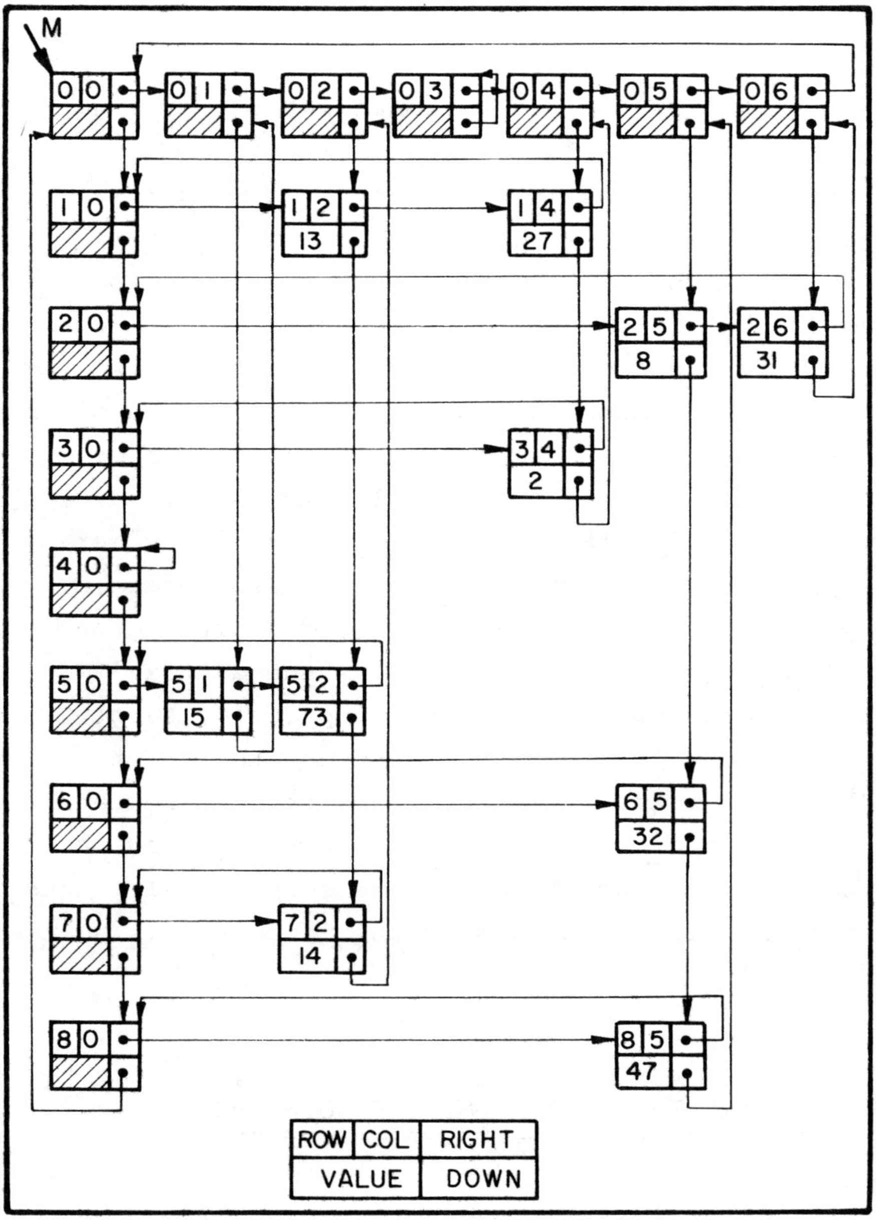

Figure 7.6

Circular List Representation of a Sparse Matrix

Each node in the structure presented in Figure 7.6 has two links, RIGHT and DOWN. The first points at the next non-zero component to its right in the same row, while the second points to the next non-zero entry directly below in the same column. The other three fields in each node are the row and column indicators (ROW and COL) and the numerical value (VALUE) of the entry represented by the node. To simplify the coding of various operations, we have included a dummy row (row 0) and a dummy column (column 0) as headers for each row and column of the matrix. Moreover, an additional dummy node, (0,0) is utilized as a header to the matrix, and it serves a very similar purpose to that of the top node in linear lists. Finally, a pointer, M, pointing at this dummy header node, identifies the matrix. If we had several such matrices in a program, each would be identified by a separate pointer to its (0,0) header node. The last nodes in each row and column have their RIGHT or DOWN links pointing back at the row or column header nodes respectively, thus closing the rings and forming the circular lists.

7.2 CODING TRICKS THAT MISUSE POINTERS

In this section, we will be discussing some special techniques for representing pointers that may, for some applications, increase the efficiency of programs. Until now, we have considered pointers as being representations of memory locations where the fields of another node can be found. While this same notation will be retained with these special techniques, the new representations will be more complicated.

7.2.1 Back Links With a Single Link

In our earlier discussions of back-linked lists, each node required two pointers. We are already aware that the additional memory consumed by the extra pointer is the major drawback of back links. Consequently, any technique for back-linking that requires only a single pointer field in a node will be most welcome. However, we pay for the storage saved by increasing the computation time for the evaluation of each link.

For each node in the list, instead of storing both the forward and backward pointers, we store the sum of the two pointers (i.e., LINK(I) contains the sum of the FORE and BACK links of node I). Then, whenever we proceed through the list, we utilize two pointers for the loop variable instead of one. In addition to CUR, a pointer to the node currently under consideration, we also retain a second pointer, PREV, to identify the previous node in the list. If we are processing the list from the top node downward, PREV is always the predecessor of CUR. However, when we are processing the list backwards (from the bottom node upwards), PREV is the successor of CUR. In order to advance from one node to the next in the direction of processing, we can use the following coding:

```
TEMP = CUR
CUR  = LINK(CUR)-PREV
PREV = TEMP
```

To change the direction in which we are processing the list, we simply interchange the values of PREV and CUR.

```
TEMP = CUR
CUR  = PREV
PREV = TEMP
```

We have already considered the advantages of this technique. The disadvantages, however, are manifold. For example, it is no longer possible to identify a list by retaining a single pointer to the topmost node in that list. It is now necessary to maintain two pointers to identify the top two nodes in the list. Moreover, if we wish to be able to process the list from either end, we must either close it as a circular list or maintain another pair of pointers identifying the last two nodes in the list. Furthermore, a core dump (i.e., a print-out of core storage when a program fails) becomes very difficult to read. Finally, one of the most important techniques of storage management, namely garbage collection, becomes practically impossible.

7.2.2 Relative Links

Instead of storing a pointer to node B in node A, we might instead store the numerical difference between the pointer to node B and the pointer to node A. This difference is called a *RELATIVE LINK*. To iterate through the nodes of this type of list, we can use the following coding:

```
P = P+LINK(P)
```

The disadvantage inherent with this technique is that extra arithmetic must be performed each time a pointer reference is made. However, it becomes particularly easy to move a list structure from one location in core to another, especially if we are using actual machine addresses as pointers. If we ensure that all nodes are placed in a single contiguous block of storage, the entire structure can be moved as a single block. Since the spacing between nodes remains constant, the relative links will not need to be changed to reflect the new position of the structure. However, it will still be necessary to update any external pointers from outside the block.

7.2.3 Offset Links

Although offset links serve the same purpose as relative links, they may be more efficient on some machines. For implementing this type of linking mechanism, we maintain a base pointer, BASE, to identify the beginning of the block of storage containing the list structure. Instead of maintaining pointers to the various nodes in the list structure, we record the differences between the pointers and the BASE pointer. Thus, to examine a particular FIELD of node P, we use the following:

FIELD(P+BASE)

FORTRAN arrays provide us with an example of offset pointers, since subscripts are essentially offsets from the beginning of the memory area assigned to the array in question.

7.3 GENERALIZED DATA STRUCTURES

In Section 7.1, we introduced the term "structural information", suggesting that data structures represent some information other than the actual values found in their components. For example, we say that the structure of the data represents the relationship(s) between its components. More specifically, in a linearly linked list, we say that node P precedes node LINK(P), while, in an array, X(I) comes before X(I+1). Consequently, if the array or list is sorted into ascending order, we can use this information to say that all the successors of node P [or element X(I)] have larger values than itself. The only difference between the array and the linearly linked list is the method of associating successive components, the latter offering a more dynamic means of manipulation. Their structural information capabilities are essentially the same. A linearly linked list can represent only simple relationships such as "greater than" or "less than", but not both.

To see how we can represent more complicated relationships than the ones possible with linearly linked lists, suppose we consider an example of such a relationship. To be specific, suppose we have a set of numerical values which we wish to store in memory so that the "highest common factor" (*hcf*) and the "lowest common multiple" (*lcm*) of any pair of the numbers can be easily determined. For any pair of numbers, *hcf* is defined to be the largest number by which both are divisible, while *lcm* is defined as the smallest number which is divisible by both. These relationships, forming what mathematicians call a *LATTICE*, can be represented in pictorial form as illustrated in Figure 7.7.

In Figure 7.7 the predecessors of each number (i.e., the ones below it to which it is connected) are its divisors, with its immediate predecessors being its maximal divisors. (For example, the maximal divisors of 12 are 6 and 4. Although 3 is another divisor of 12, it is also a divisor of 6, with the result that it is an immediate predecessor of 6.) Symmetrically, the immediate successors of each number are its smallest multiples. To find the *hcf* of any pair of numbers, we merely follow their predecessors downwards until we find a common predecessor. (For example, 6 is the *hcf* of 30 and 12, while 5 is the *hcf* of 15 and 5.) Similarly, to locate the *lcm*, we search for the first appearance of a common successor.

We could represent the lattice of Figure 7.7 using a multi-linked list structure. However, if

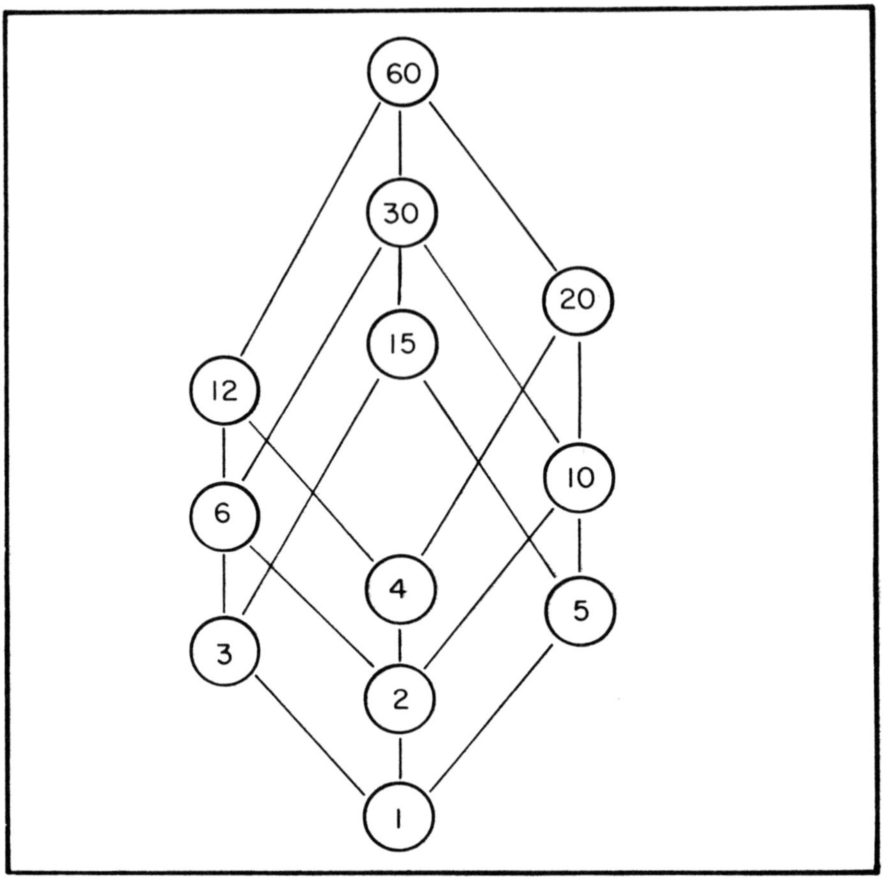

Figure 7.7

Lattice for *lcm* and *hcf*

we represent each number by a separate node, we will have, in the general case, a variable number of links originating from the nodes. Furthermore, the relationship between any pair of nodes cannot be expressed in definite terms. Consequently, the representation of the lattice requires a non-linear list structure.

To facilitate our study of non-linear list structures, we should find a way to classify the various structures that can be represented by such lists. Towards this end, we shall be using methods and terminology developed by mathematicians dealing with graph theory. Consequently, in the following pages, we shall be considering a set of definitions adopted from graph theory. These elementary concepts will be helpful to us in subsequent sections for identifying and discussing arbitrarily complex data structures.

A *GRAPH* is defined to be a set of nodes connected by entities called *EDGES*. (Actually, the standard term in graph theory for "node" is "vertex".) Each edge connects two nodes. The graph may be a *DIRECTED GRAPH* (*DIGRAPH*), in which case each edge has a direction associated with it (i.e., <u>from</u> one node <u>towards</u> another node). In a drawing of a graph, edges are drawn as lines connecting the nodes. If the graph is a directed one, the edges are drawn as arrows. Figure 7.8 presents an illustration of a directed graph.

When we can begin at a certain node, and, by following the edges, return to the starting node, we say that the nodes through which we have passed form a *LOOP*. For example, in Figure 7.8, the nodes CFDC form a loop, and nodes ABIGDCA do as well. A set of nodes like CADC do not form a loop, since a loop must proceed in the same direction as the edges. However, if the graph in Figure 7.8 were an undirected graph (i.e., the arrowheads were

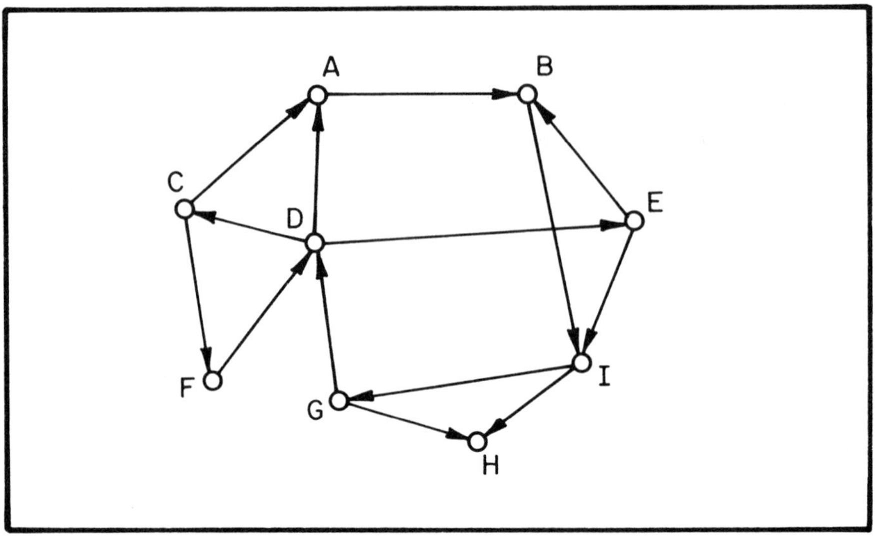

Figure 7.8

Directed Graph

erased), nodes CADC would comprise a loop.

A *TREE* can be defined as a graph in which there are no loops and which has a *ROOT* (i.e., a node from which every other node can be reached by following the edges in their proper directions). In Figure 7.9, both graphs are trees when we consider them as directed graphs. If they were undirected graphs, however, only the graph on the left would be a tree, since the one on the right would then contain a loop.

A node in a tree which has no edges originating from it is called a *LEAF*. In Figure 7.9, for example, nodes d, e, m, n, k, l, g, h, and i are the leaves of the tree on the left.

A section of a tree that can be reached along the edges from a particular node is called a *SUBTREE* or *BRANCH* of the tree. In general, we identify a subtree by its root node. For example, in Figure 7.9, subtree "f" is circled.

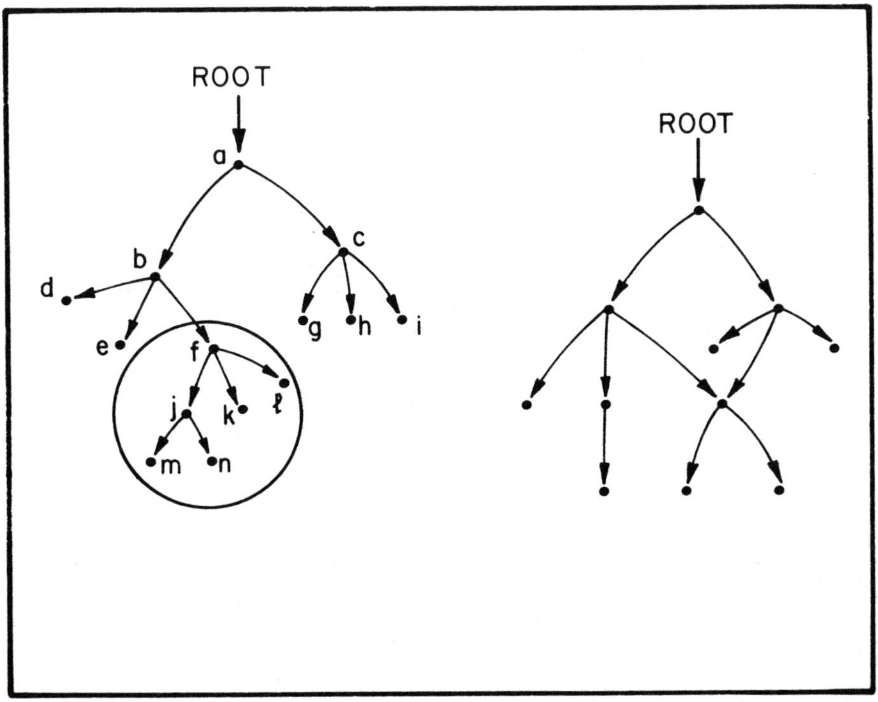

Figure 7.9

Trees

A *BINARY TREE* (*BITREE*) is a tree in which each node has at most 2 edges originating from it. None of the three graphs presented in Figures 7.8 and 7.9 are binary trees, since each has at least one node with more than 2 edges leaving from it.

In general, an n-ary tree is a tree in which each node has at most n edges originating from it.

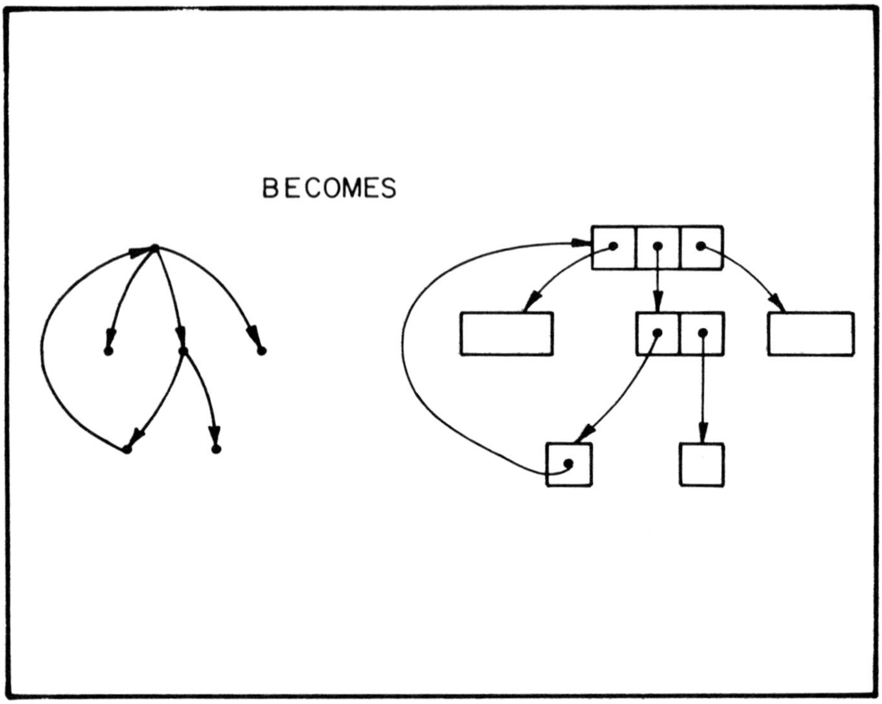

Figure 7.10

Representation Of a Graph By a Linked List

If we use the technique of representing directed graphs and trees by list structures, a node in a graph becomes a node in the list structure, while a directed edge is converted into a pointer. Figure 7.10 illustrates such a representation. However, we are immediately faced with the problem that the nodes contain different numbers of pointers, and thus require different amounts of storage. We could overcome this difficulty directly by finding machinery to handle varying node sizes. This approach would necessitate our maintaining an additional field in each node to represent the number of links contained in the node. Alternatively, we could extend each node to the size of the largest node, thus making all the nodes uniform and easier to handle, but wasting considerable memory space.

A third possible solution involves reducing the node size. Any tree can be transformed into a binary tree by using a mapping that preserves the structure of the tree. In essence, we simply replace each occurrence like

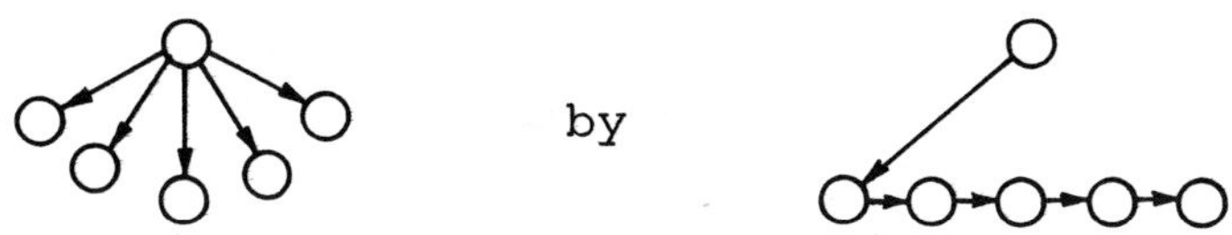

By so doing, we replace a large number of links inside a node by a linked list of its successors. Figure 7.11 illustrates the transformation of a more complicated tree structure to an equivalent binary tree.

Although we gain in uniformity by this translation, we do so at the cost of speed. For example, in Figure 7.11, to go from node A to node I, we have to follow only two links before the translation, as compared to having to traverse six links afterwards.

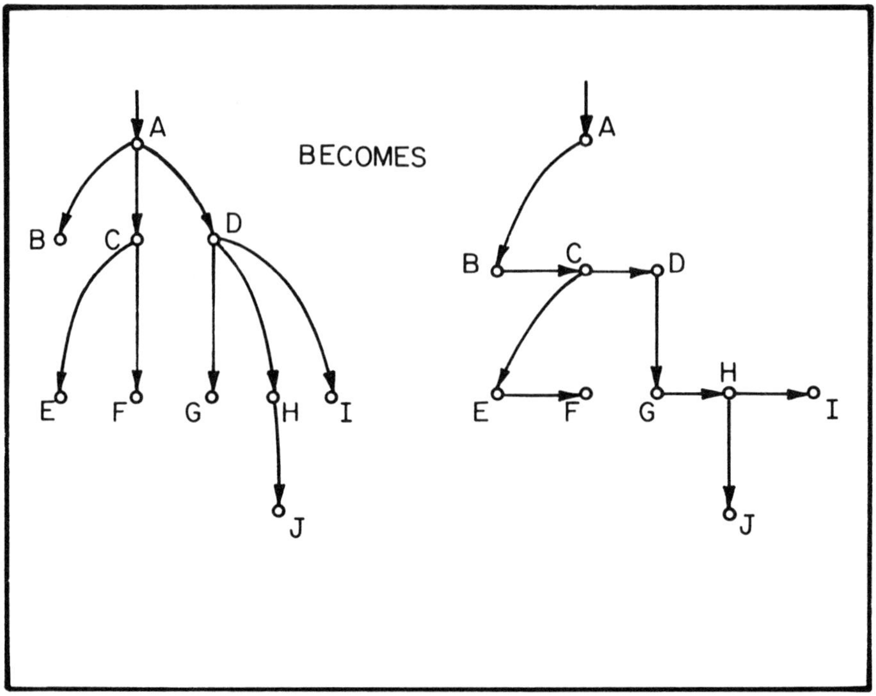

Figure 7.11

Transformation To a Bitree

The bitree is one of the most commonly employed structures in many different areas of computer science. Indeed, variations of binary trees can be used for the representation of numerous complex data structures. In subsequent sections, we shall be making a detailed examination of bitrees, their applications, and implementation.

7.4 TREES AND BITREES

In the preceding section, we defined "trees" as loop-free graphs with root nodes. In this section, we shall proceed to make some further distinctions between different types of trees, while at the same time illustrating their applications.

The strictest definition of a tree structure imposes the following three restrictions on the data structure:

(i) Loop Free: By following the links, it is not possible to traverse the same node twice.

(ii) Unique Predecessor: There is one, and only one, internal pointer pointing at any given node (roots are exceptions).

(iii) Single Root: There exists only a single node with no predecessors and from which every other node in the tree can be reached by following the links.

The first restriction is an essential one for the definition of a tree structure. However, we can relax the other restrictions (e.g., one of the nodes in the rightmost tree in Figure 7.9 has two predecessors) without incurring too many complications, provided that the particular application justifies such action [see Figure 7.12(e)]. In fact, the relaxation of the third restriction implies the relaxation of the second one (why?). For our purposes in this book we do not insist that conditions (ii) and (iii) be satisfied for every tree, even though this practice might not agree with the conventions adopted by most graph theoreticians.

As an example of the type of information that can be best represented by a tree structure, suppose we consider the following arithmetic assignment statement:

```
X = A/(2*B)+B**C*D+2*B
```

The expression on the right of the assignment operator contains several arithmetic operations to be performed. The order in which these operations are handled obviously depends upon the conventions adopted by the programming language in which such a statement is written. Most (although not all) languages employ the mathematical convention of performing multiplications and divisions after exponentiations but before additions and subtractions. Moreover, if we also assume that equal priority operations are performed in a left-to-right order, the operations in our sample expression will be executed in the following sequence:

1. Multiply 2 times B.
2. Divide A by the product of Step 1.
3. Raise B to the power of C.
4. Multiply the result of B**C by D.
5. Add A/(2*B) and B**C*D.
6. Multiply 2 times B (again).
7. Add the product of Step 6 to the sum of Step 5.

How can we represent the "true" meaning of an arithmetic assignment statement by a data structure? To properly answer this question, we have to find an unambiguous representation for a specific sequence of operations. Figure 7.12 illustrates several possible tree structures to represent our sample statement.

In Figures 7.12(a) and (b), the trees consist of two different types of nodes. The leaves are the only nodes which contain data, whereas the other nodes are comprised exclusively of pointer fields. The difference between the trees of (a) and (b) is actually only in the relative positions of the operators and their operands, although, in tree (b), we have "factored" the common operators in each one of the tree levels and placed it in front of its operands. By comparison, the trees in Figures 7.12(c), (d), and (e) consist of a single type of node, each having one data field which can contain either an operator or an operand, and also including two (or more) linking fields. Although this might be considered an improvement over the trees in (a) and (b) which have two different types of nodes, the cost of this uniformity is the significant waste of unused linking fields in the leaves of these trees. However, this cost is compensated for by a reduction in the total number of nodes required for the representation of each statement. For example, tree (a) has 24 nodes compared to only 16 nodes in the equivalent tree (c).

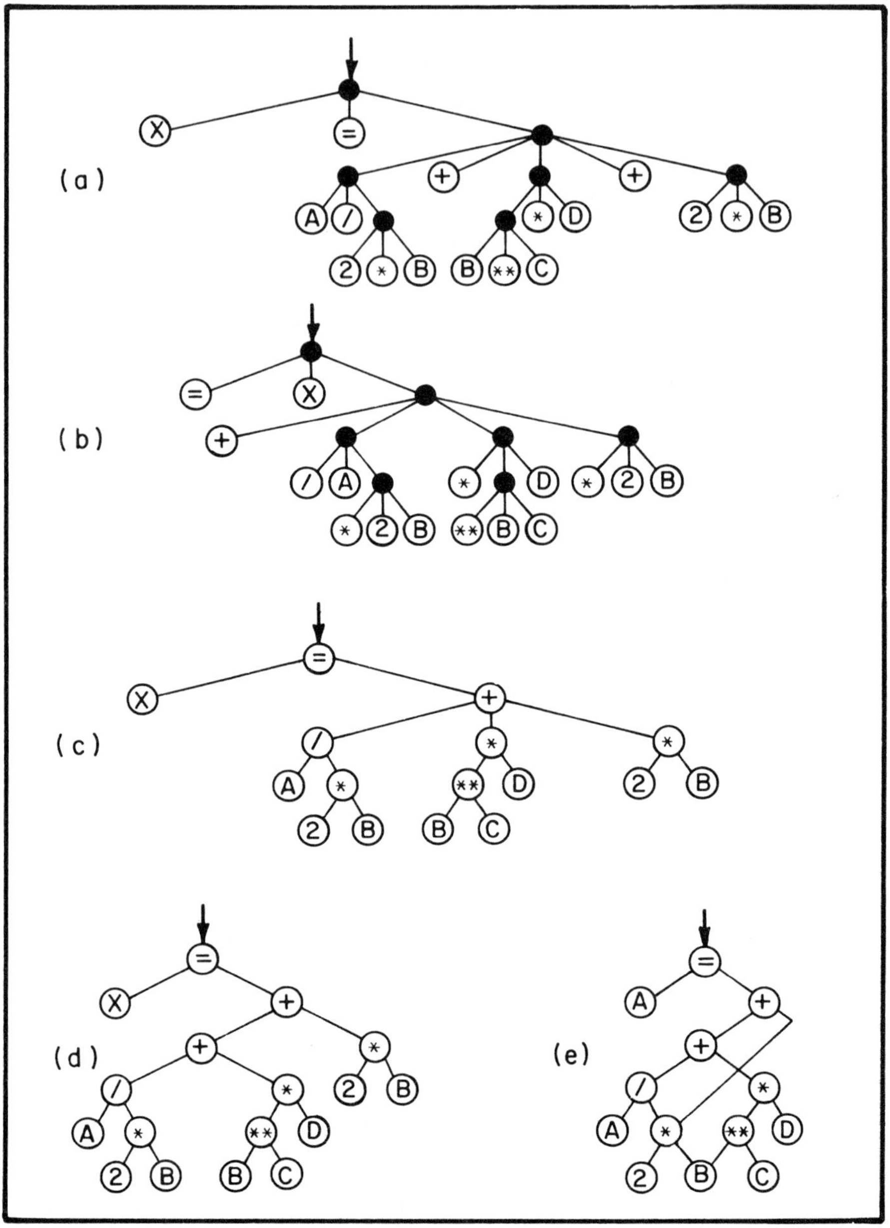

Figure 7.12

<u>Tree Representations of X = A/(2*B)+B**C*D+2*B</u>

By using the transformation procedure discussed in the preceding section, we can represent each of the three trees, (a), (b), and (c), by its equivalent bitree. However, knowing that each of our operators has two operands, we can represent the operations more "naturally" by a bitree of the type illustrated in Figure 7.12(d). In such a tree, each of the leaves is an operand, either a variable name or a constant, while the non-terminal nodes contain the operators. Furthermore, every operator has its two operands as its successors, each of which can be either a leaf or a subbitree representing a sub-expression. The advantage of such a bitree representation stems from its symmetry and recursiveness. To be more specific, whenever we process such a bitree, we do not distinguish between the tree and its branches. Consequently, by considering every node as the root of another bitree (actually a sub-tree), we can apply the process to it as if it were the root of a complete tree (i.e., a recursive application of the process).

Sometimes, a significant saving in nodes can be realized by permitting some nodes to have several predecessors. For example, the common subexpression, 2*B, appears as two different branches in tree (d). Similarly, there is more than one leaf containing the operand B. As illustrated in Figure 7.12(e), we can rearrange the links and eliminate this duplication, thus reducing the number of nodes required for the representation of the statement.

Since we shall be using bitree representations of arithmetic expressions in Chapter Nine for our discussion of programming language syntax, let us take a closer look at this form of expression. First, we should emphasize that each arithmetic expression has a definite structure as depicted by the order in which its operations are performed. Each of these operations has to be identified by an operator and its two operands. In order to transform an expression into its equivalent bitree, we have to know the conventions regarding operator priorities (part of the language syntax) adopted by the particular language. For example, consider the two FORTRAN expressions and their bitree representations presented in Figure 7.13. Except for a pair of parentheses in (b), the two expressions look identical. The two bitrees, in addition to having exactly the same number of nodes, contain identical data content in their nodes (i.e., they contain the same operators and operands). However, because of the effect of the parentheses in overriding normal operator priorities, the two bitrees differ considerably in their structure (i.e., the nodes and links are arranged differently in the two trees). The parentheses themselves do not appear in bitree(b), since they are no longer necessary. The structure of the tree itself is sufficient for representing the expression, regardless of operator conventions.

An arithmetic assignment statement, punched on a source card, is expressed in character string form, and, as such, it is readily comprehensible to human beings. However, this form is not a convenient

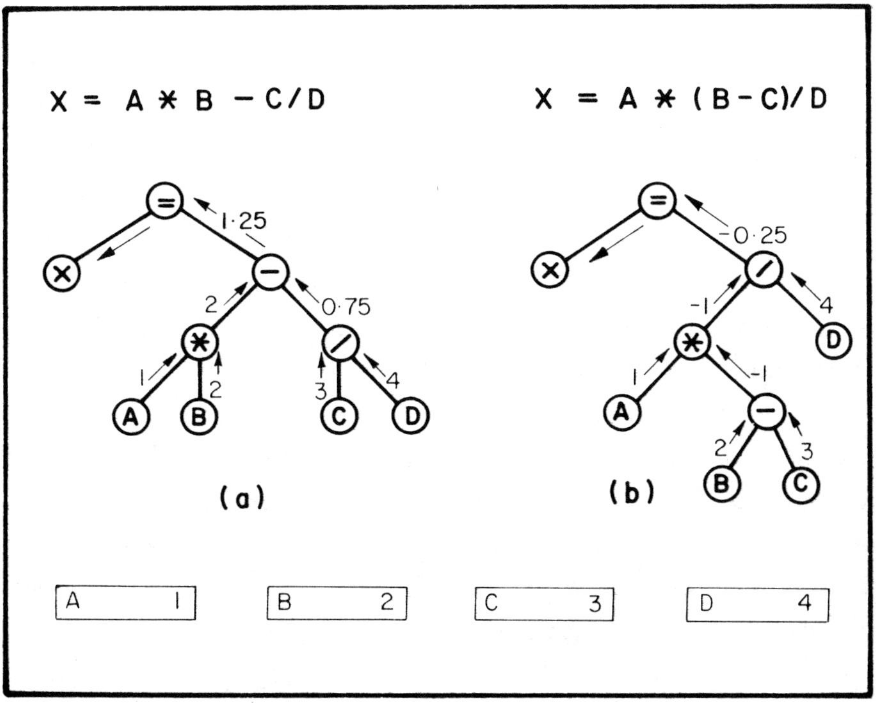

Figure 7.13

Bitree Interpretation of FORTRAN Expressions

one for processing by the computer. The bitree representation of the statement, on the other hand, can be easily processed (i.e., translated or interpreted) by a computer program. In general, to execute a statement in bitree form, we begin with the leaves of the tree and work our way up towards the root. As each leaf is examined, we obtain the value represented by that node. Subsequently, whenever both branches descending from a node are known quantities, it is possible to perform the operation specified by the node and transmit the result one step further up the tree.

To illustrate, suppose we return to the example of Figure 7.13(a), and assume that variables A, B, C, and D have the values 1, 2, 3, and 4 respectively. Leaves A and B convey their values to the '*' node, with the result that their product (2) is passed upwards as the left branch of the '-' node. Similarly, the value of the quotient when C is divided by D (0.75) is transmitted upwards as the right branch of the '-' node. Subsequently, the difference between these two values (1.25) is conveyed to the '=' node from its right branch. Finally, this value is stored in variable X as a result of carrying out the '=' operation. (A second similar analysis is presented in Figure 7.13(b).)

7.5 THE BITREE SYMBOL TABLE

In Sections 4.2 and 4.3 we introduced the concept of a symbol table and discussed some basic algorithms for searching operations on such tables. We saw that the primary operation to be performed on a symbol table is that of locating a particular entry whose name is known. Furthermore, in some applications, since this operation is performed very frequently, it is extremely important that the process be a rapid one. A second operation often performed on a symbol table is that of adding a new entry. Because a symbol table is often sorted, or at least partially sorted, this operation is usually very similar to that of finding an already existing entry, since, to add a new entry it is necessary to determine the location in the table where the entry should be inserted. Sometimes, it is desirable to add an entry to the table only if it is new. In such cases one can search for the proper location of the entry in the table, and providing it is not already present, insert it.

We also indicated in Section 4.3 how much more efficient a binary search can be, provided, of course, that we can afford to maintain the table in proper alphabetical order. We know that the addition of each new entry into such a table necessitates a mass movement of all the entries in the table following the point of insertion. The standard way to avoid such movement is to use a list structure to represent the table. A simple linear linked list will not be sufficient, however, since we cannot readily find the center of such a list without scanning through all of its nodes. If we have to scan sequentially through the nodes anyway, we might just as well perform a straightforward linear search instead.

On the other hand, we should be sure that the frequency with which new entries are added to the table warrants the maintenance of a more complicated structure. For example, if there were normally very few (perhaps none) new additions to the table, there would be no advantage in our using anything other than a standard linear array (vector) to represent the table. The extra cost of maintaining a more complex structure would not be justified, since there would be little or no occasion to utilize the extra flexibility provided by such a structure.

Nevertheless, for environments in which a list structure is warranted for the representation of the symbol table, we have to determine the type of structure which best accommodates the search operations to be performed. Our quest can be made considerably easier if we recognize that, with the binary search technique, the way in which we scan through the table appears to be tree-structured. Indeed, by continually dividing the segments of the table into halves, we have essentially subdivided the table into an actual tree structure. We can quite naturally let the symbol table be an explicit tree, and subsequently follow down through the nodes to locate a symbol. Such a representation is called a *BITREE SYMBOL TABLE*. Each node in this type of structure, in addition to containing a character string to represent the name of an entry, has two pointer fields, one pointing to the branch containing entries which appear earlier in the alphabet than the one represented by the node in question, and a second pointing to the branch whose entries appear later in the alphabet.

To find a particular entry in the table, we compare the symbol being sought with the symbol in the root node. If they are the same, our search is over. Otherwise, we have to follow one of the links from the root node down one level in the tree to a successor node. In cases where the symbol being sought precedes in alphabetical sequence the symbol in the root node, we follow the left link. Whenever this is not the case (i.e., the symbol being sought follows the root node symbol in the alphabet), we take the right link down the tree. In either event, we repeat the same comparison procedure with the next node. This process is repeated for successively lower node levels in the tree, until we either find a match or encounter a leaf of the tree (i.e., we encounter a null pointer when we attempt to move further down the tree in the appropriate direction). In the latter case, we can conclude that the symbol we are seeking does not exist in the current table. If we wish to do so, we can easily insert the new symbol in the table by constructing a new node and replacing the null pointer that terminated the search by a link to the new leaf.

As an example, consider the tree in Figure 7.14 as a symbol table maintained by a compiler. Furthermore, assume that the next symbolic name encountered in the program is the variable FALL. Consequently, the task faced by the compiler is to determine whether FALL is a new symbol, and, if it is, to insert it in the appropriate position in the tree. Beginning at the root node, it finds that FALL alphabetically precedes FORMAT, with the result that the left branch is followed down the tree. Next, after finding that FALL follows COM in alphabetical order, the compiler program takes the right branch from the COM node. Subsequently, FALL is ascertained to follow E but precede FIRE in alpha-

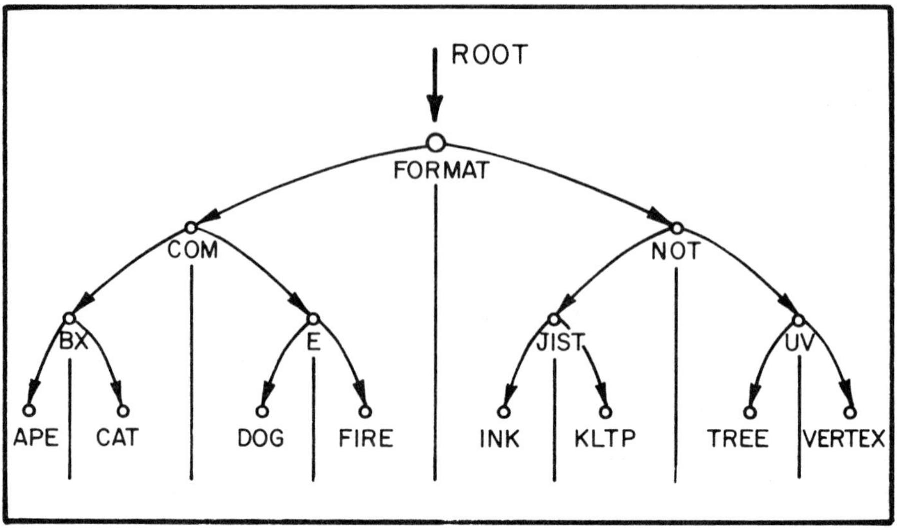

Figure 7.14

Bitree Symbol Table

betical sequence. However, a null pointer is encountered in the left link of the FIRE node, thus indicating that FALL does not exist in the current tree. As a result, a new node is constructed to represent FALL, and the left link of the FIRE node is adjusted to point at the new leaf of the tree.

Implementation of a bitree symbol table can be accomplished quite easily in FORTRAN. The nodes of the list structure can be defined to have four fields, two of which contain a character string to represent the symbol and an integer for the corresponding address (i.e., the actual meaning of the symbol) respectively. The remaining two fields contain links pointing at the left and right branches descending from the node. A single straightforward routine can be written to perform both the search and the insertion of new entries into the tree structure. We leave the detailed coding of such a routine as an exercise (see Section 7.6). However, in Section 8.5, we will be presenting a detailed example of bitree symbol table processing within the framework of our discussion of processing index terms.

In actual practice, bitrees are rarely as symmetrically structured as the one shown in Figure 7.14. The structure of a symbol table has to be designed so that it has the capacity to accept names in any order. Indeed, the detailed arrangement of the bitree depends completely upon the time sequence in which the names are added to it. For example, consider the following selection of symbols:

HEX DOG PLUTO FIGHT HAMAL BEAST CABLE ENJOY CAR.

If these symbols were added to a symbol table in this particular order, we would have the bitree shown in Figure 7.15(a). However, in the event that they had appeared originally in alphabetical order (i.e., BEAST CABLE CAR DOG ENJOY FIGHT HAMAL HEX PLUTO), the resulting bitree would appear as shown in Figure 7.15(b). A search through this latter tree would be essentially the same as a linear search.

To accelerate average search time in a bitree, it might be desirable to *BALANCE* the tree. A bitree is said to be balanced if, for every node in the tree, the number of nodes descending from its left

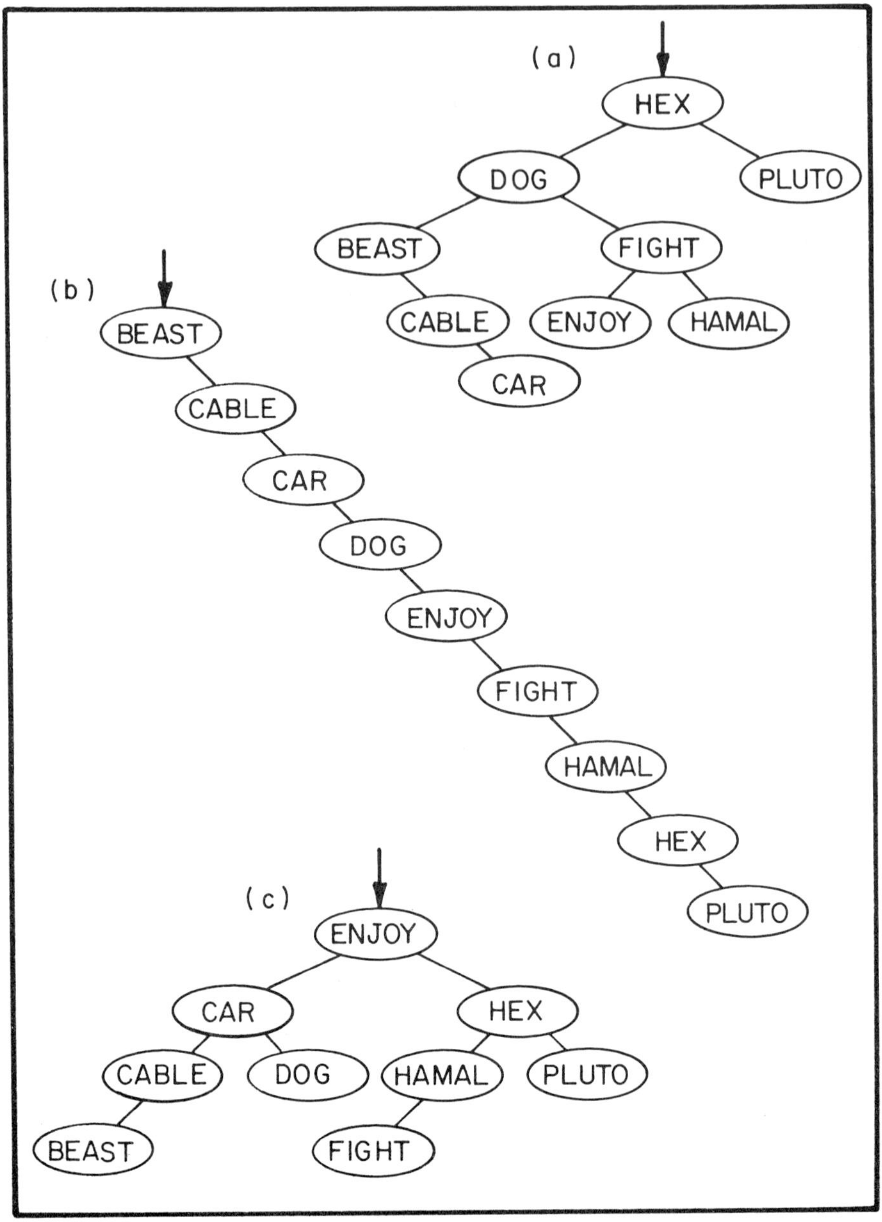

Figure 7.15

Balanced and Unbalanced Bitree Symbol Tables

branch differs by at most one from the number of nodes hanging on its right branch. (We permit a difference of one, since, if we demanded exact equality, the only trees that could be balanced would be those having $2^n - 1$ nodes, where n is any positive integer.) However, we should not be over-anxious to balance a tree, since this operation is not likely to be too useful unless it is expected that very few changes will be made to the tree after it has been balanced. As an illustration of a balanced tree, we might consider the tree in Figure 7.15(c), which is composed of the same symbols as trees (a) and (b).

7.6 EXERCISES

1\. (a) Two integers, A and B, are considered to be "congruent modulo n", written as $A \equiv B \pmod{n}$, if, and only if, $A-B = pn$ for some integer p. From this definition, it is clear that every integer is congruent modulo n to exactly one of the integers $0, 1, \ldots, n-1$. The most straightforward way of determining this value is to note the remainder after division by n. An alternative (although impractical) procedure for determining this integer is to utilize a circular linked list. If we are dealing with congruence modulo n, the list should be comprised of n nodes containing values 0 to $n-1$ in sequence, and the process of division simulated by repeated revolutions around the list. Write a function, MOD, which accepts two INTEGER parameters, A and B, and returns as its value the integer which is congruent to A modulo B.

(b) Write a mainline program which invokes function MOD from (a) to perform modular arithmetic. The program should read as data three integers (N1, N2, and N3) and an operator (one of +, -, or *). N1 and N2 should each be reduced modulo N3 (using function MOD) and the specified operation applied. Then the result of the operation should be reduced and printed.

2. The use of a bitree symbol table (Section 7.5) requires a function that returns as its value the location of a specified symbol in the table. In the case that the symbol in question does not exist in the table, a node has to be created and inserted (i.e., linked) at the appropriate point in the bitree structure. Write a FORTRAN function, LOOKUP, to implement this procedure. Each node in the structure contains three fields, SYMB, LL, and RL, corresponding to the symbol table entry, left link, and right link respectively. When the function is invoked, a pointer (ROOT) to the root of the bitree and the symbol to be located (SYMBOL) are supplied as parameters. If a node containing SYMBOL already exists in the table, the pointer value returned by LOOKUP is negative. Otherwise, the value returned should be positive.

```
INTEGER FUNCTION LOOKUP*2(ROOT,SYMBOL)
CHARACTER*6 SYMB(1000),SYMBOL
INTEGER*2 LL(1000),RL(1000),ROOT
COMMON SYMB,LL,RL
.
.
.
```

You might need a bitree node constructor routine for use with function LOOKUP. In the routine described below, NEWSYM, NEWLL, and NEWRL refer to the new symbol entry, left and right link fields respectively.

```
INTEGER FUNCTION BTCNS*2(NEWSYM,NEWLL,NEWRL)
CHARACTER*6 SYMB(1000),NEWSYM
INTEGER*2 LL(1000),RL(1000),NEWLL,NEWRL
COMMON SYMB,LL,RL
```

3. This problem requires the development of a complete system for the manipulation of sparse matrices that are represented in memory by two-dimensional circular linked lists as illustrated in Figure 7.6. This will entail writing routines to read and print such matrices, as well as the coding of functions to perform the following matrix operations: addition, subtraction, multiplication, calculation of a determinant, and finding an inverse.

The input to this system will be comprised of assembly-language-like instructions and data cards. The instruction cards are all punched in a fixed format, each containing one opcode and from one to three symbolic operands. Two optional values, NR and NC, may be included on an instruction card to determine the dimensions (i.e., number of rows and columns) of the matrix (or matrices) to be involved with the specified operation. If these fields on an instruction card are left blank, NR and NC will be read as zeros (under I FORMAT) and the appropriate dimensions will be obtained from an examination of the matrix in question. Using the opcode as a "key", the mainline program will execute the instructions <u>interpretively</u> through appropriate invocations of subroutines. The operand matrices and values of NR and NC will be the arguments in the subroutine calls. Whenever they are required, the data cards will follow immediately after the corresponding instruction card.

To facilitate the operation of the various subroutines, it will be necessary to write accompanying utility functions (CNS, DELETE, etc.). Furthermore, whenever an invalid instruction card (e.g., one requesting the multiplication of incompatible matrices, inversion of a non-square matrix, etc.) or improper data card is encountered, an error termination procedure should be carried out. This involves the printing of an appropriate error message, the termination of execution of the subroutine involved, and notification of the mainline program by the subroutine that an error has been discovered. The notification should be handled by using the parameter ERROR which will be a parameter for all of the subroutines.

Your system should include the following routines:

INTEGER FUNCTION READM(NR,NC,ERROR)

This function returns as its value a pointer to the root of a newly created representation of a sparse matrix. Each of the input data cards read by this routine should contain three fields, consisting of two integer values for the row and column positions of the element and a floating-point value for the actual matrix entry in question. As the data cards are read, this routine constructs the matrix representation, element by element, until such time as the next instruction card is encountered. If either NR or NC is zero, the number of rows or columns is determined from the largest subscript specified for a row or column on the data cards. This implies that the dummy row and column headers are constructed dynamically as the data cards are read. On the other hand, if either NR or NC is positive, the row or column headers are allocated at the start of the construction of the linked list. Furthermore, if either NR or NC is positive, and if a data card specifies a row value or column value larger then NR or NC respectively, an error termination should be initiated.

To facilitate the operation of function READM, you might find it helpful to design a function which inserts an element node into an already existing matrix list structure.

i.e., INTEGER FUNCTION INSERT(M,E)

where M is a pointer to the root of an existing matrix structure and E points at an element node.

SUBROUTINE PRINTM(M,NR,NC,ERROR)

This subroutine prints (using any format you desire) the sparse matrix represented by the list structure having node M as its root. If either NR or NC is positive, only the first NR rows or NC columns of the matrix are printed. If either NR or NC exceeds the corresponding dimension of the matrix, however, an error termination should be initiated.

INTEGER FUNCTION ADD(M1,M2,NR,NC,ERROR)

This function returns as its value a pointer to a newly created matrix structure representing the sum of matrices M1 and M2. If either NR or NC is zero, the existing dimension(s) of M1 and M2 should be used. In the case where the two matrices have different dimensions, an error termination should be initiated. However, if either NR or NC is positive, only the first NR rows or NC columns are selected from each matrix for the calculation of the sum matrix. Of course, if either NR or NC exceeds the corresponding dimension of M1 or M2, an error termination should be initiated.

INTEGER FUNCTION SUB(M1,M2,NR,NC,ERROR)

The operation and design of this routine are similar to those of the ADD function except that matrix M2 is subtracted from matrix M1.

INTEGER FUNCTION MULT(M1,M2,NR,NC,ERROR)

The operation and design of this routine are similar to those of the ADD function except that matrices M1 and M2 are multiplied to produce the new matrix. An error should be signalled if the number of columns of M1 is not identical to the number of rows of M2. If either NR or NC is positive, it is used to specify the appropriate dimension of the product matrix. Otherwise, the existing dimensions of M1 and M2 are used. If either NR or NC exceeds the corresponding dimension of M1 or M2, an error termination should be initiated.

REAL FUNCTION DETR(M,N,ERROR)

This function returns the value of the determinant of the matrix with root M. If N is positive, the determinant is calculated for the submatrix comprised of the first N rows and columns. Otherwise, the existing dimensions of M are used. If N exceeds in size either of the dimensions of M, an error termination is initiated. Similarly, if N is zero and matrix M is not square, an error condition should be indicated.

INTEGER FUNCTION INVERS(M,N,ERROR)

This function returns as its value a pointer to a newly created matrix structure representing the inverse of matrix M. If matrix M is singular (i.e., DETR(M,N,ERROR) = 0), and hence the inverse does not exist, the function returns the value zero. If N is positive, the inverse is constructed for the submatrix comprised of the first N rows and columns of matrix M. Otherwise, the existing dimensions for M are used. If N exceeds in size either of the dimensions of M, an error condition is indicated. Similarly, if N is zero and matrix M is not square, an error termination is in order.

Once the preceding routines have been developed, we can consider the construction of a mainline program as a driver for these routines. To distinguish instruction cards from data cards, we use a '.' in column one of instruction cards and leave that column blank on all data cards. Matrices are referenced through the use of single-character symbolic names appearing in the operand fields of instruction cards. Consequently, the mainline program will have to maintain a symbol table to contain the symbolic names of the matrices and corresponding pointers to the roots of the appropriate list representations. Design a symbol table lookup routine using any algorithm you desire.

The format of an instruction card is as follows:

.opcode op1 op2 op3 #rows #columns

The '*opcode*' is CHARACTER*6 and the three operand names ('*op1*', '*op2*', and '*op3*') are all CHARACTER*1. The last two fields contain integer values specifying the dimensions of the matrices in question.

Whenever data cards are being read, the end of any given sequence of cards is to be recognized by encountering the next instruction card. Data cards are used to represent matrix elements and they adhere to the following fixed format:

b̸ row# column# value

The integer values for '*row#*' and '*column#*' must always be greater than zero.

The input stream to the mainline program is assumed to contain a "batch" of jobs, each terminated with the instruction opcode '*.END*'. Whenever this instruction card is encountered, the program should "clear" memory of all matrices, "wipe out" the symbol table, and reinitialize all nodes back into the availability list, all in preparation for the resumption of processing a new collection of instructions. In the case of an error termination, the mainline program should "flush out" succeeding input cards, down to and including the next '*.END*' card, at which point, it should begin to prepare for the next job. The final end-of-data is determined through the use of an 'END=' option in a READ statement.

Following is a list of the various types of instruction cards that may be used and the appropriate actions to be taken. In each case, the fields in square brackets are optional.

.READ op1 [# of rows] [# of columns]
optional data cards

This instruction card invokes the READM function, provided there are accompanying data cards, to create a new matrix having the symbolic name '*op1*'. If a matrix with this name already exists in the symbol table, its old list representation should be erased and its nodes liberated by returning them to the availability list. If no data cards accompany the instruction cards, the value assigned to the operand matrix should be the empty matrix (i.e., a single root node).

```
e.g.,    .READ   A 5
            1   3  0.23
            1   7  1.45
            3   2  0.067
            :
```

This particular instruction card results in the creation of a list structure to represent the 5×7 matrix A (whose entries follow as data).

.*PRINT* *op1* [*# of rows*] [*# of columns*]

The operand matrix ('*op1*') is printed according to the format chosen. Once this operation has been completed, if data cards are encountered when another instruction card is expected, an appropriate error message should be printed and the data cards ignored. If the operand name does not exist in the symbol table, an error termination should be initiated. This procedure should be adopted for all undefined symbolic references encountered in the program.

.*ADD*
.*SUB* } *op1 op2 op3* [*# of rows*] [*# of columns*]
.*MULT*

For each of these instruction cards, the appropriate matrix operation is applied to matrices '*op2*' and '*op3*' and the result is assigned to '*op1*'. If '*op1*' exists in the symbol table, its old value is deleted by returning the nodes comprising its list representation to the availability list.

e.g., .*ADD* *A B C 5 7*
.*MULT* *X B A*

For any one of these instruction types, either '*op2*' or '*op3*' can be replaced by an asterisk (*) which indicates that the instruction card is to be followed by data cards from which the value of the operand in question is taken. A temporary list representation is created for the operand to be used in the specified operation, and, when the operation has been completed, the temporary structure is erased by returning its nodes to the availability list. In cases where '*op2*' or '*op3*' is replaced by an '*', it will be necessary to use function READM. However, in instances where '*op1*' is replaced by an '*', the resulting matrix is to be printed rather than saved in memory. Once the result has been printed, the temporary structure for it should be deleted.

.*DETR* *op1* [*# of rows*]

This type of instruction card results in a determinant being evaluated and its value printed as part of the following message:

THE DETERMINANT OF MATRIX *op1* IS ....

.*INVRS* *op1* *op2* [*# of rows*]

This type of instruction card causes the inverse of matrix '*op2*' to be computed and assigned to '*op1*'. If '*op1*' already exists in the symbol table, its old value is erased. Once again, either '*op1*' or '*op2*' may be replaced by an '*' with results similar to those described previously for the addition, subtraction and multiplication operations.

4. This exercise involves the development of a complete system for automating the transactions of a car rental company (as introduced in Chapters Five and Six). We shall assume that the company has five parking lots, each having a rental office and a service station. Cars are represented by nodes linked into three major linearly linked lists: cars currently rented, cars free for rental, and cars being serviced. Furthermore, each rental outlet has its own sub-lists (of its own cars) for these three categories.

   Car rental charges are classified under three ranges:

   Class 'A' - \$14/day and 12¢/mile
   Class 'B' - \$12/day and 10¢/mile
   Class 'E' (Economy) - \$8/day and 8¢/mile

   The nodes representing cars contain the following fields:

LICENS	CHARACTER*6	car license number
STATUS	CHARACTER*1	'F' - free, 'R' - rented, 'S' - service
MILAGE	INTEGER	most recently noted mileage (e.g., when rented)
SERMIL	INTEGER	mileage at time of last service
EDATE	INTEGER	expected date of return from rental †
RDATE	INTEGER	date of rental †

LINK1	INTEGER*2	link for major list (any one of 3 lists)
LINK2	INTEGER*2	link in minor list (i.e., office sublists)
LOT	INTEGER*2	parking lot number where parked or rented
CLASS	CHARACTER*1	'A', 'B', or 'E'

† Dates are expressed as integers in the form 'yyddd', where 'yy' represents the last two digits of the year, and 'ddd' is the number of the day in that year (i.e., 001 to 366). e.g., 71041 represents February 10, 1971.

Information about the operation of the various rental offices and the company as a whole is maintained in a table having six rows, one for each rental outlet and the last for company-wide information. Each row contains the following items of information:

PNAME	CHARACTER*6	name of rental office (blank for company row)
NET	REAL	income of office or company
NOTRSA	INTEGER*2	number of transactions (rentals) for class 'A' cars
NOTRSB	INTEGER*2	number of transactions for class 'B' cars
NOTRSE	INTEGER*2	number of transactions for class 'E' cars
RENT	INTEGER*2	top pointer to list of rented cars

FREE	INTEGER*2	top pointer to list of free cars
SER	INTEGER*2	top pointer to list of cars in service

The pointers in row six of the table, since this is the row for company-wide information, point at the top nodes of the major lists. By comparison, the pointers in rows one through five are pointing at the top nodes of the sublists (i.e., minor lists) for the individual rental offices.

A car is associated with a particular parking lot (and rental office) as long as it has not been moved to another lot. For example, cars that are out on rental or in service are still associated with the outlet where they were parked last. However, if a car is returned to an office other than the one from which it was rented, it then becomes the responsibility of the office to which it has been returned. In such cases, the LOT field and the chaining through LINK2 have to be updated accordingly.

We want to take advantage of the fact that the total number of cars owned by the company does not change very frequently and to provide for easy location of cars through their license numbers. As a result, we associate cars with nodes in a manner that permits them to be sorted according to their license numbers. In other words, node I is assigned to represent the car whose license number is the Ith one in ascending sequence. A pointer,

LAST, is retained to point at the last node used. Whenever a new car is added to the company's collection, LAST is incremented and the node representing the new car is inserted, by mass movement of data, into the proper position in the various arrays representing the fields of the nodes. Similarly, whenever a car owned by the company is scrapped, all nodes succeeding that car in the arrays have to be moved forward one position and LAST decremented accordingly.

The nodes in the RENT major list and sublists are ordered according to their EDATE (the top node in each list has the earliest expected return date), while those in the FREE list and sublists are ordered according to their MILAGE (the top node in each list has the lowest mileage). The SER sublists, on the other hand, are maintained in order of first-in-first-out. This type of structure can be implemented by inserting the most recent car requiring service at the bottom of the appropriate list. We shall assume that the topmost car in any service sublist is the only one in that list which has been completely serviced and hence is eligible to be removed from the list (and the major service list). In such cases of removal from a service sublist, the top pointer to that sublist has to be altered so that it points at the next car in the sublist. This new top node then represents the next car to be available from that service sublist when the next demand for a serviced car is processed. The major SER list, however, does not provide any such obvious indication of which cars have been completely serviced but merely represents an overall list of those cars in service status. Consequently, the nodes in this major list need not be arranged in any particular sequence.

Write the coding for the following routines:

INTEGER FUNCTION NEWCAR*2(LIC,MIL,CLS,PLOT)

The parameters LIC, MIL, and CLS represent the license number, mileage, and class respectively for a new car purchased by the company. In this and all succeeding routines, PLOT is an INTEGER*2 parameter which has one of the values one through five to indicate a particular rental office. In this instance, it indicates the designated parking lot for the newly purchased car. The function creates a new node for the car and inserts it into the appropriate positions in the various lists. The value returned by the routine is a pointer to the newly created node. Remember, however, that the mass movement of data in the field arrays will most likely invalidate many pointers. Your coding for this routine should maintain the integrity of the various lists and sublists by updating all necessary pointers.

INTEGER FUNCTION JNKCAR*2(CAR)

In this and all succeeding routines, CAR represents an INTEGER*2 pointer to a node representing a car. This particular function performs the necessary alterations and data movement involved with the deletion of node CAR from all lists and sublists. This entails the removal of the various field entries for node CAR from the arrays representing the node fields. If the operation is successful, the function returns the value zero. Otherwise, it returns an appropriate integer value which indicates why it has not been possible to carry out the operation. Possible reasons for this happening might be that the car is currently rented or it has been omitted by error from all of the major (or minor) lists.

SUBROUTINE TRANS(PLOT,CAR)

This subroutine performs the necessary actions for transferring car CAR to parking lot PLOT. To be eligible for transfer, CAR must be at the top of any service sublist or be on free status at an office other than PLOT. In either case, node CAR is linked into the FREE sublist of office PLOT. If CAR was formerly on service status, it should also be removed from the appropriate service lists and linked into the major FREE list. However, in instances where parameter PLOT has the value zero, CAR is transferred to the bottom of the service sublist for office LOT(CAR). In addition to changes to pointers and linkages, this latter step involves assigning the value MILAGE(CAR) to SERMIL(CAR). There may be occasions when one or more of the conditions specified for a valid transfer are violated (e.g., CAR is on rental status, CAR is on service status but not at the top of a service sublist, etc.). In these cases, appropriate error messages are printed and control returned to the calling program.

INTEGER FUNCTION REQST*2(PLOT,RCLASS)

This routine is invoked to answer a request from office PLOT to rent a car. RCLASS is a CHARACTER*1 parameter specifying the class of the requested car. First, the function searches for a free car of the desired class among the free cars of outlet PLOT. If it fails to find a suitable car, the routine continues its search in other parking lots. If it is not able to find a suitable car in any of the lots, the function returns the value zero. Otherwise, the routine returns as its value a pointer to the node representing the car in question. If the car is in a parking lot other than PLOT, the sign of the pointer is set to be negative.

SUBROUTINE RENTO(PLOT,CAR,DATE)

This subroutine performs all the necessary actions involved in renting the car CAR from office PLOT:

(i) Assign the value of DATE as the new EDATE of node CAR and change the status of CAR (i.e., 'F' to 'R').

(ii) The value of PLOT must be the same as LOT(CAR). Otherwise, an error message is issued. [Note: In cases where function REQST returns a negative value indicating that a car of the desired class is available but at an office other than PLOT, subroutine TRANS has to be invoked before

RENTO. (This might give the rental agent time to convince the customer that he should rent a more expensive car than he had originally intended.)]

(iii) Increment the appropriate one of NOTRSA, NOTRSB, and NOTRSE for PLOT and the company.

(iv) Assign to RDATE the current date (which is a COMMON variable).

REAL FUNCTION RETURN(PLOT,CAR,RMILE)

This function performs all the necessary actions involved in returning the car CAR to office PLOT, and it returns as its value the rental charges. RMILE represents the mileage on the car upon its return.

(i) Calculate the rental charges from MILAGE(CAR), RMILE, RDATE(CAR), and the current date. Add these charges to the NET of office PLOT and the company.

(ii) Update MILAGE(CAR) to RMILE, and change STATUS(CAR) (i.e., 'R' to 'F').

(iii) Transfer CAR to the FREE list of PLOT, and, if PLOT is different from LOT(CAR), perform the necessary alterations in linkages.

(iv) Assuming that cars should be serviced every 1,000 miles, check the updated value of MILAGE against SERMIL, and, if appropriate, issue a message to send the car for servicing.

INTEGER FUNCTION SEARCH*2(LIC)

This function performs a binary search through the license fields of the cars and returns as its value a pointer to the node representing the car with license number LIC (CHARACTER*6). If it is not able to locate the car in question, the function returns a zero value.

SUBROUTINE INQIRE(LIC)

This routine prints out a summary report on the car with license number LIC. The report includes all the information contained in the fields of the node representing the specified car. If the car with this license number is not locatable (i.e., function SEARCH returns a zero value when invoked by this routine), an appropriate message is printed and control returned to the calling program.

SUBROUTINE LOTREP(PLOT)

This routine prints out a complete report on all the cars associated with office PLOT. The initial output is subdivided into three sections, one for each of the different sublists (i.e., free, rented, and service) for PLOT. For each car, the information displayed is the same as that printed by subroutine INQIRE [although it would be very inefficient for LOTREP to invoke INQIRE for every car (why?)]. The report also includes the total number of cars in each of the three sublists, messages to indicate those rented cars that are overdue and those free cars which require immediate servicing, and the values of NET, NOTRSA, NOTRSB, and NOTRSE for PLOT.

SUBROUTINE COMREP

This subroutine prints a complete report on the operations of all the company's parking lots. For each rental office, the information displayed is that printed by subroutine LOTREP. Following the reports on the individual offices, there is a summary of the aggregate totals for the company. These include the total number of cars in each of the three major lists, the total numbers of rented cars that are overdue and free cars which require servicing, and the company-wide values of NET, NOTRSA, NOTRSB, and NOTRSE. Throughout the output, there are appropriate titles included to simplify reading of the report.

SUBROUTINE REORG(DOIT)

This subroutine examines the number of free cars in each parking lot in an effort to discover possible undesirable concentrations of cars at certain outlets. We assume that the offices which report the highest number of transactions are the busiest and hence should have more cars associated with them on their parking lots. The subroutine calculates the <u>desired</u> number of <u>free</u> cars in <u>each</u> class (i.e., 'A', 'B', and 'E') for <u>each</u> parking lot. For each class of car, the desired number of free cars on each lot is determined by that outlet's share of the company-wide transactions for cars of that class. (In other words, if a given outlet has initiated n% of the company's transactions for cars of a particular class, it should ideally have n% of the company's free cars of that class parked on its lot available for rental.) The printed output from this subroutine consists of the desired numbers of free cars in each class for each lot. If the parameter DOIT has the value unity, the routine then figures out a set of car transfers that will redistribute the company's stock of free cars according to the values calculated. Then it issues the necessary calls to subroutine TRANS to execute these transfers. If DOIT has some value other than unity, control is returned to the calling program without performing the transfers to perform the redistribution.

Once these subprograms have been written, develop a mainline program to perform the various services for the car rental company. The various transactions, each originating from one of the rental offices, are simulated by input data cards to the mainline routine. Since the rental agents would not know the node numbers of the cars, all references to cars in the transactions are made through their license numbers. The mainline program responds to the transaction requests by printing appropriate messages directed to the various offices, depending upon the results encountered when it attempts to accommodate the requests. Each message is preceded by the following header:

'TO LOT NO. *n*'

where *n* is the number of the rental office to which the message is directed.

The transaction cards are all punched in a fixed format with the following fields:

ACTION	CHARACTER*6	keyword specifying the requested action
LOTNO	INTEGER*2	identification number for the calling office
LICNO	CHARACTER*6	car license number
ACLASS	CHARACTER*1	class of car ('A', 'B', or 'E')
AMIL	INTEGER	mileage of car
ADATE	INTEGER	date used in transaction

The six fields of the transaction cards always appear in the following order:

ACTION LOTNO LICNO ACLASS AMIL ADATE

The ACTION field indicates the routine to be invoked and the remaining fields are used as subprogram calling arguments. For several of the transactions, some of the last five fields are not required, and, as a result, they may be left blank. The mainline program should perform comprehensive error checking on the input fields and issue error messages when needed. Any messages printed should reproduce the input transaction card in question and include a confirmation or other response when it is appropriate.

Finally, the mainline program should perform one of the following set of actions depending upon the keyword contained in the ACTION field.

NEWCAR lotno licno aclass amil -----

Create a node for a new car to be associated with office '*lotno*'.

JUNK ----- *licno* ------ ---- -----

Delete the car with license number '*licno*' from the company records.

SETDAT ----- ----- ------ ---- *adate*

Assign the value of '*adate*' to the global (COMMON) variable representing the current date.

REQUST lotno ----- *aclass* ---- -----

A car of class '*aclass*' is requested from lot '*lotno*'. The printed message in response should consist of the license number of the car that has been found and an indication whether the car was located in another lot.

RENT lotno licno ------ ---- *adate*

Rent the car with license number '*licno*' from office '*lotno*' and print a confirmation. '*adate*' is the expected date of return for the car.

RETURN lotno licno ------ *amil* -----

Return the car with license number '*licno*' to

office '*lotno*' and print a confirmation accompanied by the rental charges.

TRANS lotno licno ------ ---- -----

Transfer the car with license number '*licno*' to office '*lotno*', or to service status (if '*lotno*' is zero), and print confirmation.

SERET lotno ----- ------ ---- -----

Determine whether office '*lotno*' has any cars in its service sublist. If so, remove the topmost car from the service lists and reassign it to free status in the parking lot. Inform office '*lotno*' about the results, including those instances when the service sublist is empty.

INQURE lotno licno ------ ---- -----

Print a report on the car with license number '*licno*' in response to the request for information from office '*lotno*'.

REPORT lotno ----- ------ ---- -----

Generate a summary report for the cars at office '*lotno*'. If '*lotno*' has the value zero, print a company report.

REORG ----- ----- ------ ---- -----

Print the desired numbers of free cars of each class for every lot.

REDIS ----- ----- ------ ---- -----

Execute the necessary transfers of cars to carry out the recommendations of subroutine REORG.

5. In a multiprogramming system several different programs can reside simultaneously in the memory of the computer and share the computing capabilities of the machine. A large number of the programs operating in this type of environment may require access to secondary storage devices for the retrieval of subprograms or the manipulation of data. In addition, many operating system functions depend upon access to such secondary storage facilities.

   One of the most common devices used for secondary storage in present-day computing is a replaceable disk unit. A system usually has a specific number of disk drives on which disk volumes can be mounted. Each of these volumes may contain numerous sets of data that are required by various programs and which can be accessed simultaneously by several of the programs that share the memory of the computer. Disk volumes are maintained in a library and mounted on the system's drives as required. (Like tapes, any volume may be mounted on any drive. Unlike tapes, however, disk volumes can be shared.) A program cannot execute successfully if the disk volumes that it requires are not mounted on the system's drives.

The purpose of this exercise is to design a program to optimize the utilization of a system's disk drives so as to maximize the throughput of the system (i.e., minimize the total amount of time required for the execution of all the jobs) and minimize the total number of volume changes. Jobs submitted for execution are maintained in a queue. In this particular exercise, the program accepts "jobs" from input cards, each specifying a list of volume ID's (i.e., the disk volumes required by that job). To assist in the scheduling of these jobs, the program maintains a list of the disk volumes requested by the jobs in the queue with flags to indicate the volumes that are mounted and those that are currently being used by a job in the midst of execution. The number of volumes flagged as "mounted" should never exceed the number of drives available to the system.

After examining the disk requirements of the jobs in the queue, the program schedules the jobs and releases them for execution at the appropriate times. Jobs are released for execution one at a time, and only when an active job has completed execution and thus made its memory space available. Furthermore, only those jobs whose disk requirements can be completely satisfied (i.e., all its required volumes are currently mounted on drives) can be released from the queue for execution. If no such job can be located in the queue, the program prints a message which indicates the necessary changes of disk volumes. This is accomplished by specifying the ID's of the volumes to be replaced and the ID's of those volumes to be mounted in their place.

All communication with this program is handled through data cards. The first data card sets the system parameters. It contains two integer values NOJOBS and NODRVS, which represent respectively the maximum number of jobs that can be run simultaneously in the memory of the machine and the number of disk drives available to the system. Following the specification card is a batch (of variable size) of "job cards", each simulating a job submitted to the system. The format of these cards is as follows:

$$jobname \quad time \quad vol_1 \quad vol_2 \quad vol_3 \ldots vol_{10}$$

where '*jobname*' (CHARACTER*6) is a unique name identifying the job, '*time*' is the computer time required for the execution of the job, and 'vol_i' (i = 1,2,...,10) represents the ID (CHARACTER*6) of a disk volume required by the job. Each job card can specify any number of volume ID's between zero and ten but never more than NODRVS.

Design appropriate data structures for maintaining the information needed by this program. These structures should include the job queue, a record of the volume requirements for the various jobs and a list indicating the status of the different volumes (i.e., which ones are mounted and/or currently used by jobs in execution). The data structures should be designed so as to make the necessary manipulation as efficient as possible.

When considering the design of these structures, you should adhere to the following conditions:

(i) Neither the number of jobs in the batch nor in the queue can be predicted. At any particular time, these numbers may be very large, while, at some other point in time, the numbers may be very small.

(ii) Once a job has been released for execution, it is removed immediately from the queue to make room for other jobs.

(iii) No assumptions can be made concerning the number of disk volumes required by a particular job. There may be several jobs that do not require any disk volumes at all, and there may be others that need the maximum number possible.

(iv) Your program should make optimal use of storage while still providing for an efficient algorithm to determine whether a job may or may not be released from the queue for execution. The data structures should be designed to facilitate a fast search through the job queue and allow for the search to be terminated upon encountering the first executable job.

(v) No assumptions can be made regarding the "job mix" in the queue or the mix of volumes required by any particular job.

(vi) You may assume that the system has only a very small number of disk drives available (probably between six and sixty) as compared to the large number (perhaps hundreds) of volumes contained in the library.

When designing this job scheduling program, you should incorporate several routines, including ones to read the input job cards and construct the job queue and other list structures to represent the disk volumes available, the status of the various volumes, and their relationships to the jobs in the queue. You should also include a subroutine to scan the job queue for an executable job and release it for execution. In the event that no job in the queue can be executed with the current set of mounted disk volumes, this subroutine should notify the mainline program.

For instances when the mainline program has been informed that no executable jobs can be located in the queue, an additional subroutine should be written to determine the necessary volume changes for maximum throughput. This routine should print the appropriate change messages and update the data structures representing the disk volume status to reflect these changes. It is very difficult to devise an algorithm that will yield an absolute maximum throughput with an absolute minimum number of disk volume changes, especially when we consider the time parameter associated with each job. Consequently, you should attempt only to develop a good algorithm for volume scheduling that will permit as many jobs as possible to execute simultaneously with a near minimum number of volume changes.

You should assume that there will always be more jobs in the original batch (i.e., job cards in the input data deck) than there is room in the job queue. Your program should stop reading the job cards as soon as the queue becomes filled but continue entering them as other jobs are released for execution and removed from the queue. This process should continue until all the jobs have been entered into the queue and completed execution. Quite obviously, the volume-changing scheduler can examine only the jobs in the queue, and as a result, it cannot achieve an optimal max/min combination for the whole batch.

The overall purpose of this program is to simulate the processes of scheduling and executing a batch of jobs. After initial loading of the job queue, the program should make an initial assignment of disk volumes for all available drives and set a run-time clock to the value zero. Then as many jobs as possible are submitted for execution and their slots in the queue filled with subsequent jobs. Throughout this entire simulation procedure, the program maintains a table (having at most NOJOBS entries) of all jobs in the midst of execution. For each job in the table the information recorded consists of the job name and required execution time (both obtained from the job card), as well as the value of the run-time clock as recorded when the job started execution.

After the initial stages the simulation proceeds by the program's iterating through the following sequence of steps until all the jobs have completed execution:

(i) Increment the run-time clock.

(ii) Scan through the table of executing jobs in a search for jobs that have completed execution (i.e., current time minus starting time equals job time). If none can be found, return to Step (i). Otherwise, delete all jobs that have completed execution from the table.

(iii) Determine if there is a job in the queue that can be executed with the volumes that are currently mounted. If there are no such jobs in the queue, proceed to Step (v).

(iv) Enter the new job into execution from the job queue. Then read a new job card from the input batch (if there are any left) and insert the job into the queue. At this point, if there is room in memory for another job to execute, return to Step (iii). Otherwise, return to Step (i).

(v) Determine whether any of the currently mounted disk volumes can be replaced. Remember that a volume cannot be replaced as long as it is being used by any of the jobs in the midst of execution. You have to wait until all jobs using that particular volume have completed execution before you can replace it. If no replacements are possible, return to Step (i).

(vi) Determine whether there is a job in the queue whose volume requirements can be satisfied by mounting new volumes to replace those which are not currently being used. If no such job exists in the queue, return to Step (i). Otherwise, mount the necessary volumes for the new job and return to Step (iv) to enter that job into execution. (This is a very simplified approach for volume replacement. You may wish to attempt to devise a better algorithm that strives to minimize the number of volume changes.)

During this simulation process your program should print the starting and finishing time for the execution of each job as indicated by the run-time clock. In addition, it should print summary statistics relating the total length of time for the execution of all the jobs and the total number of volume changes.

Discuss the efficiency of the data structures that you choose for the job queue and volume status representations, and by analyzing the alternatives, justify your choice.

CHAPTER EIGHT
OPERATIONS WITH TREE STRUCTURES

8.1 SEQUENCING THROUGH TREES

Now that we have defined non-linear lists and illustrated the use of tree structures, we are ready to investigate programming techniques for processing such structures. The first question that arises in this context is the obvious one concerning the order in which we should consider the nodes of a non-linear structure when we wish to perform some operation on all of them. We have to be careful to define this sequence in such a way that we retain the structural information embedded in the data structure. We did not have any choice when we were concerned with linearly linked lists, since the only possible order in which we could process the nodes was to begin with the top node and follow the links sequentially through the remaining nodes. When dealing with bitrees, however, we shall see that the order in which we process the nodes may vary considerably from one application to another. Nevertheless, we do retain a similar way of identifying a tree structure. To be more specific, we identified a linearly linked list by a pointer to its top node, since all the nodes of the list were accessible from it. In analogous fashion, we shall be referring to a tree by a pointer to its root node, once again because all the nodes in the tree can be accessed from the root.

In order to clarify some of these ideas, let us consider a subroutine to list the symbols in a bitree symbol table in alphabetical order. As an input parameter, the subroutine should require a pointer (P) identifying the bitree whose symbols are to be printed. (The actual nodes comprising the bitree can be passed to the subroutine using COMMON storage.) For each node in the tree, the program must first print the symbols contained in the branch pointed at by the left pointer (LL) in the node (i.e., the ones appearing earlier in the alphabet than the symbol represented by the node in question). If the left pointer is the null value, of course, nothing need be printed. After printing all the symbols in the left branch, the program has to print the entry in the node itself, followed, in turn, by the symbols in the nodes of the right branch, as indicated by the pointer RL.

Each branch of the tree is itself a tree, and, as a result, it has to be processed in the same fashion as the overall tree. In other words, beginning with the root node, we have to apply our procedure <u>recursively</u> on all the nodes of the tree. Ideally, we would like to have a simple print routine which could be applied to every single subtree of the bitree symbol table in the proper sequence. This goal could be achieved in the most straightforward fashion if we were permitted in FORTRAN to invoke a subroutine inside itself. Assuming that such a subroutine call were valid, the coding for our print routine could appear as illustrated in Example 8.1.

```
C EXAMPLE 8.1 - RECURSIVE SUBROUTINE FOR PRINTING
C               THE ENTRIES OF A BITREE SYMBOL
C               TABLE IN ALPHABETICAL ORDER
C               (THIS CODING IS INVALID IN FORTRAN.)
C
      recursive SUBROUTINE PRINT(P)
C
C Make appropriate declarations of nodes in the tree.
C
      CHARACTER*6 SYMBOL(...)
      INTEGER ADDRES(...),LL(...),RL(...),P
      COMMON SYMBOL,ADDRES,LL,RL
C
C LL and RL are the left and right links respectively.
C
C Print the left branch of node P if one exists.
C
   10 IF(LL(P).GT.0)call print(LL(P))
C
C Now print the entry in node P itself.
C
   20 PRINT,SYMBOL(P)
C
C Print the right branch of node P if one exists.
C
   30 IF(RL(P).GT.0)call print(RL(P))
C
   40 RETURN
      END
```

Subroutines (such as the one in Example 8.1) that can call themselves, either directly or indirectly, are called *RECURSIVE* subroutines. Unfortunately, however, FORTRAN does not support recursion. Consequently, in order that we be able to execute our print routine, we shall have to add more instructions to the version presented in Example 8.1 so as to eliminate the recursive calls within the subroutine. Nevertheless, at this stage in our discussion, we shall consider the version in Example 8.1 as if it were valid, since it is much simpler than the legitimate version, and thus much easier to understand.

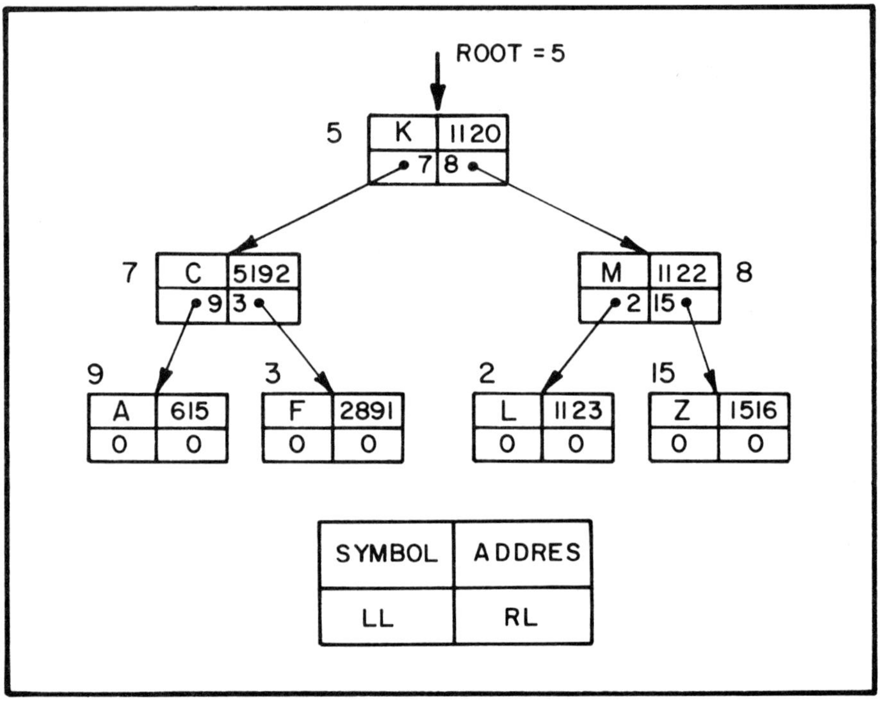

Figure 8.1

Sample Bitree Symbol Table

To further illustrate the recursive nature of our print routine, suppose we trace through its

execution when applied to the bitree symbol table in Figure 8.1. The subroutine is first invoked by

call PRINT(5)

since 5 is the value of the pointer identifying the root of the tree. PRINT then examines the left link of node 5, and, after recognizing that its value, 7, is not the null pointer, it recursively invokes PRINT(7). It is essential that we remember, however, that we are in the midst of executing PRINT(5). We have to be reminded that we are currently working on the left branch from node 5, and that it still remains for us to print SYMBOL(5), followed, in turn, by the entries in the right branch from node 5. For this purpose, we can adopt the convention of appending the word "left" to PRINT(5). Using this new notation, we can describe our present position in the recursive application of the PRINT routine as follows:

PRINT(5)left → PRINT(7).

Using our newly adopted notation for the sake of brevity, we can describe the entire processing of our bitree as follows:

The calling program invokes PRINT(5).
Consider LL(5) which has the value 7.
PRINT(5)left → PRINT(7).
Examine LL(7) which is found to be 9.
PRINT(5)left → PRINT(7)left → PRINT(9).
Determine that LL(9) is the null pointer.
Print SYMBOL(9) (i.e., 'A').

Notice that RL(9) is also the null pointer.
Return to PRINT(5)left → PRINT(7)left.
Print SYMBOL(7) (i.e., 'C').
Consider RL(7) which has the value 3.
PRINT(5)left → PRINT(7)right → PRINT(3).
Ascertain that LL(3) is the null pointer.
Print SYMBOL(3) (i.e., 'F').
Notice that RL(3) is also zero.
Return to PRINT(5)left → PRINT(7)right.
Return control to PRINT(5)left.
Print SYMBOL(5) (i.e., 'K').
Consider RL(5) which has the value 8.
PRINT(5)right → PRINT(8).
Examine LL(8) which has the value 2.
PRINT(5)right → PRINT(8)left → PRINT(2).
Consider LL(2) which is the null pointer.
Print SYMBOL(2) (i.e., 'L').
Notice that RL(2) is also zero.
Return to PRINT(5)right → PRINT(8)left.
Print SYMBOL(8) (i.e., 'M').
Examine RL(8) which has the value 15.
PRINT(5)right → PRINT(8)right → PRINT(15).
Notice that LL(15) is the null pointer.
Print SYMBOL(15) (i.e., 'Z').
Examine RL(15) which is also zero.
Return to PRINT(5)right → PRINT(8)right.
Return to PRINT(5)right.
Return to the original calling program.

In our preceding example of printing the symbols in a bitree symbol table in alphabetical order, we have defined a very precise method of traversing a tree. Since we print the left branch first for each node, we can consider this as being a left-to-right scanning of the nodes. Furthermore, we print the symbol represented by the node itself between the printouts of its left and right branches. As a result, we use the term, *LEFT-TO-RIGHT INFIX FORM*, to describe this traversing order. On the other hand, if we wish to print the contents of the bitree table in reversed alphabetical order, we have to use *RIGHT-TO-LEFT INFIX*.

ORDER	LEFT-to-RIGHT	RIGHT-to-LEFT
PREfix	P,L,R	P,R,L
INfix	L,P,R	R,P,L
POSTfix	L,R,P	R,L,P

Notation: L: Traverse the LEFT Branch.
P: PROCESS the Node.
R: Traverse the RIGHT Branch.

Figure 8.2

Tree-Traversing Orders

In dealing with bitrees, there are two additional orders in which we can process the content of a node relative to its branches. These are called *PREFIX* and *POSTFIX*. As their names imply, in the prefix order, we process (print in our preceding example) the content of the node itself before traversing its branches, whereas, in postfix order, we process the node itself after its branches. As a result, we have a total of six different ways in which we can sequence through bitrees. These six different forms are summarized in Figure 8.2.

In each of the six traversing orders, we apply the same three actions recursively on successive nodes, beginning always with the root node. However, each form is uniquely characterized by the order in which these actions are performed. To illustrate, consider the different results produced by the application of the six sequencing orders to the bitree in Figure 8.1:

	LEFT-to-RIGHT	RIGHT-to-LEFT
PREfix :	KCAFMLZ	KMZLCFA
INfix :	ACFKLMZ	ZMLKFCA
POSTfix:	AFCLZMK	ZLMFACK

The particular process applied to the bitree symbol table in the preceding example was that of printing the symbols contained in the table. However, the same sequencing orders can be applied within the context of any other type of operation or manipulation that we might wish to perform on trees. Whenever we process a tree in subsequent sections, we will use one of the six orders just introduced. Moreover, the definitions of the sequencing orders can be extended quite easily for n-ary trees. Although the prefix and postfix forms would remain unchanged, there would then be n-1 different infix forms, as determined by the choice of branches between which the node itself was processed.

Another way of regarding the traversing orders which we have been discussing is to consider them as straightening algorithms by which a tree structure can be converted into a character string. Some of the structural information, however, is obviously lost in the process, and indeed, we shall have an opportunity later to see that the strings we obtain from trees are not unique. In other words, many different trees will yield the same string under a particular order of straightening.

8.2 THE MECHANISM OF RECURSION

In Section 8.1, we saw how simple tree-traversing operations could be coded in the form of a recursive procedure. In particular, we discussed a recursive subroutine for printing the entries in a bitree symbol table in alphabetical order. (We emphasized, however, that the coding for this routine, as presented in Example 8.1, was not valid in FORTRAN.) In general, it is most convenient to write programs for the manipulation of trees in a recursive fashion, since the structure of this data type is itself of a recursive nature. Most modern programming languages support recursion, and, as a result, it is easier to write tree-processing programs using such languages (e.g., Algol, PL/1) rather than FORTRAN. Nevertheless, this convenience might be deceiving for programmers who are concerned with the efficiency of their programs. A significant overhead is involved with recursive procedures. When the programmer is not aware of the "real" processing being performed on his behalf by the built-in routine provided by the compiler in support of recursion, he may utilize recursive routines in a most indiscriminate fashion. In such cases, the result is often a very inefficient program.

Recursion is a very powerful tool that has to be used carefully. There is no justification, for example, in writing a recursive procedure for multiplying matrices, even though it may result in fewer program statements. Multiplication of matrices is an iterative process rather than a recursive one, and, as such, it does not warrant the use of recursion. The processing of tree structures, however, is a recursive process which definitely calls for the use of recursion, and such operations should be programmed (whenever possible) in a language which supports recursion. Nevertheless, to make the student aware of the cost of recursion and enable him to truly understand its implications, we have chosen to discuss in detail the implementation of recursive procedures in a language (i.e., FORTRAN) which does not support recursion.

Suppose that we return to reexamine Example 8.1 with the aim of eliminating the recursive calls, thus making the printing procedure a legitimate FORTRAN subroutine. We might first recall that, for each invocation of subroutine PRINT, we have to remember, in some fashion or other, the path through the tree by which we arrived at the particular node currently being processed (i.e., the node pointed at by the parameter P). In essence, we remember the path by storing a set of pointers to the nodes in the path. For example, in our application of subroutine PRINT to the bitree in Figure 8.1, when we processed node 2 (i.e., the one containing the symbol 'L'), we had kept a record of the pointers 5 and 8 to indicate the path which we had followed to reach that node. In addition, along with each pointer, we have to store information indicating the extent to which we have processed each of the nodes along the path. For example, to accompany the pointer 5, we indicated right branch processing, while, with the pointer 8, we recorded left branch processing. Consequently, when we have finished with node 2, we return to node 8 with full knowledge of the point at which we interrupted the processing of that node, with the result that we can then proceed to print the contents of the node itself, followed, in turn, by its right branch. In a similar fashion, after finishing with node 8 and all its successors, we return to node 5, at which time, after determining that this node has no predecessors, we have nothing left to do, thus terminating the process.

We want to study our recursive printing example within the context of a set of general rules for the implementation of recursive procedures. Towards this end, we might first observe that, for every invocation of a recursive subroutine, we have to provide a new version of all the local variables (including formal parameters) used inside the subroutine. In our print routine, we have only one such variable, the parameter P, which points at the node currently being processed. By saving the values of P for all the previous recursive invocations, we can remember the path from the root to the current node. Every time we execute a recursive call, we add a new pointer to the list of path pointers we have accumulated, and, whenever we return from a recursive activation of the subroutine, we remove the latest value of P from this list.

In the more general case, when we have more than one local variable, we maintain a separate storage area for the local variables for each recursive invocation of the subroutine. In other words, for each time that we enter the recursive routine, we add a new storage area for the most recent values of the local variables. During execution of the routine, the latest values of the local variables are the ones used, and, upon exit from the subroutine, these most recent values are deleted. This means that the penultimate values of the local variables will be used when the previous invocation is resumed.

In addition to saving the values of the local variables upon entry to the subroutine, we also have to record the return address, as with any subroutine call, so that we know the statement from which to resume execution upon return to the calling routine.

(In the recursive case, the calling and called subroutines are one and the same.) Saving the return point will indicate, inside the PRINT subroutine, the stage at which execution should be resumed in the processing of the predecessor node (i.e., whether to resume at statement 20 or statement 40 in Example 8.1).

In Example 8.2 we have inserted the necessary instructions to convert Example 8.1 into an executable FORTRAN subroutine. We have included two vectors, PSTACK and RSTACK, in which we save respectively the values of the pointer P and the return addresses. A special pointer, STP (STack Pointer), is utilized to designate the current entries in these vectors. Consequently, wherever we used P in Example 8.1, we now use PSTACK(STP). Moreover, before executing a "recursive call", we save the return address in RSTACK(STP), and then assign the new value of P, PSTACK(STP+1), to be the left or right pointer of the current node P, PSTACK(STP), according to the branch we are following. Finally, we increment STP so as to make its new value current before branching to the beginning of the routine to execute our simulated recursive call.

In the coding of Example 8.2, the RETURN statement of Example 8.1 has been replaced by a set of instructions that restore the penultimate values of the stack variables by decrementing STP and resuming execution at the point designated by the value saved in RSTACK(STP) (i.e., either statement 20

```
C EXAMPLE 8.2 - VALID FORTRAN VERSION OF EXAMPLE 8.1
C               (LEFT-TO-RIGHT INFIX PRINTING
C               OF A BITREE SYMBOL TABLE)
C
      SUBROUTINE PRINT(ROOT)
C
      CHARACTER*6 SYMBOL(1000)
      INTEGER ADDRES(1000),ROOT
      INTEGER*2 LL(1000),RL(1000)
      COMMON SYMBOL,ADDRES,LL,RL
C
      INTEGER*2 PSTACK(100),RSTACK(100),STP
C
      STP = 1
      PSTACK(1) = ROOT
C
C Begin the recursive part of the procedure.
C
   10 IF(LL(PSTACK(STP)).GT.0)GO TO 100
   20 PRINT,SYMBOL(PSTACK(STP))
   30 IF(RL(PSTACK(STP)).GT.0)GO TO 300
C
C Return from the recursion.
C
   40 STP = STP-1
      IF(STP.LT.1)RETURN
C
C Restore the previous stack value, and then
C transfer to the appropriate point of return.
C
      K = RSTACK(STP)
      GO TO (20,40),K
C
C Recursive call on the left branch.
C
  100 RSTACK(STP) = 1
      PSTACK(STP+1) = LL(PSTACK(STP))
      STP = STP+1
      GO TO 10
C
C Recursive call on the right branch.
C
  300 RSTACK(STP) = 2
      PSTACK(STP+1) = RL(PSTACK(STP))
      STP = STP+1
      GO TO 10
C
      END
```

or statement 40). Since we cannot manipulate addresses in FORTRAN, we employ a COMPUTED GO TO statement with the value of RSTACK(STP) as an index. Because we have only two possible points of return, we need only save in RSTACK the values 1 and 2. In the general case, however, where we might have several possible return points, we can assign an index number to each possibility, and then branch accordingly.

Execution of our printing routine is terminated when we perform a return from a recursive call to find that STP has been reduced to zero. This indicates that we have returned to the root of the tree, thus completing the sequencing through the nodes. The actual recursive calls in Example 8.1 (i.e., statements 10 and 30) have been replaced by branches to statements 100 and 300 respectively. In both cases, we save the proper return address and assign a new value for P [actually PSTACK(STP+1)] in preparation for a new recursive application of the printing process.

Vectors PSTACK and RSTACK are used in a very specific way to support recursion. In particular, we are always concerned with only a single value in each vector, the one identified by STP. By incrementing STP, we can add new values to the vectors, and conversely, by decrementing STP, we can delete values. Once values have been deleted, they are never used again. This stacking concept is so very commonly used in various areas of computer science that it has acquired a special name — *PUSH-DOWN STACK*.

Sometimes, a push-down stack is called a "first-in-last-out queue" to describe the order by which values are stored in, and removed from, the stack.

In order to support recursion, one must always utilize a push-down stack. Conceptually, we can consider every entry in a stack as containing several items. For example, we can regard PSTACK and RSTACK as comprising a single stack with two items on each level. Most modern programming languages (e.g., Algol, PL/1, APL) support recursion as part of the language facilities. For such languages, stacks are maintained by the run-time routines provided by the compiler. In FORTRAN, however, we have to simulate these operations in order to have recursive-like routines.

One of the major problems encountered in the simulation of recursion is the determination of the size of the push-down stacks. For example, in our print routine, the stack has to be large enough to contain the longest possible path through the tree. In cases like the bitree symbol table, where the construction (i.e., shape) of the tree is data dependent, this might create severe difficulties. Fortunately, we can use other methods to list the entries in a bitree symbol table that avoid recursion. We shall be considering such methods further in Section 8.4.

In the general case, however, when we are processing trees in postfix or prefix order, we might be forced to use recursion, either explicitly (in the cases of languages which support it), or

```
C EXAMPLE 8.3 - LEFT-TO-RIGHT POSTFIX LISTING OF
C               A BITREE SYMBOL TABLE
C
      SUBROUTINE POSTPR(ROOT)
C
      CHARACTER*6 SYMBOL(1000)
      INTEGER ADDRES(1000),ROOT,P
      INTEGER*2 LL(1000),RL(1000)
      INTEGER*2 PSTACK(100),RSTACK(100),STP
      COMMON SYMBOL,ADDRES,LL,RL
C
      STP = 0
      P = ROOT
C
C Push down PSTACK and store the pointer.
C
    1 STP = STP+1
      IF(STP.GT.100)STOP
      PSTACK(STP) = P
C
C Begin the recursive part of the procedure.
C
   10 IF(LL(P).GT.0)GO TO 100
   30 IF(RL(P).GT.0)GO TO 300
   20 PRINT,SYMBOL(P)
C
C Restore P and pop up the stacks.
C
   40 STP = STP-1
      IF(STP.LT.1)RETURN
C
      P = PSTACK(STP)
      K = RSTACK(STP)
      GO TO (30,20),K
C
C Recursive call on the left branch.
C
  100 RSTACK(STP) = 1
      P = LL(P)
      GO TO 1
C
C Recursive call on the right branch.
C
  300 RSTACK(STP) = 2
      P = RL(P)
      GO TO 1
C
      END
```

implicitly through the use of stacks. In such instances, whenever we have a new value to enter into the stack, we will have to check to see that the stack is not already full. As an illustration, the coding in Example 8.3 produces a postfix listing of a bitree. For simplicity, we have chosen our previous example of a bitree symbol table, even though there is no practical use for postfix listing in such symbol tables. However, the sequel operations have been rearranged to demonstrate another way of handling the stack which permits us to have only one stack-full check point.

8.3 PUSH-DOWN STACKS

The push-down stack is a very important concept in computer science, and one that we will be using frequently in subsequent chapters. Consequently, before we initiate our discussion of methods for sequencing through trees without stacks (Section 8.4), we would like to generalize the idea of this new data type. For convenience, we shall also be introducing general-purpose FORTRAN routines to manipulate stacks for us.

A push-down stack can be considered as a data structure that bears a close analogy to a spring-mounted stack of dishes in a cafeteria. One can add dishes to the top of the stack, and remove dishes from the top. However, one does not add dishes to, or remove them from, the center or bottom of the stack. In similar fashion, a push-down stack can be implemented as a vector of data entries. Entries may be added to one end, or deleted from that end, but never added to, or taken from, the center or the other end of the vector.

For our general-purpose stack routines, we shall represent a push-down stack by a one-dimensional array. The first element of the array will be used as the stack pointer (previously STP) pointing to the top entry in the stack. The bottom entry in the stack is represented by the second element of the array, the next-to-bottom entry of the stack by the third element, and so forth. The top entry in the stack is represented by the $(n+1)^{st}$ element of the array, assuming that there are n entries in the stack. As an example, consider the stack presented in Figure 8.3. This stack has three entries, 'X' at the top as represented by STACK(4), 'Q' in the middle as represented by STACK(3), and finally 'R' at the bottom as represented by STACK(2). STACK(1) has the value 4 to indicate the position of the top entry in the stack.

The two most basic operations to be performed on a push-down stack are to *PUSH DOWN* and *POP UP* the stack. Pushing down the stack entails adding a new element to the top of the stack. Within the context of our implementation of stacks, this means incrementing the stack pointer and then inserting the new entry. This operation is called "push down" by analogy to the stack of dishes, since, when a

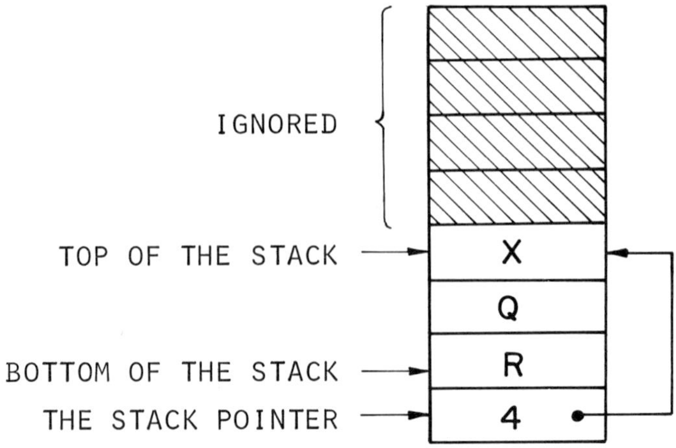

Figure 8.3

Vector Representation of a Push-Down Stack

person adds a dish to the top of the pile, he pushes all the others down one level. By comparison, popping up the stack consists of physically removing the top element from the stack. For our purposes, this entails decrementing the stack pointer.

The third operation that we shall be performing on a push-down stack is, strictly speaking, unnecessary, but it is a very convenient one. It involves selecting a particular entry in the stack for further examination, without altering the stack in any way. If we had a complete disregard for computer time, we could accomplish this selection by a sequence of push-down and pop-up operations. Such action would, however, be very inefficient.

We shall use subprograms PUSH, POPUP, and EXAMIN, as coded in Examples 8.4, 8.5, and 8.6 respectively, to exhibit explicitly these three operations on push-down stacks whenever they arise. In these routines we assume that we have exclusively INTEGER*2 stacks. Whenever we need stacks with different types of entries, we will have to define new stack routines for them. For each of our stack manipulation routines, we pass the stack vector as a parameter. Unfortunately, we also have to pass the size of the vector as a parameter to the routines. (This is required only in WATFIV, since, in standard FORTRAN, there are ways of programming by which we can avoid the need to pass its length along with each vector.)

```
C EXAMPLE 8.4 - PUSH-DOWN OPERATION
C
      SUBROUTINE PUSH(STACK,L,VAL)
C
C PUSH adds the value VAL to the top of STACK.
C
      INTEGER*2 STACK(L),VAL
C
      STACK(1) = STACK(1)+1
      IF(STACK(1).GT.L)GO TO 99
C
      STACK(STACK(1)) = VAL
      RETURN
C
   99 PRINT,'STACK FULL'
C
      STOP
      END
```

```
C EXAMPLE 8.5 - POP-UP OPERATION
C
      SUBROUTINE POPUP(VAL,STACK,L,*)
C
C POPUP removes the top entry from
C STACK and assigns its value to VAL.
C
      INTEGER*2 STACK(L),VAL
C
C If STACK is empty, the alternative
C return point is used.
C
      IF(STACK(1).LT.2)RETURN1
C
      VAL = STACK(STACK(1))
      STACK(1) = STACK(1)-1
C
      RETURN
      END
```

```
C EXAMPLE 8.6 - STACK-ACCESS OPERATION
C
      INTEGER FUNCTION EXAMIN*2(STACK,L,I)
C
C EXAMIN returns as its value the Ith entry of STACK.
C If I = 1, EXAMIN will return the top entry.
C If I = 2, EXAMIN will return the second entry, etc.
C
      INTEGER*2 STACK(L)
C
      K = STACK(1)+1-I
      IF(K.LT.1.OR.K.GT.L)GO TO 88
C
      EXAMIN = STACK(K)
      RETURN
C
   88 PRINT,'EXAMIN OUT OF RANGE'
C
      STOP
      END
```

Operations on push-down stacks are so common in computer science that special notations have been developed for their representation. We shall be using these notations in our subsequent flowcharts. The various notations are explained below, accompanied in each case by the equivalent implementation using our stack manipulation routines. In these explanations, S is a symbolic name for a stack, and K is a simple variable.

K←S : Assign to K the value of the topmost element in stack S. The stack itself remains unchanged.

```
        K = EXAMIN(S,L,1)
or
        K = S(S(1))
```

S←K : Replace the top entry in the stack by the value of K.

```
        S(S(1)) = K
```

S↑ : Pop up the stack and throw away its previous top entry.

```
  CALL POPUP(DUMMY,S,L,&999)
C Go to statement 999 if stack is empty.
```

$S{\downarrow}\leftarrow K$: Push down the stack and insert the value of K as the new topmost entry.

```
CALL PUSH(S,L,K)
```

$K\leftarrow S{\uparrow}$: Assign K the value of the topmost entry in the stack, and then pop up the stack.

```
CALL POPUP(K,S,L,&999)
```

$K\leftarrow{\uparrow}S$: Pop up the stack, and then assign to K the value of the new topmost element.

```
CALL POPUP(DUMMY,S,L,&999)
K = S(S(1))
```

Combinations of these notations can be used to indicate further operations. For example,

$${\uparrow}S\leftarrow K \quad \text{and} \quad {\uparrow}{\uparrow}S\leftarrow K$$

specify that stack S is popped up once or twice, respectively, before replacing the top stack entry by the value of K.

We can now employ these stack notations for describing the various algorithms used to sequence through trees. For example, Figure 8.4 displays, in flowchart form, the algorithm for postfix listing of a bitree (as formerly introduced in Example 8.3). In this flowchart, we use S and R to represent the two stacks, PSTACK and RSTACK, respectively. Since the two stacks have a common stack pointer, STP, we

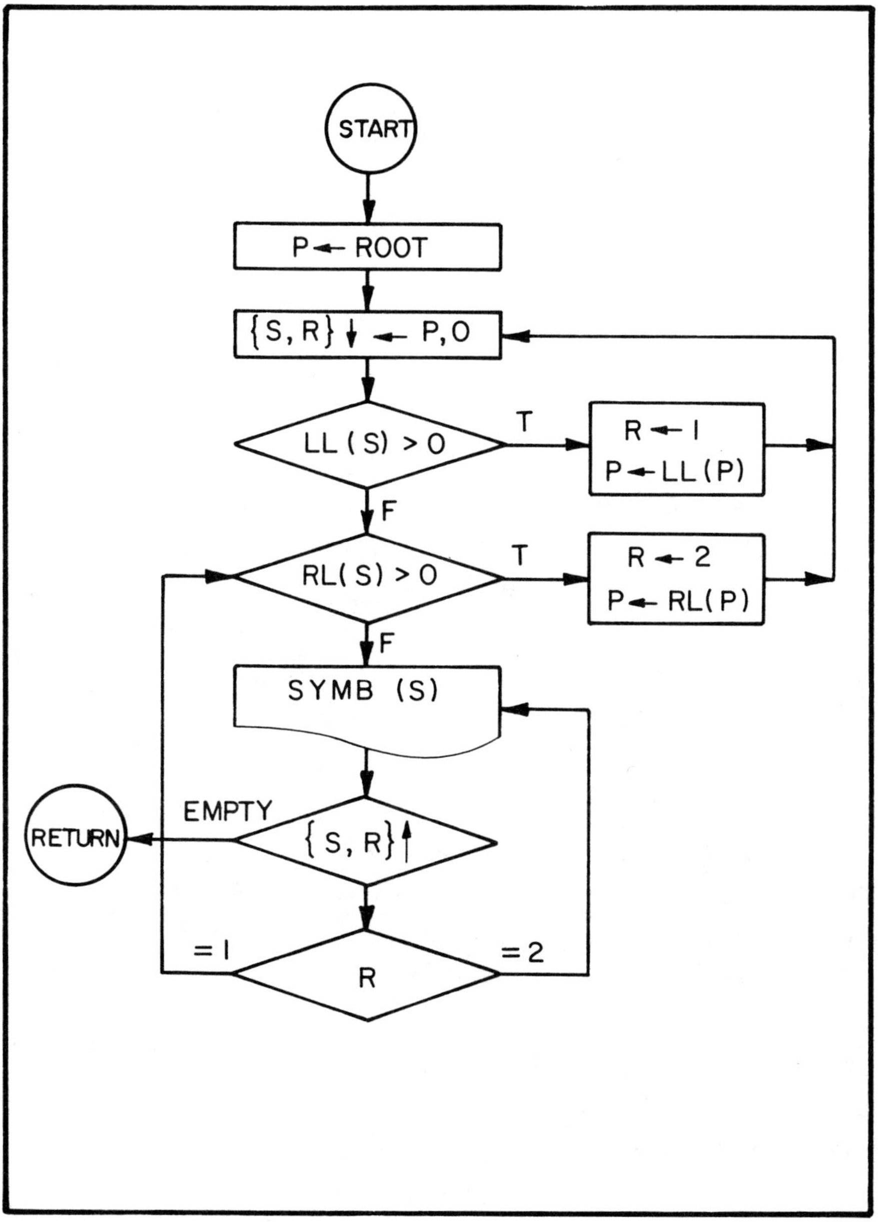

Figure 8.4

<u>Postfix Listing of a Bitree Using Stacks</u>

can combine their operations. The common operations are designated by enclosing the stack symbols in braces (e.g., {S,R}↓←P,0 indicates that we push down both stacks, S and R, and insert the values P and 0 at the tops of S and R respectively). Finally, it should be clear that LL(S) and RL(S) represent the left and right links respectively of the node designated by the pointer value currently at the top of stack S.

As a further illustration of our stack notations, Figure 8.5 presents a flowchart describing an algorithm for infix listing of a bitree symbol table. This latest algorithm is a slightly improved version of the one presented earlier in Example 8.2. This improvement is based upon the observation that, once a symbol has been printed, there is no longer any need to maintain a pointer to the node containing that symbol. Consequently, instead of pushing down the stack and inserting the right branch pointer as the new top entry, we merely replace the value currently on top of the stack with a pointer to the right branch. In addition to eliminating the need for RSTACK, this revision also reduces the required stack size, since we now have to retain pointer values only upon proceeding to the left. The pointer values in the stack no longer trace the complete path from the root to the current node, however, since we now save pointers in the stack only to those nodes in the path whose entries have not yet been printed.

This latest simplification is not valid for postfix listing, since, in this case, the node

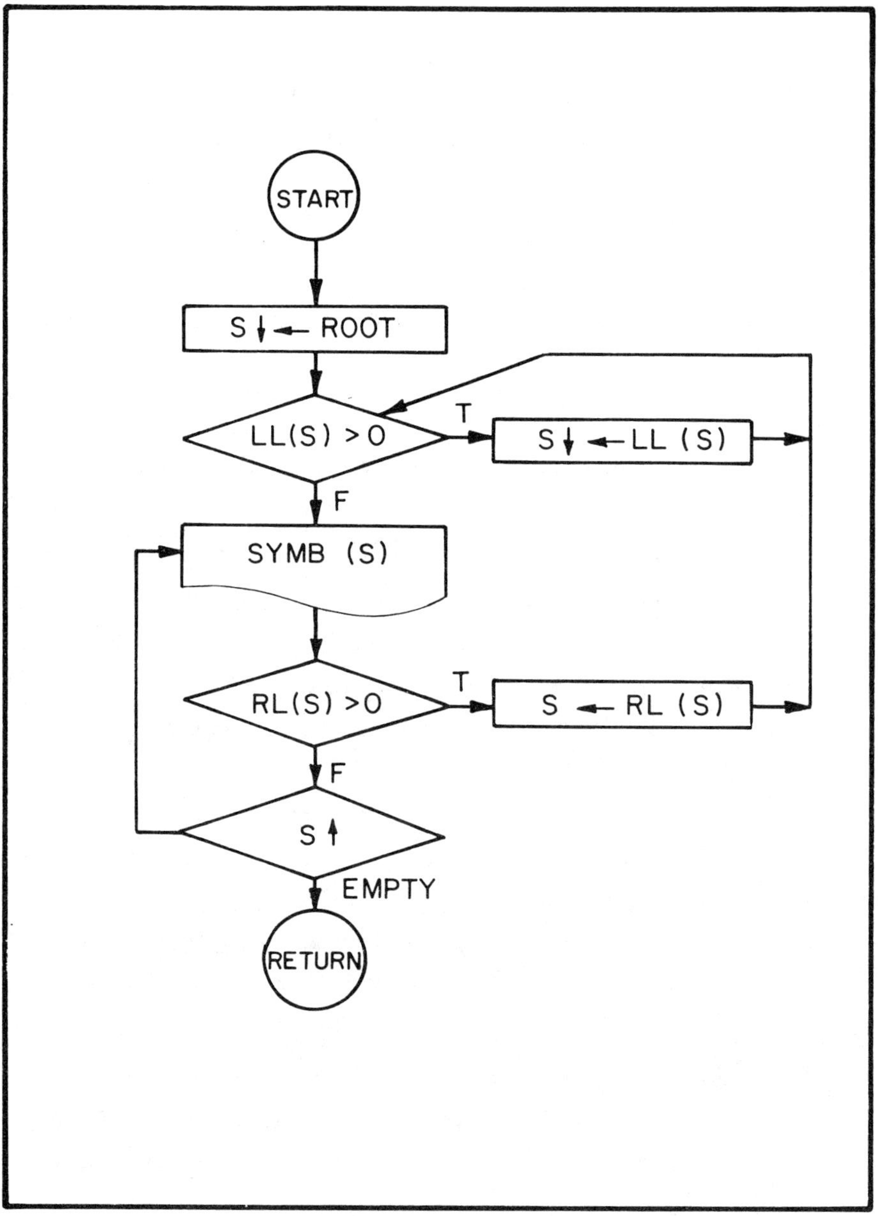

Figure 8.5

Infix Listing of a Bitree Using a Single Stack

itself is considered only <u>after</u> all its branches. For such a listing, we must use two stacks and maintain a complete record of the path from the root. This is very unfortunate, since, as we shall have occasion to see, the postfix order of traversing trees is the most useful one, and it will be used frequently in later examples.

8.4 NON-RECURSIVE METHODS FOR PROCESSING TREES

In the previous sections of this chapter we have developed techniques for sequencing through trees using recursive procedures or their equivalent push-down stacks. These methods are very straightforward and relatively easy to implement, especially with languages that support recursion. Nevertheless, the overhead involved with the recursion and the extra unpredictable amount of storage required for the stacks may make such algorithms impractical. For some applications, once again by trading off computing time versus memory space, we can eliminate the need for push-down stacks. This can be accomplished by adding some mechanism for computing the path we are following through the tree or using the links of the tree as temporary storage indicators of the path.

For the infix order of processing trees, we can devise an algorithm that will be more efficient than the recursive one with respect to both time and storage. For other orders, we can eliminate the need for stacks by increasing the time required for processing the trees. In this section we discuss two such methods. The first utilizes the unused links in the leaves as the tree is being constructed. The second method, on the other hand, alters the pointers in the link fields as it progresses through the tree so as to maintain a record of the path being followed. When proceeding backwards up the tree at any stage, the algorithm restores the links to their former values.

8.4.1 Threaded Trees

The first method is based upon the simple observation that most of the link fields in a tree structure contain the null pointer, and, as such, they are not used effectively. From graph theory (or by applying some common sense), we can see that a tree with N nodes has only N-1 edges. Consequently, if we have K linking fields in each node, we are using effectively only N-1 of N*K links, with the result that N*(K-1)+1 links contain the null pointer. In particular, bitrees (K = 2) have N+1 null pointers. The basic idea behind this approach is to utilize these unused links as back pointers so that we can use them to sequence through the tree.

The most effective way of utilizing the links of a leaf node is to set them to point at the predecessor or the successor of that node in the left-to-right infix order. More specifically, an empty left link is set to point at the node's predecessor in the left-to-right infix order, whereas an empty right link is set to point at the node's successor in the same order. This technique provides for a very simple procedure for infix processing, while still being very easy to incorporate in the construction of the tree.

Figure 8.6 illustrates a typical bitree with its back links adjusted for an infix order. There are two links which still contain the null pointer. These are respectively the left link of the first node in the infix order and the right link of the last node in that order. When processing the tree in a left-to-right order, we will use only the right back links as we progress from each node to its successor. On the other hand, if we wished to process the tree in the reverse order (i.e., right-to-left infix), we would use only the left back links in an analogous fashion.

Before we proceed to investigate how we might actually construct such back links in a bitree, we should emphasize the difference between the concept of a predecessor and/or successor in the left-to-right infix ordering and that of a predecessor and/or successor in the actual structure of the tree itself. The former relationship (indicated by light black arrows in Figure 8.6) reflects the order in which the nodes are processed in an infix sequence, whereas the latter (indicated by dark black arrows in Figure 8.6) is independent of any individual processing order.

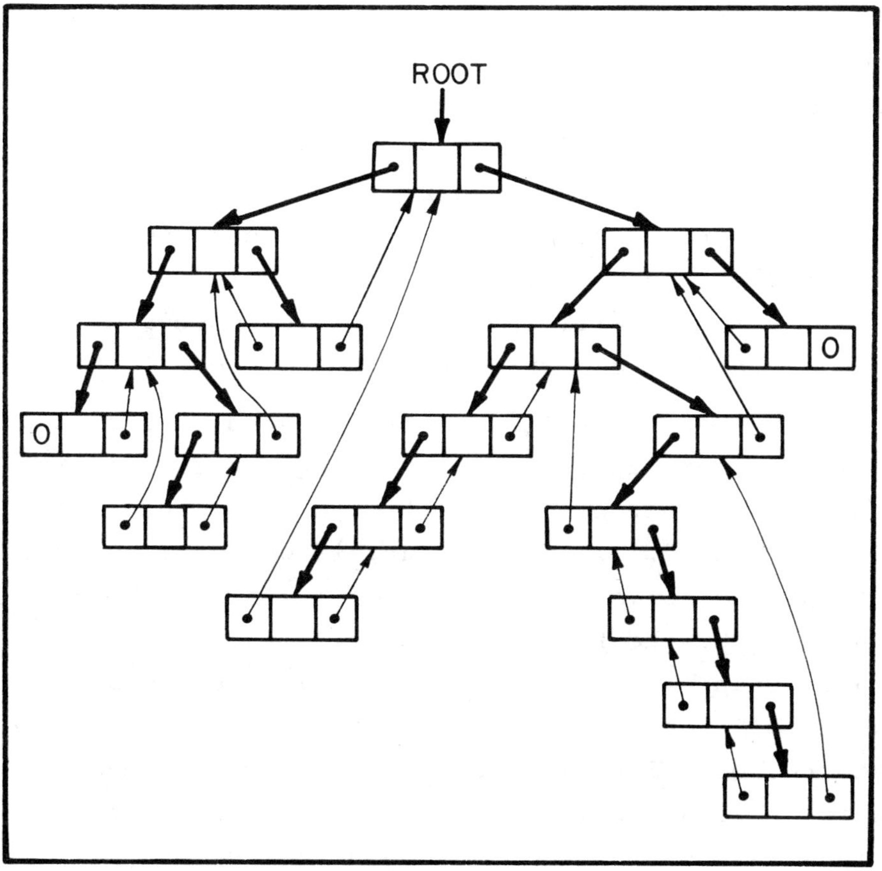

Figure 8.6

Example of a Threaded Bitree

Before we write the actual FORTRAN coding to process a bitree which includes appropriate back pointers, we first have to find some way to distinguish the back links from the regular links of the tree. We can achieve this by simply setting the sign of the back link values to be negative. This is equivalent to using one bit in the link field as an indicator of its type. Until now, whenever we encountered a link whose value was less than unity, we automatically concluded that it was a null pointer. However, now we have to distinguish between links whose values are negative and those which are zero. The former will be recognized as being back links for the left-to-right infix order, while the latter will indicate the leftmost and rightmost nodes respectively in the bitree.

In a few cases (bitree symbol tables included), however, we can determine whether a link is a back pointer by merely comparing it with the pointer to the node itself. In particular, if we never perform deletions, a forward (i.e., normal) link can be identified by the fact that LINK(P) is always greater than P, assuming that we allocate storage sequentially and never release it. If this is the case, the back link will always satisfy the inverse condition LINK(P).LT.P. In our coding to process a bitree symbol table having both forward and backward links (Examples 8.7 through 8.10), we use the sign to indicate back links. However, we could just as easily adopt the other method of comparing pointers, since the example satisfies the conditions specified for its use.

Subroutine PRINT, as presented in Example 8.7, prints the entries in a bitree symbol table in alphabetical order (i.e., left-to-right infix) without using stacks. The coding is based upon the assumption that the back links have been set properly within the tree. Beginning with the root node (as designated by the parameter ROOT), the routine follows the left links of successive nodes until it arrives at the leftmost node in the tree. This will be the first node printed in the left-to-right infix order. After processing this node, the routine begins the search for its successor in the infix sequence. If the node just processed is a leaf, its right link will be a back pointer to the desired successor node. On the other hand, if the node is not a leaf, its right link will be a pointer to its right branch. In the latter case, we follow this pointer and initiate a new search for the leftmost node in the right branch subtree. (This sought-after node will have its left link set as a back pointer to the node from which the search was originated.) Upon encountering this successor node, we print its entry and resume a new search for the next node to be processed. The routine terminates execution as soon as it finds the (one and only) null pointer in the right link field of the rightmost node in the original tree. (To print the entries of the bitree in a right-to-left infix order, we would follow a similar algorithm, except that the words "left" and "right" would be exchanged in this paragraph.)

As we indicated earlier, the coding for our print routine assumes that the back links have been constructed properly within the bitree. As a result, we have to construct the entire bitree before invoking the print subroutine. This can be accomplished by using a mainline program (Example 8.8) in conjunction with two functions, SYMTA (Example 8.10)

```
C EXAMPLE 8.7 - PRINTING A BITREE SYMBOL
C               TABLE USING BACK LINKS
C
      SUBROUTINE PRINT(ROOT)
C
C This subroutine prints the bitree
C in left-to-right infix order.
C
      CHARACTER*6 SYMB(1000)
      INTEGER*2 LL(1000),RL(1000),ROOT,P
      COMMON SYMB,LL,RL
C
      P = ROOT
      IF(P.LT.1)RETURN
C
C Find the leftmost node of the (sub)tree.
C
   10 IF(LL(P).LT.1)GO TO 20
      P = LL(P)
      GO TO 10
C
C Print the node and follow the right link.
C
   20 PRINT,SYMB(P)
      P = RL(P)
C
C A negative right link is a back link; a zero
C indicates the rightmost node in the tree; and a
C positive right link points to a subtree.
C
      IF(P)30,40,10
C
   30 P = -P
      GO TO 20
C
   40 RETURN
      END
```

and BTCNS (Example 8.9). The mainline program reads a variable number of symbolic names from data cards, one name per card, and invokes SYMTA to build the tree structure using these names. SYMTA, in turn, calls upon function BTCNS to create new nodes as they are needed. The latter function has three parameters to correspond to the three fields in each node (i.e., a symbolic name, a left link, and a right link). This construction function is identical to the ones discussed in Chapter Six, with the exception of the field names. When the entire bitree has been completed, the mainline program then calls upon subroutine PRINT to print the symbol table.

```
C EXAMPLE 8.8 - MAINLINE ROUTINE
C
      CHARACTER*6 SYMB(1000),SYM
      INTEGER*2 LL(1000),RL(1000),ROOT/0/,SYMTA
      COMMON SYMB,LL,RL
C
   10 READ(5,20,END=40)SYM
   20 FORMAT(A6)
C
C Print the symbol and its location.
C
      PRINT,SYM,SYMTA(ROOT,SYM)
      GO TO 10
C
C Print the complete binary tree.
C
   40 CALL PRINT(ROOT)
C
      STOP
      END
```

Now that we have a general feeling for what has to be done, let us consider the construction of the bitree and the operation of function SYMTA in more detail. When SYMTA is invoked for the first time, it finds that the tree indicated by ROOT is empty (i.e., ROOT = 0), with the result that it creates a root node (by invoking function BTCNS) with its two links containing null pointers. Then the mainline program reads a new symbolic name and

```
C EXAMPLE 8.9 - NODE CONSTRUCTION ROUTINE
C
      INTEGER FUNCTION BTCNS*2(NEWSYM,NEWLL,NEWRL)
C
      CHARACTER*6 SYMB(1000),NEWSYM
      INTEGER*2 LL(1000),RL(1000),NEWLL,NEWRL,AVAIL/1/
      COMMON SYMB,LL,RL
C
      BTCNS = AVAIL
      IF(AVAIL.LE.1000)GO TO 10
C
      PRINT,'INSUFFICIENT STORAGE'
      STOP
C
C Nodes are allocated sequentially
C from the availability list.
C
   10 AVAIL = AVAIL+1
C
      SYMB(BTCNS) = NEWSYM
      LL(BTCNS) = NEWLL
      RL(BTCNS) = NEWRL
C
      RETURN
      END
```

calls upon SYMTA to search through the tree for a match. If the new symbol is already in the table, SYMTA returns as its value a pointer to the node in the tree which contains that symbol. Otherwise, if a match is not found, the function has to attach a new node containing the new symbol to the node with which our search terminated. (Once again, the value returned by the function will be a pointer to this newly created node containing the given symbol.) Furthermore, SYMTA has to attach this new node to the right or left link of the former leaf node, according to the results of the last comparison made during the search for a match.

```
C EXAMPLE 8.10 - BITREE CONSTRUCTION FUNCTION
C
      INTEGER FUNCTION SYMTA*2(ROOT,SYMBOL)
C
C SYMTA returns as its value a pointer
C to the node containing SYMBOL.
C
      CHARACTER*6 SYMB(1000),SYMBOL
      INTEGER*2 LL(1000),RL(1000),ROOT,BTCNS,NULL/0/
      COMMON SYMB,LL,RL
C
      SYMTA = ROOT
      IF(ROOT.GT.0)GO TO 10
C
C Create the root node for a previously empty tree.
C
      SYMTA = ROOT = BTCNS(SYMBOL,NULL,NULL)
      RETURN
C
C Compare SYMBOL to existing nodes in the bitree.
C Return if a match is found; otherwise, create a
C new node through the left or right link of SYMTA.
C
   10 IF(SYMBOL.LT.SYMB(SYMTA))GO TO 20
      IF(SYMBOL.GT.SYMB(SYMTA))GO TO 30
      RETURN
C
   20 IF(LL(SYMTA).LT.1)GO TO 25
      SYMTA = LL(SYMTA)
      GO TO 10
C
   25 SYMTA=LL(SYMTA)=BTCNS(SYMBOL,LL(SYMTA),-SYMTA)
      RETURN
C
   30 IF(RL(SYMTA).LT.1)GO TO 35
      SYMTA = RL(SYMTA)
      GO TO 10
C
   35 SYMTA=RL(SYMTA)=BTCNS(SYMBOL,-SYMTA,RL(SYMTA))
      RETURN
C
      END
```

When a new node is being added to the bitree, we can maintain the back links by following a very straightforward procedure. We copy the value of the link which has to point to the new node into the equivalent field in the new node, and then set the other link in the new node to be a back link pointing at the node to which it is attached. For example, suppose that our most recent search has terminated at node P without finding a match, and that the results of the last comparison have shown that the new symbol comes later in the alphabet (i.e., is numerically greater) than the symbol in node P. This means that the new node has to be attached through the right link of node P. By invoking BTCNS, we create a new node and rearrange the various links. More specifically, we first copy the back link found in RL(P) into the right link field of the new node, thus maintaining the proper successor sequence. (The node which was formerly the successor in infix order of node P now becomes the successor of the newly created node.) Subsequently, we set RL(P) to be a forward pointer to the new node. Finally, we set the left link of the new node to be a back pointer to node P, since P is now the predecessor of the new node in the infix sequence. (A similar procedure is followed when we are linking the new node to the left link of an already existing node.)

Trees with the type of back links described in this section are sometimes called *THREADED TREES*. This type of tree can also be processed in the prefix or postfix order without using stacks, but the search for the successors in these cases becomes prohibitively long. As a result, we will not devise the equivalent procedures for processing bitrees in these orders. Instead, we leave them as exercises to illustrate the impracticality of such procedures.

8.4.2 Recording Stack Entries Inside Tree Links

Unlike the method discussed in Section 8.4.1, the procedure considered in this section is equally suitable for all orders of processing. It effectively uses the link fields of the nodes to store the information formerly contained in the entries of the push-down stack. As we proceed down through the tree structure, this is accomplished by temporarily altering one of the links in each node to point backwards at the node previously considered in the processing sequence. When the procedure progresses backwards through these temporary back links, it restores the appropriate pointers to their former forward values.

The algorithm for left-to-right postfix processing is illustrated by the flowchart in Figure 8.7. This procedure utilizes three external pointers while traversing the bitree. During the forward progression through the tree, P points at the node currently under examination, while S points at the last node considered prior to P. The relative positions of nodes S and P remain the same during the retreat back through the nodes, in that S continues to point at the last node examined prior to node P during the forward part of the algorithm. We maintain S so that, during the forward progression through the tree, we can assign its value to the appropriate back links. Furthermore, when we start

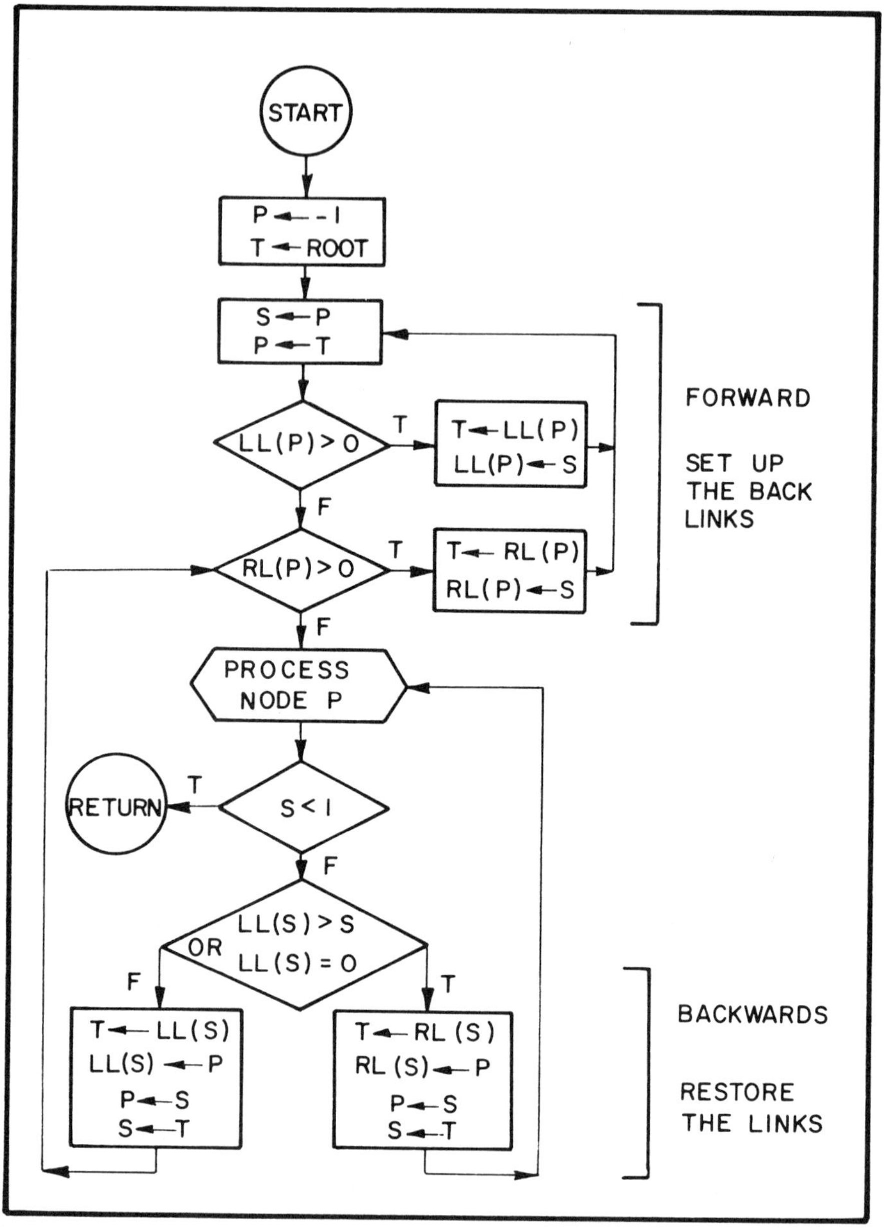

Figure 8.7

Postfix Processing Using Link Modification

to retreat back up the tree, we need the value of S to indicate the node whose forward links should be restored. The third pointer, T, is a temporary pointer which serves as an advancing pointer for S and P in the direction of the processing. More specifically, during the forward part of the algorithm, T is used to point at the next node to be examined following P, whereas, in the backward portion of the algorithm, it points to the node which was considered prior to node S during the forward progression to node P. Finally, we assign a special value of -1 as the initial value of S so that, when this value is encountered during the backward part of the algorithm, we know that it is time to terminate the processing of the bitree.

As we proceed downwards through the tree, we alter one of the links in each node to point at the preceding node which is specified by S. Once again, however, we have the problem of distinguishing the back pointers from the regular forward pointers. This distinction is especially important during a retreat back up the tree, since we have to know which link we followed before so that we can restore its forward value. We can use either of the two methods discussed in Section 8.4.1, namely the sign indicator or the relative value of the pointer. In Figure 8.7, since we have already used the former method in an earlier example, we have adopted the latter method for identifying back pointers.

It is worthwhile paying special attention to the large decision box in the backward portion of the flowchart in Figure 8.7. It is there that we determine which of the links of node S we followed earlier to reach the current node P. Upon testing the left link of S, if we find that its value is smaller than that of S, we then have reason to suspect that this is the link we followed before. However, before accepting this conclusion (and subsequently following the 'F' exit from the decision box), we have to check that the value of LL(S) is not zero. (It would be zero in the event that there is no left branch originating from node S.) Assuming that LL(S) is indeed a back link, we restore its previous forward value to point at node P. Then, by assigning the value of S to P and setting S to have the former value of LL(S) (i.e., the back pointer value temporarily stored in T), we proceed one step backwards up the tree. At this point, we examine the right link of node P (formerly S) for possible advance to its right branch.

On the other hand, if the decision made during the backwards portion of the algorithm is that the left link of S is either the null pointer or a legitimate forward pointer, we assume that we have advanced from node S to node P through the right link of S. Then, in an analogous fashion to the retreating procedure followed earlier with the left link, we restore RL(S) to point forward at node P and readjust the values of P and S. However, in this case, we proceed to process node P immediately, since, with postfix ordering, the node itself is processed last after both its branches. After

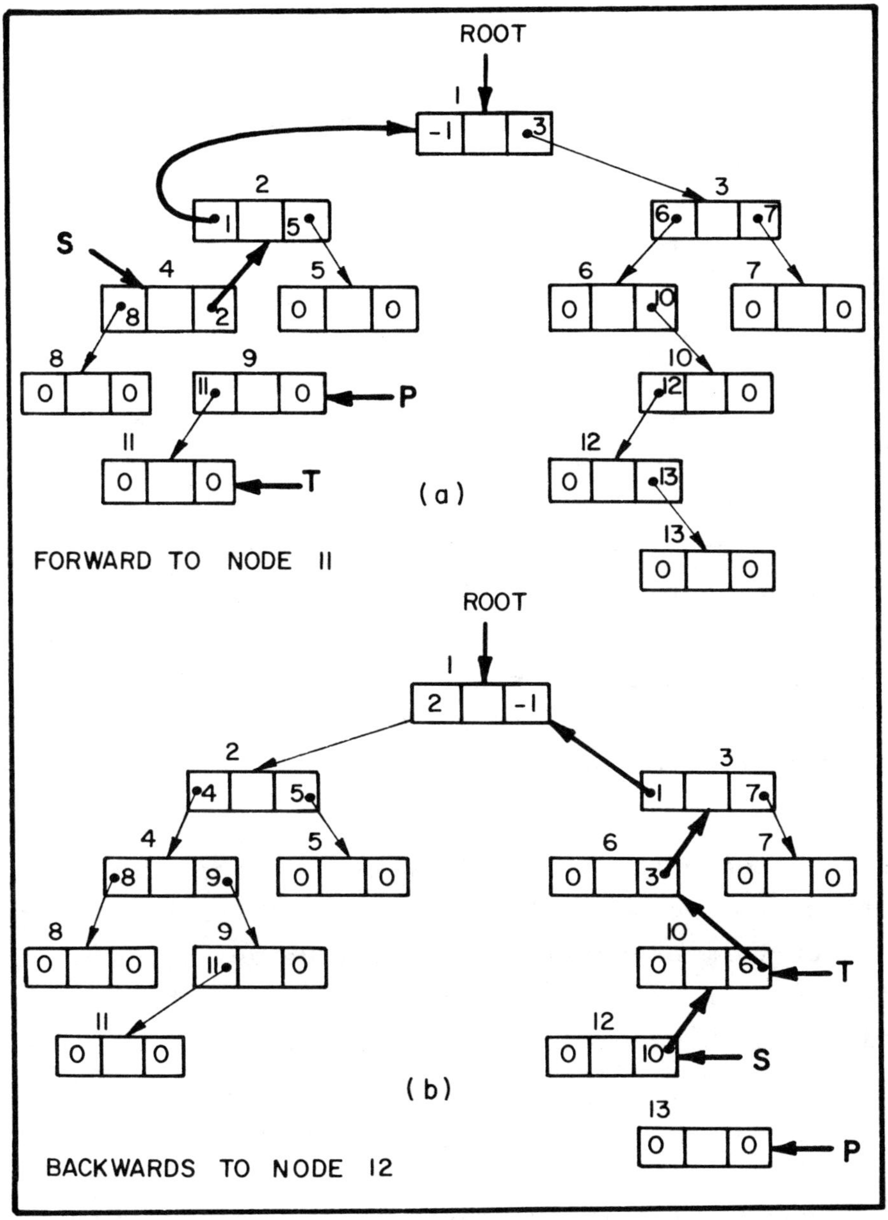

Figure 8.8

Example of Link Modification Technique

P has been processed, we continue our retreat backwards to its predecessor.

Figure 8.8 demonstrates two instances in the postfix processing of a typical bitree using this algorithm. In particular, Figure 8.8(a) shows how we advance from node 9 to node 11, as well as indicating the back links plotting the path from node S (4) to the root. Similarly, Figure 8.8(b) shows the regression from node 13 back to node 12. It might prove very helpful for readers to follow through the complete application of this processing algorithm to the entire tree. [The original bitree, before the application of the procedure, can be reconstructed by pairing the left half of tree (b) with the right half of (a).] The order in which the nodes of this bitree are actually processed is as follows: 8, 11, 9, 4, 5, 2, 13, 12, 10, 6, 7, 3, 1 (i.e., postfix order).

At this stage we have decided not to present FORTRAN coding for this algorithm. In the next section, however, within the context of an example of index-term processing, we shall be using a similar algorithm for printing a bitree. Detailed FORTRAN coding will be included at that time.

8.5 PROCESSING INDEX TERMS - A REAL-LIFE EXAMPLE

In this section we present an example of designing and processing data structures for the solution of a specific and realistic problem. Beginning with a precise definition of the problem, we proceed to examine the detailed considerations involved in selecting the proper data structures to facilitate the most efficient processing of the data for carrying out the operations specified in the definition of the problem. Following this, we conclude with a detailed description of the FORTRAN program which constitutes a solution to the problem.

When we were writing this book, we were confronted with the problem of composing an index for inclusion at the end of the book. We had to collate all the index terms scattered throughout the book, each accompanied by the page number on which it appears. We realized that several of the index terms might appear on more than one page. Furthermore, with some of the terms, we foresaw that we would want to associate several subterms, each of which would have its own list of page numbers. In the index listing, the major terms have to be printed in alphabetical order, each term followed by its subterms which must also be listed alphabetically. Moreover, each of the terms and subterms has to be followed by a list of its page numbers arranged in ascending numerical sequence.

Once we had decided on the desired output, we turned our attention to considering the form of the input. First, we marked all the index terms throughout the book. Then, in order to simplify the preparation of the input cards on which this information was to be punched, we decided to make the input format-free. Besides, after noticing that the lengths (i.e., numbers of characters) of the terms and subterms varied considerably, we realized that there was little sense in trying to force them into a fixed-format input form. Actually, we wanted to handle these terms as variable length character strings anyway. After considerable thought, we decided to use the input form described in the subsequent paragraph.

The input consists of a variable number of statements separated by semicolons, each statement containing a major term, a qualified subterm (i.e., a subterm accompanied by a major term), or an unqualified subterm. In the last case, the subterm is to be considered as being associated with the most recent major term encountered in the input stream. Major terms are separated from their subterms by a period, and the page numbers are separated from one another and from the term with which they are associated by commas. If a statement does not include a major term, the first non-blank character in it should be a period. However, if a statement contains only a major term, the period does not appear in it at all. (In the index listing of this book, the major terms are those lying flush against the left margin, whereas the subterms are indented beneath their associated major terms.) The acceptable input forms can be summarized as follows:

[*MAJOR TERM*][.*SUBTERM*],*PAGE NO*[, , , , , *PAGE NO*];

the components enclosed in square brackets may be omitted.

Now that we know the forms of our input and output, we can concentrate our attention on the design of a program to actually implement this indexing procedure. In planning such a program, we should distinguish three major tasks to be performed. First, we have to scan the input, extracting information from it, and, at the same time, checking that the statements are valid ones. Second, after extracting the term(s) and associated page numbers from an input statement, we have to include them in the index. This operation involves a search through the existing terms and insertion of the information into the appropriate place in the structure. Finally, after all the statements have been read, we have to print the entire index as prescribed in the problem definition.

The efficiency of the program, especially that of the last two tasks, depends to a large extent on the data structures used for the representation of the index list. For example, whenever the program accepts a term, it has to perform a search through the existing terms to determine if it is new. The same is true for subterms and page numbers. Consequently, the index has to be organized in such a way as to allow for efficient searching procedures.

Furthermore, the specifications for the printing of the index require that the major terms, subterms, and their page numbers be properly sorted within themselves. This suggests that it might be advantageous to sort the information as it is extracted from the input stream so that the search procedures can be made more efficient. Since we anticipated numerous major terms, we were led to the choice of a bitree structure for these terms. (We have already discussed the advantages and disadvantages of this technique in previous sections.) Admittedly, there are other searching techniques that are more efficient than the bitree method. For this particular application, however, since we do have the specific requirement of sorted output, we can tolerate the inefficiencies that might arise from unbalanced trees in exchange for the advantage of having all the terms arranged in alphabetical order when the input stream has been exhausted.

Based on the assumption that each major term would have only a few subterms (and several none at all), we did not think it was justified to construct a bitree for each list of subterms. The same was true for the page number lists. Nevertheless, these lists will be changed quite frequently as new entries are extracted from the input stream. Such alterations can be handled easily by using simple linearly linked list structures to represent the lists of subterms and page numbers. These linked lists will always be maintained in the proper order.

Now that we have defined the type of list structures to be used to represent the various lists, we can decide what types of nodes are needed for the implementation of the indexing procedure. Since we have three different types of lists, we require three different types of nodes: major term, subterm, and page number nodes. These three types are illustrated in Figure 8.9.

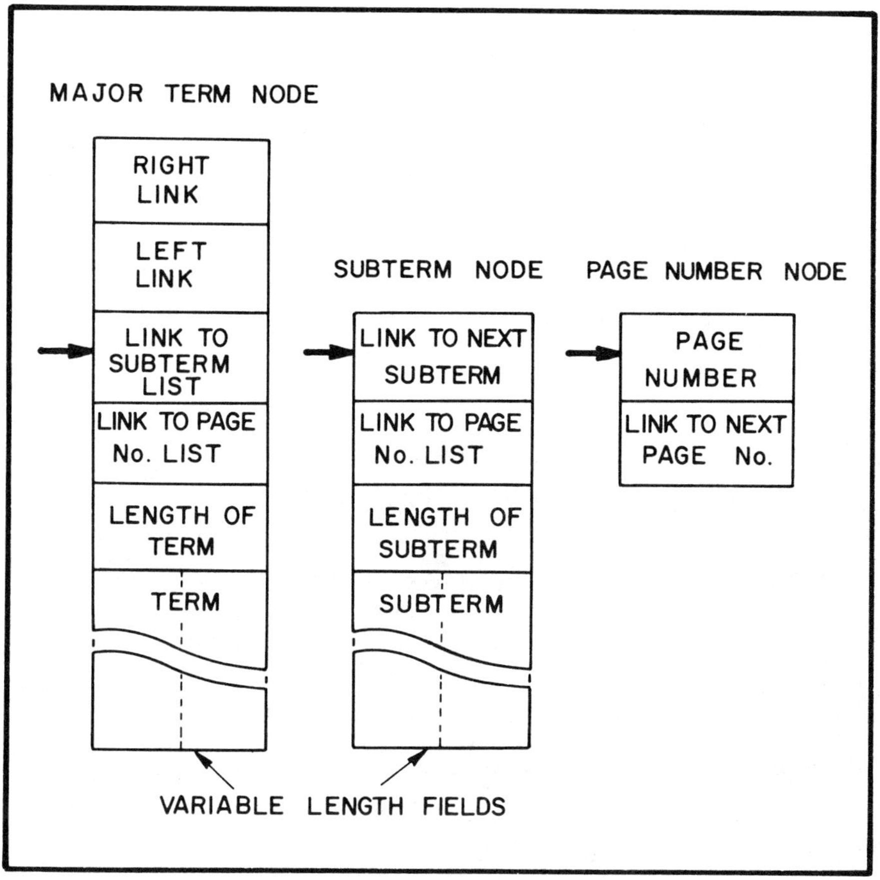

Figure 8.9

Node Formats For Index Term Processing

The major term and subterm nodes are almost identical, except for the addition of left and right links for the bitree in the major term nodes. The link field used for linking the subterm nodes into a linear list is used in the major term node to point at its first subterm (i.e., the one appearing first in alphabetical sequence). By comparison, the page number nodes are comprised of only two fields, one for the actual page number and the other to serve as a link to the next node in that list (whose page number is larger than its own). Each of the term and subterm nodes has a field which contains a pointer to the top node (i.e., the one with the smallest page number) of the page number list associated with it. Furthermore, each of the term and subterm nodes contains an actual index term, and, as already mentioned, because of the large range of lengths of these terms, we would like to store them as variable length character strings. Consequently, each of the term and subterm nodes will have a field containing a character string and a length field which records the number of characters in that string.

The data structure which we have been discussing for the solution of the index term problem would be effective almost independently of implementation. The node formats can be easily realized and efficiently processed, even in assembly language. In our FORTRAN program we will use the language almost as if it were the assembly language of our computer so as to gain in efficient processing. In so doing, we do not employ the customary vector-for-each-field method for the implementation of the various nodes, since this type of realization would be extremely wasteful for our particular index structure. Instead, we adopt the more natural method of having the various fields of each node occupy contiguous storage locations.

We would like to avoid a commitment of any data area as a specific field of a node, since we want to exercise the liberty of allocating storage for the different nodes dynamically as required. As a result, we construct all the nodes in a common data area which is declared, in WATFIV, as a large vector (DATA) of half-word integers. We equivalence this vector with a CHARACTER*1 vector (CHAR) so as to facilitate the convenient storage of the characters comprising the index terms in this area. (In standard FORTRAN the characters would be handled in their integer form.) We use the half-word integers for the pointers and length fields of our nodes. Moreover, for storing the actual index terms, we store two characters in each half-word integer, padding a blank in the last character position of a term if it has an odd number of characters. The length field in each term node, however, contains the actual number of characters in the index term.

With this implementation, fields of nodes will be selected by their displacement from the pointer which points at the node rather than by their field names. For example, if P is a pointer to a subterm node, its fields are selected in the following manner:

DATA(P): the field containing the pointer to the next subterm node in the linearly linked list of subterms

DATA(P+1): the field containing the pointer to the smallest page number node associated with the subterm

DATA(P+2): the field containing the length (i.e., number of characters) of the subterm.

Similarly, we can make use of the CHAR vector to reference individual characters of the index term as follows:

CHAR(2*P+5): the first character of the subterm

CHAR(2*P+4+DATA(P+2)): the last character of the subterm.

The fields of major term and page number nodes are referenced in a similar fashion.

The advantage of this implementation lies with the flexibility of not having to allocate a specific number of nodes in advance for each of the three types. Instead, we allocate the necessary amount of storage from vector DATA as it is needed for the construction of any type of node. This practice supports very nicely the idea of variable node sizes which result from having variable length character string fields in the major and subterm nodes.

To further illustrate the structure of the index, Figure 8.10 presents a typical major term node and its associated subterm list. Each of these term nodes has an associated page number list. To simplify the processing of the index nodes, we decided that a pointer to a major term node would not point to its first field (i.e., the right link field). Instead, it will point to the field

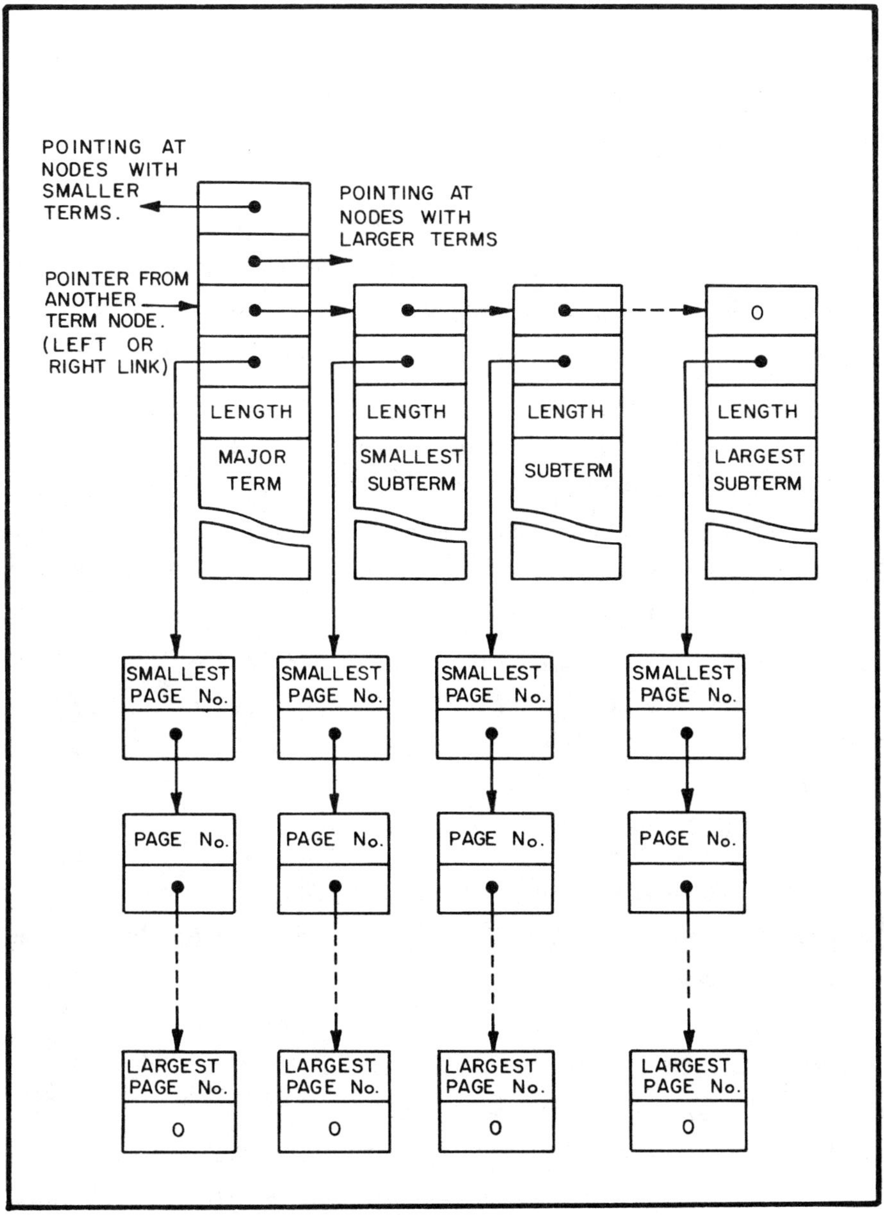

Figure 8.10

Index Structure

containing the subterm list pointer (i.e., the third field in a major term node). This means that, if P is a pointer to a major term node, DATA(P-1) represents the left link field of the node and DATA(P-2) is the right link field. The remaining fields of the major term node will be referenced precisely like those of a subterm node. By adopting this approach, we unify the mechanism for sequencing through subterm nodes, in that we always follow the link which is found in the field indicated by the scanning pointer (i.e., DATA(P)). Similarly, we locate the page list pointer of any node by always looking at the field immediately following the one pointed at by the scanning pointer. (This may be the fourth field in a major term node or the second in a subterm or page number node, but it will always be referenced as DATA(P+1).) This practice frees us from having to distinguish between the various types of nodes when we wish to locate subterm or page number pointers.

For scanning the input stream, we have developed a modified version of NECAR, the source scanning routine introduced in Chapter Four. In addition to performing all the basic character-by-character scanning of the input cards, this routine (Example 8.11) uses three optional return addresses to return to the calling program, depending upon whether the character encountered is a blank, an alphabetic or special character (excluding delimiters), or a digit. If a delimiter (period, comma, semicolon, or end-of-data signal) is encountered, the standard RETURN is used. A secondary entry point, NEDEL (NExt DELimiter), can then be used to reenter the subroutine to determine precisely which delimiter has been located.

```
C EXAMPLE 8.11 - SOURCE SCANNING ROUTINE
C
      SUBROUTINE NECAR(CC,*,*,*)
C
C Subroutine NECAR reads one character at a time.
C Multiple returns are employed to indicate
C the type of character encountered.
C
      CHARACTER C,CC,CARDIN(72),CARD*72,IC(4)
      INTEGER INP/72/
C
C Arrange storage so that C references
C the rightmost byte of I.
C
      EQUIVALENCE (I,IC),(IC(4),C),(CARD,CARDIN)
C
      I = 0
      INP = INP+1
C
C If necessary, read and print a new card.
C
      IF(INP.LE.72)GO TO 30
C
   10 READ(5,20,END=40)CARD
   20 FORMAT(A72)
      PRINT,'      ',CARD
      INP = 1
C
   30 CC = C = CARDIN(INP)
C
C Check for alphabetic, numeric, blank, and special
C characters using the table of values in Figure 3.1.
C
      IF(I.GE.240)RETURN3
      IF(I.GE.108)RETURN2
      IF(CC.EQ.' ')RETURN1
      IF(I.GE.76.AND.I.NE.94.AND.I.NE.107)RETURN2
C
   40 RETURN
C
```

```
C The entry NEDEL determines whether a delimiter
C is a period, comma, semicolon, or end-of-data.
C
      ENTRY NEDEL(*,*,*,*)
C
      IF(C.EQ.'.')RETURN1
      IF(C.EQ.',')RETURN2
      IF(C.EQ.' ')RETURN3
      IF(I.EQ. 0 )RETURN4
C
      RETURN
      END
```

Subroutine NECAR is invoked mainly from subroutine GETERM (Example 8.12) which is used for collecting the characters comprising an index term (or subterm) from the input stream into our storage area. The parameter for this collection routine, NEW, is a pointer to the half-word integer into which the length of the new term is to be stored. The individual characters of the term are placed in consecutive bytes following the length field. Preceding and trailing blanks are not included in the length count. If, however, a delimiter or digit is encountered as the first non-blank character of the term, the non-standard return (as specified by the second parameter) is taken to reflect the fact that an invalid data item has been discovered in the input stream.

In performing a binary search through the major term bitree and a linear search through the lists of subterms, we need to compare two variable length character strings which are stored in our data area. For this purpose, we have written subroutine CVLCS (Compare Variable Length Character

```
C EXAMPLE 8.12 - INDEX TERM CONSTRUCTOR
C
      SUBROUTINE GETERM(NEW,*)
C
C Subroutine GETERM builds a term using NECAR.
C
      INTEGER*2 DATA(12000),NEW
      CHARACTER CHAR(24000)
      EQUIVALENCE (DATA,CHAR)
      COMMON DATA
C
C I is starting location in CHAR for a new term.
C
      I = 2*NEW+1
C
C Search for the first non-blank character.
C
   10 CALL NECAR(CHAR(I),&10,&30,&20) †
C
C RETURN1 signifies an invalid term.
C
   20 RETURN1
C
C Collect characters comprising the new term.
C
   30 N = I
   40 I = I+1
      CALL NECAR(CHAR(I),&40,&30,&30)
C
C The length of the term is determined (by
C truncating preceding and trailing blanks)
C and put in DATA(NEW).
C
      DATA(NEW) = N-2*NEW
C
      RETURN
      END
```

† Because of a "bug" in the current version of WATFIV, this statement should be replaced by:

```
   10 CONTINUE
      CALL NECAR(CHAR(I),&10,&30,&20)
```

Strings). Two of its parameters, A and B, are pointers to the length fields of the two nodes containing the character strings to be compared. Once again, we have utilized non-standard returns in this routine. (In fact, there is no standard return at all.) The first optional return is taken if the string designated by A follows in alphabetical sequence (i.e., is numerically larger than) the string indicated by B. Conversely, if string A precedes string B in alphabetical order, the third return is taken. Finally, in the case where the two strings are identical, the second return is taken. The coding for CVLCS is presented in Example 8.13.

Now that we have examined subroutines NECAR, GETERM, and CVLCS, we can proceed to explore the mainline program (Example 8.14) for the implementation of our index term procedure. Following our declaration and storage allocation statements, we initialize our common DATA area. Then we construct a dummy root node for our major term bitree having the dummy term 'M', in the hope that the major index terms will split evenly on both sides of the root node, thus avoiding badly unbalanced trees. Following this initialization, we find the coding for reading major terms and performing the search through the major term bitree. The pointer NEXT is used to indicate the next available position in the DATA area. When a new term has been read, its length (i.e., number of characters) is stored in the appropriate position in the unused portion of the DATA area (i.e., NEXT+4 for the major term and

```
C EXAMPLE 8.13 - CHARACTER STRING COMPARISON ROUTINE
C
      SUBROUTINE CVLCS(*,A,*,B,*)
C
C Subroutine CVLCS compares variable
C length character strings.
C
      INTEGER*2 A,B,DATA(12000)
      CHARACTER CHAR(24000)
      EQUIVALENCE (DATA,CHAR)
      COMMON DATA
C
      LENGTH = DATA(A)
      IF(DATA(A).GT.DATA(B))LENGTH = DATA(B)
C
      IA = 2*A
      IB = 2*B
C
C The first comparison is character by character.
C
      DO 10 I=1,LENGTH
      IF(CHAR(IA+I).GT.CHAR(IB+I))RETURN1
   10 IF(CHAR(IA+I).LT.CHAR(IB+I))RETURN3
C
C If control has not been returned, then
C compare the lengths of the two strings.
C
      IF(DATA(A)-DATA(B))40,30,20
C
   20 RETURN1
   30 RETURN2
   40 RETURN3
C
      END
```

NEXT+2 for a subterm). If the result of the search through the bitree is that the new major term has not previously appeared in the input stream, a new node is constructed for it. This node is then linked into its proper position in the bitree structure, and NEXT is advanced to point at the next available storage position.

Following the coding for the binary search and the creation of major term nodes, we encounter the coding for subterm node creation. This section is essentially the same as that for major terms, with the exception of the difference in the method of search. The subterm nodes, unlike the major ones, are contained in a simple linearly linked list.

The third main subsection of the mainline program contains the coding for processing page numbers from the input stream. Page numbers are read in character form, one digit at a time, and then translated into appropriate numeric values. This scheme allows us to check for the presence of invalid (i.e., non-numeric) characters which may have been mistakenly punched as part of a page number, thus avoiding premature termination of execution in such cases. If we find a valid page number, a node is created for it and inserted into its proper position in the appropriate list.

The coding in the mainline program is executed for each new statement found in the input stream. Portions of the program are bypassed according to the delimiters encountered in the input statement. This is accomplished by invocations of the NEDEL entry inside subroutine NECAR which results in transfers of control in the appropriate sections of the program. The program is also designed to recognize various error conditions in the input statements. If it encounters an invalid constituent in the input stream, it proceeds to ignore (i.e., flush out) all the characters which follow until it encounters the next semicolon (indicating the end of the statement). Then, until it finds a new major term in the input stream, it appends all unqualified subterms and page numbers to the dummy root node, since it does not know the major term to which such terms should be properly attached. For every invalid statement encountered, an appropriate error message is printed (following the printout of the statement) so that the user can correct any mistakes in his data for a subsequent run of the program.

In the mainline program of Example 8.14, an end-of-file or out-of-storage condition terminates processing of the input stream and leads to the printing of the entire index listing. Since this printing procedure is actually part of the mainline program, its type-declaration and storage allocation statements are included in Example 8.14. However, to subdivide our consideration of the overall program, we have isolated the print routine as a separate section of coding in Example 8.15. (The coding in Example 8.15 belongs immediately after that of Example 8.14.)

```
C EXAMPLE 8.14 - MAINLINE ROUTINE
C
      INTEGER*2 DATA(12000),SIZE/12000/,NEXT/8/
      INTEGER*2 NEWL,PAGE,PNTR,SUBT,TERM,TRML
      INTEGER*2 COUNT/0/,BACK,LINK,O
      CHARACTER CHAR(24000),C
      CHARACTER CK(4),SK*4,OC(25),OUT*25
C
C CHAR is overlaid on DATA to permit both the
C storage of integers and characters.
C Further overlays are made to facilitate
C page number conversion and printout.
C
      EQUIVALENCE (DATA,CHAR),(K,CK),(C,CK(4))
      EQUIVALENCE (OC,OUT),(CK,SK)
      COMMON DATA
C
      DO 10 I=1,SIZE
   10 DATA(I) = 0
C
C Initialize dummy bitree root node and pointers.
C
      TERM = SUBT = DATA(1) = 4
      DATA(6) = 1
      CHAR(13) = 'M'
C
C Check for sufficient available storage.
C
   20 IF(NEXT+50.GT.SIZE)GO TO 490
C
C NEWL points to the new term's length field.
C
      NEWL = NEXT+4
C
C Read in the new major term.
C
      CALL GETERM(NEWL,&70)
C
C Initiate a search through bitree for new term.
C
      TERM = 1
   30 TERM = DATA(TERM)
C
C TRML points to length field of an existing term.
C
      TRML = TERM+2
```

```
C
C Compare the two terms using subroutine CVLCS.
C
      CALL CVLCS(&50,TRML,&60,NEWL,&40)
C
C Follow right link (TERM-2) or left link (TERM-1)
C through the bitree and continue search.
C
   40 TERM = TERM-1
   50 TERM = TERM-1
      IF(DATA(TERM).GT.0)GO TO 30
C
C If the major term is not found in the bitree,
C create the necessary linkage.
C
      TERM = DATA(TERM) = NEXT+2
C
C Zero out the links of the new major term.
C
      DATA(TERM-2) = DATA(TERM-1) = 0
      DATA(TERM) = DATA(TERM+1) = 0
C
C Advance pointer to the next available storage.
C
      NEXT = NEXT+5+(DATA(NEWL)+1)/2
C
   60 SUBT = TERM
C
C Transfer to subterm, page number, a new major
C term, or print routine according to delimiter.
C
   70 CALL NEDEL(&110,&160,&20,&500)
C
      PRINT,'**** INVALID TERM'
      TERM = SUBT = 4
C
C If an invalid component is encountered, flush out
C the characters up to the next semicolon.
C
   90 CALL NECAR(C,&90,&90,&90) †
  100 CALL NEDEL(&90,&90,&20,&500)
      GO TO 90
C
C Beginning of section for subterm processing:
C NEWL points to length field of new subterm.
```

```
C
  110 NEWL = NEXT+2
      CALL GETERM(NEWL,&140)
C
C Start linear search for location of new subterm.
C
      SUBT = TERM
  120 PNTR = SUBT
      SUBT = DATA(SUBT)
      IF(SUBT.LT.1)GO TO 130
      TRML = SUBT+2
C
C Compare the two subterms using subroutine CVLCS.
C
      CALL CVLCS(&130,TRML,&140,NEWL,&120)
C
C If the subterm is not found in the linear
C list, create the necessary linkage.
C
  130 DATA(NEXT) = DATA(PNTR)
      SUBT = DATA(PNTR) = NEXT
      DATA(SUBT+1) = 0
C
C Advance pointer to the next available storage.
C
      NEXT = NEXT+3+(DATA(NEWL)+1)/2
C
C Transfer to error condition, page number, a new
C major term, or print routine according to delimiter.
C
  140 CALL NEDEL(&150,&160,&20,&500)
C
C Print error message and branch to "flush" routine.
C
  150 PRINT,'**** INVALID SUBTERM'
      SUBT = 4
      GO TO 90
C
C Beginning of section for page number processing:
C N is a page number and K is a (numeric) character.
C
  160 K = N = 0
  170 CALL NECAR(C,&170,&180,&200) †
C
C Print error message and branch to "flush" routine.
C
  180 PRINT,'**** INVALID PAGE NUMBER'
      GO TO 100
```

```
C
C Conversion of page number from character to
C integer (one digit at a time) — see Figure 3.1.
C
  200 N = 10*N+K-240
      CALL NECAR(C,&210,&180,&200)
C
C Start linear search for location of page number.
C
  210 PAGE = SUBT
  220 PNTR = PAGE
      PAGE = DATA(PAGE+1)
      IF(PAGE.LT.1)GO TO 230
C
C Compare page numbers.
C
      IF(DATA(PAGE)-N)220,240,230
C
C If page number is not found in the linear
C list, create the necessary linkage.
C
  230 DATA(NEXT) = N
      DATA(NEXT+1) = DATA(PNTR+1)
      DATA(PNTR+1) = NEXT
C
      NEXT = NEXT+2
C
C Transfer to error condition, page number, major
C term, or print routine according to delimiter.
C
  240 CALL NEDEL(&180,&160,&20,&500)
  250 CALL NECAR(C,&250,&180,&180) †
      GO TO 240
C
  490 PRINT,'** INSUFFICIENT DATA AREA'
```

† Because of a "bug" in the current version of the WATFIV compiler, this statement should be treated in the same fashion as statement 10 in Example 8.12.

The major term bitree is traversed using the link modification method discussed in Section 8.4.2. In our present case, however, the printing is done in a left-to-right <u>infix</u> order, as compared to the postfix order considered earlier. During the forward progression through the bitree, the pointers BACK, TERM, and PNTR correspond to S, P, and T respectively in Figure 8.7. However, during the retreat back through the tree, the sequence of actions has been modified to be more compatible with our current implementation of nodes. Following the printing of each major term and its associated page numbers is a printout of all its subterms and their page numbers. The dummy root node, of course, is bypassed during the printing of the structure.

```
C EXAMPLE 8.15 - PRINT ROUTINE
C
  500 PRINT 996
  996 FORMAT('1')
      BACK = -1
C
C Initialize TERM to point at the dummy root.
C
      TERM = DATA(1)
      GO TO 520
C
C Create back links and update PNTR, BACK, and TERM.
C
  510 PNTR = DATA(LINK)
      DATA(LINK) = BACK
      BACK = TERM
      TERM = PNTR
C
C Check left link for forward pointer.
C
  520 LINK = TERM-1
      IF(DATA(LINK).GT.0)GO TO 510
C
```

```
C Inhibit printing of dummy root.
C
  530 IF(PNTR.EQ.4)GO TO 575
C
      OUT = ' '
      O = 0
  535 LENGTH = DATA(PNTR+2)
C
C COUNT records number of major terms and subterms.
C
      COUNT = COUNT+1
C
C TRML is starting location in CHAR and LENGTH is
C the number of characters to be printed.  OC is the
C output line and O is a current pointer for OC.
C
      TRML = 2*PNTR+4
      DO 537 I=1,LENGTH
  537 OC(O+I) = CHAR(TRML+I)
C
      O = O+LENGTH
      PAGE = PNTR
C
C PAGE now points to individual page numbers.
C
  540 PAGE = DATA(PAGE+1)
      IF(PAGE.LT.1)GO TO 570
      O = O+1
      OC(O) = ','
C
C Maximum of 25 characters per line.
C
      IF(O.GT.20)GO TO 570
C
C Access to page number through core-to-core I/O.
C
  550 WRITE(SK,995)DATA(PAGE)
  995 FORMAT(I4)
C
      DO 560 I=1,4
      IF(CK(I).EQ.' ')GO TO 560
      O = O+1
C
C Put page number in OC.
C
      OC(O) = CK(I)
  560 CONTINUE
      GO TO 540
```

```
C
C Print a line and prepare for succeeding line.
C
  570 PRINT,'    ',OUT
      OUT = ' '
      O = 4
C
C If there are any more page numbers, loop back.
C
      IF(PAGE.GT.0)GO TO 550
C
      O = 2
      PNTR = DATA(PNTR)
C
C If there are any more subterms, loop back.
C
      IF(PNTR.GT.0)GO TO 535
C
C Check the right link for a forward pointer.
C
  575 LINK = TERM-2
      IF(DATA(LINK).GT.0)GO TO 510
C
C Upon completion of printing, BACK
C will have the value -1.
C
  580 IF(BACK.LT.1)GO TO 600
C
C K is a flag to determine whether a right
C or left link was traversed.
C
      K = 1
      IF(DATA(BACK-1).GT.BACK.OR.
     *   DATA(BACK-1).EQ.0)K = 2
C
C Restore left (or right) link and update PNTR,
C BACK, and TERM to retreat back through the tree.
C
      PNTR = BACK
      BACK = DATA(PNTR-K)
      DATA(PNTR-K) = TERM
      TERM = PNTR
      GO TO (530,580),K
C
  600 PRINT,COUNT,'INDEX TERMS AND SUBTERMS'
C
      STOP
      END
```

8.6 FORMAL MANIPULATION OF ARITHMETIC EXPRESSIONS

In Section 7.4 we indicated how the structural information imbedded in arithmetic expressions could be represented by tree structures. It is important to realize that, regardless of the programming language used, the meaning of an arithmetic statement (i.e., the sequence of operations and their operands) can only be described as a tree structure. In this section, we will develop programming methods for the manipulation of arithmetic expressions in their bitree form. Once again, as we did with the polynomial manipulation system of Section 6.4, we are essentially developing a special-purpose language with a new type of data — the arithmetic expression. The internal representation of this new data type is the bitree, since it is the data structure which best lends itself to efficient manipulation for the particular operations to be performed on expression data.

Formal manipulation of expressions is a scientific application sometimes called *FORMULA MANIPULATION*. The classic example of such an application is a procedure that accepts an expression as input and differentiates it with respect to a specified variable. The output of such a procedure, of course, is another expression. It should be clearly understood that we wish to manipulate the expressions themselves rather than their numerical values. (It is in the latter context that we are used to thinking of such expressions when we are dealing with numerical applications.) The operations that we might wish to perform on arithmetic expressions include the usual arithmetic operations of taking two expressions and producing a third one representing their sum, difference, product, quotient, etc.. In addition, we might want to compare expressions or determine whether two expressions are equivalent. (In general, this is a very difficult procedure unless we impose some restrictions or force a canonical form on our expressions. Indeed, for most interesting classes, determining whether expressions are equivalent is an uncomputable task.) Alternatively, we might wish to ascertain whether a certain expression is a proper subexpression of another. These are only some of the numerous operations which could be performed, depending upon the application in question.

Special-purpose languages that manipulate data of type EXPRESSION have already been developed. FORMULA-ALGOL, for example, is an extension of the language Algol in which a new data type, known as FORM, was added. This language provides the aforementioned operations and more as part of its language facilities. Variables of type FORM are bitrees which represent expressions (classified as FORMULAE in the language terminology). In this section, we will attempt to show how some of these operations can be implemented in FORTRAN, while placing special emphasis on the techniques for manipulating bitrees. In particular, as an introduction to Chapter Nine in which we will be discussing some compiling and translating techniques, we would like to illustrate the notion of the formal structure associated with expressions.

8.6.1 Implementation of Expression Trees

A data variable of type EXPRESSION will be represented by a pointer which will usually point to the root of the bitree which represents its current value. Figure 8.11 illustrates one way in which we can represent expressions using our conventional implementation of links and nodes in FORTRAN. In the bitree itself, we have three fields in each node, including the two customary link fields. The third field contains a type indicator, which, in the case of a non-terminal node, specifies the arithmetic operation (i.e., +, -, *, **, etc.) associated with the node. In the case of a terminal node (i.e., leaf), however, this indicator identifies the type of the elementary data item represented by the node. For our example, we have only two types of leaves, namely variables and constants (TYPE = -2 and -1 respectively). We use the left link field in a leaf representing a variable as a pointer to the symbol table entry corresponding to that variable. In the case of a leaf representing a constant, however, we use its left link field to store the actual value of the constant.

For simplicity, we maintain a symbol table with entries for all variables, both primitive and type EXPRESSION, used in our program. We assume that all variables are half-word INTEGER type so that we can maintain their current values in the

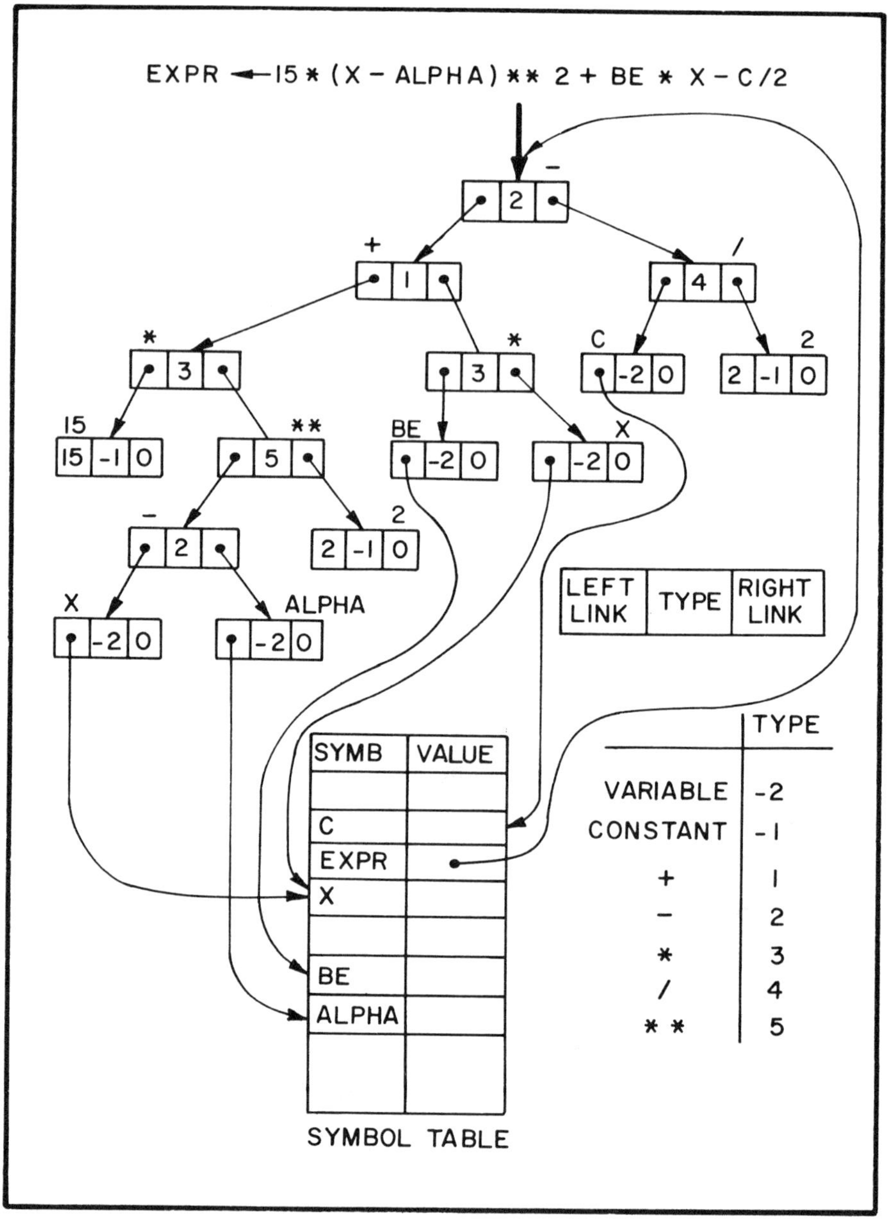

Figure 8.11

<u>FORTRAN Implementation of Expression Bitrees</u>

VALUE section of the symbol table. For a variable of type EXPRESSION, the value entry in the table contains a pointer to the root of the bitree representing its current value. (If this value is zero, it is an empty expression.) Admittedly, this scheme is definitely not an efficient one, since we are wasting considerable storage in the unused fields of the leaves. A more efficient scheme, using the idea of a common storage area for nodes (as illustrated in Section 8.5 for index terms), could be employed in this instance. Nevertheless, because they provide a simpler notation that contributes to the simplicity of the program and its explanation, we use the conventions for bitree expressions illustrated in Figure 8.11.

As we always do when we are discussing a new data type, we have to construct input/output procedures for our new data structure. In our present example, we expect the input and output data to be in the form of character strings representing the expressions. However, the mappings from character string to expression bitree and back again depend upon the syntax of the specific language used in the program. Since we will be discussing syntax and syntactic analysis of programming languages in the next chapter, we defer any further discussion of the input/output routines until that time. Consequently, for the present, we assume that bitrees representing expressions somehow exist in the data area of our program. We can input and output expressions by merely reading and printing the contents of the various fields of the nodes in the bitrees. However, we should remember that we do not store operators as characters in our example. Instead, for each operator, we store a code number indicating its type. Although this scheme might make a simple printout difficult to understand, it simplifies considerably the processing of the bitrees.

8.6.2 Numerical Evaluation of Expressions

As a first example, suppose we consider a function for evaluating the current numeric value of an expression. More specifically, we want to develop a procedure that will carry out the computation represented by an expression. By the very nature of the data structure used to represent expressions (i.e., each branch of an expression bitree is itself a separate expression), this process will be a recursive one. To evaluate an expression, we evaluate all its subexpressions recursively. (This type of recursive procedure has already been illustrated in Section 8.1.) Example 8.16 illustrates the recursive function EVAL which accepts as a parameter a pointer to an expression bitree and returns as its value the current numeric value of that expression. For simplicity, we assume that all values are half-word integers, with the result that the value fields in the symbol table, as well as the EVAL function itself, can be declared to be of this type.

The coding of the recursive evaluation function, as presented in Example 8.16, is very straightforward (although not valid FORTRAN). We

```
C EXAMPLE 8.16 - RECURSIVE FUNCTION FOR EVALUATING
C                EXPRESSIONS (NOT VALID IN FORTRAN)
C
      INTEGER recursive FUNCTION EVAL*2(P)
C
      INTEGER*2 TYPE(..),LL(..),RL(..),VALUE(..),P
      CHARACTER*6 SYMB(..)
C
      COMMON/BITREE/TYPE,LL,RL/SYMTA/SYMB,VALUE
C
      K = TYPE(P)+3
      GO TO (10,20,20,40,50,60,70,80),K
C
   10 EVAL = VALUE(LL(P))
      RETURN
C
   20 EVAL = LL(P)
      RETURN
C
   40 EVAL = eval(LL(P)) + eval(RL(P))
      RETURN
C
   50 EVAL = eval(LL(P)) - eval(RL(P))
      RETURN
C
   60 EVAL = eval(LL(P)) * eval(RL(P))
      RETURN
C
   70 EVAL = eval(LL(P)) / eval(RL(P))
      RETURN
C
   80 EVAL = eval(LL(P)) ** eval(RL(P))
      RETURN
C
      END
```

begin by executing a COMPUTED GO TO statement whose index value is determined by the type of the node at the root of the expression bitree. In the simplest case, if the node is a leaf, we return the current value of the variable or constant represented by that node as the value of the function. For a variable, this value can be found in the symbol table (statement 10), whereas, for a constant, it is located in the left link field of the node (statement 20). If, however, the node at the root of the argument tree contains an operator rather than an operand, we recursively evaluate the subexpression trees which comprise the operands for that operator. This is accomplished by invoking the EVAL function with the left and right links of the operator node as arguments. The values returned from these two function calls are combined to calculate the original returned value, depending upon the type of operator as specified in the TYPE field of the root node. Each successive invocation of function EVAL is carried out in the same fashion as the original call, in the sense that each subexpression tree is treated as if it were a completely new tree.

As we compute the current value of an expression, we are effectively traversing the expression bitree in a left-to-right postfix order. Furthermore, we should note that operations like EVAL are very common with a special kind of translator called an interpreter (to be discussed further in Chapter Nine). Interpreter programs execute source language statements directly without first translating them into equivalent machine language coding. The EVAL function is precisely the kind of process performed by an interpreter when it executes a statement. Of course, before such statements can be executed, they must be converted into their bitree representations.

```
C EXAMPLE 8.17 - RECURSIVE FUNCTION FOR EVALUATION
C                OF EXPRESSIONS - REARRANGED
C
      INTEGER recursive FUNCTION EVAL*2(P)
C
      INTEGER*2 TYPE(..),LL(..),RL(..),VALUE(..),V,P
      CHARACTER*6 SYMB(..)
      COMMON/BITREE/TYPE,LL,RL/SYMTA/SYMB,VALUE
C
C Determine whether node P is a leaf of
C the bitree and branch accordingly.
C
    1 IF(TYPE(P).GT.0)GO TO 5
C
      IF(TYPE(P).EQ.-1)EVAL = LL(P)
      IF(TYPE(P).EQ.-2)EVAL = VALUE(LL(P))
      GO TO 100
C
    5 V = eval(LL(P))
C
   15 EVAL = eval(RL(P))
C
   16 K = TYPE(P)
      GO TO (40,50,60,70,80),K
C
   40 EVAL = V+EVAL
      GO TO 100
C
   50 EVAL = V-EVAL
      GO TO 100
C
   60 EVAL = V*EVAL
      GO TO 100
C
   70 EVAL = V/EVAL
      GO TO 100
C
   80 EVAL = V**EVAL
C
  100 RETURN
C
      END
```

Our expression-evaluation example reiterates how straightforward it is to write tree-processing programs in recursive form, assuming, of course, that you are using a language which supports recursion. We shall illustrate once again how to implement this procedure as a valid FORTRAN function, although, since we have already considered this problem quite extensively in preceding sections, our discussion will not be too exhaustive.

First, we rewrite our recursive function in a form that will be more convenient for conversion into proper FORTRAN. More specifically, by "factoring out" the recursive evaluations of the operand subtrees, we minimize the number of statements from which a recursive call is initiated. This revised version is illustrated in Example 8.17. In addition, we attempt to reduce the number of variables which are local to the recursive part of the program, since we are going to need a push-down stack for each of these local variables. We use a local variable, V, to store the result of the evaluation of the left branch. The result of the right branch evaluation, however, does not require a local variable, since, after this computation has been completed, there are no further recursive calls initiated from this particular level of execution of the procedure. As a result, the value returned from the right branch evaluation can be saved in the temporary variable reserved for the function result, EVAL.

```
C EXAMPLE 8.18 - PROPER FORTRAN FUNCTION FOR
C                RECURSIVE EVALUATION OF
C                EXPRESSION BITREES
C
      INTEGER FUNCTION EVAL*2(ROOT)
C
      INTEGER*2 TYPE(..),LL(..),RL(..),VALUE(..)
      CHARACTER*6 SYMB(..)
      COMMON/BITREE/TYPE,LL,RL/SYMTA/SYMB,VALUE
C
      INTEGER*2 ROOT,P,PSTACK(100),RSTACK(100),
     *          VSTACK(100),V
C
      P = ROOT
C
C Determine whether node P is a leaf of
C the bitree and branch accordingly.
C
    1 IF(TYPE(P).GT.0)GO TO 5
C
      IF(TYPE(P).EQ.-1)EVAL = LL(P)
      IF(TYPE(P).EQ.-2)EVAL = VALUE(LL(P))
      GO TO 100
C
C Recursive call for the evaluation of left branch.
C
    5 CALL PUSH(PSTACK,100,P)
      CALL PUSH(RSTACK,100,1)
      P = LL(P)
      GO TO 1
C
C Recursive call for the evaluation of right branch.
C
   15 CALL PUSH(PSTACK,100,P)
      CALL PUSH(RSTACK,100,2)
      CALL PUSH(VSTACK,100,EVAL)
C
C After saving the result of the left branch
C evaluation, call recursively to the right.
C
      P = RL(P)
      GO TO 1
C
C Arrival at statement 16 means that EVAL now
C contains the result of the right branch evaluation.
C
   16 CALL POPUP(V,VSTACK,100,&200)
```

```
C
C After retrieving the value of the left subtree
C in V, branch to the appropriate arithmetic
C operation associated with node P (as before).
C
      K = TYPE(P)
      GO TO (40,50,60,70,80),K
C
   40 EVAL = V+EVAL
      GO TO 100
C
   50 EVAL = V-EVAL
      GO TO 100
C
   60 EVAL = V*EVAL
      GO TO 100
C
   70 EVAL = V/EVAL
      GO TO 100
C
   80 EVAL = V**EVAL
C
C Return from recursive calls.
C
  100 CALL POPUP(P,PSTACK,100,&200)
      CALL POPUP(K,RSTACK,100,&200)
      GO TO (15,16),K
C
  200 RETURN
      END
```

This revised version of our recursive function can be converted directly into its equivalent FORTRAN function, as illustrated in Example 8.18. We have to provide three push-down stacks: one for the argument pointer (PSTACK); a second for the return address to distinguish between left and right branch invocations (RSTACK); and a third for the local variable V in which we save the values of left branch evaluations (VSTACK). For the manipulation of these stacks, we use the PUSH and POPUP routines introduced in Section 8.3 (Examples 8.4 and 8.5

respectively). In the coding of Example 8.18, statement 1 is the apparent entry to the recursive part of the procedure. Following statements 5 and 15, we include the coding to simulate recursive invocations for the left and right branches respectively. As part of the right branch recursive call, the computed value of the left branch is saved in VSTACK. Finally, after the calculation of the function value for a particular invocation of the recursive part of the routine, a recursive return is simulated by the statements following statement 100. It is at this point where the stacks are popped up and a return branch is taken to the return address specified by the appropriate entry of RSTACK.

8.6.3 Arithmetic Operations With Expressions

Now that we have seen how expressions can be represented by bitrees and conveniently manipulated in this form, we can discuss further operations with expression data. More specifically, we would like to perform various arithmetic operations with expressions. For example, suppose we consider how we might create an expression to represent the sum of two given expressions. First, we remember that, in general, an expression is identified by a pointer to the root of its bitree representation, and, in certain instances, this bitree may be degenerated to being a single constant or variable node. To perform an arithmetic operation with two operand expressions, we have to create a new node and set its left and right links to point at its two operands.

The TYPE of this new node will represent the desired operation.

This is a very straightforward process, and, if we use a bitree node-construction function, it can be achieved by a single function call. For this purpose, assume that we have available the function

BTCNS(NEWTYP,NEWLL,NEWRL)

which finds a storage area for a new node, initializes its fields to have the values of its arguments, and finally returns as its value a pointer to the newly created node. Then, if we want the pointer E to point at a bitree representing the sum of the expressions A and B (i.e., A and B are pointers to the root nodes of the bitrees representing the expressions), we simply use the following:

E = BTCNS(1,A,B)

As a result, A and B become the left and right link values of a new root node in the bitree representing the sum, and, since 1 is the type code representing the addition operator, we use it as the type indicator for the new node.

The addition of two expressions, as we have described it, appears to be a very trivial process. However, we usually expect the arithmetic operation routines to perform some simplifications in certain situations. For example, with the addition operation, if either of the two operand expressions is a constant with the value zero, we do not need the new node. Moreover, if both expressions are

ADD	SUB
E ← E + 0	E ← E - 0
E ← 0 + E	(0 ← E - E)

MULT	DIV
0 ← E * 0	0 ← 0 / E
0 ← 0 * E	E ← E / 1
E ← 1 * E	(1 ← E / E)
E ← E * 1	

EXP

1 ← E ** 0

E ← E ** 1

Figure 8.12

Simplification Rules for Arithmetic Operations

constants, then we should create a new node representing their constant sum. It is not acceptable to have expressions like E ← 2*X+0 or E ← 7+5. We can easily write a function to perform all the necessary checks and create the proper representation for the sum expression.

We have to observe a set of simplification rules for the other arithmetic operations as well. Based upon these rules, we could write functions to perform the five basic arithmetic operations: ADD, SUBtract, MULTiply, DIVide, EXPonentiate. The desired simplifications to be used with these functions are summarized in Figure 8.12. These elemen-

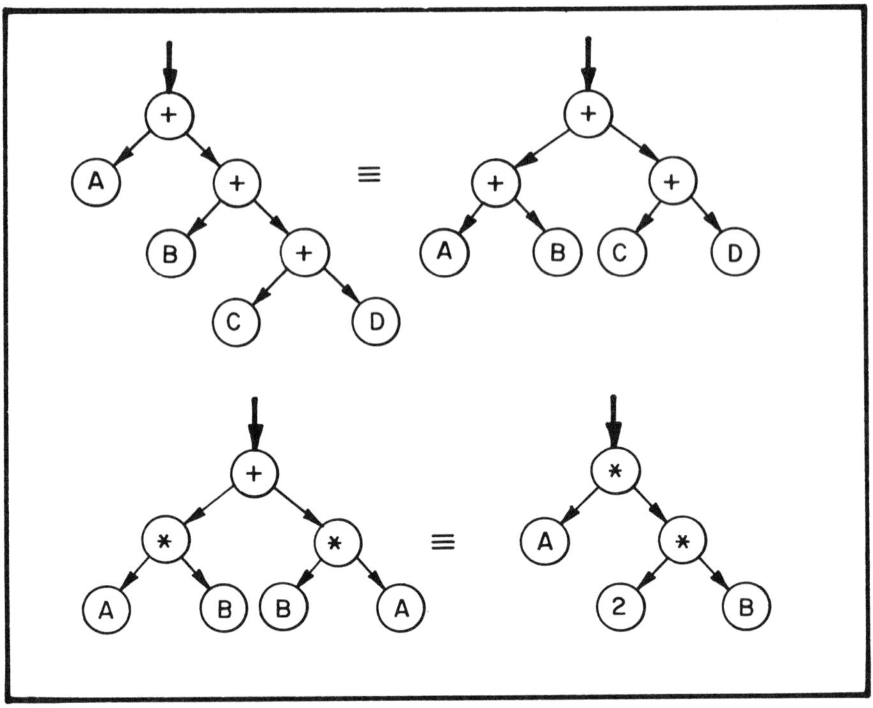

Figure 8.13

Equivalent Expressions Represented
by Different Bitrees

tary rules do not include the obvious case where both operands are constants and the result reduces to a single constant node. The two SUB and DIV simplification rules that have to detect whether the two operands are equal would be difficult to implement. We can easily check if two expressions are similar (i.e., they have identical bitrees, allowing, of course, for the commutativity of '+' and '*'). However, as illustrated in Figure 8.13, two expressions can be equivalent (i.e., represent the same arithmetic computation) and yet be represented by two completely different bitrees.

We have chosen to present the detailed coding (including provision for the simplification rules) for only one of the five arithmetic operation functions, namely the MULT routine as illustrated in Example 8.19. The remaining functions are left as exercises.

In a discussion of formula manipulation operations, we are, in effect, developing a programming language with variables of type EXPRESSION. There are two different ways in which such variables can be used. For example, in our language, if we write a statement like E ← A+B, where E, A, and B are variables of type EXPRESSION, it is not clear how such a statement should be interpreted. Following the conventions of most programming languages, such a statement means that the current values of the variables A and B are to be added and the result assigned to variable E. In our example, the current values of A and B are the two bitrees representing their expression values at the time the statement is executed.

However, there are occasions when we might wish to create an expression E with the property that A and B are its proper subexpressions. In other words, if the values of A and/or B change at any time in the future, we want the change(s) to be reflected in the value of the expression E. As a result, for this second interpretation, we have to devise some new conventions. Whenever we wish to

```
C EXAMPLE 8.19 - EXPRESSION MULTIPLICATION
C
      INTEGER FUNCTION MULT*2(E1,E2)
C
      INTEGER*2 TYPE(..),LL(..),RL(..),VALUE(..)
      CHARACTER*6 SYMB(..)
      COMMON/BITREE/TYPE,LL,RL/SYMTA/SYMB,VALUE
C
C E1 and E2 are pointers to expression bitrees.
C
      INTEGER*2 E1,E2
C
      IF(TYPE(E1).EQ.-1)GO TO 20
      IF(TYPE(E2).EQ.-1)GO TO 30
C
C Arrival at statement 10 indicates that
C no simplification is to be performed.
C
   10 MULT = BTCNS(3,E1,E2)
      RETURN
C
   20 IF(TYPE(E2).EQ.-1)GO TO 40
      IF(LL(E1).EQ.0)GO TO 50
      IF(LL(E1).NE.1)GO TO 10
C
C If control reaches this point, then E1
C must be the constant value unity.
C
      MULT = E2
      RETURN
C
   30 IF(LL(E2).EQ.0)GO TO 50
      IF(LL(E2).NE.1)GO TO 10
C
C If control reaches this point, then E2
C must be the constant value unity.
C
      MULT = E1
      RETURN
C
C Both operands must be constants at this stage.
C
   40 MULT = BTCNS(-1,LL(E1)*LL(E2),0)
      RETURN
C
```

```
C One of the operands must be zero at this point.
C
   50 MULT = BTCNS(-1,0,0)
      RETURN
C
      END
```

discuss a variable (as an entity in itself) rather than its (current) value, we shall precede its symbolic name by a period. Consequently, our second interpretation, as applied to the addition of expressions A and B, would be written as E ← .A+.B. Furthermore, we should be able to intermix the two types of variable usage within the same statement.

One implementation of these two interpretations of EXPRESSION variables is illustrated in Figure 8.14. When the value of an expression is referenced as an operand for an arithmetic operation, the operand pointer in the new root node created for that operation is set to point at the bitree value of the EXPRESSION variable. However, if the actual formal expression itself is required, the appropriate operand pointer is set to point at the corresponding symbol table entry (to indicate that we are dealing with a variable rather than its value). In particular, Figure 8.14(a) illustrates the results of three arithmetic operations involving expressions A and B as they are assigned to E1, E2, and E3 respectively. Then, in Figure 8.14(b), we see the effect of assigning a new value to variable B. In the symbol table entry for B, the value pointer is adjusted so that it points to the updated

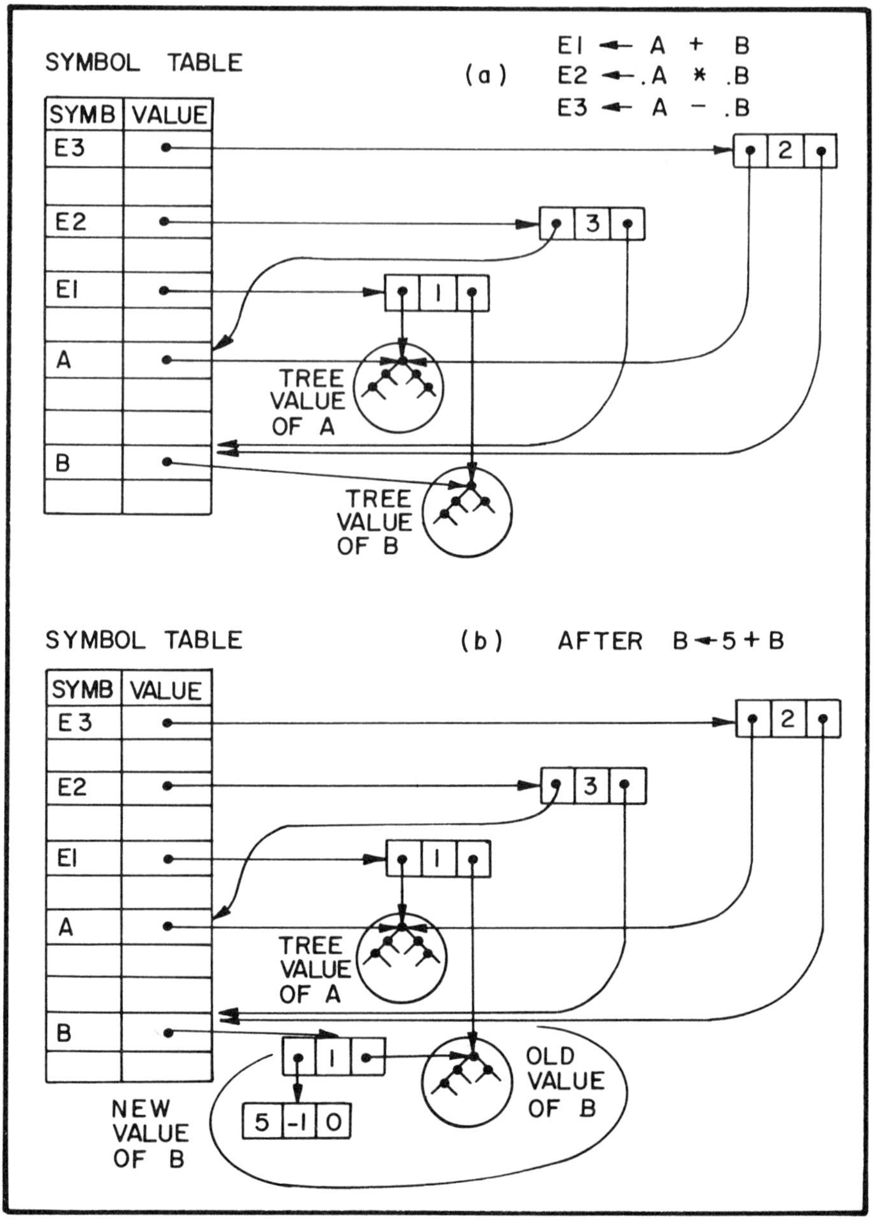

Figure 8.14

<u>Illustration of Formal Manipulation of Expressions</u>

bitree representing B. As a result, because the assignments to E2 and E3 involved symbolic references to B, their values are also updated, since their right operand pointers are also pointing (indirectly) at the new bitree value of B. By comparison, since the expression E1 did not involve any symbolic reference to B, its right operand pointer continues to point at the old value of B.

Although we have not yet explicitly mentioned the fact, it should be obvious that some type of "flag" must be maintained in the symbol table entries for distinguishing between primitive and EXPRESSION variables. Under these circumstances, whenever access is made to a variable (TYPE = -2), a check is made to determine whether the variable is a primitive one, in which case its value is located in the VALUE section of the symbol table, or one of type EXPRESSION, in which case the VALUE entry is a pointer to the root of its bitree representation. (This does, of course, require some modification to function EVAL.

8.6.4 Formal Differentiation of Expressions

As a further example of expression manipulation, we consider how to perform the operation of formally differentiating an expression with respect to a specific variable using our implementation of expression bitrees. Suppose that E is a pointer to the root node of an expression bitree and VAR is a pointer to a symbol table entry for a variable (primitive or EXPRESSION). We want to write a function, DERV(E,VAR), which returns as its value a pointer to a bitree representing the derivative of expression E taken with respect to the variable indicated by VAR. The implementation of such a function is very straightforward (see Example 8.20). For example, the derivative of a constant is always the constant zero. In addition, the derivative of a variable is unity if that variable is the same as VAR and zero otherwise. For operators, we utilize the well known differentiation formulae for algebraic expressions. As a specific illustration, the derivative of a sum is the sum of the derivatives, and, as a result, we call function DERV recursively on the left and right branches of the node representing the addition operator. The results of these recursive calls are used for the construction of the desired derivative expression. Furthermore, in order to obtain as simple a result as possible with function DERV, we use our simplifying arithmetic operation functions for the construction of the derivative expression bitrees.

```
C EXAMPLE 8.20 - RECURSIVE DIFFERENTIATION FUNCTION
C
      INTEGER recursive FUNCTION DERV( E,VAR)
C
      INTEGER*2 TYPE(..),LL(..),RL(..),VALUE(..)
      CHARACTER*6 SYMB(..)
      COMMON/BITREE/TYPE,LL,RL/SYMTA/SYMB,VALUE
C
      INTEGER*2 E,VAR,ADD,SUB,MULT,DIV,EXP
      INTEGER*2 ONE,ZERO
      COMMON ONE,ZERO
C
C ZERO and ONE are pointers to nodes representing
C the constants 0 and 1 respectively.
C
```

```
      K = TYPE(E)+3
      GO TO (10,20,20,40,50,60,70,80),K
C
   10 IF(LL(E).NE.VAR)GO TO 20 †
C
C The derivative is ONE for a variable
C which is the same as VAR.
C
      DERV = ONE
      RETURN
C
C The derivative is zero for a constant
C or a variable other than VAR.
C
   20 DERV = ZERO
      RETURN
C
C The following subsections of the program involve
C recursive calls to DERV and invocations of the
C various arithmetic operation functions.
C
   40 DERV = ADD(derv(LL(E),VAR),derv(RL(E),VAR))
      RETURN
C
   50 DERV = SUB(derv(LL(E),VAR),derv(RL(E),VAR))
      RETURN
C
   60 DERV = ADD(MULT(derv(LL(E),VAR),RL(E)),
     *             MULT(derv(RL(E),VAR),LL(E)))
      RETURN
C
   70 DERV = DIV(SUB(MULT(derv(LL(E),VAR),RL(E)),
     *                  MULT(derv(RL(E),VAR),LL(E))),
     *             MULT(RL(E),RL(E)))
      RETURN
C
   80 DERV = MULT(MULT(RL(E),
     *                   EXP(LL(E),SUB(RL(E),ONE))),     ††
     *              derv(LL(E),VAR))
      RETURN
      END
```

† We are assuming here that VAR is a primitive (rather than EXPRESSION) variable.

†† We are making the simplifying assumption here that RL(E) is <u>not</u> a function of VAR.

After observing the differentiation procedure illustrated in Example 8.20, we should appreciate the importance of the simplifications performed by the arithmetic operation functions. For example, Figure 8.15 illustrates a simple expression and its derivative expression bitrees. In particular, Figure 8.15(b) shows the bitree that would result if we did not perform the elementary simplifications and merely continued to create operator nodes without checking their operands. By comparison, Figure 8.15(c) illustrates the result we obtain from Example 8.20 when we perform the appropriate simplifications. However, as demonstrated in Figure 8.15(d), the result in (c) is not really good enough, since a human being would have simplified the derivative expression still further.

The problem of writing good computer programs for simplifying expressions is a most difficult one, and it is usually studied in the area of computer science known as "artificial intelligence". The number of specific patterns that we have to check for is infinite if we are going to perform a good simplification. However, this problem can be somewhat simplified if we impose some canonical form on the expressions. On the other hand, we find very soon that the problem of normalizing arbitrary expressions can become equally formidable.

Nevertheless, the process of expression simplification requires a mechanism for determining whether two trees (or branches) represent <u>equivalent</u> expressions. In particular, many of the simplifi-

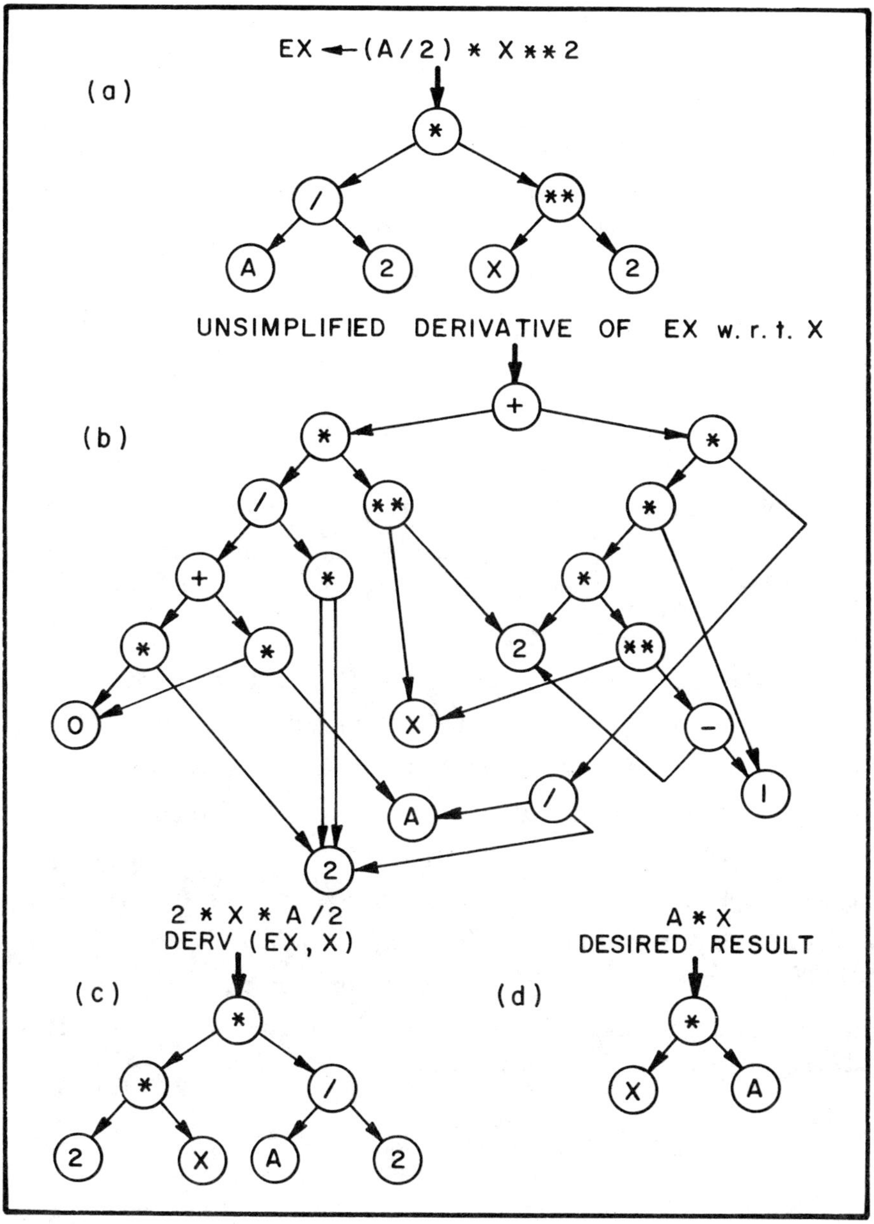

Figure 8.15

Differentiation — With & Without Simplification

cation rules require a comparison of branches of a bitree for equivalence. At this stage, however, the best we can do (without investigating extensive procedures) is to compare the trees themselves for similarity. This comparison would become much more effective (i.e., closer to determining equivalence) if the trees were simplified before the comparison. (We have to be careful here not to imitate the cat that chases his own tail.)

As a final example, we introduce a very simple comparison function, SIMLAR, for testing two bitrees for similarity. To be similar, two bitrees must be identical, except in cases where the root node is a '+' or '*' operator node, when, taking into account the commutativity of '+' and '*', we accept cases where the left branch of the first tree is identical to the right branch of the second tree and the right branch of the first tree is identical to the left branch of the second tree. The coding for this recursive function is presented in Example 8.21. The function accepts as parameters two pointers to roots of the expression bitrees which are to be compared. It returns the logical value .TRUE. if the bitrees are similar and .FALSE. otherwise.

```
C EXAMPLE 8.21 - RECURSIVE FUNCTION TO TEST WHETHER
C                TWO EXPRESSION BITREES ARE SIMILAR
C                (NOT PROPER FORTRAN)
C
      LOGICAL recursive FUNCTION SIMLAR*1(A,B)
C
      INTEGER*2 TYPE(..),LL(..),RL(..),VALUE(..)
      CHARACTER*6 SYMB(..)
      COMMON/BITREE/TYPE,LL,RL/SYMTA/SYMB,VALUE
C
      INTEGER*2 A,B
C
C A and B point to the bitrees to be compared.
C
C Check the root nodes first and act accordingly.
C
      SIMLAR = .FALSE.
      IF(TYPE(A).NE.TYPE(B))RETURN
C
      K = TYPE(A)+3
      GO TO (10,10,10,20,30,20,30,30),K
C
C At this stage, compare the values of leaf nodes.
C
   10 IF(LL(A).NE.LL(B))RETURN
      SIMLAR = .TRUE.
      RETURN
C
C Institute check for commutativity of + or *.
C
   20 SIMLAR = simlar(LL(A),RL(B)).AND.
     *         simlar(RL(A),LL(B))
      IF(SIMLAR)RETURN
C
C Institute check for identical bitrees.
C
   30 SIMLAR = simlar(LL(A),LL(B)).AND.
     *         simlar(RL(A),RL(B))
C
      RETURN
      END
```

8.7 EXERCISES

1. (a) Using the flowchart in Figure 8.4, write a FORTRAN subroutine to list a bitree symbol table in left-to-right postfix order.

   (b) Modify the subroutine in part (a) to do a right-to-left postfix listing.

2. (a) Making use of the flowchart in Figure 8.5 (i.e., using only one stack), write a FORTRAN subroutine to list a bitree symbol table in alphabetical (i.e., left-to-right infix) order.

   (b) Modify the subroutine in part (a) to list the symbol table in reverse alphabetical (i.e., right-to-left infix) order.

3. In Examples 8.7 through 8.10, we adopted the convention of using negative signs to indicate back links. From the properties of a bitree symbol table, we indicated that positive back links could also be used so that relative pointer values would differentiate between forward and backward pointers. Rewrite Examples 8.7 and 8.10 to employ positive back links.

   Is there any advantage to using one method over the other?

What would happen if we deleted a node (comment on both methods)?

4. In addition to being used for an infix listing, the threaded trees technique can also be employed to traverse a bitree in either prefix or postfix order. Note that, although we will not require stacks, the amount of work to determine a successor (or predecessor) increases prohibitively. Rewrite Examples 8.7 and 8.10 to perform either a prefix or postfix listing (left-to-right). Under what circumstances would we use back links instead of stacks for such listings?

5. The procedure for processing a bitree by recording the path in the nodes of the tree itself, as shown in the flowchart of Figure 8.7, can be easily modified to perform any one of the six orders of listing a bitree symbol table (Figure 8.2). Write a FORTRAN subroutine that will achieve this goal.

```
SUBROUTINE PRINT(ROOT,I)
      .
      .
      .
      .
```

ROOT is a pointer to the root of a bitree and I is a code indicating the sequencing order ($1 \le I \le 6$).

6. The index terms in Section 8.5 are stored in a bitree structure. To simplify the PRINT routine and utilize the N+1 null pointers, we can use a threaded bitree. Use your own discretion to decide whether to use negative or positive (i.e., relative) back links, and rewrite Examples 8.14 (mainline) and 8.15 (print routine) according to your decision.

7. Write valid FORTRAN coding to test for similarity between two bitrees, as outlined in Example 8.21. Upon <u>each</u> call of function SIMLAR (i.e., recursive call), what information must be stored (i.e., local variables, parameters, returning statement number, etc.)?

8.(a) Following the simplification rules listed in Figure 8.12, write the following four FORTRAN function subprograms: ADD,SUB,DIV,EXP. You need not check for similarity of the bitrees in SUB and DIV.

(b) Employing function SIMLAR (Exercise 7), we can now check for similarity of bitrees in SUB and DIV. Rewrite these two functions to incorporate the new simplifications.

9. Rewrite function EVAL of Example 8.18 to incorporate EXPRESSION variables. To distinguish

an EXPRESSION variable from a primitive variable, you could maintain a "flag" in the symbol table entries. Another method might involve the introduction of a third type of leaf (TYPE = -3) for EXPRESSION variables.

10. With the aid of the FORTRAN functions written in Exercise 8, write valid FORTRAN coding for the recursive function DERV of Example 8.20.

11. It is quite conceivable that we might wish to know the number of nodes on the right and left branches respectively of a particular bitree or subbitree. Write the coding for the following FORTRAN subroutine to find this information:

```
SUBROUTINE COUNT(LCOUNT,RCOUNT,NODE)
       .
       .
       .
       .
```

NODE is a pointer to any node in the bitree. LCOUNT and RCOUNT are INTEGER variables used to store the number of nodes contained on the left and right branches respectively of the bitree or subbitree originating from the node NODE.

12. (a) Write a FORTRAN subroutine to delete a node from a bitree symbol table. Assume that the symbol table has no back links. The tree structure must be maintained after the deletion operation (i.e., make the appropriate changes in links).

```
SUBROUTINE DELETE(ROOT,P)
     .
     .
     .
     .
```

ROOT points to the bitree from which P is to be deleted.

(b) From a bitree symbol table represented as a threaded tree, delete a node using a modified version of DELETE from part (a).

13. (a) Given an arbitrary branch (subbitree) of a bitree symbol table, we may wish to rearrange its nodes so that the same number of nodes, or, at most, a discrepancy of one node, is contained on both branches of the new root node. This rearrangement should not destroy the greater-than-less-than relationship represented by the tree structure. Write the coding for the following FORTRAN function to create the new subbitree:

```
INTEGER FUNCTION NUMBAL(NODE)
     .
     .
     .
     .
```

NUMBAL returns as its value a pointer to the new root node of the rearranged subbitree and NODE is a pointer to the root node of the originally given subbitree. The result of invoking this function will be a new tree structure which maintains the same type of relationship as the original tree, yet has an equal number of nodes (or a difference of one) contained on both branches of NUMBAL. In some cases, NODE and NUMBAL will have the same value (when?).

13.(b) It may be advantageous to balance a bitree symbol table if it has reached the stage where it is to be referenced frequently but seldom altered (i.e., adding a symbol). Using the definition of a "balanced tree" (as given in Section 7.5), it is apparent that the average search time would be minimized in such a tree. Write the following FORTRAN function subprogram to balance a bitree symbol table:

```
INTEGER FUNCTION BALANC(ROOT)
     .
     .
     .
```

This function acts as a driver routine in coordinating successive invocations of function NUMBAL in order to balance a bitree symbol table. BALANC returns as its value a pointer to the root of the final balanced tree which is produced from the bitree having root node ROOT. Remember that all trees do not have perfect balance — i.e., only those bitrees with $2^n - 1$ nodes are perfectly balanced. The balancing operation should always maintain a tree structure throughout execution — i.e., it is not sufficient to string the nodes into a linear list and then create a bitree.

13.(c) The procedure of part (b) is only one method of balancing a bitree symbol table. Can you think of another method? How do you feel your algorithm compares with the one presented in part (b)?

14. To combine the operations of the last three exercises, write a mainline routine to coordinate these subroutines and functions. Do the following:

(i) create a balanced bitree
(ii) delete a node
(iii) determine if the bitree symbol table is still balanced
(iv) balance the new tree if necessary.

This will entail the use of SYMTA (modified to construct a tree with no back links), COUNT, BALANC, NUMBAL, and DELETE.

15. We can define the *HEIGHT* of a node in a tree structure as being the number of nodes on the path leading from the root to that node. Write the following FORTRAN subprograms:

(a)
```
INTEGER FUNCTION HIGHST(ROOT,HEIGHT)
INTEGER LL(1000),RL(1000),DATA(1000)
INTEGER ROOT,HEIGHT
COMMON LL,RL,DATA
   .
   .
   .
```

This function returns as its value a pointer to the highest node in the bitree structure having root ROOT. The highest node is defined to be the one with the greatest height. This routine also returns the height of the node in question via the parameter HEIGHT. If there is more than one such node having this maximum height, the function returns a pointer to the first one encountered. Each node in the bitree has three fields, two for left (LL) and right (RL) links, and the third for a data value (DATA).

(b)
```
INTEGER FUNCTION LOWLEF(ROOT,HEIGHT)
```

This routine is similar to that of (a) except that it returns a pointer to the leaf node with the smallest height.

15.(c) SUBROUTINE STBYHT(ROOT)

This routine prints the data of all the nodes of the bitree with root ROOT in ascending order of height. Your routine may destroy the bitree in the process of sorting. Nodes having the same height should be printed in left-to-right order.

CHAPTER NINE
THE PROGRAM AS AN OBJECT FOR MANIPULATION

9.1 INTRODUCTION

In earlier chapters we have studied various programming techniques. We have seen how to manipulate information represented in the form of character strings, usually involving the scanning of such strings and breaking them up into separate pieces according to some predetermined rules. Moreover, we have considered ways of representing and manipulating complicated structured data in the form of complex structures of nodes and links.

In this chapter we shall discuss the application of these programming techniques to the manipulation of computer programs. After all, a source program punched on cards can be regarded as being merely a sequence of character strings, each containing 80 characters. We can read programs from cards in the same manner as we read any other character string data. First, however, we should consider what kind of manipulations are meaningful for program data and define precisely what operations we want to perform on such data.

Modern computers derive much of their power from the ability to execute programs that manipulate or generate other programs. As an illustration, WATFIV is just another computer program. It reads FORTRAN source statements from cards, analyzes them, and then, after organizing the symbolic names in the symbol table and assigning storage for them, translates the source program into equivalent machine language coding. Finally, it arranges to have the machine coding executed. Computer programs that translate programming language source into machine language are called *COMPILERS*.

In general, programming languages are designed to assist users in implementing the solutions to their problems. Some languages, known as *GENERAL-PURPOSE* languages (e.g., FORTRAN, Algol, PL/1), aim at supplying users with specific tools which will enable them to implement their algorithms for solving a wide variety of problems. These languages do not provide a packaged solution for a particular type of problem, but are intended instead for more general usage. The main advantage in utilizing these languages lies with the elimination of the detailed work involved with programming in machine language. By comparison, *SPECIAL-PURPOSE* languages are designed to provide special packaged solutions to specific classes of problems, leaving to the user only the responsibility for modifying them to satisfy his own individual requirements. One example of this type of language is RPG (Report Program Generator) which translates the user's specifications into a program for scanning through data and producing summaries and reports in specific output formats.

Irrespective of the category to which it belongs, any programming language is designed to be convenient for use by the human programmer by adopting his conventions for expressing the specific problems he is trying to solve or the algorithms he is attempting to implement. The compiler has the task of translating the program statements, each expressed in a form that is easily comprehended by humans, into the equivalent machine language instructions required for their execution. The invention of compilers in the 1950's was one of the most important developments in the field of computer science. By eliminating the cumbersome and highly technical task of coding in maching language, compilers have made computers more accessible to a much wider class of people. Special-purpose programming languages are presently being utilized on a widespread basis by people interested only in the problems for which these languages have been developed and who very often have little or no understanding of how the computer operates (e.g., the use of RPG by accountants and paymasters with no computing background).

What are the advantages of using high-level programming languages and how do they relate to the machines for which they generate programs? In response to these questions, we should first examine the complexities of using lower-level languages. At the lowest level we speak about *MACHINE LANGUAGE*, the only language whose instructions can be executed directly by the hardware of the computer. These are the detailed instructions that are stored in the memory of the computer in a special coded form. In the case of most computers, they are very elementary instructions which direct the computer to perform some simple operation (e.g., arithmetic, logical, etc.) on some operands that are identified by their locations in memory or as the contents of various registers in the arithmetic unit of the machine. These commands are stored in the memory of the machine along with the data used by the program. (This is the basis for the term *STORED-PROGRAM COMPUTER*.) Most contemporary machines have a wider and much more powerful repertoire of instructions than did their predecessors, but, nevertheless, these instructions are still at a very elementary level compared to those of higher-level languages.

We can obviously program a computer to solve any problem within its capacity by using hand-generated machine language instructions. This will, however, be a very time-consuming, elaborate, and error-prone task if we are dealing with a problem of any significance. When we are programming in machine language, it is necessary to keep a record of the operation codes for the various instructions, remember the addresses of the operands for the instructions, and finally assign the allocation of memory space for all the data and instructions. Some of these chores can be handled by a computer program called an *ASSEMBLER*. Such programs allow us to code our machine instructions in symbolic form by permitting the use of symbolic names for operands and mnemonics for the operation codes.

An assembler program translates a set of assembly language source statements into the equivalent machine language instructions. Programming in assembly language is significantly simpler than its counterpart in machine language, and, for this reason, the availability of assemblers made computers more versatile tools for users. Nevertheless, we are not able to reduce the number of instructions required to solve a problem by using assembly language. In contrast with higher-level languages where one statement is usually translated into several machine language instructions, each assembly language instruction is translated into one (and only one) machine instruction. Different assemblers provide different facilities for the low-level language programmer, depending on the varying requirements of the computers for which they were written. In spite of this, however, the programmer still has to understand the detailed specifications of the machine instructions and express his procedures at the lowest level of complexity.

There are two approaches to the further simplification of the programming process, the first of which is the use of high-level language compilers. The utilization of high-level languages frees the user from the need to be concerned with machine addresses, registers for arithmetic computation, and so forth, all of which are an essential part of lower-level computing. In addition, as mentioned earlier, high-level languages provide the user with the facilities to express his algorithms in a much more natural notation. The programmer does not have to be aware of any machine language operations, and, in some cases, he may even wish to run his program on several different machines. In view of these goals, a high-level language is designed to satisfy the user's notations and conventions rather than those of the computer.

Finally, and most important, high-level languages enable the user to be brief in the description of his algorithms. This brevity, of course, is achieved by making the compiler do most of the detailed work of generating the executable program. Each statement in a high-level language is usually compiled into several machine language instructions. In addition to allowing less scope for errors, brevity also makes it possible to write programs in a much shorter period of time. Moreover, because they are more easily comprehended by humans, such programs are easier to debug than their lower-level equivalents.

Another technique for further simplifying the programming process is the utilization of *MACRO PROCESSORS*. The idea of a macro originally stemmed from the observation that, with only small modifications, specific sequences of machine language instructions tend to be repeated several times in a single program. Consequently, the first step in the use of a macro is the definition stage through which the particular sequence of instructions is assigned a unique symbolic name and the coding comprising the sequence is specified, including formal parameters which represent the part of the sequence which will vary from one appearance to another. This group of instructions can be inserted into a program at any point merely by specifying its name and an appropriate list of parameters. These parameters are used to modify the original macro definition by replacing the formal parameters defined in the body of the macro.

Macros were first introduced as an extension of assembly language facilities, but they were later also found to be useful for extending the power of high-level language programming and doing string manipulations. It is quite possible to combine the use of compilers and macro processors. There are in existence macro processors which generate source language for compilers (e.g., the preprocessor of PL/1, which provides macro processing facilities for the production of PL/1 source statements), and conversely, compilers that translate the source language into the input stream of a macro processor. Macros represent a very powerful programming tool, and we shall be considering them in further detail in Section 9.8.

9.2 PROGRAMMING LANGUAGE TRANSLATORS - AN OVERVIEW

In later sections of this chapter, we shall consider some of the basic processes involved in programming language translation. In the meantime, however, before we become involved with this discussion, we would like to take a brief look at programming language translators in general so that we can gain further understanding of the various types of translators and their different modes of operation.

At this stage, we know that, if a program written in any language other than machine language is submitted for execution, it first has to undergo the process of translation into machine language coding. The translated code is executed only if the translation stage has been successful. The translator program itself is just another piece of coding which is executed like any other program. Its input is the source language program and its output is the generated machine language coding known as *OBJECT CODE*.

The translation process can be performed in many different ways, depending upon the specific requirements placed on the design of the translator. Translation of high-level languages is by no means unique, as witnessed by the fact that different compilers can produce different object code for the same source program. These different sets of object code, however, when executed, will all produce the same results as specified by the high-level language program. The basic differences between programming language translators stem from the varying approaches to translation adopted in their designs. Each one is intended to satisfy different requirements and operate in different environments.

What are these different requirements? To answer this question, we should first consider three modes of program execution.

Testing

Programs in this category are in the testing stage during which the programmer runs his program in order to detect and correct erroneous source statements and errors in the logic or performance of the program. A particular version of a program in this mode is usually compiled and executed at most once, or perhaps not executed at all if there are any severe errors, so that the programmer can study the results, correct any errors, and run it again. During this debugging stage, the programmer is interested more in rapid and inexpensive compilation than in efficiency of the translated program.

Production

Programs in the production stage have been well debugged. Having reached the point where they are not expected to change, these programs are to be reexecuted numerous times with different sets of input data. Compiler programs are one example of production programs in that they are executed many times each day for the translation of different subject programs from the source language into machine coding. In the case of such production programs, we are interested in having efficient and effective object code. Once a program of this type has been translated, since it is going to be reexecuted several times in the same form, the object code is saved and executed every time the program is needed.

Conversational

Programs in this mode interact with the user during their execution. This involves the use of some sort of terminal device through which the user can input data to the program, accept output from the program, or modify the program either during the execution stage or before execution has been initiated. There are numerous variants to this mode of operation. In some cases, a conversational system can provide an efficient way of debugging programs known as *ON-LINE DEBUGGING*. This gives the user the capacity to execute and debug sections of his program as he is constructing it rather than having to complete the entire program before debugging. In other instances, where specific services such as on-line entry of data or updating of data already existing in the system are desired, a well debugged program can be utilized for a production type of operation (e.g., tic-tac-toe, on-line order-entry and inventory control, computer-assisted instruction, etc.).

In subsequent subsections, we shall consider three different types of programming language translators and see how each of them complies with the varying modes of execution that we have been discussing.

9.2.1 The Standard Compilation Process

The most common procedure for translating and executing high-level (including assembly) language programs is known as the *COMPILE-LINK-GO* procedure. This process can be used for both debugging purposes and the creation of reusable machine coding for production type execution. It is a somewhat complicated process, however, and one which does not easily satisfy the requirements of a debugging environment. The reasons for this will become more apparent as we describe in detail the entire process of program translation and execution. Figure 9.1 describes in block form the different procedures that are implemented and the flow of data that takes place during this process.

The source is usually punched on cards, although, in some cases, it might be maintained on a secondary storage device like a disk file or magnetic tape. The advantages of these input media lie in their speed, convenience, and flexibility. Magnetic tapes, for example, offer better storage density and can be read much faster than the equivalent decks of cards containing the same information. On the other hand, contemporary multiprogramming systems make the input from cards almost as efficient

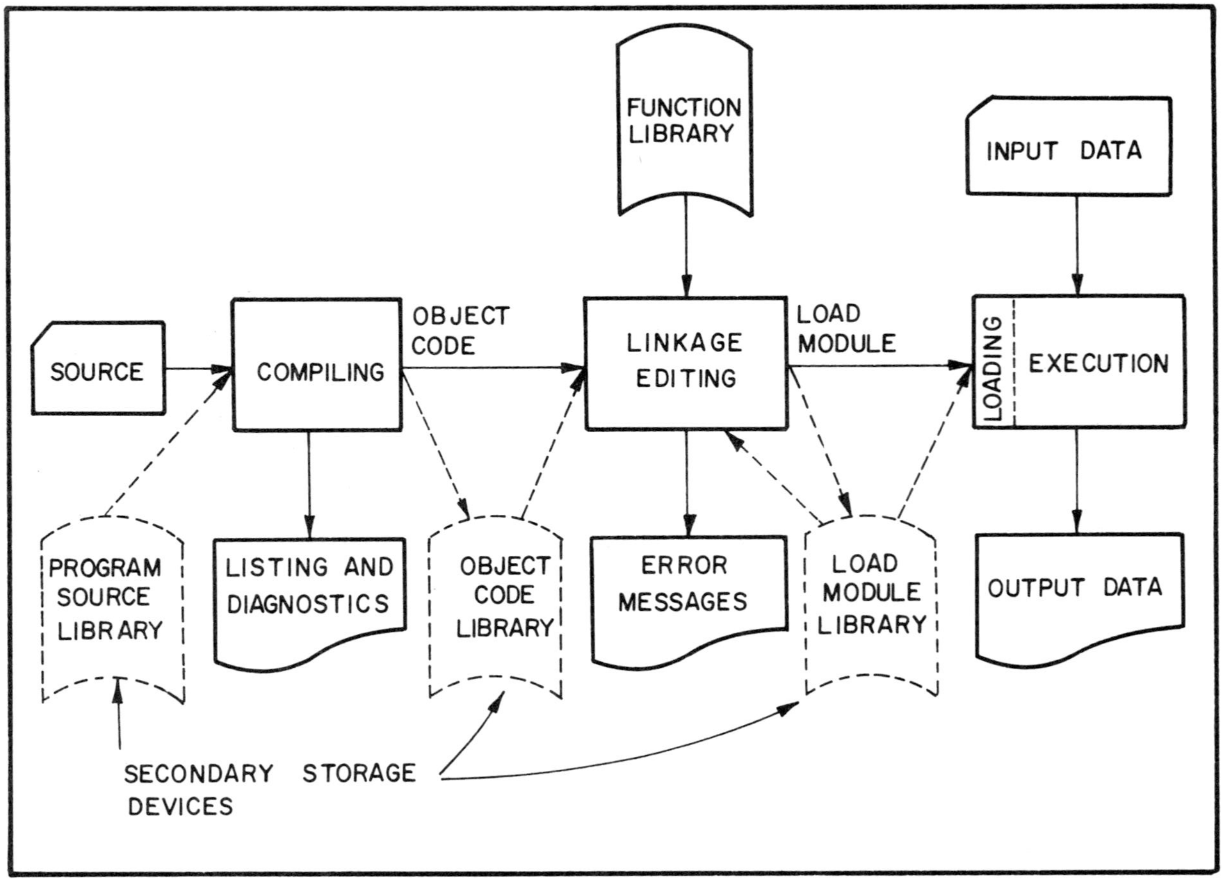

Figure 9.1
The Standard Compilation Process

as the input from secondary storage devices by copying the decks onto a disk file (i.e., *SPOOLING*) before submitting them as input to the compiler. In cases where an interactive system for the creation and modification of programs is available (e.g., University of Waterloo WITS system), the maintenance of a program source library on disk has the advantage of eliminating the chore of keypunching.

In any event, regardless of the original input media, the actual input to the compiler program is in the form of card images represented by 80-byte character strings. After accepting these character strings as input, the compiler, through a process that we shall be describing in more detail throughout the remainder of this chapter, produces the object code. Simultaneously, the compiler produces a listing of the source program and includes any error messages, statistics, and diagnostics pertaining to the compiled program.

For most compilers, however, the object code produced at this stage is not yet in an executable form. The source program might have made references to built-in functions and the compiler might have inserted calls to some run-time routines such as I/O, subscript calculation, or storage management. The machine language code for these routines is maintained in a library, usually on a disk file. Before the compiled program can be executed, the code for these routines has to be linked with the object code of the source program.

In cases where a large program is being produced, it is usually advisable to compile the source program in modules and debug them individually. As we progress with the program, the subroutines already compiled and debugged can be maintained, in object code form, in another library. This avoids the need to recompile those parts of the program that have already been debugged every time we rerun the program.

The task of combining the machine object code of functions and subroutines with the object code of a source program is called *LINKAGE EDITING*. Different operating systems take different approaches to the problem of linkage editing. However, the basic idea of combining the additional code with the object code of the source program and inserting the addresses of the added routines in the instructions from which they are invoked is common to all of them. The output from the linkage editing step is already an executable piece of machine language code. Such segments of executable code are known in S/360 terminology as *LOAD MODULES*, and they are stored in libraries for further use at a later time. They can be brought into the computer and executed after being loaded by the operating system. Only coding in this form can be loaded and executed by the machine.

The linkage editor program of the S/360 can accept load modules as additional input and perform linking and editing operations on them. All the system programs, such as compilers, linkage editor,

I/O routines, and other operating system functions, are maintained by the system, in load module form, in the system libraries. As a result, they are ready for loading and execution upon a user's request. It is very important, at this stage of our discussion, to reiterate that compilers and linkage editors are really nothing more than programs. When a user wishes to run a program coded in a particular language, he has to inform the operating system which language he is using so that the proper compiler can be loaded for translating his source coding. The linkage editor, however, is common to all languages, and it operates on object modules or load modules without distinguishing which compiler or assembler generated them.

The preceeding discussion has described very briefly the process of translation that takes place for most high-level and assembly languages. However, there are two major deviations from that scheme: *IN-CORE COMPILERS* and *INTERPRETERS*. In the next two subsections, we shall consider these exceptions in further detail.

9.2.2 In-Core Compilers

We have already seen how the standard process of compilation and execution involves three steps. The compiler program, the linkage editor program, and finally the user's program are loaded, one after the other, into the same storage area allocated by the operating system for the job. Moreover, between each pair of steps, the subject program, in its different forms, is stored on a secondary storage device and then retrieved later by the next step. This process can be very time consuming and often very wasteful, especially for simple programs that are not going to be executed very frequently (i.e., a load module is not needed) or programs in the debugging stage where the user is mainly interested in the correctness of the program (efficient execution comes later).

These considerations led to the idea of in-core compilers, some examples of which are WATFOR, WATFIV, ALGOLW, and PL/C. For these compilers, the primary goals are fast compilation, extensive diagnostics, and thorough program checking. The price for achieving these aims is the inability to generate reusable object code and the possibility of executing inefficient object programs. Such compilers are particularly suitable for processing programs run by students as part of their course work. Since they are not writing large production programs that will be executed very frequently, students do not need a load module for their programs. For the few times that such programs are reexecuted, the cost of recompiling every time can be easily afforded. Of these programs, many will be discarded as soon as they have been successfully debugged. Consequently, we need fast compilers that provide a large number of compilations for a very small price. Extensive error diagnostics usually accompany this type of educational software to provide further assistance to inexperienced programmers.

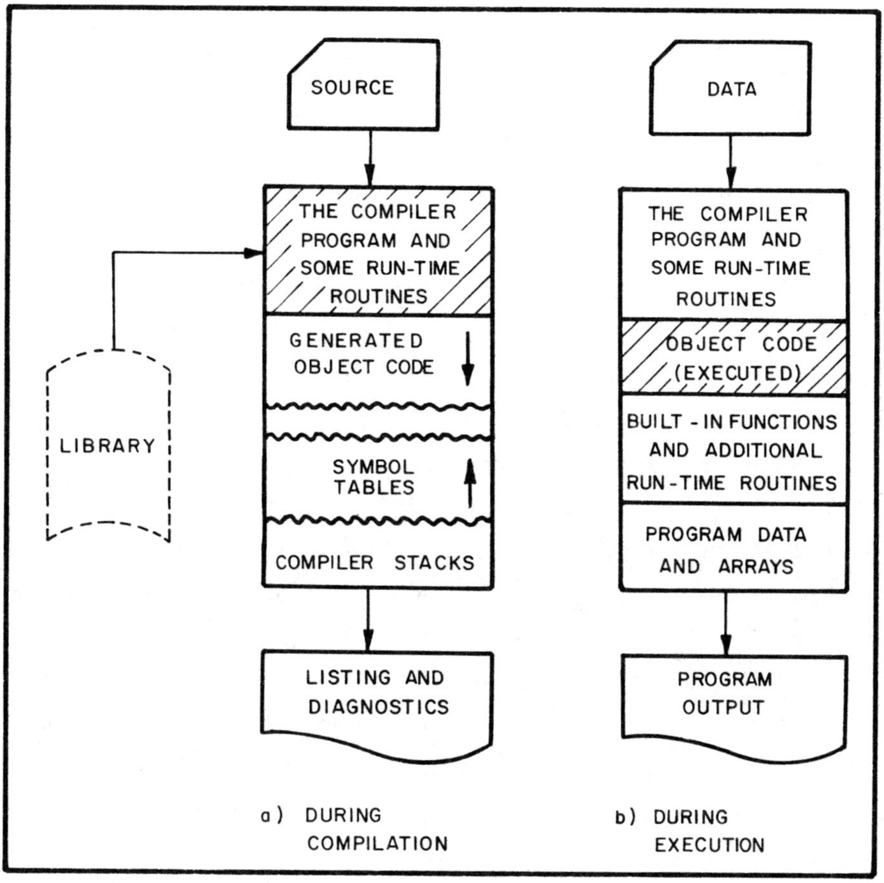

Figure 9.2

In-Core Compilation

The concept behind in-core compilers is illustrated in Figure 9.2. The three steps of compilation, linkage, and execution are all merged into one. The compiler program, once it has been loaded, stays in core throughout the execution phase, thus providing some of the run-time facilities as well. In this way, as soon as one subject program completes execution, the compiler is still in core to process the next job. This scheme is especially efficient for *BATCH PROCESSING*, where we group several jobs into one input stream. The compiler is loaded only once for the compilation and execution of all the batched jobs.

As illustrated in Figure 9.2, during the compilation stage the compiler generates the object code for the subject program and uses the rest of the storage for symbol tables and other working areas. The object code generated might be significantly different from that which would be generated by a standard compiler for the same program. This discrepancy results from the difference in objectives associated with the two types of compilers. The main objective for in-core compilers is rapid compilation, whereas, for standard compilers, the primary goal is efficient object code. In general, the code generated by an in-core compiler will make more use of run-time routines in an effort to reduce the amount of object code generated.

Once the subject program has been successfully compiled, it progresses towards execution. The compiler, after loading any additional built-in functions and run-time routines required by the program, allocates the rest of the storage (previously used for the symbol tables) for the data and array variables used in the subject program. Execution of the subject program then proceeds under the close supervision of the compiler program. In an effort to reduce the number of routines loaded for the execution of a particular program, the compiler includes in its own storage area the more commonly used built-in functions and run-time routines. The loading of the additional routines and the establishment of the necessary links can be performed by the compiler itself, thus avoiding the use of conventional linkage editing techniques.

9.2.3 Interpreters

Interpreters carry the concept of "no reusable object module/fast compilation" to an extreme but for different reasons than in-core compilers. Interpreters, in fact, eliminate the regular object code completely. The source program is read and executed, one statement at a time. Some preliminary syntax analysis might be performed on each statement before it is saved for execution, but, in any case, no object code is generated.

This policy is adopted for one of two reasons. First, the operations specified by the language may be extremely data dependent. Some languages, of which APL and LISP are examples, relax the requirements of strict data type declarations for every data item. In such languages the type of a symbolic name, instead of being fixed at compile time, can be altered at different times during the execution of a program so that the variable represents different types of operands. At any particular stage of execution, the type associated with any variable name will depend upon what type of operand has been most recently assigned to it. For example, a symbolic name could be assigned a simple constant value at one point in the program and be used as a vector or matrix at some other stage. Consequently, when a source statement is encountered for execution, there is no use in generating reusable object code, since the next time the same statement is to be executed, the types of the variables involved might have been changed, thus altering the coding which would be appropriate for the operation(s) specified.

As an illustration, suppose we consider the following APL statement:

$$Z \leftarrow X + Y$$

This same statement can be used to specify the addition of any two operands, either fixed-point or floating-point. These operands may be simple variables, vectors, matrices, or in some cases a mixture, depending upon the last assignments made to X and Y. The object code which would be appropriate would vary with each of these possibilities. Therefore, since there is no guarantee that the types of X and Y will remain the same from one execution of this source statement to another, the most reasonable action would be to invoke the appropriate operator routine for each execution. The necessity of having to make these function calls, and thus interpretively process the program instead of being able to generate reusable object code, is the consequence of relaxing the need for strict data type declarations.

A second reason for using interpreters is the interactive execution and debugging of programs in cases where the system provides for interaction between the user and the computer through remote key-driven terminals (e.g., teletypes and other communication terminals). In such instances, we want to provide the user with facilities to "watch" his program being executed; manually provide data to the program whenever it is needed; and, most important of all, permit him to modify his coding at any stage in the processing of the program (e.g., in the middle of interrupted execution). The conventional idea of object code generation would certainly not be suitable for this purpose. Interpreters have the advantage that, if the user changes any part of the program, no significant recompilation is required.

The complete interpretation process is illustrated in Figure 9.3. Once the interpreter program has been loaded into core, it is available to serve one or several users simultaneously in multiprogramming or time-sharing environments. As is the case with in-core compilers, the interpreter program is loaded into core only once to serve the various users. The source is obtained either from punched cards or from communication terminals through a communication control program. After receiving the source and performing some preliminary checking on it (some interpreters might perform syntactic checking), the interpreter stores it away in its memory. After accepting part or all of the source program, the interpreter executes the source, and,

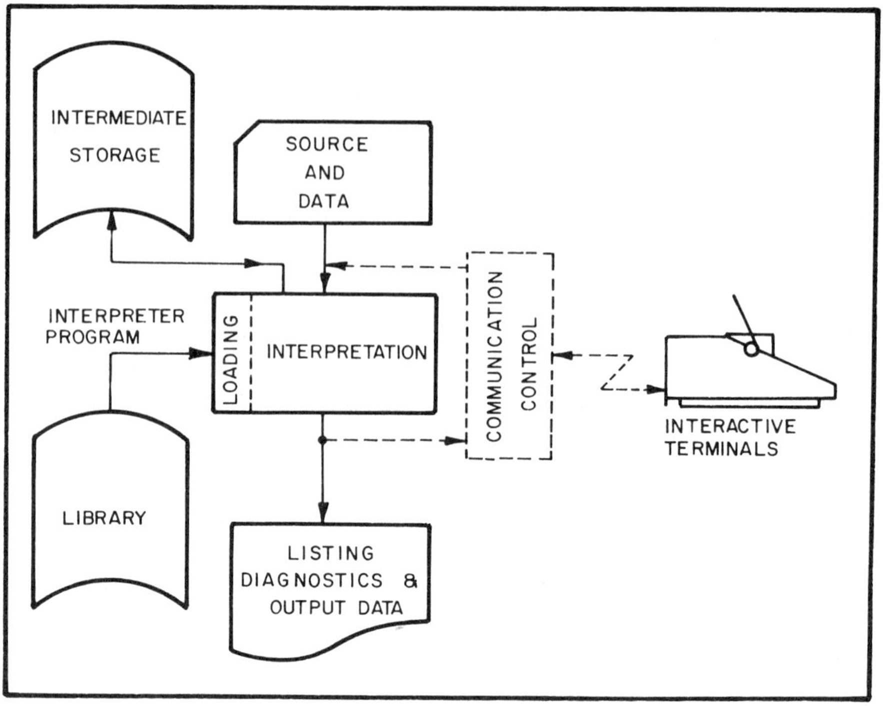

Figure 9.3

The Interpretation Process

in the process of doing so, demands data from the input unit and generates the output and messages which can be printed or transmitted back to the interactive user for inspection or correction.

The disadvantage of interpreters is their slow execution time. The interpretation of source statements is a much slower process than the execution of the equivalent object code. This is especially true when the program involves loops, since the same statements in the loop range are reinterpreted many times, thus resulting in very slow and inefficient execution. Interpreters are available for languages like FORTRAN on many different systems. Examples of languages which are mainly interpreted, rather than compiled, are LISP, APL, and CPS.

In order to maintain a complete picture of the various translators available, we should include mention of *INCREMENTAL COMPILERS*. Such compilers are designed to generate object code for a single source statement at a time with facilities to replace the object code for any given statement according to changes in the source. They are used mainly for on-line debugging and modification of programs. This technique avoids the inefficiencies inherent with interpreters (which execute directly from source) while still retaining the ability to modify a program in the midst of execution. The design and implementation of such compilers, however, seems to involve considerably more effort than interpretive techniques.

In summary, we have examined three different types of translation process. The Compile-Link-Go procedure is the only one of the three which is really suitable for the generation of large production type machine language programs. In-core compilers, on the other hand, are best suited to a debugging environment, while interpreters are the obvious choice to be used in those conversational mode cases where the user wishes to have the ability to change the program in the middle of execution. All of these translation processes, however, share the common feature that each involves a basic pattern whereby the source language is read and verified, and then certain actions are followed (i.e., generation of object code or immediate execution) depending upon the specifications of the source program. In succeeding sections of this chapter, we shall explain this general notion of translation in further detail and discuss its implementation as it applies to the conventional type of compiler.

9.3 THE TRANSLATION PROCESS

We use the general term *TRANSLATOR* as a generic name for many different types of programs. The common property of all these programs is reflected in the definition of translators as programs that accept structured input data and analyze it according to some predetermined set of *SYNTAX* rules, and then subsequently perform some actions, as prescribed by the result of the input analysis, according to some other set of rules called the *SEMANTICS* specifications. This definition makes a clear distinction between the two steps involved in the translation process. The first step, referred to as the *SYNTAX RECOGNITION* stage, analyzes the input source and produces an intermediate representation of the structure of the input. This product is fed to the second stage where the desired output is generated. This second step is usually referred to as the *SEMANTICS GENERATION* phase. Conceptually, we can associate with the first step a set of syntax rules which constitutes the definition of an acceptable input structure. Similarly, we would like to associate with each of the input structure constituents a set of desired actions to be activated. This two-stage process is illustrated in Figure 9.4.

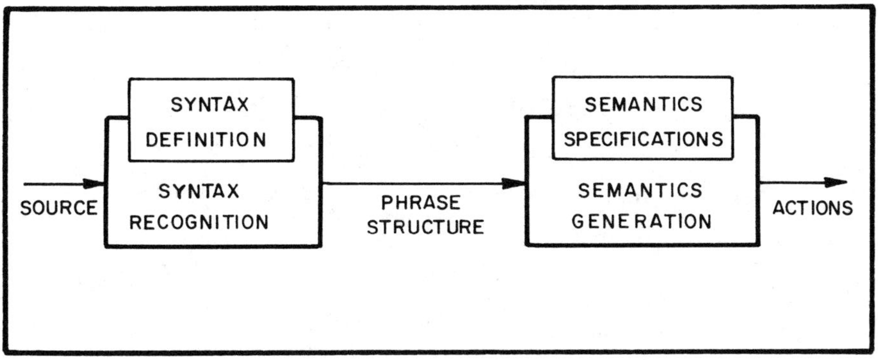

Figure 9.4

The General Translation Process

If the translator is a compiler, the first step of the translation process is dependent upon the specific language for which the compiler has been written. The second step, of course, depends upon the specific machine language into which the source is to be translated. The intermediate representation is completely independent of both the source and target languages. Conceptually, we should be able to take a translator initially designed to translate language A into language B, and by replacing its first (i.e., syntax recognition) step with another one which implements the syntax rules of language C, create a translator from language C into language B. In a similar fashion, replacement of the second (i.e., semantics generation) step should result in a different target language.

Actually, although real-life compilers do not strictly follow the preceding definition, their translation processes can always be decomposed into the two distinct steps of syntax recognition and semantics generation. The syntax recognition step has the additional responsibility of rejecting input that does not conform to the syntax rules of the source language. In the case of a compiler, we would expect it to recognize the invalid source and print an error message to indicate the presence of an incorrect statement in the program.

The intermediate representation, sometimes called the *PHRASE STRUCTURE*, is effectively a tree structure representing the true meaning of the source. In Chapter Eight we saw how tree structures can represent the structure of arithmetic expressions. This idea is carried further to include all types of source statements. The input source and output target languages are considered to be in string form. This is certainly true for programming language source, and we may consider the object code generated as the result of the semantics actions as being in some kind of string form.

Our definition of the translation process has been made very general deliberately so as to include other programs that utilize mechanisms similar to those of compilers, although we shall be devoting most of our discussion in this chapter to the principles of compilers. Nevertheless, it should be understood that the very same principles are applicable to other translating programs. In order to illustrate the broad scope of translators, we shall briefly consider some programs that fall into this category.

Computer programs that attempt to translate one natural language (e.g., English, French, etc.) into another are obviously included in our definition of translators. The syntax rules of the source language are applied during the first step of the translation, thus producing what is known as the *PARSING TREE* of a source sentence. This structure is the intermediate representation. In this tree, syntactic units of the source statement, such as verbs, subjects, and articles, are identified and isolated. The second step accepts this parsing tree, and with the help of a dictionary and other specifications of the target language, produces the desired translation.

Another example of a translator is a computer program designed to read addresses of letters and direct the letters into appropriate bins. For this purpose, one might devise a strict set of rules defining what he would accept as a valid mailing address. The source, which in this case would be the mailing address, would be checked by the first step of the program to determine if it conformed with this set of rules. The intermediate representation might be a table or tree identifying the specific components of the address. Notice that words like "St.", "Mr.", and "Apt." act as key words, playing a similar role to the various key words in FORTRAN (e.g., DO, INTEGER, GO TO, etc.). In this particular case, the second step is very simple. Once the address has been found to be valid, a specific set of actions has to be initiated to direct the letter to its proper destination.

Figure 9.5 illustrates the block diagram for the process carried out by a compiler program. The syntax recognition step can be divided into a source scanning phase and a syntactic analysis phase. As we saw earlier, in Chapter Four, the source scanning procedure produces operator-operand pairs (or tables). The syntactic analysis phase accepts the operator-operand pairs of a source statement and converts them into the equivalent tree representation like the ones introduced in Sections 7.4 and 8.6. An interpreter would evaluate these trees in a similar fashion to that demonstrated in Section 8.6. Compilers, however, have to generate object code for the specific target language from that intermediate representation. This code generation would be performed during the second (i.e., semantics generation) step. Symbol tables and other information about the source are passed forward from this syntactic step to the object code generation step.

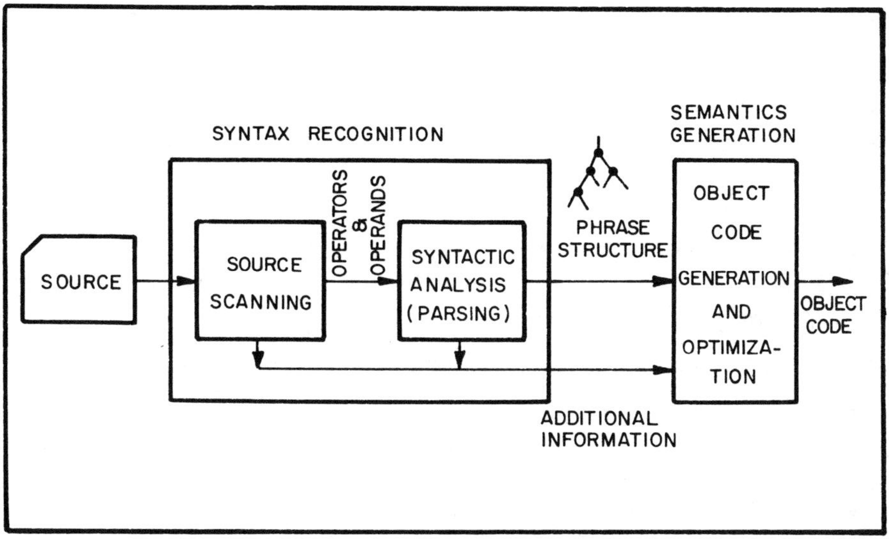

Figure 9.5

An Overview of Compilation

In subsequent sections of this chapter, we shall be considering the syntactic analysis and code generation processes in considerably more detail.

9.4 INTRODUCTION TO SYNTACTIC ANALYSIS

In this section we shall consider several different algorithms for performing the syntactic analysis of programming languages. In each case, we shall be using FORTRAN as the sample source language. As a prelude to considering the various algorithms, however, we shall recall that the syntax recognition phase of the translation process involves two main areas of responsibility. First, it has to generate the phrase structure representation of the source. In addition, it has to verify the validity of the source statements, and, whenever appropriate, produce the necessary error messages. If the source statement does not comply with the syntax rules of the language, it is impossible to create a correct bitree representation for further processing.

The major portion of the syntax rules for the FORTRAN language concerns the order in which operators contained in arithmetic expressions should be executed in the translated object code of the source program. This area of concern is usually referred to as *OPERATOR PRECEDENCE*. By adopting the standard mathematical conventions for arithmetic operators, FORTRAN associates, for example, a higher priority with the multiplication operator than with the (binary) addition or subtraction operators. In the expression A+B*C, for example, the multiplication, B*C, is performed before the addition, A+(B*C). In a similar fashion, we can order all other language operators in a priority list to be used in the conversion of the source into its phrase structure. For FORTRAN, and indeed for most other mathematically oriented languages, an ordered list of operators can be constructed and priority numbers associated with each operator. A typical list is illustrated in Figure 9.6.

OPERATORS	PRIORITY
** and unary + or -	8
* and /	7
+ and - (binary)	6
relational operators (.EQ.,.NE.,.GT.,.LT.,.GE.,.LE.)	5
.NOT.	4
.AND.	3
.OR.	2
=	1
) and $ (end-of-statement symbol)	0
(and # (start-of-statement symbol)	-1

Figure 9.6

Operator Priority List

Priority values are (arbitrarily) assigned to the operators in a manner that reflects the precedence prescribed by the syntax rules of the language. These priorities determine the sequence in which the various operators are executed when they are encountered in an arithmetic expression. In the case of two operators having different priorities, the operator with higher priority is to be executed first, and, in keeping with this convention, it will eventually occupy a lower-level position in the resulting bitree than the other operator (i.e., more towards the leaves of the tree and further away from the root). To illustrate, consider the expression A+B*C. Since '*' has a higher priority than '+', we obtain the bitree given

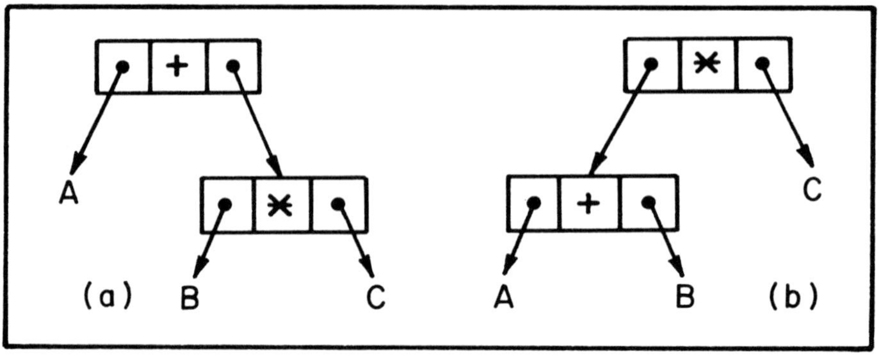

Figure 9.7

Bitree Representations of A+B*C (a) and (A+B)*C (b)

in Figure 9.7(a). By comparison, if the priorities were reversed, we would obtain the bitree presented in Figure 9.7(b).

In a similar manner, if we consider the assignment statement A = B+C, we know that the addition, B+C, is performed before the resulting value is assigned to variable A. Indeed, the other possible grouping, (A=B)+C, would be most inappropriate. Such alternatives, of course, are prevented by assigning both '*' and '+' higher priorities than '='.

Other operators, such as IF, DO, or GO TO, may be incorporated into an operator precedence list if it is desirable to have a single parsing procedure for all types of statements. In fact, with languages that have a better defined syntax than FORTRAN (e.g., Algol), this becomes a necessity. However, for simplicity and clarity of explanation, we shall confine ourselves at this point to a consideration of FORTRAN arithmetic expressions.

The symbols '(' and ')', unlike the other operators we have been discussing, are not true operators in the usual sense. They are merely the mechanism by which a programmer can override the standard precedence rules of the language. Although they do not appear in bitree representations of expressions, parentheses can have considerable effect on the structure of such trees if they are used in the source statement. We will have to handle these symbols differently from the other standard operators. For convenience, we have assigned priorities of 0 and -1 to the right and left parentheses respectively. Similarly, we have included two special symbols as operators, '#' and '$', which are used as signals to initiate and terminate the parsing process. The roles played by these symbols will become more readily apparent when we study the various algorithms for syntactic analysis in more detail.

In addition to establishing priorities, the syntax rules of the language also have to specify the order in which equal priority operators are to be executed. In FORTRAN, equal priority operators are executed from left to right except in the case of successive exponentiation operators. For example, A*B/C is taken to mean (A*B)/C, whereas A**B**C is interpreted by many compilers as meaning A**(B**C).

The push-down stack is a tool which is utilized by all syntactic analysis procedures. In the process of generating the phrase structure, the syntactic units are temporarily stored in a push-down stack. Different algorithms utilize the stack (or stacks) in different ways, but all such procedures require a stack for one purpose or another. This will be best demonstrated in our subsequent discussions of various simple syntactic analysis procedures. For all of these procedures, however, we shall assume that source scanning has already been performed by a program similar to the routine discussed in Chapter Four.

9.4.1 Creating The Bitree Representation

As our first algorithm for syntactic analysis, we introduce a procedure for converting a source arithmetic expression into its equivalent bitree representation. This procedure can also be used directly as an input routine for the symbolic manipulation system discussed in Section 8.6. The algorithm begins by inserting syntactic units into a stack until such time as a subbitree can be generated. Then the topmost entries in the stack are removed and the subtree for these entries is created. Subsequently, a pointer to the root of this subtree is inserted as the new top entry in the stack. As a result, we have three types of entries in the stack: one for operators, a second for operands, and a third for subtree pointers. The latter are considered as operands for the purpose of possible later inclusion as branches of other generated expression trees.

In order to determine when a subexpression tree can be created from the three entries on the top of the stack, we compare the priority of the topmost operator in the stack (which is always the penultimate entry) with that of the operator currently under consideration as the most recent syntactic unit obtained from the source statement. If the priority of the operator currently being considered is less than or equal to that of the topmost operator in the stack, a subtree is created. The root of this subtree will contain the operator just removed from the stack, while the left and right branch nodes will contain the operands previously located below and above that operator respectively in the push-down stack (i.e., the top three stack entries are replaced by one operand-like entry). On the other hand, if the priority of the operator currently being considered is greater than that of the topmost operator in the stack, we insert this new operator as the new topmost stack entry. Then we continue to push syntactic units into the stack until another operator is encountered, at which time another priority comparison is performed, and the whole process is repeated once again.

Left and right parentheses are handled as special cases. When a left parenthesis is encountered, the usual priority comparison is ignored and it is inserted automatically into the push-down stack. Later, when the right parenthesis is encountered, all the stack operators located above the matching left parenthesis will be cleared off the stack as successive expression bitrees are created. This means that the left parenthesis eventually becomes exposed as the topmost operator in the stack for comparison with the right parenthesis. At this point, the left parenthesis is deleted from the stack, the right parenthesis is discarded, and the next syntactic unit is selected from the source statement for further examination.

In a similar fashion, the statement delimiter '$' causes a clearing of the stack entries until the point where the delimiter '#' surfaces to the top of the stack. This situation signals the end of the conversion process. The symbols '#' and '$' are arbitrarily chosen to act as delimiters for the expression. The former is automatically inserted into the stack as the first step in the conversion procedure, and, since it has the lowest priority associated with it, it conveniently facilitates the automatic insertion of the '=' operator into the stack and the later termination of the conversion procedure. The terminator symbol '$' is merely the symbolic representation of whatever mechanism you may wish to adopt as a means of recognizing the end of the expression.

A flowchart for this conversion procedure is displayed in Figure 9.8. It is, however, only a skeleton chart describing the basic logic of the algorithm, and the detailed coding of this routine is left as an exercise (see Exercise 1 in Section 9.9). For a complete conversion procedure, one also has to handle other problems such as the creation of symbol table entries for variables and performing

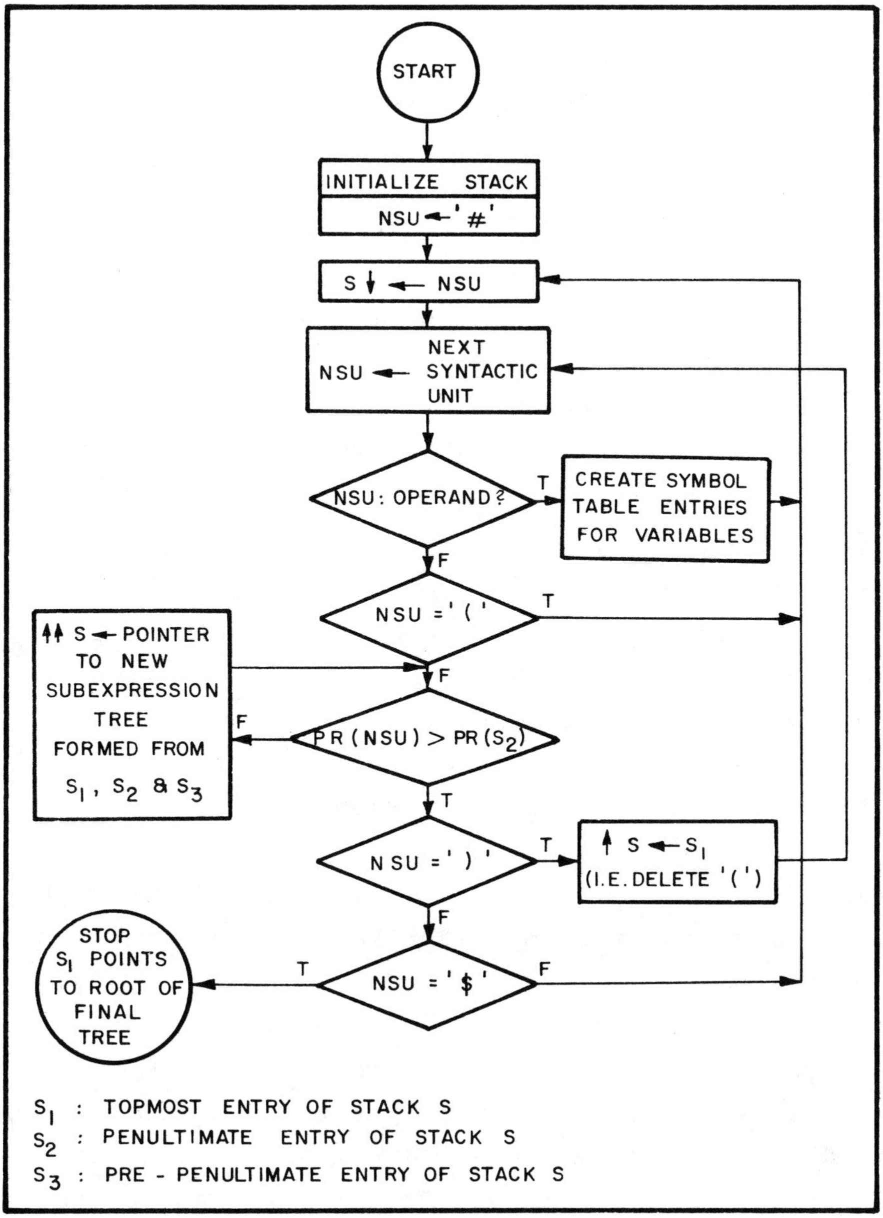

Figure 9.8

<u>Conversion From FORTRAN To Bitree Representation</u>

a thorough validity check on the source statement. In the flowchart of Figure 9.8, S_1, S_2, and S_3 designate the topmost entry, the penultimate (i.e., second from the top) entry, and the prepenultimate (i.e., third from the top) entry respectively in the push-down stack S. These three components comprise the subexpression tree that is generated for each operator, with S_2 serving as the root, and S_1 and S_3 comprising the right and left branches respectively. The various stack operations are described in the notation introduced in Section 8.3.

If we follow the algorithm presented in Figure 9.8, a syntactically incorrect expression will either result in the creation of an invalid tree structure or cause the procedure to terminate prematurely. If a check for invalid delimiter pairs is not performed as part of the text scanning process, the invalid operators will eventually be assigned as leaves of a subexpression tree. Our algorithm is also designed on the assumption that operators and operands appear alternatively throughout the source statement with the exception of parentheses and delimiter symbols. This simplifying assumption is not valid for all programming languages, and, even in FORTRAN, it makes the processing of unary minus a very difficult operation. Furthermore, this algorithm processes all equal priority operators from left to right without provision for any exceptions to the rule (e.g., successive exponentiation operators).

As an illustration of the application of this algorithm, suppose we consider the following typical arithmetic assignment statement:

X = A+B*C+(P/Q-7)

To initiate the procedure, we automatically insert the start-of-statement symbol '#' into the push-down stack. Then the first syntactic unit, X, is encountered and placed immediately in the stack. Subsequently, upon finding the '=' operator, we compare its priority with that of '#' and, since it is greater, we insert the '=' operator as the new topmost stack entry. Then, following the automatic placement of operand A in the stack, we meet the operator '+', and, since its priority is greater than that of '=', we add it to the stack. In a similar fashion, B, '*', and C are inserted into the stack. This sequence of steps can be summarized as follows:

Stack	Syntactic Units Remaining
#	X=A+B*C+(P/Q-7)$
#X	=A+B*C+(P/Q-7)$
#X=	A+B*C+(P/Q-7)$
#X=A	+B*C+(P/Q-7)$
#X=A+	B*C+(P/Q-7)$
#X=A+B	*C+(P/Q-7)$
#X=A+B*	C+(P/Q-7)$
#X=A+B*C	+(P/Q-7)$

At this point in the implementation of our algorithm, we encounter another '+' operator. Upon comparison of its priority with that of the topmost stack operator '*', we find that it is time to generate a subexpression tree and rearrange the push-down stack. This subtree will have '*' as its root node with B and C as left and right operands respectively. Then, after completing the pop-up and insertion operations with the stack, we proceed to compare the '+' operator once again with the new topmost stack operator. In this case, the new stack operator being compared is also '+', and, since the two operators involved in the comparison have the same priority, another subexpression tree is generated for the '+' operator currently in the stack. This sequence of operations is summarized as follows:

After the stack has been rearranged following the generation of the second subexpression tree, we are left to compare the same '+' operator with the new topmost stack operator '='. Since '+' has higher priority than '=', we finally insert the '+' operator into the stack. Following this step, of course, the symbol '(' is automatically placed on top of the stack without a priority comparison. These two steps, as well as the next few that follow, can be summarized in our usual notation. For the sake of conserving space, we shall denote the tree structure already generated by merely using an arrow with the expression A+B*C.

```
#X=    ↓     +                    (P/Q-7)$
     A+B*C
```

```
#X=    ↓     + (                   P/Q-7)$
     A+B*C
```

```
#X=    ↓     + ( P                  /Q-7)$
     A+B*C
```

```
#X=    ↓     + ( P /                 Q-7)$
     A+B*C
```

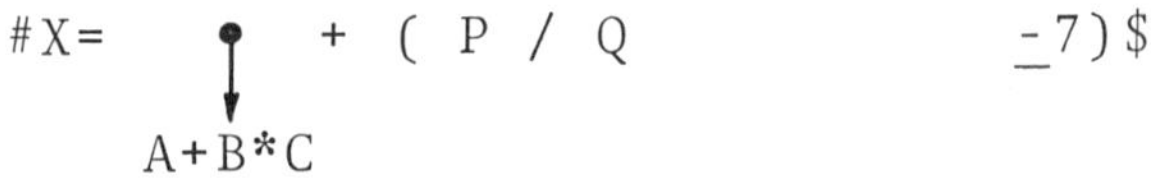

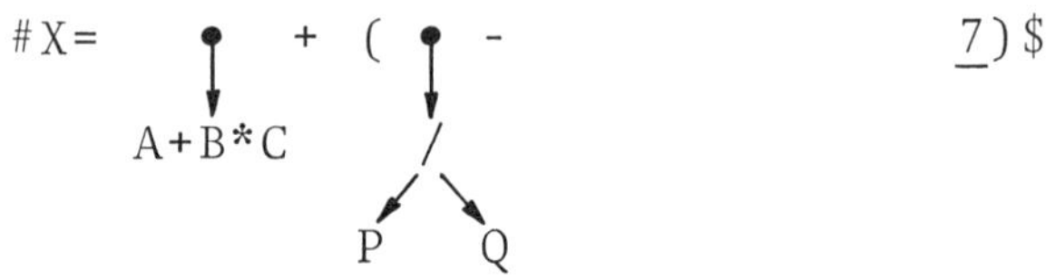

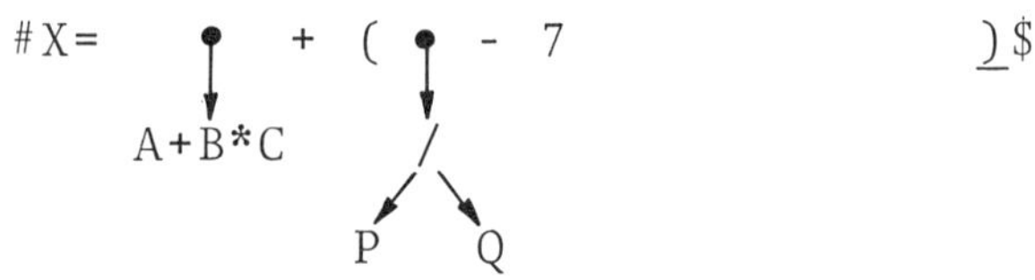

At this stage, we encounter a right parenthesis whose priority is compared to that of '-' which is the latest topmost stack operator. The result of this comparison is the generation of yet another subexpression tree for the operator '-'. Subsequently, after making the necessary stack rearrangements, we find that we are comparing the right parenthesis with the new topmost stack operator which is a left parenthesis. This necessitates the deletion of the '(' operator from the stack and the elimination of ')' from further consideration. To delete '(' from the stack, we pop up the stack, and then replace the new top entry [i.e., '('] by the previous topmost entry (in this case a pointer to the subexpression tree for '-') which was saved prior to popping up the stack. Once again, we summarize the preceding steps:

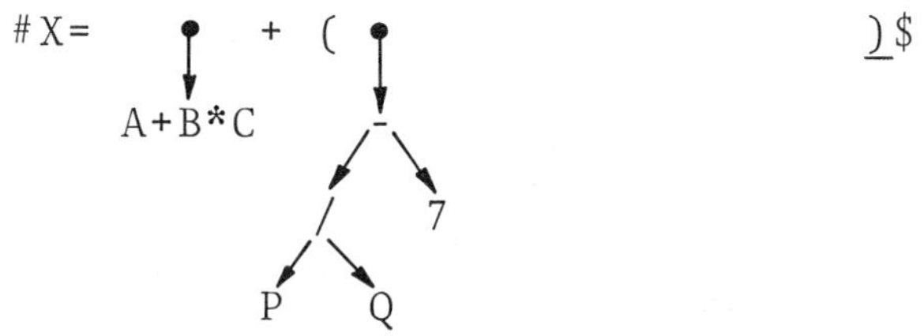

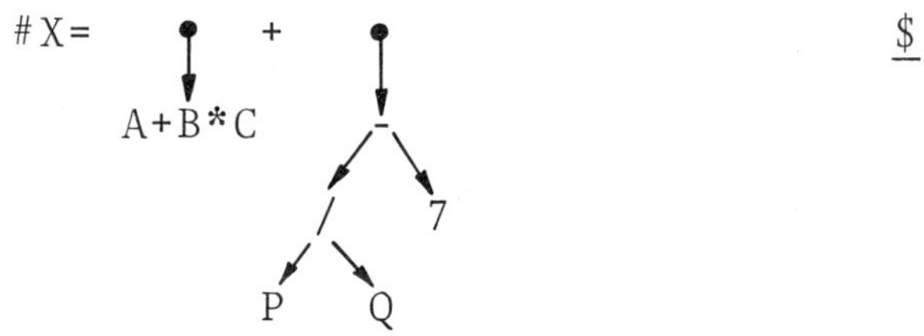

Now that we have met the end-of-statement symbol '$', we clean all the entries off the stack and create new subexpression trees for the two remaining stack operators '+' and '='. Then, faced with the comparison of the two delimiter symbols '#' and '$', we terminate the procedure and leave at the top of the stack a pointer to the final expression tree generated for the original statement. These final steps are illustrated as follows:

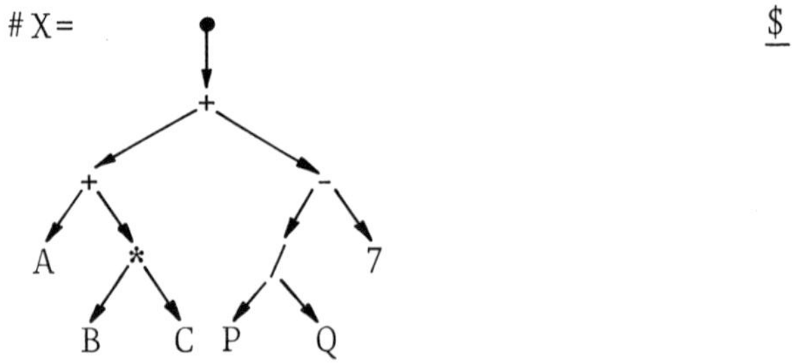

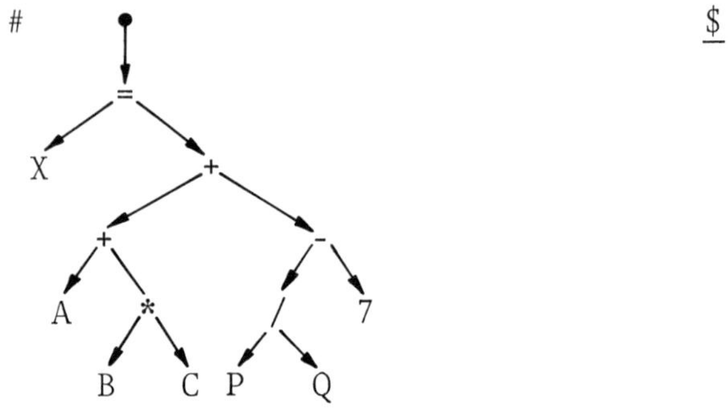

9.5 THE POSTFIX NOTATION

In the preceding section we considered the bitree as being the syntax-free representation of the source, and, as such, it is one example of what we call the "phrase structure" of the statement. However, it is cumbersome to generate a bitree, and, for most applications, with the noteworthy exception of the creation of bitree representations for formal expression manipulation, it is not really necessary. Ideally, we would like to use some representation which is equivalent to the bitree in that it contains not only the same data but also the relevant structural information represented by the tree. Indeed, it is much more convenient to handle the phrase structure in string form rather than as a tree.

The expression evaluation function of Section 8.6.2, in performing the computations prescribed by the expression, effectively traversed the tree in a postfix fashion. The two operands of each operator node were evaluated before the operator itself was applied to the operands. This fact leads us to believe that the relevant structural information contained in an expression bitree can be captured in a postfix listing of the tree. In general, however, a postfix listing would not be a unique representation of a bitree (i.e., several different trees can have the same postfix listing). Nevertheless, in the specific case of expression trees, since we can distinguish between operators and operands, and, because the number of operands associated with an operator is fixed, we can conclude that such trees can be faithfully represented by their postfix listings.

As an illustration of such a listing, suppose we consider the sample assignment statement examined in Section 9.4.1.

```
X = A+B*C+(P/Q-7)
```

Taking the postfix listing of the expression tree representing this statement, we would derive the following phrase structure representation:

```
X A B C * + P Q / 7 - + =
```

This equivalent form of source statements is known as *POLISH POSTFIX NOTATION* in memory of the Polish mathematician who discovered its significance for language translation. All the information needed for the second phase of the translation process is properly contained in this type of string. With this notation, there are no longer any rules about operator precedence. The order in which operations are to be performed is simply defined from left to right with each operator having its two operands preceding it. Moreover, there is no need for including parentheses in these new strings.

The language translation process for most machines could be significantly simplified if we could convince programmers to code source statements in postfix form instead of the customary infix pattern. This suggestion is unacceptable, however, since mankind has developed and used the infix form with implicit hierarchy of operators for many generations, and it is unlikely that he will change this convention merely to simplify computer language translation. It is interesting to notice, nonetheless, that a step in this direction has been taken in the design of the language APL. Although statements are still coded in infix form, this language has completely abolished the notion of operator precedence. In APL the operators are executed strictly from right to left (an arbitrary decision) with each binary operator having its two operands located on its left and right sides respectively. Since the traditional infix form is retained in the language, however, APL still requires parentheses.

9.5.1 Evaluating Expressions In Postfix Notation

The principle involved in evaluating Polish Postfix expressions is similar to the one used by the expression evaluation function of Section 8.6.2 when it utilized the postfix order of traversing through the nodes in a recursive evaluation process. With postfix notation, however, the process of evaluation becomes extremely simple. The actual procedure can be described as follows:

(i) Initiate the scanning of the postfix string with the leftmost entry.

(ii) Continue scanning the string from left to right until an operator is encountered. If the end of the string is encountered, the procedure is terminated, since the string will then be reduced to containing a single numerical value which is the desired result.

(iii) Replace the operator encountered in Step (ii) and the two operands preceding it in the string by the numerical value obtained through the application of the operator to its two operands.

(iv) Proceed to Step (ii).

To illustrate this evaluation procedure, suppose we consider the expression A+B*C+(P/Q-7) which, in postfix notation, would be given as ABC*+PQ/7-+. Furthermore, assume that the variables have the following values at the time of execution:

A = 10 B = 2 C = 3 P = 20 Q = 5

The first operator encountered in the left-to-right scan is '*', and, when it is applied to the values of its two predecessors in the string, B and C, we obtain the numerical value 6. Then, after replacing 'BC*' in the string by this value, we have the following:

A 6 <u>+</u> P Q / 7 - +

The next operator found in the string is '+', and this calls for the addition of 6 to the value of A. Upon obtaining the value 16, we insert it into the string in place of 'A6+' to obtain the following

16 P Q <u>/</u> 7 - +

In a similar fashion, we divide P by Q to get the value 4, and then we subtract 7 from this result as a consequence of meeting the '-' operator as we proceed further along the string. Finally, we add the value produced by the subtraction (i.e., -3) to the value 16, thus yielding the final answer of 13. These steps are summarized as follows:

16 4 7 <u>-</u> +
16 (-3) <u>+</u>
13_

In order to implement this procedure without destroying the postfix representation of the statement, we have to use a push-down stack for storage of the interim results. This will usually be the case when the statement has to be executed several times, each with a different set of values. In such instances, we want to maintain the form of the postfix string for successive computations. This procedure, applied to the same example considered previously, is illustrated as follows:

Stack		Postfix Expression
	Evaluate A.	ABC*+PQ/7-+
10		
	Evaluate B.	ABC*+PQ/7-+
10,2		
	Evaluate C.	ABC*+PQ/7-+
10,2,3		
	Multiply.	ABC*+PQ/7-+
10,6		
	Add.	ABC*+PQ/7-+
16		
	Evaluate P.	ABC*+PQ/7-+
16,20		
	Evaluate Q.	ABC*+PQ/7-+
16,20,5		
	Divide.	ABC*+PQ/7-+
16,4		
	Get the constant.	ABC*+PQ/7-+
16,4,7		
	Subtract.	ABC*+PQ/7-+
16,-3		
	Add.	ABC*+PQ/7-+
13		
	Finished!	

9.5.2 Translation Into Postfix Notation

Now that we have seen the importance of, and the convenience involved with, using the postfix notation as an intermediate representation of the source statement, we can introduce some procedures for performing the translation from FORTRAN infix notation into postfix. It is obvious that we could generate the bitree representation of the source and then reduce the tree to its equivalent postfix string (using one of the algorithms discussed in Sections 8.3 and 8.4). At this point, however, we shall devise a much more efficient algorithm for direct translation from the source to the corresponding postfix string.

As is the case with all syntactic analysis procedures, the postfix translation algorithm which we shall consider utilizes a push-down stack for the storage of operators encountered in the source statement. In this particular case, the algorithm can be illustrated very clearly by the railroad track diagram presented in Figure 9.9. Each syntactic unit of the source is portrayed as being placed on a freight car awaiting future delivery to the shunt track. This shunt track corresponds to our push-down stack. The amount of time spent on the shunt track before ultimate transfer to the target track will vary according to the syntactic unit involved. The transfer of freight cars from one track to another takes place one car at a time.

The algorithm illustrated in Figure 9.9 is very similar to the one described in Section 9.4.1 with the major exception of the difference in the manner of handling operands in the input source. With our new procedure, each new syntactic unit is examined, and, if it proves to be an operand, it is moved directly to the target track. In the case of encountering an operator, however, we conduct our customary operator priority comparison. We

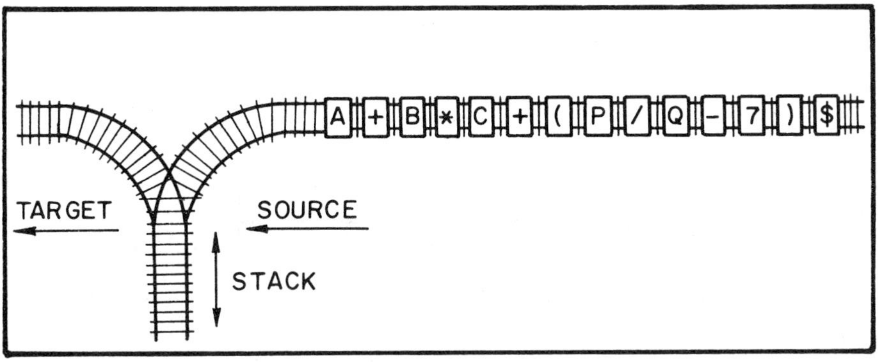

Figure 9.9

Railway Diagram For FORTRAN To Postfix Conversion

compare the priority of the input operator with that of the operator on the first car in the shunt (now the topmost entry in the stack as compared to before when it was the penultimate stack entry). If the priority of the incoming operator is greater than that of the operator in the shunt, the new operator is moved onto the shunt track. Otherwise, the first car in the shunt is transferred to the target track, and another comparison is initiated involving the same input operator and the one on the car which has now moved to the first position in the shunt. This procedure terminates when the end-of-statement symbol is compared with the start-of-statement symbol on the shunt. It is worthwhile to notice that, in keeping with the basic notion of a push-down stack, only the topmost stack entry is involved with any of the shifting operations.

Figure 9.10 contains a flowchart for this syntactic analysis procedure. As a matter of

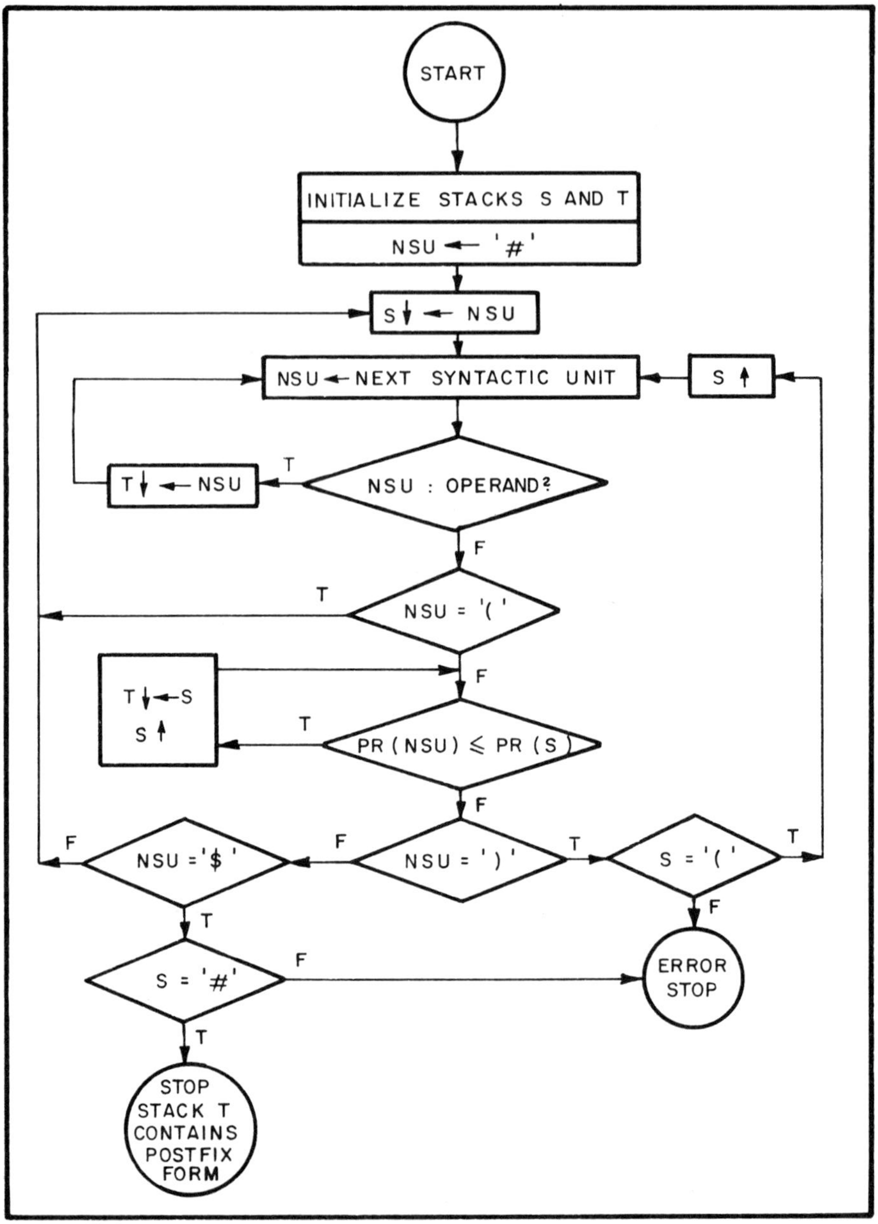

Figure 9.10

<u>Conversion From FORTRAN To Postfix</u>

convenience, we treat the target track as if it were a stack into which we move the operands from the source and the operators from the shunt stack as required. This target stack is never popped up, and, upon completion of the algorithm, it will contain the postfix form of the input source. Operands are moved directly to the target stack, whereas each operator (with the exception of '(' which is inserted automatically into the shunt stack) is maintained in the shunt stack until its second operand (which follows it in the source) has been moved to the target stack. In the latter case, if the next operator from the source is of lower or equal priority, the operator at the top of the shunt stack is moved to the target stack. Otherwise, it is maintained in the shunt stack and pushed down by the higher priority operator(s) until such time as it resurfaces to the top of its stack and is compared with an operator having lower or equal priority. With this scheme, operators are moved to the target stack in the order of their execution which is precisely the same order in which they appear in the postfix notation.

To illustrate this procedure, suppose we consider the same arithmetic expression examined in preceding sections:

A+B*C+(P/Q-7)

The step-by-step conversion of this expression to postfix form is summarized as follows:

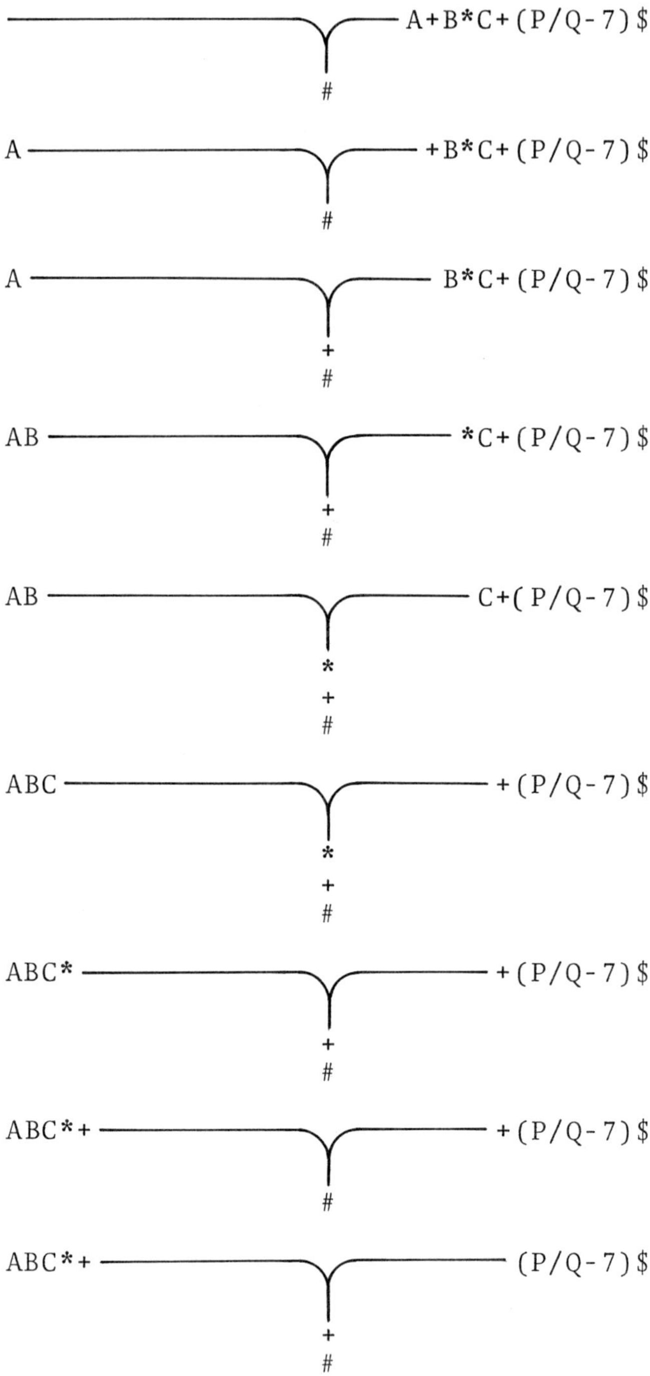
A+B*C+(P/Q-7)$
#
A
+B*C+(P/Q-7)$
#
A
B*C+(P/Q-7)$
+
#
AB
*C+(P/Q-7)$
+
#
AB
C+(P/Q-7)$
*
+
#
ABC
+(P/Q-7)$
*
+
#
ABC*
+(P/Q-7)$
+
#
ABC*+
+(P/Q-7)$
#
ABC*+
(P/Q-7)$
+
#

```
ABC*+ ─────────┐┌───────── P/Q-7)$
               ││
               (
               +
               #
```

```
ABC*+P ────────┐┌───────── /Q-7)$
               ││
               (
               +
               #
```

```
ABC*+P ────────┐┌───────── Q-7)$
               ││
               /
               (
               +
               #
```

```
ABC*+PQ ───────┐┌───────── -7)$
               ││
               /
               (
               +
               #
```

```
ABC*+PQ/ ──────┐┌───────── -7)$
               ││
               (
               +
               #
```

```
ABC*+PQ/ ──────┐┌───────── 7)$
               ││
               -
               (
               +
               #
```

```
ABC*+PQ/7 ─────┐┌───────── )$
               ││
               -
               (
               +
               #
```

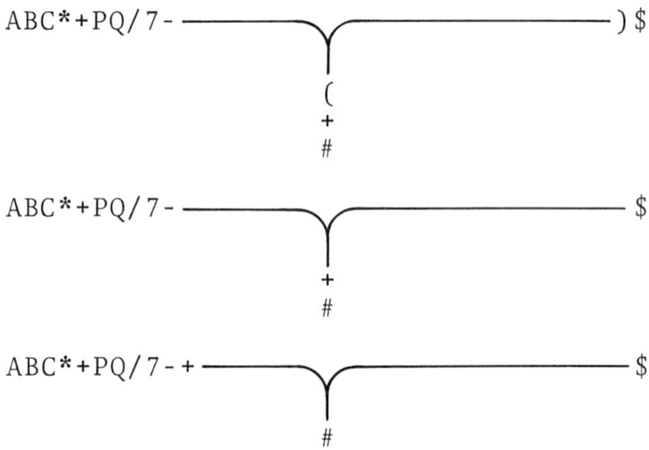

9.5.3 The Jump Table Algorithm

There are numerous algorithms for syntactic analysis, most of which generate the postfix form as their output. However, at this stage of our discussion, rather than investigate any significantly different approaches, we would like instead to consider only a slightly modified version of the procedure described in the preceding subsection. The main purpose for this is to introduce a new programming technique known as the *JUMP TABLE*. This technique can be illustrated very nicely as part of a syntactic analysis program.

In the procedure described in Section 9.5.2, the parentheses and statement delimiters had to be treated as special cases. Furthermore, error checking had to be performed by ad hoc coding. For example, the flowchart of Figure 9.10 illustrates a simple check for matching parentheses, but this requires two additional decision points in the algorithm. However, the algorithm still does not allow for exceptions such as two consecutive exponentiation operators to be treated any differently than any other pair of consecutive equal priority operators. Including provision for such an exception would have necessitated even further additions to the flowchart.

The jump table technique, in addition to simplifying the analysis procedure, provides for easy handling of exceptions and inclusion of further error checking. In general, this technique can be used to advantage in cases where many decisions have to be made and different courses of action followed based upon those decisions. In such instances when this technique is utilized, changes in the syntax specifications do not necessitate any changes in the actual body of the program. All we need do is modify the contents of the jump table that "drives" the rest of the program.

The basic idea of a jump table is very straightforward. In our syntactic analysis procedures, different courses of action are taken depending upon the topmost operator in the stack and the operator representing the syntactic unit currently under examination. Although the priority values associated with the various operators have helped us to devise a relatively simple procedure for determining the proper action, they are really not sufficient if we want to have a more comprehensive algorithm. As an improvement to the procedure, we shall construct a table having one row for each possible operator on top of the stack and one column for each operator that can be encountered as the next syntactic unit. Each entry of this table will indicate, in coded form, which action is to be taken in the instance where we are comparing the two operators in question.

From a detailed examination of Figure 9.10, we can isolate five different actions to be determined by a given pair of operators:

M: Move - Move an operator from the shunt stack to the target, and then initiate another comparison test.

S: Stack - Push the current syntactic unit (an operator) into the shunt stack.

D: Dump - Pop up the shunt stack to eliminate a left parenthesis [in instances where '(' is compared with ')'].

E: Error - This indicates an invalid source statement.

F: Finish - Terminate the procedure when '$' is compared to '#'.

Now we can devise a jump table to specify the correct action to be taken for any given pair of operators, as illustrated in Figure 9.11(a). Each entry in this table is one of the letters M, S, D, E, and F, as an indication of which of the preceding five actions should be followed. For example, the entry in the '=' row and '-' column of

TOP STACK ENTRY	NEXT SYNTACTIC UNIT **	*	/	+	−	=	(	)	$
**	S	M	M	M	M	E	S	M	M
*	S	M	M	M	M	E	S	M	M
/	S	M	M	M	M	E	S	M	M
+	S	S	S	M	M	E	S	M	M
−	S	S	S	M	M	E	S	M	M
=	S	S	S	S	S	E	S	E	M
(	S	S	S	S	S	E	S	D	E
#	S	S	S	S	S	S	S	E	F

a) THE JUMP TABLE

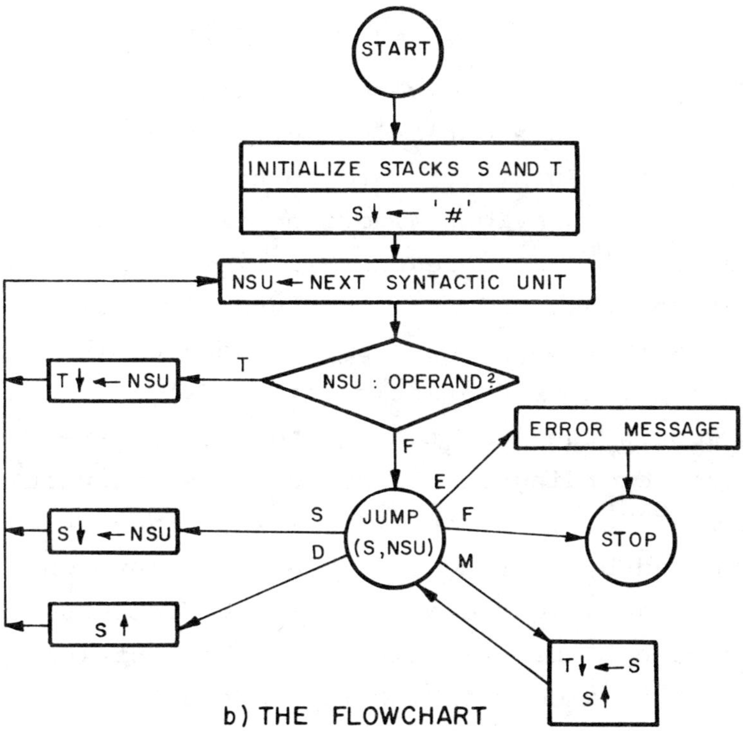

b) THE FLOWCHART

Figure 9.11

The Jump Table Algorithm

the table has the value 'S' to indicate that, when the topmost stack operator is '=' and the syntactic unit currently under consideration is '-', the operator '-' should be inserted into the shunt stack. This specific table has been designed to include error checking to detect illegal appearances of '=' and the presence of unmatched parentheses. In addition, it can handle the special case of two consecutive exponentiations by specifying 'S' as the action to be performed when two '**' operators are encountered instead of the customary entry 'M' which is specified for all other equal priority cases.

The procedure used with the jump table of Figure 9.11(a) is presented in the flowchart of Figure 9.11(b). In addition to being significantly simpler than the previous algorithm discussed in Section 9.5.2, it has more capabilities. The heart of the entire algorithm is a compound five-way transfer instruction. The topmost operator in stack S and the next syntactic unit (NSU) are used for a lookup in the jump table, and the transfer is carried out according to the appropriate entry in the table. In FORTRAN, this multi-way transfer can be implemented by storing the integers 1 through 5 in the jump table (corresponding to the letters we have been using) and utilizing the table entries as the "driver" in a COMPUTED GO TO statement.

Alas, however, we never get something for nothing. The advantages inherent with the additional flexibility and reduction in size of the program coding have to be weighed against the amount of storage consumed by the jump table. A table designed to accommodate the complete set of FORTRAN operators can become prohibitively large, especially when we remember that its size grows proportionally to the square of the number of operators handled. Nevertheless, as we have indicated, the utilization of a jump table is a very effective technique which requires only a small amount of coding and is very easy to modify to accommodate any changes in syntax specifications.

9.6 GENERATION OF OBJECT CODE

In Section 9.3 we indicated that the semantics generation step for the general translation process is not carried out until after completion of the syntax recognition phase. The phrase structure generated by the first stage of the process is passed forward to the semantics generation phase as input. In the case of a compiler, the semantics generation stage involves the creation of object code, and it is this basic procedure of code generation which we shall consider in this section. For our purposes, we shall assume that the phrase structure is presented in Polish Postfix form.

In order to examine the code generation process in more detail, we first have to select a sample assembly language as the target language for our compiler. For this purpose, we have chosen the hypothetical language, SPECTRE MAP, which has been used for teaching purposes in the introductory computer science course at the University of Waterloo. (Readers not familiar with this language should read through Appendix C before proceeding. Only a very surface knowledge of this language is necessary for comprehension of the material in this section.)

Suppose we examine the machine language coding that we would expect to be generated as a translation of a FORTRAN arithmetic assignment statement. In particular, consider the following statement and its corresponding postfix form:

```
X = A*(B-C)/D
X A B C - * D / =
```

The translation of this source statement into SPECTRE MAP coding, as performed by a straightforward compiler, should appear as follows:

```
CLA B       -
SUB C
STO T1

LDQ A       *
MPY T1
STQ T2

LDQ T2      /
DIV D
STQ T3

CLA T3      =
STO X
```

T1, T2, and T3 are symbolic names representing temporary memory locations where intermediate results of computations may be stored. The assignment of these temporary locations is performed by the compiler when it is generating the object code. These locations are not unique for any given statement in that the same temporary memory locations can be shared by object code generated for different statements. By examining the coding generated for the preceding statement, we can see that, with the exception of the '=' operator, each operator contained in the FORTRAN statement is translated into a sequence of three SPECTRE MAP instructions. The order in which these operators are translated is the same as the order of appearance of the operators in the postfix form of the statement. The order of the operators in the postfix form, you will recall, reflects the order in which the operators are to be executed.

The sequence of machine language instructions produced for each operator is dictated by the specific requirements of the subject machine for which the compiler is generating the coding. In the particular case of the SPECTRE computer, we have to load the first operand into the AC (accumulator register) for addition and subtraction and into the MQ (multiplier-quotient register) for division and multiplication. Furthermore, the result of addition and subtraction appears in the AC, whereas, for multiplication and division, the product and quotient respectively are placed in the MQ after the computation has been performed. These conventions are peculiar to the SPECTRE computer, however, and other machines will have other different requirements.

Nevertheless, in spite of the differences between various machines, we can observe that, basically, for each operator, we have to fetch one of the operands into some register, then perform the actual operation, and finally store the result of the computation in some temporary location. This pattern holds true for each of the operators in our FORTRAN statement with the exception of the assignment operator. For this particular case, there is no computation involved. Instead, a value is merely fetched from the most recently used temporary location and stored in the memory location associated with the target operand.

Throughout our examples, we assume that the variables referenced are all of type INTEGER. This assumption, however, does not destroy the generality of our explanation. If the variables involved were of type REAL, the actual machine language instructions generated would indeed be different, since we would be involved with floating-point arithmetic. Nonetheless, the basic pattern of fetching one operand into a register, performing an arithmetic operation, and storing the result in a temporary location, would be preserved. The fact that the registers involved might be different is also of no consequence if we are considering only the basic concepts behind the code generation process.

Other FORTRAN statements can be translated in a similar way. IF statements, for example, generate coding to load the logical or arithmetic value of the expression in parentheses and perform a branch accordingly. DO statements, on the other hand, are slightly more complicated, and they are usually broken down into a sequence of more simplified operations involving the initialization, incrementing, and testing of the loop index variable.

As a prelude to further discussion of the code generation process, suppose we recollect our algorithm for evaluating statements in postfix notation as presented in Section 9.5.1. The algorithm for generating object code from the postfix form is essentially the same, except that, instead of performing the actual calculations implied by the various operators, we create the appropriate machine language coding. The push-down stack utilized for storage of the intermediate results in the evaluation algorithm is replaced by the use of temporary memory locations in which the intermediate values are stored at execution time. These modifications to the algorithm of Section 9.5.1 are very trivial ones.

Our procedure for generating object code maintains a table which contains the specific instructions to be generated for the various operators. The operands for these instructions are taken from the postfix form of the source statement (each operator in the postfix string is immediately preceded by its two operands) and the result of each operation is stored in a temporary memory location (T1, T2, etc.). The symbolic names of these temporary locations are inserted into the push-down stack in place of the intermediate results which were formerly saved there as part of the evaluation procedure.

An instruction translation table for the SPECTRE machine is presented in Figure 9.12. As each sequence of instructions is selected from this table during the creation of object code, the appropriate operands are taken from the stack (where they were stored earlier after being extracted from the postfix string). In addition, the procedure maintains a counter which is incremented every time a temporary location is required, and it is the value of this counter which is used for T# as the target cell for the store command.

```
+       CLA op1
        ADD op2
        STO T#

-       CLA op1
        SUB op2
        STO T#

*       LDQ op1
        MPY op2
        STQ T#

/       LDQ op1
        DIV op2
        STQ T#

=       CLA op2
        STO op1
```

Figure 9.12

<u>SPECTRE Instruction Translation Table</u>

To illustrate the detailed operation of this code generation procedure, suppose we consider the following example:

FORTRAN: X = A+B*C+(P/Q-7)

POSTFIX: X A B C * + P Q / 7 - + =

First, we initialize the temporary counter to zero. Then we begin to examine entries from the postfix string, moving the operands directly to a push-down stack and generating code for the operators. For our example, this procedure is applied for operands X, A, B, and C as indicated in the following sequence of steps:

Stack	Postfix
X	X A B C * + P Q / 7 - + =
X A	X A B C * + P Q / 7 - + =
X A B	X A B C * + P Q / 7 - + =
X A B C	X A B C * + P Q / 7 - + =

At this point, we generate the code for the '*' operator. This involves fetching the instructions from the table, inserting the operands from the top of the stack, incrementing the temporary location counter, and inserting its value for T#. This sequence of steps produces the following object code:

```
LDQ B
MPY C
STQ T1
```

Then we insert T1 into the stack to replace the operands of the multiplication operator.

Stack	Postfix
X A T1	X A B C * + P Q / 7 - + =

As we continue scanning from left to right in the postfix string, we encounter the '+' operator which signals the need to increment the temporary location counter and generate further coding. Upon completion of this step, we once again replace the operands in the stack by the name of the temporary location of the result (T2).

```
CLA A
ADD T1
STO T2
```

Stack	Postfix
X T2	X A B C * + P Q / 7 - + =

The remaining steps in the application of this code generation procedure to our example are summarized as follows:

Stack	Coding	Postfix
X T2 P Q		X A B C * + P Q / 7 - + =
	LDQ P DIV Q STQ T3	(division)
X T2 T3 7		X A B C * + P Q / 7 - + =
	CLA T3 SUB =7 STO T4	(subtraction of literal 7)

```
X T2 T4                     X A B C * + P Q / 7 - + =
          CLA T2
          ADD T4     (addition)
          STO T5

X T5                        X A B C * + P Q / 7 - + =
          CLA T5
          STO X      (assignment)
```

9.7 CODE OPTIMIZATION

The object code generated by a compiler is usually less efficient than the machine language coding that could be generated by a human programmer. In the early development stages of compilers, since computing power was relatively limited, this fact was a cause for major concern in the computing field. Consequently, one of the goals in the original design of the first FORTRAN compilers was to have the generated object code be as efficient as possible, or, in other words, to *OPTIMIZE* the code produced. It is interesting to note that many of the restrictions imposed by earlier versions of FORTRAN, such as simple (linear) subscript expressions, restricted forms of DO statements, and limits placed on the number of subscripts or nested DO loops, were developed with the intention of facilitating better optimization and hence more efficient object code. This emphasis on code optimization is still an important feature of today's compilers, even though the computing power available has increased tremendously from earlier years and some of the earlier language restrictions have since been removed.

The basic idea involved in code optimization is to examine the generated object code with the intention of removing from it any redundant instructions and/or rearranging the coding so as to produce more efficient code. When we are compiling a program for debugging purposes, this feature is not so important, since the program will have to be recompiled numerous times before it reaches its final form. It is extremely important, however, when a program has been completed and is due to enter production execution. Optimization can be performed at different levels, and accordingly, the time and cost involved with the compilation increases directly with the extent to which the optimization process is carried out. As a result, we often find today that numerous languages have several compilers available for them, each one differing in the level of optimization it performs. Indeed, still other compilers will perform different levels of code optimization as specified by parameters supplied by the user prior to compilation.

To illustrate the discrepancies between hand-generated and compiler-created machine language coding, suppose we examine the following FORTRAN arithmetic assignment statement:

```
X = A*(B-C)/D
```

The compiler-generated object code for this expression, assuming that no optimization has been performed, was presented at the beginning of Section 9.5. By way of comparison, a human programmer could code this same expression as follows:

```
CLA B
SUB C
STO T1
LDQ A
MPY T1
DIV D
STQ X
```

The compiler-generated code is grossly inefficient, even for this simple statement, and the extent of its inefficiency, when compared to carefully written human coding, increases considerably with the complexity of the expression.

The process of object code optimization can be considered in two forms, often referred to as *LOCAL* and *GLOBAL* optimization. The first technique involves the optimization of small subsections of the generated coding without being concerned with any overall features displayed in the program. The second form, on the other hand, considers the whole source program in an attempt to improve the efficiency of the object code generated. We shall now investigate each of these forms of optimization in further detail.

9.7.1 Local Optimization

Local optimization involves the examination of, and whenever possible, the improvement of small subsections of the object code, and it usually takes the form of eliminating totally useless instructions.

In fact, it is sometimes called "peephole optimization" because of the fact that it entails looking at very small pieces of object code and changing them without being concerned with the overall context in which they are used. The classical case of peephole optimization, for example, is the removal of store-load combinations. Whenever a pair of instructions like

```
STO X          STQ X
CLA X    or    LDQ X
```

is encountered in the generated code, the CLA or LDQ instruction is recognized as being completely redundant and it is eliminated.

Local optimization entails the detection and improvement of many special cases like the store-load combination. For example, it would be very helpful to detect sequences of instructions like

```
STO T
CLA T
ADD Y
```

and replace them by the following single line:

```
ADD Y
```

This action is appropriate, of course, only if T is a temporary location (T#) and its value is not required by the program. If, however, T is a variable from the source program, the best that can be done is to reduce this three-line sequence to

```
STO T
ADD Y
```

Another possibility is the rearrangement of the order of instructions when translating commutative operations so as to allow for possible further optimization. For example, instead of generating

```
CLA T1
ADD T2
STO T3
```

the compiler could generate

```
CLA T2
ADD T1
STO T3
```

The desirability of such an action would depend upon the coding immediately adjacent to this section. In addition, by recognizing that T1 and T2 are not really needed, a further optimization could be performed by generating

```
CLA T2
ADD T1
STO T1    (reset temporary counter to 1)
```

To illustrate some of these optimization techniques, consider the following assignment statement and the corresponding object code generated by a non-optimizing compiler:

FORTRAN: X = (A-B)+(C-D)

POSTFIX: X A B - C D - + =

CODING:

```
CLA A
SUB B
STO T1
CLA C
SUB D
STO T2 <------------------------- eliminate
CLA T1 }                 { CLA T2 <-
ADD T2 }  interchange    { ADD T1
STO T3 }
CLA T3 }  eliminate
STO X
```

By performing the indicated interchange of instructions and the elimination of unnecessary store-load sequences, we could reduce the coding to the following:

```
CLA A
SUB B
STO T1
CLA C
SUB D
ADD T1
STO X
```

The optimization of this coding can be carried even further to recognize the presence of a redundant pair of parentheses, (C-D), and simplify the coding to

```
CLA A
SUB B
ADD C
SUB D
STO X
```

This latter step, however, might not be acceptable as optimization in all instances, since, in some cases, the programmer might have had some purpose in inserting the redundant pair of parentheses, and this purpose would not be apparent to the compiler at the time it is generating the object code.

Another form of local optimization entails recognizing the presence of repeated subexpressions within an expression. For example, in the following statement

```
X = (3+A*B+C)*3*(3+A*B+D)
```

the expression 3+A*B appears twice. It would be more efficient to remove it from the statement and use the following coding instead:

```
T1 = 3+A*B
X = (T1+C)*3*(T1+D)
```

This revised version would be faster during execution because 3+A*B would be evaluated only once.

This form of optimization is easy to perform on the postfix string form itself, since it is necessary only to recognize that two substrings of the original string are identical. Moreover, because of the ease with which subexpressions can be isolated and rearranged in expression bitrees, it is also quite convenient to carry out this type of optimization in an explicit tree structure representing the statement. One could refine this procedure even further to recognize that two different expressions are actually equivalent (i.e., they represent the same computation). For example, A+B and B+A could be identified as being essentially the same expression. Recognition of this and similar identities, however, requires more than a simple check for equality as we demonstrated earlier in Section 8.6.4 when we considered the problem of checking for equivalent bitree representations of expressions. Consequently, most compilers are restricted to checking for the simplest cases of equivalent expressions in the source program, since, the more complex the identity, the harder it is to recognize and the less likely it is to be useful.

A constant danger faced by compilers is the possibility that a programmer might have deliberately coded a statement in a manner that at first seems inefficient, in order to avoid roundoff errors, arithmetic overflows, or other problems. Apparent optimization can sometimes be numerically undesirable (even catastrophic), or, for more general data types, have unfavourable affects on run-time or store. In deciding to what extent the object code optimization process should be applied, the designer of a compiler has to make a decision without being able to fully anticipate the thoughts of particular users.

9.7.2 Global Optimization

As we mentioned earlier, global optimization entails an examination of the complete program in an effort to improve the object code generated. This type of optimization can be performed by both the compiler and the programmer. The FORTRAN H compiler for the S/360, for example, furnishes an excellent illustration of this form of code optimization. First, the compiler reads the entire source program into core storage and transforms it into list structures for convenience in processing. Then a detailed analysis of the branching and looping structure in the program is performed. From the IF statements, GO TO instructions, DO loops, and so forth, the compiler detects almost all the programming loops existing in the program. Furthermore, it constructs tables of information pertaining to the 128 most commonly used variables in the program and notes where each of these variables is used and assigned a value.

In addition, if an arithmetic expression occurs inside a loop in spite of the fact that none of its variables are changed in the loop, the compiler is designed to move the expression outside the loop. This implies that the expression in question can be evaluated once outside the loop instead of several times inside the loop. This movement of expressions by the compiler applies even to fragments of address calculations for subscripts. Furthermore, the compiler can perform additional optimization by taking advantage of the fact that, if an expression occurs twice without any of its variables being altered between the two occurrences, it need really occur only once. By saving the value when it is first calculated, the compiler avoids the duplication by using the saved value the second time. It is also equipped to delete any instructions in the source program that it detects as being completely useless. This could be the case, for example, if the source program assigns a value to a variable which is never used again in the program.

The S/360 has sixteen fast general registers and four floating-point registers in which all the arithmetic is performed. These are analogous to the AC and MQ registers in the SPECTRE computer except that there are considerably more of them. Information can be retrieved from these registers faster than from any other memory storage available. Consequently, in order to utilize them in the most efficient manner, we should allocate them so that they are used to store the values which are needed most frequently in the program at various stages of execution. The FORTRAN H compiler, for example, begins by examining the program's innermost loops and assigns its registers to variables that are heavily used locally and to temporary results that are used later in the loops. This improves the efficiency of the most frequently executed parts of the program. In addition, if a value is kept in a register inside a loop and in main memory storage outside the loop, it should be inserted back into main storage whenever an exit is made from the loop. This need be done only if the value is required later outside the loop.

In addition to carrying out various forms of global optimization, the FORTRAN H compiler also performs numerous sorts of peephole optimization. Indeed, the writers of this compiler claim that, for small programs having a simple loop structure, their compiler will generate "perfect" object code, or, in other words, machine language coding that could not be improved by an expert human programmer. Regardless of the validity of this claim, it is readily apparent that the object code generated by this compiler is extremely efficient. As an illustration, we might compare the relative efficiencies of object programs generated by FORTRAN H and WATFIV. Although the ratio will vary with the source program in question, the coding generated by FORTRAN H is approximately twenty times faster than that produced by WATFIV. Remember, however, that WATFIV was not designed for production type execution, but was developed instead for debugging purposes and the processing of small programs. The compilation speed of WATFIV is considerably faster than that of FORTRAN H.

FORTRAN H is a complete FORTRAN compiler that was, in fact, itself written in FORTRAN. Nevertheless, in spite of the fact that it was written in a high-level language, when it is used to compile itself, it still performs efficiently. As a result, its authors now claim that, since this degree of object code optimization has been demonstrated to be practical, there is no longer any need (or excuse) for anyone to program large systems in assembly language. Not everyone, of course, shares their confidence.

9.8 MACRO PROCESSORS

Programming in high-level languages involves certain inherent restrictions and inefficiencies.

For one thing, most programming languages are quite inflexible. A compiler is a very complex program which is quite difficult to change to satisfy the specific requirements of an individual program. A FORTRAN compiler, for example, translates only valid FORTRAN statements. If a programmer had a collection of FORTRAN programs which made frequent use of some special operation, say the concatenation of character strings, and he wished to include a new operator in the language (like the operator '||' in PL/1), he would find that his task involved considerable effort. To begin, he would have to familiarize himself at a very detailed level with the logic and operation of the compiler. Then he would have to make the appropriate modifications to the compiler so that it would be able to handle the new operator, debug the revised version, and then use the new compiler which he had developed. Admittedly, he could instead write a FORTRAN subroutine to perform the concatenation, but this alternative would not really be what he wanted, and besides, it would yield a very inefficient object code.

The preceding example illustrates the fact that a compiler involves an inherent inefficiency when it is used in ways for which it was not intended. As a further illustration, suppose that we had a FORTRAN compiler for the SPECTRE computer. In addition, assume that this compiler did not have a built-in function for absolute value and that we wanted to develop this facility. We could write a FORTRAN function subprogram to compute the absolute value of its argument. However, this would mean that, every time we wished to compute the absolute value of some quantity, the compiler would not merely insert the two appropriate machine language instructions. Instead, it would generate the object code to go through the procedure of setting up a parameter list, calling the subprogram, copying the single argument value into the local cell reserved for the subprogram parameter, and so forth. Finally, after computing the desired value, the subprogram would return to the calling program with the result. In addition to the inefficiency inherent with this process, the body of the subroutine, since it was the result of FORTRAN compilation, would calculate the absolute value in a most inefficient manner. There would be no way whatsoever of inducing the compiler to simply insert as on-line object code the load-register-set-sign-positive instruction sequence (i.e., CLA X and SSP) which would yield the desired absolute value directly. This would be by far the most efficient way to compute the absolute value in SPECTRE.

For some applications, especially in the production environment where the efficiency of the generated object code is of prime concern, it appears that we need a more flexible tool than the high-level language compiler. Macro processors, although they were first introduced only as extensions to assembly language processors, can supply us with some of the desired flexibility. Originally, the idea behind a macro was to identify a commonly used set of assembly language instructions by a symbolic name. This sequence of instructions could then be repeated at various points in the program, each time with different parameters, by merely specifying the symbolic name and the appropriate lists of parameters.

As an illustration, suppose we wish to add a CALL statement to SPECTRE MAP. This new statement will be used to call subroutines that accept a single argument which we can assume should be placed in the MQ prior to transfer to the subroutine. For example, if we want to make use of a subroutine SIN with an argument X, we want to be able to invoke the subroutine using the following coding:

```
CAL SIN,X
```

The SPECTRE machine has no such instruction in its repertoire of commands, and, as a result, we have to make do with the following coding:

```
LDQ X
TSL SIN
```

However, CAL can be defined as a macro, and, as such, it can appear as an operation code in the source. The macro processor scans through the assembly language source and copies each line of the source text as it is encountered, except that, whenever it finds a statement with CAL in the operation code field, it replaces the single statement by two statements like those above. So, for example,

```
CAL COS,P
```

would be converted into

```
LDQ P
TSL COS
```

In developing a macro processor, we have to recognize that our new translation process entails two distinct stages. First, we have to be able to recognize the appearance of a macro call when we find its name in the operation code field. Once this has been accomplished, we have to determine its arguments by searching for commas and blanks which act as delimiters for these arguments. This phase of the operation is the syntactic analysis process. Following this part of the procedure, we enter the semantics generation phase in which we have to generate the correct SPECTRE MAP instructions which will eventually perform the correct operations.

Both compilers and macro processors involve translation from one language to another. With the latter, however, through the utilization of *MACRO DEFINITIONS*, the programmer has the capacity to specify some of the syntax instead of having it immutably fixed in the language. The following coding, for example, is an illustration of a macro definition for the macro CAL:

```
     MAC
&LAB CAL &SUB,&ARG
&LAB LDQ &ARG
     TSL &SUB
     MEN
```

The special operation code MAC is used to identify the text that follows as a macro definition. The second line illustrates how the macro should be called whenever it is to be used. The user has to specify the macro name (CAL) in the operation code field and list the appropriate parameters. In the macro definition, ampersands (&) are employed as markers to identify parameters for the macro. The specific label associated with the macro call (i.e., &LAB) is effectively just another parameter. However, for consistency with other labels in the source, it is placed in the label column rather than among the other parameters. The remaining parameters for our example are &SUB and &ARG which represent the subroutine to be called and the subroutine argument respectively.

The remaining statements, down to but excluding the operation code MEN, comprise the *BODY* of the macro and specify the coding into which the macro call should be expanded. The &-parameters indicate where the arguments are to be inserted, and, when a macro call is expanded, every occurrence of an &-parameter in the body is replaced by the corresponding argument provided in the call. If no actual argument is provided, the &-parameter is merely deleted. Finally, MEN (Macro ENd) is used to identify the end of the macro definition.

To illustrate the application of this algorithm, suppose we consider the following assembly language input to our macro processor:

```
     MAC
&LAB CAL &SUB,&ARG
&LAB LDQ &ARG
     TSL &SUB
     MEN
     CLA =16
     ADD Q
     STO Q
     CAL SIN,Q
      :
      :
```

Upon encountering the first statement, the macro processor recognizes the MAC operation code as initiating a macro definition. The succeeding statements, down to and including MEN, are read and stored in a table called a *MACRO TABLE*. These statements are not reproduced as part of the output from the macro processor. The name of the macro (CAL) is then entered into a special macro opcode table together with a pointer to the location in the macro table where the body of the macro has been saved. From this point onward, CAL will be recognized as a valid operation code.

The three statements following MEN, since they do not involve macro calls or additional macro definitions, are simply reproduced as output. Then the macro call (CAL SIN,Q) is encountered, and the macro processor ascertains that it is indeed a macro call from the fact that the operation code (CAL) appears in the macro opcode table. In the macro parameter table, symbols LAB, SUB, and ARG are associated with the character strings '   ' (since the label field is blank for the macro call), 'SIN', and 'Q' respectively. From this point onward, statements are copied as output from the body of the macro. However, each time that one of the symbols LAB, SUB, or ARG is encountered following an ampersand, the appropriate choice from the strings '   ', 'SIN', and 'Q' is substituted for the formal parameter name and preceding ampersand. Consequently, when the macro processor meets the statement

```
        CAL SIN,Q
```

it does not reproduce the statement as output, but instead generates the following expanded version:

```
LDQ Q
TSL SIN
```

Upon completion of this step, the macro processor continues processing the rest of the source deck. For the portion of the source that we have considered, however, the complete generated output has been as follows:

```
CLA =16
ADD Q
STO Q
LDQ Q
TSL SIN
```

The advantage of the macro definition for CAL is that it enables us to simplify the coding for subroutine calls considerably. In our particular example, instead of two statements we need only one. While this saving is not itself that significant, we can appreciate the fact that the saving would be considerably more significant if we were dealing with a more general subroutine call where several arguments for the subroutine were involved. In addition, the CAL opcode suggests what we are attempting to do much more clearly than LDQ and TSL. This may reduce the frequency of coding errors, especially in the more customary case where there are numerous lines of coding involved, and it certainly makes the resulting program easier to read and debug.

As a second illustration of a SPECTRE MAP macro, consider the following input source for our macro processor:

```
         MAC
&LAB     CLC  &OP,&X,&Y,&Z
&LAB     CLA  &X
         &OP  &Y
         STO  &Z
         MEN
         LDQ  X
TOP      CLC  ADD,SUM,X,SUM
         STQ  C
         CLC  SUB,A,=1,B
         ADD  Z
```

The first six statements define a macro called CLC which has five parameters. These include the macro label (&LAB), three instruction operands (&X, &Y, and &Z), and an operation code (&OP). In most instances, this variable operation code will be either ADD or SUB, since the macro was developed with the viewpoint of its being an abbreviation for both of the following two types of instruction sequence which appear frequently in many programs:

```
CLA X                CLA X
ADD Y        or      SUB Y
STO Z                STO Z
```

Nevertheless, in spite of our original intentions for this macro, if an appropriate situation were to arise where we wanted to insert some other operation code for &OP, there would be nothing to prevent our doing so.

In the preceding source input for our macro processor, we have included two macro calls. The first illustrates the case where the argument X does not correspond to the parameter &X. This does not present any problem, since &X is only a dummy representation for the actual character string which will be inserted during the expansion produced by the macro call. The second macro call includes the use of '=1' as an argument to correspond to &Y.

The complete output generated by our macro processor for this particular input is presented below:

```
        LDQ X
TOP     CLA SUM  )
        ADD X    }      TOP   CLC ADD,SUM,X,SUM
        STO SUM  )
        STQ C
        CLA A    )
        SUB =1   }            CLC SUB,A,=1,B
        STO B    )
        ADD Z
```

It is important to reiterate that a macro processor does not process assembly language statements as such. Instead, it produces an expanded version of the source which can then be submitted to an assembler processor as input. Figure 9.13 presents a block diagram for the operation of a simple assembly-language-oriented macro processor. The source is assumed to contain valid assembly language statements, and, as a result, it is very straightforward to identify the operation codes in each source statement and detect the presence of macro definitions (which are eliminated from the output) and macro calls requiring expansion.

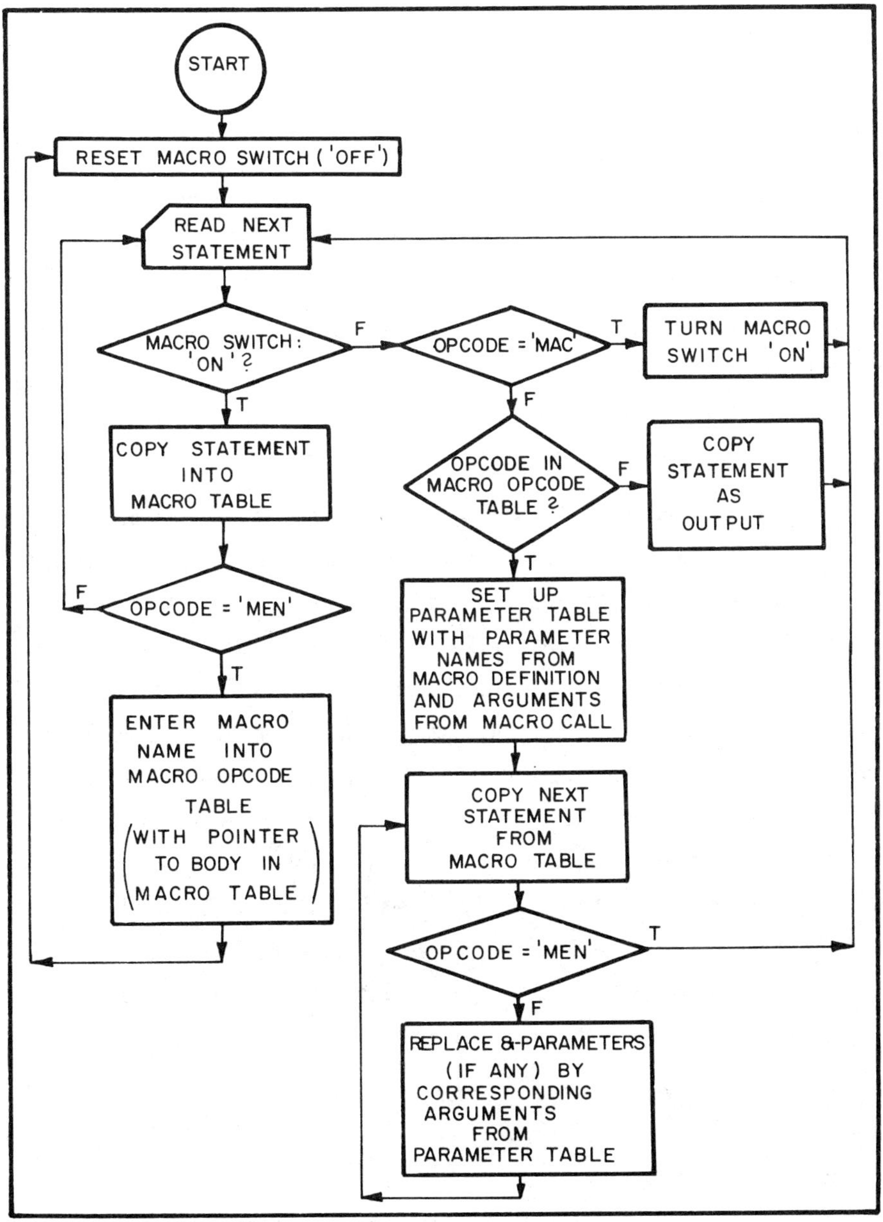

Figure 9.13

<u>An Assembly-Language-Oriented Macro Processor</u>

The advantage of having a macro processor available is greater flexibility. Instead of having an assembler that merely recognizes CAL or CLC statements as special cases, we have a processor that permits the programmer to make his own definitions and thereby enrich the language he is using. It is certainly much easier to define a macro than it is to change an existing assembler. Furthermore, a programmer need only maintain his own collection of macros rather than his own version of the complete assembler program.

Nevertheless, our macro processor retains the restriction that its source and target languages are essentially assembly-level languages. Although the availability of macro facilities with SPECTRE MAP makes the language considerably more flexible to use, we are still faced with much of the inherent clumsiness of the assembly language. To overcome this obstacle, considerable attention has been devoted to including macro facilities with certain high-level programming languages. In fact, the use of macro processors with high-level languages constitutes a major area for current research in the field of programming languages.

The concept of a macro processor, as illustrated in Figure 9.13, has been generalized in a very straightforward manner. As we have indicated, the input to a macro processor is a long character string (comprised of all the input source statements) and the output is another long character string. This output string represents a modification of the input string through the deletion of macro definitions and the expansion of macro calls. This led to the development of macro processors as general-purpose string processors. Special characters in the input identify macro definitions, each one including a list of parameters and a sequence of coding comprising the definition, and, whenever the symbolic name of a macro is encountered in the input, it is replaced by the expanded body of the macro with appropriate modifications for the parameters. Such general-purpose string processors are relatively easy to implement and they can be utilized for the generation of source programs for any compiler (e.g., the preprocessor available with PL/1) or assembler that is desired. The advantage of their use is the added ability to define all kinds of new operations in the subject language and to be able to invoke them through their symbolic names.

In conclusion, we would like to point out that the facilities of macro processors have been enhanced in several different ways. For example, in existence today we find macro processors providing the capabilities to nest macros, or, in other words, to include a macro call within the definition of another macro (including recursive macro facilities). In addition, some macro processors have been developed to include provision for making the expansion of parts of the macro body conditional upon some logical expression involving the arguments of the macro, conditional GO TO statements, and other similar high-level language features. This implies that, in the process of expanding the macro, different code sequences can be generated for different values of the parameters.

9.9 EXERCISES

In the following exercises you may assume that all FORTRAN and postfix statements consist exclusively of one-character syntactic units (i.e., one-letter variable names and single-digit constants). To conform with this assumption, you may use the special symbol '@' to specify exponentiation. Although this decision limits the generality and scope of variable names and constants, it does simplify considerably the scanning and processing of the source.

1.(a) In Section 9.4.1, we described a routine for converting a FORTRAN arithmetic assignment statement into its equivalent bitree representation. Write a FORTRAN function subprogram to implement this procedure. The function should accept as a parameter a character string image of a source statement and return as its value a pointer to the bitree representation. The resulting tree structure should comply with the conventions described in Section 8.6.1. Each node in the tree should have three fields, one for a TYPE indicator and the others for left and right links. For each leaf node representing a variable, the left link should point to the location of that operand in a symbol table (linear or otherwise) constructed by your function. In the case of a leaf representing a constant operand, the value of the constant should be stored in the node's left link field. An example of such a bitree representation is presented in Figure 8.11. Include in the coding for your bitree construction function checks for possible syntax errors (e.g., unmatched parentheses) in the source statement and provisions for printing appropriate messages if such errors are detected.

1. (b) Write a mainline program that reads as data several FORTRAN arithmetic assignment statements and invokes the function of part (a) to create the equivalent bitree representations.

(c) The algorithm involved in part (a) processes all equal priority operators from left to right without provision for any exceptions to the rule. Consequently, it processes A**B**C as (A**B)**C. Modify the function of part (a) to process A**B**C as A**(B**C).

(d) The conversion procedure implemented in part (a) was designed on the assumption that, with the exception of parentheses and delimiter symbols, operands and operators appear alternatively in the source statement. Modify the function of part (a) to accommodate unary minus. How will this extra provision change the tree structure?

2. (a) Write a FORTRAN function subprogram to perform the reverse operation to that involved with Exercise 1(a). More specifically, your routine should accept as a parameter a pointer to a bitree representation for a FORTRAN source statement and return as its value a character string image of the reconstructed FORTRAN statement. For the processing of operator nodes in the tree structure, this procedure will necessitate a conversion from a TYPE indicator entry to the actual operator itself. In the case of leaf nodes, variable names and constants can be obtained from the symbol table and the left link fields respectively. Essentially, this conversion process entails the left-to-right infix listing of a bitree. However, it involves a further level of complexity, since it will be necessary in many cases to insert parentheses in the output statement to force operator priority. (It is worthwhile noting that the TYPE indicator provides the relevant information of an operator priority table.) One instance where it may be necessary to insert parentheses, for example, is the case of an operator appearing lower in the tree structure (i.e., further from the root) than some other operator having higher priority. This situation is illustrated in Figure 9.7(b).

(b) Expand the mainline program of Exercise 1(b) so that, for each bitree representation created, the program invokes the function from Exercise 2(a) to reconstruct the corresponding FORTRAN source statement.

3.(a) In Section 9.5, we described two algorithms for performing the conversion of a FORTRAN source statement into Polish Postfix notation. The second of these two methods (i.e., the jump table algorithm of Figure 9.11) is really only an extension of the first (Figure 9.10). Write the FORTRAN coding for two functions, one to implement each of these procedures. In both cases, the function should accept as a parameter a character string representing an arithmetic assignment statement and return as its value another character string representing the equivalent postfix form. Both algorithms utilize two stacks and perform the conversion directly from FORTRAN to postfix without creating an intermediate bitree representation. The jump table, however, although it requires considerable memory for storage (i.e., the table entries must include provision for all possible operator pairings), is much more adaptable for processing operator exceptions (e.g., successive exponentiation) and incorporating error checking.

(b) Write a mainline program to read a series of FORTRAN source statements and invoke the functions from part (a) to create the equivalent postfix strings. Compare the execution times of the two procedures when they are applied to the same source statements. Under what circumstances would one of the algorithms be preferable to the other?

3. (c) Extend the jump table to include provision for handling multiple assignment statements.

e.g., X = A = B = C-D+4

(d) How would you incorporate unary minus into each of the two algorithms?

4. This exercise requires the writing of an interpreter for executing a subset of FORTRAN source statements. Each source statement is read as data, translated into postfix notation, and then executed. You may assume that the source is composed exclusively of arithmetic assignment statements (with no multiple assignment). This assumption implies that we require only <u>one</u> "pass" over the input stream in order to execute all the source coding. This interpretive process can proceed in two phases (parts (a) and (b) of this exercise).

(a) Phase one involves the translation of FORTRAN source statements to their equivalent postfix forms and the creation of a symbol table to contain all variable names and their corresponding values. Modify the coding for your jump table routine in Exercise 3 so that it creates the appropriate symbol table entries while it is converting each source statement. Include provision for the printout of relevant error messages in cases where syntax errors are detected in the source.

4.(b) Phase two entails the execution of the source statements directly from the postfix forms obtained in phase one. The algorithm for this procedure is described and illustrated in Section 9.5.1. Write the coding for a subroutine which implements this algorithm. The subroutine should accept as an input parameter a character string representation of a postfix string. Evaluation of the postfix form begins with the second syntactic unit (why?), and, when the '=' is encountered, the evaluation process is terminated. Then the symbol table value of the first syntactic unit is updated to reflect the execution of the '=' operator. During the processing of each postfix string, a symbol table lookup is required whenever a symbolic operand is encountered. However, constants appearing in the postfix string will have to be converted from character string form to equivalent numerical form before they can be used as operands in performing an arithmetic operation. For each postfix string supplied as input, the subroutine should print the first symbolic name in the postfix form (i.e., the variable preceding '=' in the corresponding FORTRAN statement) and its new value after the source statement has been executed. Error checking in phase two should consist of diagnosing undefined variables.

4.(c) Write a mainline program which reads as data a series of FORTRAN arithmetic assignment statements and invokes the subprograms of parts (a) and (b) to interpretively execute the source. Output should include a reproduction of the source deck to be executed. Use an 'END=' parameter with a READ statement as a means of recognizing the end of the source. Test your program on the following sequence of source statements:

```
I = 7
J = 5
K = I*J/(I-J)
L = M+K*I/J
```

5.(a) Write a subroutine to generate the equivalent SPECTRE MAP object code for a given arithmetic assignment statement expressed in postfix notation using the algorithm described in Section 9.6. The single input parameter to this routine is a character string representation of the postfix form to be translated. As output parameters, the routine produces two CHARACTER vectors to store the generated coding, one for the opcodes and the other for the corresponding operands. (Since we are excluding the possibility of transfer statements in the source, we do not need to include a third vector for labels.) The coding for this routine can assume that no exponentiation operators are present in the postfix form.

5.(b) Write a mainline program to supply a series of postfix strings to the subroutine of part (a) for translation into SPECTRE MAP coding. For each string translated, the output should include a reproduction of the string and the generated object code. Your program may read the postfix strings in the form of CHARACTER data directly from data cards. Alternatively, it could read a series of FORTRAN assignment statements as source data and invoke the jump table routine of Exercise 3 to create the postfix strings.

6.(a) Write a subroutine to optimize a given sequence of SPECTRE MAP coding. Two CHARACTER vectors can be used to serve as both input and output parameters for this routine. Upon entry to the subroutine, they will contain the opcodes and operands respectively for the statements to be optimized, and, upon exit from the routine, they will store the optimized version. The level of optimization performed need only be "local" (as described in Section 9.7.1), and operand names like T1, T2, ... can always be assumed to represent temporary memory locations. The optimization performed should include the elimination of redundant store-load combinations, the interchanging of statements for commutative operations (i.e., addition and multiplication) to facilitate deletion of instructions, and the reutilization of temporary locations whenever possible by decrementing the temporary storage counter.

6.(b) Write a mainline program to supply sequences of SPECTRE MAP coding to be optimized by the routine of part (a). For each sequence considered, the output should include both the original and optimized versions. The sequences of coding to be optimized may be read directly from data cards as character string data. Alternatively, your program could read FORTRAN assignment statements as source data and combine the routines of Exercises 3, 5(a), and 6(a) to form a three-phase operation.

7.(a) Write a subroutine to interpretively execute a sequence of SPECTRE MAP coding. The coding is passed to the routine in two CHARACTER vectors of the form described in Exercise 6(a) (i.e., no labels). The operations included in the assembly language coding are restricted to addition, subtraction, multiplication, and division, and all operands are assumed to be of type INTEGER. Your routine should construct a bitree symbol table for the operand names (and their values) as they are encountered. Any literals appearing as operands can be assumed to consist of one digit following the '=' sign and must be converted from character string form into appropriate numerical form for carrying out the specified operation. Whenever an output instruction (i.e., opcode OUT) is encountered in the coding, the subroutine should print the value of its operand (obtained from the symbol table). Finally, the appearance of an STP opcode in the source terminates processing by the subroutine. Error checking in this routine consists primarily of diagnosing undefined variables.

7.(b) Write a mainline program to supply sequences of SPECTRE MAP coding to be interpretively executed by the subroutine of part (a). The sequences of coding to be executed may be read directly from data cards as character string data. Once again, as an alternative, your program could read FORTRAN assignment statements as source data and combine the routines of Exercises 3, 5(a), 6(a), and 7(a) to form a four-phase operation.

8. The routines in Exercises 4 through 7 can be combined to form a four-phase operation for processing FORTRAN source statements (FORTRAN → postfix → object code → optimized code → interpretive execution). Incorporate GO TO and arithmetic IF statements into this procedure. For simplicity you may assume that all IF statements have been simplified so that they have only a single operand value inside the parentheses. For example, the statement

```
IF(J-K*2)1,2,3
```

would be coded as follows for inclusion in our restricted source deck:

```
I = J-K*2
IF(I)1,2,3
```

Now that we are permitting transfer statements in our source, the postfix forms of all statements should be maintained as variable length character strings in one long CHARACTER vector. A special symbol may be used as a terminal delimiter for each postfix form in the vector. There is no special postfix form for GO TO and IF statements. Consequently, the mainline program of Exercise 4 should be revised to include a simple scan of each FORTRAN source statement to determine whether it is an assignment statement. If it is, the routine of Exercise 4(a) is invoked to create the appropriate postfix form and the corresponding symbol table entries. Otherwise, the statement should be inserted directly into the vector holding the converted representation of the source with all imbedded blanks removed. For example,

GO TO 6

would be entered into the vector as the character string 'GOTO6'. In addition, the mainline program should record all statement numbers from the source in a separate table, each statement number accompanied by a pointer to the beginning of the representation in the CHARACTER vector for the statement with which it is associated.

Since transfer statements can now appear as part of the source, the subroutine of Exercise 4(b) can no longer consider the source only one statement at a time. Instead, it has to be modified to accept and interpretively execute the source as a collective unit stored in the CHARACTER vector. The subroutine has to make decisions whenever IF statements are encountered and process transfers via the statement number table. Finally, since none of the statements (postfix or otherwise) in the vector representing the source will contain any imbedded blanks, the subroutine can terminate processing of the source as soon as it encounters the first blank.

In Exercise 5 SPECTRE MAP object coding is generated from the postfix representation of the source. Now that we are permitting transfer statements, there is a need for a third CHARACTER vector as an output parameter from the subroutine to contain labels generated by processing of the transfers. The revised input parameter to the routine will be the new CHARACTER vector which contains the entire source for processing. Special sequences of assembly language coding will have to be generated for GO TO and IF statements. A separate label symbol table should be created as well for the labels appearing in the generated object code. Each node could contain a label name, the corresponding FORTRAN statement number, and a pointer to the appropriate statement in the SPECTRE MAP coding produced.

For the code optimization process of Exercise 6, the only significant change involves the inclusion of a third parameter vector for labels. However, the routine for interpretively executing SPECTRE MAP coding in Exercise 7 should also be modified to utilize the label symbol table as a means of accommodating transfer statements.

9. Write a FORTRAN program to implement the operation of the assembly-language-oriented macro processor depicted in Figure 9.13. The rules for defining a macro and expanding a macro call are presented in Section 9.8. Essentially, all statements may be handled as character strings with appropriate substitutions made during the macro expansion process. There are three tables associated with the macro processor: one each for macro names, bodies, and parameter lists; although two or more of these tables could be combined into a single

stack for implementation. Furthermore, since the lengths of macro bodies vary considerably, you may wish to adopt for your macro table a storage approach (similar to that employed in Section 8.5) using variable length character strings.

APPENDIX A

POSITIONAL NOTATIONS

ARABIC, BINARY, HEXADECIMAL

A.1 ARABIC NUMERALS

Everyone in our Western civilization is well aware that the number "ten" plays a very special role as the *BASE* of our present number system. This system of notation for numbers, which we first learned in elementary school, is called the *ARABIC* system (although it was probably developed by the Hindus about 500 A.D.) because it was introduced into Europe by the Arabs when they conquered Spain in the eighth century. The earliest Arabic manuscripts using this system date from the ninth century, and it was during this period that a famous Arabic textbook author, al-Khowârizmî, wrote a much celebrated book expounding the principles of decimal (base-10) arithmetic. It is interesting to note that historians of mathematics have found that the term "algorithm" was derived from this author's name. Actually, the modern spelling is an extension of the earlier version, "algorism", which originally meant "the process of doing arithmetic using Arabic numerals".

The convenience of the Arabic system lies in the fact that it is a *POSITIONAL* notation. We need only the ten symbols or *DIGITS* 0, 1, 2, 3, 4, 5, 6, 7, 8, 9 (notice the word "digit", meaning finger). Any number larger than nine is written as a combination of these digits in such a manner that the position of each digit indicates how it should be interpreted. In defining the Arabic notation for a natural number such as 294, we multiply the digit farthest to the right by 10^0 or 1. Then, moving from right to left, we multiply the remaining digits by successively increasing integer powers of ten. Finally, we sum the products to arrive at the value two hundred and ninety-four.

It is obvious that the ordering of the digits involved is extremely important. For example,

$$2056 = 2(10)^3+0(10)^2+5(10)+6$$

whereas

$$6502 = 6(10)^3+5(10)^2+0(10)+2.$$

Actually, 6502 is the value of the polynomial

$$6x^3+5x^2+0x+2 \text{ when } x = 10.$$

Indeed, we can regard every natural number in Arabic notation as the value of a polynomial where $x = 10$, with the implicit understanding that the coefficients, required to be one of the digits from 0 to 9 inclusive, are the only things actually written. It is interesting to note the importance of the rather sophisticated invention of a symbol for zero in positional notation. Without it, we would have considerable difficulty in distinguishing between such numbers as 18, 180, 108, 1080, and 1800. In fact, it was man's failure to recognize the necessity of having such a symbol that delayed the invention of a positional system.

The Arabic notation for decimal fractions is interpreted in a manner very analogous to that for natural numbers. Digits to the right of the decimal point are multiplied by successively decreasing integer powers of ten, beginning with the power -1 for the digit immediately adjacent to the decimal point. As is true for natural numbers, the sum of these products is the value of the number represented by that particular set of digits. For example,

$$0.325 = 3(10)^{-1}+2(10)^{-2}+5(10)^{-3}.$$

Similarly, non-terminating decimal fractions are really only infinite series; to illustrate, we see that

$$0.2035\ldots = 2(10)^{-1}+0(10)^{-2}+3(10)^{-3}+5(10)^{-4}+\ldots$$

It is interesting to note that Arabic numerals were once written from right to left with the most significant digit at the right end (e.g., seventy-two would be expressed as 27). Despite this early convention, however, our present left-to-right order for expressing numbers has remained standard throughout the various periods of transition.

If our sole concern with numbers were to record them, as historians record dates, then one system of notation would seem to be as good as another. However, if we are going to add, subtract, multiply, and divide numbers, then some systems are clearly superior to others. The primary reason why the various ancient systems of notation (e.g., Egyptian, Babylonian, Greek, Chinese, Roman, etc.) have come to be of so little value is that our present positional notation is the only one which is practical for doing calculations with any degree of speed or accuracy. Despite its obvious advantages over previous methods, however, the Arabic system was adopted generally by Europeans only after a long fight against the repressive forces of tradition and resistance to change. In fact, this notation was not very widely used in Europe until as late as the sixteenth century, more than 700 years after the Arabs had first introduced it. The British Pound System still utilizes measurements which do not accommodate themselves well to decimal fractions (e.g., 12 inches to a foot, 3 feet to a yard, etc.).

A.2 OTHER POSITIONAL SYSTEMS

We have seen that the convenience in the manipulation of Arabic numerals lies in the positional nature of the notation, a characteristic which makes possible the use of only ten digits and such devices as carrying. The question arises whether or not we might have such positional notations which are not based on powers of ten. It has often been suggested that our system is decimal because of the fact that we have ten fingers on which we first learned to count. Suppose, however, that we had all been born with only eight fingers. Then it is likely that we would have written our numbers in powers of eight, and thirty-five would be expressed as 43, meaning "four eights and three units". In such a system, we would have only eight digits: 0, 1, 2, 3, 4, 5, 6, and 7. Any numbers larger than seven would be expressed as a combination of these digits. Actually, this *OCTAL* number system was first proposed by King Charles XII of Sweden early in the eighteenth century. He felt that such a notation would be more convenient for calculation than the decimal system.

Still other bases could be used equally well. In expressing a number using base three, we have only the digits 0, 1, and 2. Consequently, thirty-five is expressed in base three as 1022, since $35 = 1(3)^3+0(3)^2+2(3)+2$. Similarly, using base-five notation, we express thirty-five as 120, since $35 = 1(5)^2+2(5)+0$. Actually, we are merely discussing different ways of writing the same familiar numbers. In other words, we are discussing different systems of notation, or different (written) languages. When we say that the number which is written as 17 in our usual decimal language can be expressed as 32 in base-five language, we are merely translating from one language to another. Consequently, the same symbol, say 24, can mean different things according to the base used or the system of notation in which it is intended to be interpreted. In Figure A.1, each horizontal line contains just one number rewritten in several different languages.

Base 10	Base 5	Base 3	Base 7	Base 9
24	44	220	33	26
31	111	1011	43	34
8	13	22	11	8

Figure A.1

Examples of Different Notations

These new notations look strange only because we have been raised since early childhood to interpret numerals automatically in base 10. The processes of adding, subtracting, multiplying, and dividing could be handled just as easily using another base. However, we would find it clumsy unless we memorized new tables of addition and multiplication for the other base as thoroughly as we have memorized those of base 10. To avoid possible confusion as to which language or base a number such as 24 is expressed, we may either state the base in words as we have done so far, or we may use a subscript such as 24_8 to indicate that base 8 is being used. Such subscripts will always be written in the familiar base 10, since that is our "native" language. If no subscript is used nor any explicit remark made, base 10 is always to be assumed throughout the rest of this appendix.

In general, we define a positional notation using base r (often called *RADIX* r) by the following rule:

$$(\ldots d_3 d_2 d_1 d_0 . d_{-1} d_{-2} d_{-3} \ldots)_r$$
$$= \ldots + d_3 r^3 + d_2 r^2 + d_1 r + d_0 + d_{-1} r^{-1} + d_{-2} r^{-2} + d_{-3} r^{-3} + \ldots$$

where all d_i's are integers satisfying the property that $0 \le d_i < r$ (i.e., at most r distinct digits appear in the expression for any number in base-r notation). The dot appearing between d_0 and d_{-1} is called the *RADIX POINT* (usually referred to as the decimal point when $r = 10$).

A.3 BINARY NOTATION

The positional notation having 2 as a base is called the *BINARY* system. Such a system has only two unique digits, 0 and 1, and consequently all larger numbers are represented by various combinations of 0's and 1's. For example, 23 is expressed as 10111 in binary notation (i.e., the value of the polynomial $x^4+0x^3+x^2+x+1$ where $x = 2$).

It appears that the first publication discussing the binary system was written by a Spanish bishop, Juan Caramuel Lobkowitz (late 17th century). Although he discussed number representations using bases 2, 3, 4, 5, 6, 7, 8, 9, 10, 12, and 60 in detail, he gave only trivial examples of arithmetic operations in non-decimal systems. Early in the 18th century, however, Leibnitz wrote a very illustrative article dealing with binary addition, subtraction, multiplication, and division. While he did not recommend binary notation for practical calculations, he did emphasize its importance in number theory, in light of the fact that number-sequence patterns are very often more apparent in binary form than they are in the more common decimal notation. As a consequence, binary notation can often be useful for solving some mathematical problems and games (puzzles).

Arithmetical calculations in the binary system follow their own rules corresponding to the familiar "carry" and "borrow" associated with the decimal system. We might illustrate these rules by considering several examples. The decimal equivalents accompanying each example are provided for comparison purposes.

Addition	Binary Example	Decimal Equivalent
1. $(0)_2+(0)_2 = (0)_2$	01011	11
2. $(0)_2+(1)_2 = (1)_2$	+01110	+14
3. $(1)_2+(1)_2 = (0)_2$ with $(1)_2$ carried to the left.	11001	25

Subtraction	Binary Example	Decimal Equivalent
1. $(0)_2 - (0)_2 = (0)_2$	10101	21
2. $(1)_2 - (1)_2 = (0)_2$	-01100	-12
3. $(1)_2 - (0)_2 = (1)_2$	01001	9
4. $(0)_2 - (1)_2 = (1)_2$ with $(1)_2$ borrowed from the left.		

Multiplication	Binary Example	Decimal Equivalent
1. $(0)_2 \times (0)_2 = (0)_2$	11101	29
2. $(0)_2 \times (1)_2 = (0)_2$	1101	13
3. $(1)_2 \times (1)_2 = (1)_2$	11101	377
	00000	
	11101	
	11101	
	101111001	

Division	Binary Example	Decimal Equivalent
Combine rules for multiplication and subtraction.	111	7
	101 ⟌ 100011	5 ⟌ 35
	101	
	111	
	101	
	101	
	101	
	0	

A.4 HEXADECIMAL NOTATION

There is no reason why we cannot have positional number notations having as bases numbers larger than ten, providing, of course, that we can invent new digits. As an illustration, *HEXADECIMAL* notation utilizes base 16, and consequently has sixteen distinct symbols for representing numbers. The characters 0, 1, 2, 3, 4, 5, 6, 7, 8, 9, A, B, C, D, E, and F, serve as the sixteen hexadecimal digits, where the letters A to F are arbitrarily chosen digits corresponding to ten through fifteen respectively. Any numbers larger than fifteen must be represented by various combinations of these digits, and interpreted as being the sum of the products of the specified digits and the appropriate powers of 16. The relationship existing between the decimal, binary, and hexadecimal notations is indicated in Figure A.2.

The value of hexadecimal notation is especially apparent in its relationship with the binary system. We can easily convert from one notation to the other. Any number expressed in hexadecimal form can be written in binary notation by expanding each hexadecimal digit to an equivalent four-bit binary value. Conversely, a binary number can be expressed in hexadecimal form by dividing the bits into groups of four, and replacing each group by the equivalent hexadecimal digit. Consequently, we can use hexadecimal notation as a short and convenient means of representing large and cumbersome bit-strings.

Decimal	Binary	Hexadecimal
1	0001	1
2	0010	2
3	0011	3
4	0100	4
5	0101	5
6	0110	6
7	0111	7
8	1000	8
9	1001	9
10	1010	A
11	1011	B
12	1100	C
13	1101	D
14	1110	E
15	1111	F
16	10000	10

Figure A.2

Decimal, Binary, and Hexadecimal Equivalents

Examples: Integer Conversion

(i) $(7AE8)_{16} = (\underbrace{111}_{7}\ \underbrace{1010}_{A}\ \underbrace{1110}_{E}\ \underbrace{1000}_{8})_2$

(ii) $(\underbrace{1}_{1}\ \underbrace{0011}_{3}\ \underbrace{1101}_{D}\ \underbrace{1111}_{F})_2 = (13DF)_{16}$

In conversion of binary integers to hexadecimal integers, we proceed from right to left in breaking up the bits into groups of four.

Examples: Fractional Conversion

(iii) $(.7AE8)_{16} = (.\underbrace{0111}_{7}\ \underbrace{1010}_{A}\ \underbrace{1110}_{E}\ \underbrace{1000}_{8})_2$

(iv) $(.1001\ 1110\ 1111\ 1)_2 = (.\underbrace{1001}_{9}\ \underbrace{1110}_{E}\ \underbrace{1111}_{F}\ \underbrace{100\overset{*}{0}}_{8})_2$

$= (.9EF8)_{16}$

* Trailing zeros have been added to create a cluster of 4 digits.

In conversion of binary fractions to hexadecimal fractions, we proceed from left to right in breaking up the bits into groups of four.

The specific conversion algorithms used in converting binary representations to hexadecimal notation (and vice versa) cannot be used in general to convert from one base to another. The primary reason for studying more general conversion algorithms stems from our use of digital computers, although being skilled at such conversions may sometimes prove useful to a mathematician in other areas. Since the decimal number system is our natural language, we obviously wish to submit data to, and receive output from, a computer in base-ten notation. However, since the computer's native notation is not decimal, the machine must be supplied with conversion routines to make the two-way transitions.

A.5 CONVERSION FROM DECIMAL NOTATION

In order to convert the decimal notation for a given integer, N, to an equivalent representation using another base, r, we must first devise an algorithm. The algorithm for such a conversion is a very straightforward one. It is clear that there must exist integers

$$n,\ d_0,\ d_1,\ d_2,\ \ldots,\ d_n,$$

satisfying the relationship

$$N_{10} = (d_n r^n + d_{n-1} r^{n-1} + d_{n-2} r^{n-2} + \ldots + d_2 r^2 + d_1 r + d_0)_{10},$$

where

$n \geq 0$ and $0 \leq d_i < r$ for $i = 0,1,2,\ldots,n$.

In order to find the representation that we are seeking, we must determine the values of

$$d_0,\ d_1,\ \ldots,\ d_n.$$

Using base-10 arithmetic, we divide N by r to obtain a remainder, d_0, and a quotient,

$$d_n r^{n-1} + d_{n-1} r^{n-2} + d_{n-2} r^{n-3} + \ldots + d_2 r + d_1.$$

If we divide this new quotient by r, we obtain d_1 as the next remainder. Repeated division of successive quotients by r produces as remainders d_2, d_3, ..., d_n respectively. Thus, if we continue this division process until we encounter a zero quotient, we will have determined the values of all the d_i's. To find the base-r representation of N, we need only convert each base-10 digit, d_i, to its base-r equivalent.

<u>Example (i)</u>: $(421)_{10} = (?)_2$ [Decimal to Binary]

2	421	remainder 1
2	210	remainder 0
2	105	remainder 1
2	52	remainder 0
2	26	remainder 0
2	13	remainder 1
2	6	remainder 0
2	3	remainder 1
2	1	remainder 1
	0	

The binary number is read as directed by the arrow. Therefore $(421)_{10} = (110100101)_2$.

<u>Example (ii)</u>: $(31465)_{10} = (?)_{16}$ [Decimal to Hexadecimal]

16	31465	remainder $(9)_{10} = (9)_{16}$
16	1966	remainder $(14)_{10} = (E)_{16}$
16	122	remainder $(10)_{10} = (A)_{16}$
16	7	remainder $(7)_{10} = (7)_{16}$
	0	

Therefore $(31465)_{10} = (7AE9)_{16}$.

The algorithm for converting decimal fractions to an equivalent base-r notation is quite similar to the algorithm for converting integers. We can always express any fraction as the sum of a series (perhaps infinite) of products, each involving r raised to a negative integer power.

i.e., $N = (d_{-1}r^{-1}+d_{-2}r^{-2}+d_{-3}r^{-3}+\ldots)_{10}$,

where d_{-1}, d_{-2}, d_{-3}, ... are non-negative integers less than r.

In order to determine the base-r representation we are seeking, we must first find the values of d_{-1}, d_{-2}, d_{-3}, etc..

Using base-10 arithmetic, we multiply the entire decimal fraction by r to obtain

$$[d_{-1}+(d_{-2}r^{-1}+d_{-3}r^{-2}+\ldots)]_{10}$$

i.e., the digit carried over to the left of the decimal point after multiplying is d_{-1}.

If we further multiply only the portion remaining to the right of the decimal point by r, we will obtain d_{-2} as the new digit carried to the left of the decimal point. Repeated multiplication of successive parts lying to the right of the decimal point will subsequently produce d_{-3}, d_{-4}, d_{-5}, ... as the digits carried to the left. We terminate this repetitive process when the portion remaining to be multiplied at any stage is zero. However, we often encounter cases where a simple base-ten fraction may require several (perhaps infinitely many) digits for an equivalent representation in another base. In such cases, we must decide the precision required in the new base, and terminate when we obtain the appropriate number of digits. Once we have determined the values of d_{-1}, d_{-2}, d_{-3}, etc., we merely convert each one of them to its equivalent base-r representation.

Example (iii): $(.6875)_{10} = (?)_2$ [Decimal to Binary]

```
   .6875
      ×2
|  -----
|  1.375
|     ×2
|  -----
|  0.75
|    ×2
|  -----
|  1.5
|   ×2
|  -----
v  1.0 <---- STOP
```

The binary equivalent of the original fraction is comprised of the single digits to the left of the decimal points as directed by the arrow.

Therefore $(0.6875)_{10} = (0.1011)_2$.

Example (iv): $(.125)_{10} = (?)_{16}$ [Decimal to Hexadecimal]

```
 .125
  ×16
 -----
 2.000 <-- STOP
```

Therefore $(.125)_{10} = (.2)_{16}$.

Example (v): $(.69)_{10} = (?)_{16}$ [Decimal to Hexadecimal]

$$
\begin{array}{rl}
.69 & \\
\times 16 & \\
\hline
\underline{\underline{11}}.04 & (11)_{10} = (B)_{16} \\
\times 16 & \\
\hline
\underline{\underline{0}}.64 & (0)_{10} = (0)_{16} \\
\times 16 & \\
\hline
\underline{\underline{10}}.24 & (10)_{10} = (A)_{16} \\
\times 16 & \\
\hline
\underline{\underline{3}}.84 & (3)_{10} = (3)_{16} \downarrow
\end{array}
$$

Therefore $(.69)_{10} = (.B0A3\ldots)_{16}$.

Continue this process as long as desired, or until the portion to the right of the decimal point is zero.

The two algorithms discussed in this section are especially convenient for conversion from base-ten notation to another base, since all the arithmetic is done in the familiar decimal system. These same algorithms, however, may be used to convert from any base to another base, provided that all the arithmetic is performed using the first base.

A.6 CONVERSION TO DECIMAL NOTATION

In converting integers expressed in base-r notation to an equivalent decimal form, we merely use the polynomial form of a natural number expressed in positional notation. In most cases, in order to minimize the number of multiplications involved, it is best to use the nested form of polynomial evaluation.

i.e., $N_r = (d_n d_{n-1} d_{n-2} \ldots d_2 d_1 d_0)_r$

$$= (D_n r^n + D_{n-1} r^{n-1} + D_{n-2} r^{n-2} + \ldots D_2 r^2 + D_1 r + D_0)_{10}$$

$$= \left\{ D_n r + D_{n-1} \right] r + D_{n-2}] r + \ldots] r + D_2] r + D_1] r + D_0 \Big\}_{10},$$

where (i) $(D_i)_{10} = (d_i)_r$, $i = 0,1,2,\ldots,n$

(ii) $]r$ indicates that <u>everything</u> to the left of "]" is multiplied by r.

<u>Example (i):</u> $(110101010)_2 = (?)_{10}$ [Binary to Decimal]

$$(110101010)_2 = \{1(2)^8 + 1(2)^7 + 0(2)^6 + 1(2)^5 + 0(2)^4 + 1(2)^3 + 0(2)^2 + 1(2) + 0\}_{10}$$

$$= \{1(2)+1]2+0]2+1]2+0]2+1]2+0]2+1]2+0\}_{10}$$

$$= (426)_{10}$$

<u>Example (ii):</u> $(7AE8)_{16} = (?)_{10}$ [Hexadecimal to Decimal]

$$(7AE8)_{16} = \{7(16)^3 + 10(16)^2 + 14(16) + 8\}_{10}$$

$$= \{7(16)+10]16+14]16+8\}_{10}$$

$$= (31464)_{10}$$

For converting fractions expressed in base-r notation into an equivalent decimal form, we utilize the similar basic definition of a fraction expressed in positional notation.

$$\text{i.e., } N = (.d_{-1}d_{-2}d_{-3}\ldots)_r$$

$$= (D_{-1}r^{-1}+D_{-2}r^{-2}+D_{-3}r^{-3}+\ldots)_{10},$$

where $(D_i)_{10} = (d_i)_r$ for $i = -1,-2,-3$, etc.

<u>Example (iii)</u>: $(.11011)_2 = (?)_{10}$ [Binary to Decimal]

$$(.11011)_2 = \left\{1(2)^{-1}+1(2)^{-2}+0(2)^{-3}+1(2)^{-4}+1(2)^{-5}\right\}_{10}$$

$$= (1/2 + 1/4 + 0 + 1/16 + 1/32)_{10}$$

$$= (.84375)_{10}$$

<u>Example (iv)</u>: $(.A4)_{16} = (?)_{10}$ [Hexadecimal to Decimal]

$$(.A4)_{16} = \left\{10(16)^{-1} + 4(16)^{-2}\right\}_{10}$$

$$= \left(\frac{10}{16} + \frac{4}{256}\right)_{10}$$

$$= (.640625)_{10}$$

In summary, we have considered algorithms for converting both integers and fractions from one notation to another, some utilizing arithmetic performed in the first base, others employing arithmetic done in the second base. In general, if ten is one of the bases involved, we try to use an algorithm which utilizes decimal arithmetic, since computation in our familiar base-ten system is usually much easier for us than arithmetic performed in other bases. We should realize, however, that algorithms which are best suited for hand conversion may not necessarily be practical for use as computer conversion routines. Furthermore, as we have illustrated, conversion algorithms for integers are not the same as those used for converting fractions. For conversion of numbers having both integral and fractional parts, we must handle each part separately.

A.7 HEXADECIMAL TABLES

Before attempting the numerous exercises presented at the end of this appendix, the interested reader may wish to check his skill at performing hexadecimal arithmetic by consulting the tables presented in Figures A.3 and A.4. They should be of some benefit in doing several of the exercises.

	1	2	3	4	5	6	7	8	9	A	B	C	D	E	F
1	02	03	04	05	06	07	08	09	0A	0B	0C	0D	0E	0F	10
2	03	04	05	06	07	08	09	0A	0B	0C	0D	0E	0F	10	11
3	04	05	06	07	08	09	0A	0B	0C	0D	0E	0F	10	11	12
4	05	06	07	08	09	0A	0B	0C	0D	0E	0F	10	11	12	13
5	06	07	08	09	0A	0B	0C	0D	0E	0F	10	11	12	13	14
6	07	08	09	0A	0B	0C	0D	0E	0F	10	11	12	13	14	15
7	08	09	0A	0B	0C	0D	0E	0F	10	11	12	13	14	15	16
8	09	0A	0B	0C	0D	0E	0F	10	11	12	13	14	15	16	17
9	0A	0B	0C	0D	0E	0F	10	11	12	13	14	15	16	17	18
A	0B	0C	0D	0E	0F	10	11	12	13	14	15	16	17	18	19
B	0C	0D	0E	0F	10	11	12	13	14	15	16	17	18	19	1A
C	0D	0E	0F	10	11	12	13	14	15	16	17	18	19	1A	1B
D	0E	0F	10	11	12	13	14	15	16	17	18	19	1A	1B	1C
E	0F	10	11	12	13	14	15	16	17	18	19	1A	1B	1C	1D
F	10	11	12	13	14	15	16	17	18	19	1A	1B	1C	1D	1E

Figure A.3

Hexadecimal Addition and Subtraction Table

Example (i): 6 + 2 = 8

8 - 2 = 6

Example (ii): F + A = 19

19 - A = F

	1	2	3	4	5	6	7	8	9	A	B	C	D	E	F
1	01	02	03	04	05	06	07	08	09	0A	0B	0C	0D	0E	0F
2	02	04	06	08	0A	0C	0E	10	12	14	16	18	1A	1C	1E
3	03	06	09	0C	0F	12	15	18	1B	1E	21	24	27	2A	2D
4	04	08	0C	10	14	18	1C	20	24	28	2C	30	34	38	3C
5	05	0A	0F	14	19	1E	23	28	2D	32	37	3C	41	46	4B
6	06	0C	12	18	1E	24	2A	30	36	3C	42	48	4E	54	5A
7	07	0E	15	1C	23	2A	31	38	3F	46	4D	54	5B	62	69
8	08	10	18	20	28	30	38	40	48	50	58	60	68	70	78
9	09	12	1B	24	2D	36	3F	48	51	5A	63	6C	75	7E	87
A	0A	14	1E	28	32	3C	46	50	5A	64	6E	78	82	8C	96
B	0B	16	21	2C	37	42	4D	58	63	6E	79	84	8F	9A	A5
C	0C	18	24	30	3C	48	54	60	6C	78	84	90	9C	AB	B4
D	0D	1A	27	34	41	4E	5B	68	75	82	8F	9C	A9	B6	C3
E	0E	1C	2A	38	46	54	62	70	7E	8C	9A	A8	B6	C4	D2
F	0F	1E	2D	3C	4B	5A	69	78	87	96	A5	B4	C3	D2	E1

Figure A.4

Hexadecimal Multiplication Table

Example (i): 2 × 4 = 08

Example (ii): F × 2 = 1E

Example (iii): C × D = 9C

A.8 EXERCISES

1. Perform the following operations in binary arithmetic:

   (a) 101 + 11 + 110110 + 110101 - 1101 - 1010

   (b) 1111 - 111010 + 110111 - 110 + 100100

   (c) $(111)^2 - (110)^2$

   (d) $(1101)^3 - (101)^3$

   (e) 11011 × 101101

   (f) 101111001 ÷ 10111

   (g) 101.1011 × .1101

   (h) 11.01 - 1.0101 + 0.11 × 101.11

2. Perform the following <u>additions</u> using hexadecimal arithmetic:

(i)		(ii)		(iii)	
	4A5E7		B19C		48AD0
	B73C		6FF		B3EF

3. For each pair of hexadecimal values given in Exercise 2, <u>subtract</u> the second number from the first.

4. (a) Convert the following hexadecimal numbers to equivalent binary notation:

(i) FA1234 (iv) 11111111

(ii) 12345678 (v) ABCEDFFD

(iii) FEDCBA98

4.(b) Convert the following sixteen-bit binary values to their corresponding hexadecimal representations:

(i) 1010101010101010

(ii) 0111111010110001

(iii) 1111111111111111

(iv) 0001001101111111

5.(a) Convert the following decimal numbers to their corresponding binary and hexadecimal representations.

(i) 46 (iv) 127

(ii) 32 (v) 32767

(iii) 7632 (vi) 1234567

(b) Convert the hexadecimal numbers in Exercise 4(a) to their corresponding decimal representations.

(c) Convert the binary numbers in Exercise 4(b) to their corresponding decimal representations.

6. Perform the following arithmetic operations using <u>hexadecimal arithmetic</u>:

(i) FFFF + DDDD

(ii) F3B × AB

(iii) 1234 × 1111

(iv) E1 ÷ F

(v) 15C ÷ 9

(vi) 56ABF3 ÷ D

7. (a) $(.111110001111101)_2 = (?)_{16}$

(b) $(.7AFC3)_{16} = (?)_2$

(c) $(.1)_{10} = (?)_{16}$

(d) $(.1111)_2 = (?)_{10}$

(e) $(.25)_{10} = (?)_2$

(f) $(.63ADF)_{16} = (?)_{10}$

(g) $(12.125)_{10} = (?)_{16}$

(h) $(135.732)_{10} = (?)_{16}$

APPENDIX B
CHARACTER VARIABLES WITH WATFIV

B.1 CHARACTER VARIABLES (FORTRAN IV EXTENSION)

At a meeting held during the SHARE XXVIII Conference in San Francisco in February, 1967, the SHARE FORTRAN Project proposed that IBM adopt a new type of variable as an extension to the FORTRAN language supported by IBM's compilers. The following material is taken from Appendix B of the minutes of that meeting of the FORTRAN Project, since it defines, for the most part, WATFIV's implementation of CHARACTER variables.

1. In-Core Formatting and CHARACTER Variable Type

   Character data is recognized as a legitimate data form which may be manipulated to a limited extent. The general effect to the language is:

   (i) CHARACTER is a variable type.

   (ii) Core-to-core READ and WRITE statements allow in-core formatting.

   (iii) Implicit record-size for CHARACTER arrays for FORMAT statement control is defined in the Type statement (not in the READ and WRITE statements).

(iv) A WRITE statement may be used to define a variable.

2. Variable Type: CHARACTER

A variable of type CHARACTER represents a character string (literal data). The standard and optional length specifications which determine the number of characters that are reserved for each CHARACTER variable are:

Variable Type	Default	Optional
CHARACTER	1	>1 (≤256)

A programmer may declare a variable to be of type CHARACTER by use of the:

- IMPLICIT specification statement.
- Form of the explicit specification statement: CHARACTER.

(a) IMPLICIT Statement

The type CHARACTER is permitted in the IMPLICIT statement with a specified length. If the length is omitted, the standard length of 1 is assumed.

Example:

```
IMPLICIT CHARACTER*80 (A-D),CHARACTER ($,Z)
```

All variables beginning with the characters A through D are declared as CHARACTER type, each variable or array element 80 characters in size. All variables beginning with the characters $ and Z are declared as CHARACTER. Since no length specification is explicitly given, one character (the standard length for CHARACTER) is allocated for each variable.

(b) <u>CHARACTER Statement: A Form of the Generalized Type Statement</u>

CHARACTER$*\underline{s}$ $\underline{a}*\underline{s}_1(\underline{k}_1)/\underline{x}_1/,\underline{b}*\underline{s}_2(\underline{k}_2)/\underline{x}_2/,\ldots,\underline{z}*\underline{s}_n(\underline{k}_n)/\underline{x}_n/$

where: – $*\underline{s},*\underline{s}_1,*\underline{s}_2,\ldots,*\underline{s}_n$ are optional. Each $\underline{s}$ represents one of the permissible length specifications.

– $\underline{a},\underline{b},\ldots,\underline{z}$ represent variable or array names.

– $(\underline{k}_1),(\underline{k}_2),\ldots,(\underline{k}_n)$ are optional. Each $\underline{k}$ is composed of one through seven unsigned integer constants separated by commas, representing the maximum value of each subscript in the array. Each $\underline{k}$ may be an unsigned integer variable only when the CHARACTER statement in which it appears is in a subprogram.

– $/\underline{x}_1/,/\underline{x}_2/,\ldots,/\underline{x}_n/$ are optional and represent initial data values.

The information necessary to allocate storage for arrays (dimension information) may be included within the statement. However, if this information does not appear in a CHARACTER statement, it must appear in a DIMENSION or COMMON statement (see "DIMENSION Statement" or "COMMON Statement" sections).

Initial data values may be assigned to variables or arrays by use of /$\underline{x}_n$/, where $\underline{x}_n$ is a constant or list of constants separated by commas. This set of constants may be in the form "*r* * constant", where *r* is an unsigned integer called the "repeat constant". The initial data values may only be literal constants, and must be the same length as, or shorter than, the corresponding variables or array elements. Initial data values will be truncated from the right and diagnosed if too long, and they will be padded with blanks on the right if too short (see Example 2 below).

An initially defined variable or a variable of an array may not be in blank common. In a labeled common block they may be initially defined only in a BLOCK DATA subprogram.

The CHARACTER statement overrides the IMPLICIT statement. If the length specification is omitted (i.e., *$\underline{s}$), the standard length of 1 is assumed. If an array is used in a subprogram and is not in COMMON, the size of this array may be specified implicitly by an INTEGER variable of length 4 which can appear explicitly in the SUBROUTINE statement or implicitly in COMMON (adjustable dimensions).

Example 1:

```
CHARACTER*80 CARDS(10),LINES*132(56,2),TCARD
```

This statement declares that the variable TCARD and the arrays named CARDS and LINES are of type CHARACTER. In addition, it declares the size of the array CARDS to be 10 and array LINES to be 112 (2 groups of 56 each). Each element of the array LINES is assigned 132 characters for a total of 14,784 (112 times 132) for the array. Each element of the array CARDS and the variable TCARD is assigned 80 characters (the length associated with the type). The array CARDS is assigned a total of 800 characters.

Example 2:

```
CHARACTER X*3(4)/'ABC','DEFG','HI','JKL'/
```

This statement declares that array X has four elements, three characters each, which are initialized as follows:

X(1)	ABC
X(2)	DEF
X(3)	HIb̸
X(4)	JKL

The statement is incorrectly written, and the value specified for X(2) has been altered by truncating.

3. DIMENSION Statement

CHARACTER type array names may appear in DIMENSION statements.

4. COMMON Statement

CHARACTER type variables or array names may appear in COMMON statements.

5. NAMELIST Statement

CHARACTER type variables or array names may appear in NAMELIST statements.

6. DATA Statement

CHARACTER type variables, array element names, or array names may appear in DATA statements. The data values may only be literal constants, and they must be the same length as, or shorter than, the corresponding variables or array elements. Initial data values will be truncated from the right and diagnosed if too long, and they will be padded with blanks on the right if too short (see Example 2 under "CHARACTER Statement" above).

7. EQUIVALENCE Statement

CHARACTER type variables, arrays, or array elements may appear in EQUIVALENCE statements. CHARACTER type data may be equivalenced to other than CHARACTER type data but implies storage sharing only.

Example:

```
CHARACTER A*5,B*2,C*1
CHARACTER D*1(5)
EQUIVALENCE (D(1),A),(D(2),B),(D(5),C)
:
```

These statements cause the following alignment of characters:

```
A-----
B --
C    -
```

The use of the array D enables equivalencing to characters in the middle of the variable A.

8. CALL Statement

CHARACTER variable names, array element names, array names, and literal constants may appear as parameters in a CALL statement.

9. Function Reference

CHARACTER variable names, array element names, array names, and literal constants may appear as parameters in a function reference.

Example:

```
      CHARACTER CARD*80
      :
      READ(5,1)CARD
    1 FORMAT(A80)
      IF(COMPAR(CARD,'END',4))2,3,2
    3 STOP
    2 CONTINUE
      :
```

An 80-character image is read into the element CARD. A function, COMPAR, is used to compare the first four characters of CARD with 'END' and used to return a positive, negative, or zero numeric value which is used conditionally to terminate the program.

10. Statement Function Statements

Non-subscripted CHARACTER variable names may appear as parameters in a statement function statement.

11. SUBROUTINE Statements

CHARACTER variable names and array names may appear as parameters in a SUBROUTINE statement.

12. FUNCTION Statement

CHARACTER variable names and array names may appear as parameters in a FUNCTION statement.

13. Core-To-Core Input/Output Statements

An additional type of I/O statement provides for core-to-core transmission of data under FORMAT control. There are two core-to-core I/O statements: READ and WRITE. In a core-to-core operation, no actual input/output takes place; data conversion and transmission take place between an internal buffer and the elements specified by a list.

(a) WRITE Statement

WRITE(a,b)list

Where: *a* is a CHARACTER array, array element, or variable name which specifies the starting location of the internal buffer to which data is to be transmitted.

b is a statement number of a FORMAT statement, an array name, or array element indicating the beginning location of a FORMAT statement which describes the data to be transmitted.

list is a series of variable or array names, separated by commas, which may be indexed and incremented. They specify the number of items to be written and the location in storage from which the data is taken.

This form of the WRITE statement causes the data items specified by *list* to be converted to character strings, according to the FORMAT specified by *b*, and placed in storage beginning at the first character element specified by *a*.

Characters are placed into the buffer, starting with the first character position of the first element specified by *a*, in consecutive character positions. When a new record is begun, it starts at the first character position of the next element.

The number of characters for a record caused to be generated by the FORMAT statement and *list* should not be greater than the size of the elements specified by a. If fewer characters are generated than are necessary to fill the element, it is filled out with trailing blanks.

Example 1:

```
      CHARACTER M*12(1)
      :
      I = 15
      J = 7
      :
      WRITE(M,2)I,J
    2 FORMAT(2H(F,I2,1H.,I1,1H))
      :
```

These statements might be used to create, for later use, a FORMAT stored in variable M. The FORMAT so created would appear as:

(F15.7)b̸b̸b̸b̸b̸

where b̸ represents the character blank. Since an execution-time FORMAT must be stored in an array, variable M is dimensioned to have one element. However, if we were to use M strictly as an internal buffer and not as a FORMAT, it would not need to be dimensioned.

Example 2:

```
      CHARACTER M*12,N*132,FMT(12)
      EQUIVALENCE (M,FMT)
      .
      .
      .
      K = FUNC(A,B,C,D)
      .
      .
      .
    2 WRITE(M,4)K
    4 FORMAT(1H(,I3,6HX,1H*))
    6 WRITE(N,FMT)
      .
      .
      .
```

These statements prepare a character string 132 long for use in printer plotting. The print position K is determined by the function FUNC. Statement 2 creates a FORMAT stored in variable M, which, for a value of K of 96, would appear as:

(b̸96X,1H*)b̸b̸

Statement 6 then uses the above FORMAT (in variable FMT) to prepare a character string 132 long in variable N which consists of all blanks except for an asterisk in the ninety-seventh character.

(b) READ Statement

READ(*a*,*b*)*list*

Where: *a* is a CHARACTER array, array element, or variable name which specifies the starting location of the internal buffer from which data is to be transmitted.

b is either the statement number of a FORMAT statement or a character array element indicating the beginning location of a FORMAT statement which describes the data to be transmitted.

list is a series of variable or array names, separated by commas, which may be indexed and incremented. They specify the number of items to be read and the locations in storage into which the data is placed.

This form of the READ statement causes the character string beginning at the first character element specified by a to be converted to data items, according to the FORMAT specified by b, and stored in the elements specified by list.

Characters are obtained from the buffer, starting with the first character position of the first element specified by a, from consecutive character positions. When a new record is begun, it starts at the first character position of the next element.

The FORMAT statement and list should not require more characters from an element than the length of that element. A new record is begun when specifically requested by the FORMAT.

Example:

```
      CHARACTER*80 R(10)
      :
      DO 20 I=1,10
    3 READ(R(I),5)J
    5 FORMAT(I1)
      GO TO (11,12,13,14,15,16,17,18,19),J
   11 READ(R(I),21)(A(K),K=1,10)
   21 FORMAT(1X,10F8.3)
      GO TO 31
   12 READ(R(I),22)K1,K2,K3,K4
   22 FORMAT(1X,4I5)
      GO TO 32
   13 READ(R(I),23)X,Y,Z
   23 FORMAT(1X,3E20.9)
      etc.
      :
```

These statements illustrate a method of processing randomly ordered input cards of varying format and data content. The card type is identified by a digit from one to nine in the first column. Statement 3 converts the digit from character form to integer form. The GO TO then transfers to the READ/FORMAT combination prepared to process the specified format.

14. Input/Output List

CHARACTER variable names, array element names, and array names may appear in input/output lists.

15. Replacement Statement: A = B

A replacement statement in which all variables, constants, or array elements are of type CHARACTER is permissible. In such a statement, the item of the left side may only be a CHARACTER variable name or a CHARACTER array element; the item on the right side may be a CHARACTER variable name, a CHARACTER array element, or a CHARACTER (literal) constant.

The element on the right side must be the same length as, or shorter in length than, the element on the left side. The value of the right element will be truncated from the right during replacement and diagnosed if too long, and it will be padded with blanks on the right if too short.

Note: The term "literal constant" should be replaced in language definition by "character constant".

B.2 ADDITIONAL CHARACTER FEATURES SUPPORTED BY WATFIV

The features of CHARACTER variables given in this section were not described in the SHARE proposal of the last section, and hence, they are considered as extensions to that proposal.

It should also be mentioned that WATFIV supplies no particular alignment for CHARACTER variables, unless they are forced to some half-word, full-word, or double-word boundary by COMMON and/or EQUIVALENCE statements.

1. Use as Subscripts

Subscripts may be of LOGICAL or CHARACTER value. The first character (leftmost byte) in the quantity is used as the low-order byte of a four-byte integer to form the actual subscript. For example, A('123') is the same as A(241), since the internal representation of the character '1', taken as an integer value, is equivalent to 241.

Example:

```
      CHARACTER*1 TRANSL(255),CARD(80)
      .
      .
      .
      DO 1 I=1,80
    1 CARD(I) = TRANSL(CARD(I))
      .
      .
      .
```

The preceding loop will translate each character of a card according to the translation table TRANSL.

2. Use with Relational Operators

CHARACTER variables may be used as operands of relational operators provided both operands are of type CHARACTER. All values are treated as if they were in IBM S/360 EBCDIC representation.

Example:

```
CHARACTER A*1,B*5,C*5(10)
:
IF(A.EQ.C(I))GO TO 10
:
IF(B.LE.'AAAAA')GO TO 30
:
```

For the purposes of the comparison when operands of unequal length are involved, the shorter operand is considered as if padded on the right with blanks to the length of the longer operand. A warning message is issued at compile time when operands of different lengths are used.

Note that this feature is highly dependent upon the S/360 machine representation of EBCDIC characters.

APPENDIX C
SPECTRE MACHINE AND ASSEMBLY LANGUAGE CODING

C.1 THE SPECTRE COMPUTER

The SPECTRE computer is a hypothetical machine designed and used at the University of Waterloo since 1965 as a teaching aid to introduce concepts in machine and assembly language programming and the internal organization of a computer. Since it was to be used only for teaching purposes, this simplified machine was designed to include only those features which were considered basic to an understanding of how a stored-program digital computer actually operates. Once a beginner has mastered these basic concepts, he can, if he so desires, continue with a more intensive study of a real computer. In order that students have an opportunity to run and debug their SPECTRE machine and assembly language programs, an in-core processor was developed to simulate the operation of this hypothetical computer.

In the remainder of this appendix, we shall describe very briefly various aspects of the SPECTRE computer and programming in SPECTRE machine and assembly language. This description has been kept very brief on the assumption that readers have had some exposure to machine and assembly language prior to reading this book. In particular, we have limited ourselves to a discussion of those features which will facilitate a better understanding of the material in Sections 9.6, 9.7, and 9.8.

The SPECTRE computer is a decimal machine. Its memory unit contains one thousand memory locations, each capable of storing one signed ten-digit integer in the range -9999999999 to +9999999999. For example, -7 would be recorded as -0000000007 in SPECTRE memory. Each of the memory cells has a unique address between 000 and 999 inclusive.

The arithmetic unit of the SPECTRE computer consists of two registers, each capable of holding one signed ten-digit integer. The accumulator register (AC) is used primarily for addition and subtraction and the multiplier-quotient register (MQ) for multiplication and division.

Machine language instructions for the SPECTRE computer are coded in the form of ten-digit integers that can be stored in memory along with the data to be manipulated. Each instruction has the form

00000XXWWW

where 'XX' is a two-digit operation code which instructs the machine to perform a specific task (e.g., an arithmetic operation, a transfer, etc.) and 'WWW' designates the address of the operand for that instruction. For example, +0000031500 instructs the machine to output the contents of cell 500 on the printer. The sign of an instruction is always positive and the leading five zeros are ignored.

The SPECTRE computer is a serial machine. This means that, in the absence of branching instructions to the contrary, the control unit finds successive instructions in consecutive memory cells. It does this by using an Instruction Address Register (IAR) which stores the three-digit address of the memory cell containing the next instruction to be executed following completion of the instruction currently being processed. The contents of this register are automatically incremented just prior to the actual execution of every instruction. Processing of a branching instruction merely involves setting the value of the IAR to be the operand cell address so that the appropriate transfer of control is achieved.

The only input unit available with the SPECTRE computer is a standard punched-card reader. As a result, both instructions and data are loaded into memory from cards. Each load card contains a ten-digit integer value to be loaded into memory and a three-digit address specifying the cell into which the integer is to be loaded. Because of the sequential nature of the SPECTRE machine, instructions which are to be executed consecutively must be loaded into contiguous memory cells. Once the loading of memory has been completed, the IAR is initialized and execution begins under the direction of the control unit.

C.2 SPECTRE MAP ASSEMBLY LANGUAGE

The assembly language for the SPECTRE computer is SPECTRE MAP. In this language, three-character mnemonics replace two-digit operation codes and symbolic names are used in place of three-digit numerical memory cell addresses. These symbolic names can have from one to six characters (letters of the alphabet or digits) with the restriction that the first character must be alphabetic. Each SPECTRE MAP source card has the following three fields, any of which may be left blank under certain circumstances:

LABEL OPCODE OPERAND

For example, the SPECTRE MAP source statement

```
BEGIN  INP X
```

instructs the machine to read a value from a data card into cell X. In addition, the symbolic label BEGIN is to be associated with the memory cell assigned to contain this instruction.

SPECTRE MAP permits the use of literal (i.e., constant) operands instead of symbolic ones. A literal consists of an '=' sign followed by a signed or unsigned constant having from one to ten digits. For example, if we wished to insert the value -55 into the accumulator, we could use the following instruction:

```
CLA = -55
```

When this instruction is executed, the value -0000000055 is loaded into the AC register.

The translation from SPECTRE MAP assembly language into SPECTRE machine language is performed by an assembler program. This assembly process is carried out in two stages. During the first phase, the assembler constructs a symbol table containing all the labels used in the source program and the corresponding memory cell addresses which are assigned to those labels. In addition, at the end of the first pass through the source program, the assembler assigns memory cells for the storage of all literal values which appear in the program. During the second stage of the translation process, the assembler uses the information gathered during the first phase to produce the equivalent SPECTRE machine language version (i.e., the object module) of the SPECTRE MAP source program. This object code can then be loaded into memory and executed under the direction of the control unit.

C.3 SELECTED OPERATION CODES

In Sections 9.6 through 9.9, numerous references are made to various SPECTRE MAP operation codes and instructions. The following list includes brief descriptions of the meanings of these operation codes. This list represents only a selected subset of the opcodes available.

ADD - Add the operand value to the current AC value and place the sum in the AC.

CLA - Clear the AC and insert a copy of the operand value.

DIV - Divide the number in the MQ by the operand value. The quotient is placed in the MQ and the remainder in the AC.

LDQ - Clear the MQ and insert a copy of the operand value.

MPY - Multiply the value in the MQ by the operand value and place the product in the MQ.

OUT - Print the value of the operand on the printer.

SSP - Set the sign of the AC to be positive.

STO - Store a copy of the AC contents in the operand cell specified.

STP - Halt execution.

STQ - Store a copy of the MQ contents in the operand cell specified.

TRA - Branch (unconditionally) to the operand cell specified to find the next instruction for execution.

TSL - After the IAR contents have been incremented (an automatic prelude to executing each new instruction), the new IAR contents are inserted into the rightmost three digit positions of the memory cell specified as the operand address of the TSL instruction. Then a branch is made to the memory cell immediately following that operand cell to find the next instruction for execution. The TSL operation code is used primarily as a transfer-and-store-linkage command for transferring to subroutines. After execution of the subroutine in question has been completed, control is returned to the appropriate point in the calling program by utilizing the return address which was inserted earlier into the address portion of the cell specified as the operand of the TSL.

The five operation codes listed below are all conditional transfer commands. In every case, the transfer is conditional upon the AC contents. If the specific branching condition is satisfied, the control unit looks for its next instruction for execution in the memory cell specified as the operand of the transfer opcode. However, if the transfer condition is not satisfied, the control unit finds its next instruction in its normal sequential manner.

TLE - Transfer if the AC value is less than or equal to zero.

TMI - Transfer if the sign of the AC is negative.

TNZ - Transfer if the AC value is non-zero.

TPL - Transfer if the sign of the AC is positive.

TZE - Transfer if the AC value is zero.

A complete description of SPECTRE machine and assembly language may be found in a booklet called "An Introduction to the SPECTRE Computer". This booklet, written and published by the Applied Analysis and Computer Science Department at the University of Waterloo, is available through the University's bookstore.

INDEX